Stormy Weather

Stormy Weather

THE MUSIC AND
LIVES OF A CENTURY
OF JAZZWOMEN

by Linda Dahl

PANTHEON BOOKS
NEW YORK

Grateful acknowledgment is made to the following for permission to reprint
previously published material: *The Detroit News:* Jim Dulzo, "Alive! and
Well," October 5, 1979. Copyright © 1979 by the *Detroit News*, a division of the
Evening News Association. Reprinted by permission. *Down Beat:* Excerpted
articles from various issues of *Down Beat* magazine. Reprinted by permission.
Frank Driggs: *Women in Jazz* by Frank Driggs. Copyright © (p) 1977 by Frank
Driggs. Reprinted by permission. *Jazz Forum:* Barbara van Rooyen and Pawel
Brodowski, "Betty's Groove," January 1979; and Charles Gans, "T.A.L.T.
Conference: A Conversation with Toshiko Akiyoshi and Lew Tabackin,"
February 1980. Reprinted by permission. *Jazz Times:* Article by Don Nelson,
April-May 1981. Reprinted by permission from *Jazz Times*, 8055 13th St., Silver
Spring, MD. 20910. Macmillan Publishing Co., Inc.: *Big Bill Blues:* William
Broonzy's Story, as told to Yannick Bruynoghe. Copyright © 1955. Published by
Cassell Ltd., Macmillan Publishing Co. acting as proprietor. Reprinted by
permission of Macmillan Publishing Co., Inc. *The New York Times:* "A Salute
to Women in Jazz Will Open" by John W. Wilson, June 25, 1978. Copyright ©
1978 by The New York Times Company. Reprinted by permission. Oxford
University Press: Robert C. Toll, *Blacking Up: The Minstrel Show in
Nineteenth-Century America*, 1974. Reprinted by permission. Prestige Re-
cords/Fantasy Records: Liner notes from Prestige #7647 (Mary Lou Williams).
Reprinted by permission of Fantasy Records. Houghton Mifflin Company: A
brief quote from *Alec Wilder and His Friends* by Whitney Balliett, originally
published in *The New Yorker*. Copyright © 1968, 1972, 1973, 1974 by Whitney
Balliett. Reprinted by permission of Houghton Mifflin Company. *Sing Out!*
magazine: Irene V. Jackson, "Black Women and Afro-American Song Tradition," *Sing Out!* magazine, 25, no. 2. Copyright © 1976 by Sing Out!, Inc.
Reprinted by permission.

Library of Congress Cataloging in Publication Data
Dahl, Linda, 1949–Stormy weather.
Bibliography: p.
Includes index.
1. Women jazz musicians—United States. I. Title.
ML82.D3   1984   785.42'088042   83-19456
ISBN 0-394-53555-3
ISBN 0-394-72271-X (pbk.)

Manufactured in the United States of America
First Edition

Contents

v

Acknowledgments

Many people shared their expertise and enthusiasm for jazz with me on the *Stormy Weather* project. I would like to thank the following:

My editors, Joy Johannessen and Wendy Goldwyn; Peter Keepnews for many helpful suggestions; and my agent, Susan Zeckendorf, for her encouragement and faith in me. Libraries and other institutions also deserve a thank you. Especially the people at the Institute for Jazz Studies at Rutgers University, Newark, New Jersey, and Dan Morgenstern and Ed Berger in particular; the William Ransom Hogan Jazz Archive at Tulane University in New Orleans, Louisiana, particularly Curtis D. Jerde and Bruce Raeburn; and the staff of the Music Division of the Lincoln Center Library for the Performing Arts, New York, New York.

There were many, many others, too numerous to mention by name, who helped me prepare this book. All of the musicians and others who agreed to be interviewed are cited in the text. Finally, I want to thank my parents, Robert A. Dahl and Marilyn DeCamp Dahl, for their encouragement. I dedicate this book to them.

Preface

To understand the experience of most women in jazz, we need to keep in mind that jazz is not only an art form but also a subculture. And arguably, even more than other art forms, the music we call jazz depends on its community, for the young jazz musician is trained on the job, really; the apprentice learns from the leader, the members of the group, the gig itself. The musician has thus been especially vulnerable to others' opinions and ideas, to peers and role models who train, explain, encourage, give job referrals, confer artistic recognition. The true lone genius of jazz—a Charlie Parker, say, or perhaps a Lester Young—is as rare in jazz as in any other creative endeavor. Most musicians strive for their own sound *after* having learned everything they can from the ones who went before. (This was true even for Bird and Prez and Monk, even as they developed their unique sounds.)

Jazz as art/subculture has apparently embraced paradoxical positions. It is, for example, a populist as well as a highly sophisticated music. It is both highly individualistic and communal; very competitive yet often very supportive; defensive but aggressive; artistically rich yet financially poor. So aspiring maverick soloists have to deal with the need to balance their drive toward self-expression against the constraints imposed by the group. And the jazz player generally can expect few rewards of the kind heaped on pop artists, since he or she shares the fate of many creative artists—in America, especially—which is to be misunderstood, ignored, underpaid. Still, the male jazz musician accepts and takes for granted that at every step he'll be dealing with other men—from club owners to booking agents to band-leaders, fellow players, reviewers and writers in the press: a male-dominated profession. The language that describes jazz, and jazz musicians, reflects this reality. Full of masculine metaphors, the sense of fraternity or of a male club is everywhere evoked. A fraternity that both offers a refuge from the hostile or square-seeming outside world and which also provides camaraderie-cum-healthy competitiveness. The actor in this world of music is with good reason commonly called the "jazzman."

For most of jazz history, until quite recently, it has appeared that few women were part of this community of musicians. The reasons for this are explored throughout *Stormy Weather*, but perhaps it is well to mention here a few factors that have tended to keep women from playing jazz. Clearly, the qualities needed to get ahead in the jazz world were held to be "masculine" prerogatives: aggressive self-confidence on the bandstand, displaying one's "chops," or sheer blowing power; a single-minded attention to career moves, including frequent absences from home and family. Then too, there was the "manly" ability to deal with funky and often dangerous playing atmospheres, nightclubs infested with vice and run by gangsters. These frequently went hand in hand with a tendency to drink vast quantities of hard liquor, or sometimes take hard drugs, while continuing to play coherently into the dawn. A woman musician determined not to be intimidated by such a tough, smoke-filled atmosphere (where one's peers were probably all men) often paid penalties designed to put her in her place—the loss of her respectability being high on the list, as well as disapproval, ridicule and sometimes ostracism. And sprinkle the sexist resistance to jazzwomen with a generous helping of male fear of increased economic competition, since jobs in jazz are highly prized and relatively scarce. For a black woman, there was also often heavy pressure not to compete with black men for jazz jobs, which at times came to represent both symbolic and concrete proof of the male's abilities in a culture that denigrated his manhood. The jazzman was—and is—an intellectual of music, a highly literate man in his way. His standing and prestige were not to be given up lightly. (And white players too were sometimes openly hostile to the notion of sharing the bandstand with white jazzwomen, especially during the swing era and the big-band days of the forties.)

Yet for all of that, the historian of women's music finds, as I did, a long and quite illustrious group of women who have participated in jazz from the beginning. Often they've been buried in footnotes, or in the memories of other musicians. A minority to be sure—and they probably will be for some time to come: women playing jazz, recording it, leading bands, writing, arranging, producing albums, managing groups, concertizing. Names of performers and songwriters appear from the latter part of the nineteenth century—notably, Mammy Lou, an ex-slave. Women who've been ignored almost completely in the articles, the reviews, in otherwise often excellent histories of the music. Under-recorded or, sadly, not recorded at all. Their slim oeuvre long out of print. A blanket of silence. From time to time, mention is made of women in the jazz press, as when they were played up as a gimmick by many promoters, a lucrative act during the swing era and beyond. But they were rarely taken seriously.

The assumption about women in jazz was that there weren't any, because jazz was by definition a male music. Therefore, women could not play it. Therefore, they did not do so. When confronted by women who belied the assumptions, women who competently played trumpets, saxophones, drums, a deaf ear was turned. Their achievements were explained away: "It's only a woman—what can you expect"; or, "Wow, amazing for a woman!" These were the two horns of a dilemma on which many a female jazz career was impaled.

Researching many of the women's contributions to jazz is like what I imagine collecting butterflies to be—you go out with your net to many a remote, even secretive spot to track your shy and elusive quarry. Colorful, bright specimens, many of these women in jazz, far from the mainstream, and some of them downright eccentric. There are lots of them making music in small cities, pokey college towns, black neighborhoods, cheesy cocktail lounges—where record producers and jazz reviewers hardly venture. Ladies who have turned their backs on the business side of music, and who have validated themselves through their music. When I was putting together *Stormy Weather* over a period of several years, I was inspired by the personalities of the jazzwomen—the famous and the obscure, the white and the black, the old and the young. Their grit and determination and pride in their work often helped me keep going when I felt up to my ears in old newspaper dust. The struggles of these women in and out of music, their salty and witty views on life, work, men and the pursuit of happiness, lie at the heart of this book. I wanted not only to fill in the blanks of jazz history by citing their achievements, but also to capture some of the vividness of their lives. Because these are real foremothers, taboo-breakers, independent "mamas."

Who are the jazzwomen? They are the well-known, the stars of song. They are the blues "royalty" of the twenties. Ma Rainey, Bessie Smith, Ida Cox. Scores of others. The well-known singers of today, most of whom started in the thirties, a few in the forties. Ella Fitzgerald, Sarah Vaughan, Carmen McRae. The ever-felt presence of Billie Holiday. Big-band singers, called "canaries" or "warblers" during the swing era. Helen Forrest, Helen O'Connell, Mildred Bailey, Peggy Lee and Anita O'Day—talented white band singers who became stars in their own right. And many, many more. Brazilian, Swedish, British, Japanese. Scat singers. Avant-garde. A whole section of *Stormy Weather* is devoted to women who sing; another chapter explores the vocal art of jazz improvisation in light of the statements of the instrumentalists.

And speaking of instrumentalists, we find there are dozens and dozens of women in jazz who have played or are playing every instrument. Their earliest work, seen in context of the social and cultural history from which they came, is examined in another section of this book. In New Orleans, piano was the instrument of choice of women in the teens and twenties, but there were women playing brass instruments in marching bands, and saxophones, upright bass, *before* the twentieth century. Early black traveling units, circus bands, family bands—like little Lester Young's aunts, and his sister Irma, all on sax. And there was lively activity elsewhere—composers and pianists Lil Hardin Armstrong and Lovie Austin in Chicago, for example, and a raft of women leading bands in New York and elsewhere on the East Coast. The piano players—a group of very swinging players who developed their own sound from the thirties on, around the nation—are here, led by the great Mary Lou Williams, player, composer, arranger. Here too are dozens of women instrumentalists who played from the twenties on. The famed trumpeter Valaida Snow; saxophonists L'Ana Webster Hyams and Vi Redd; trombonist Melba Liston; vibist Margie Hyams. These players of traditionally "masculine" instruments often bucked nearly insuperable odds. We preface their stories with an essay about sex taboos and instruments—a glance at various attitudes about women playing horns, etc., at different times and places around the world. Bands and bandleaders deserve a special chapter to themselves, for women were so often excluded from men's bands, and from at least the 1800s in the U.S. they banded together in order to play. The swing era saw the rise of a number of interesting all-female units, especially the Melodears, and our featured orchestra, the International Sweethearts of Rhythm. The last chapter of the text discusses the reemergence of the all-woman band since the seventies and sums up the players and the happenings in jazz to the eighties.

The jazzwomen, their music and their lives. They're all here in a rough chronology that accepts the division of jazz into stylistic periods that span ten to fifteen years. Women not featured in the text (usually because their contributions were very marginal, or information about them was next to nonexistent) are included in one of several appendices in the back of the book. A bibliography and discography will guide the reader further. I have intended *Stormy Weather* to be a survey that both gives the achievements of women in jazz and conveys something of the personalities involved. The last section of the book features a collection of interview-profiles with ten women working in jazz. Highly individualistic, they have in common their dedication to the music, as well as the desire not to be treated as exceptions to the "rule" about jazz as a manly profession. These women continue to ask for something that the earliest jazzwomen asked for too—and that is simply that we will *listen* to them.

—LINDA DAHL

Part One

THE

FORMATIVE YEARS:

OUTSIDE THE

FRATERNITY

1890s–1920s

Chapter One

THE ONES THAT GOT AWAY

---

*Jazz is a male language. It's a matter of speaking
that language and women just can't do it.*

ANONYMOUS MALE JAZZ PIANIST, 1973

The root of jazz is Africa uprooted; jazz had its beginnings in slavery, when European melodies, harmonies and instruments were combined with, and refashioned for, African-born rhythms. And the purpose of the music was African-born, too; perhaps most significant of the elements that made up slave music was the approach to feelings, a codified straining toward personal expression that ignored a preconceived ideal of sound. This was what most distinguished it from the European aesthetic, with its stress on "perfect" tonality. The music of black slaves married the pain and pleasure of physical life with a permeating spirituality; one of its great, enduring strengths was that it did not sever the life of the body from that of the spirit.

Such an earthy mingling of the sweat and sorrow of the body with loftier projections of the soul must have been completely foreign to the general white population, with its inherited assumption of guilt toward expressions of merriment. Throughout the nineteenth century (and, one could argue, well into the twentieth), white Americans retained in diluted form a significant degree of acquiescence to Puritan attitudes. Such attitudes were boldly declared as early as 1647, when the Reverend John Cotton warned his

3

flock that "to sing man's melody is only a vain show of art. God cannot delight in praise where man of sin has a hand in making the melody."[1] Much modified, of course, this mistrust of music persisted in the general culture throughout the slavery period and after.

Blacks were intimately involved with music as an integral part of slave life, just as the white indentured workers, the prostitutes and thieves who were given passage to the colonies, and the waves of immigrants from all over Europe were involved in their folk music. But it was the blacks, uprooted from their homeland by force and made to survive in sorrow in America, whose music has the most to do with the foundations of jazz. And black women certainly contributed their share to the development of this music. During slavery they made up songs that both drew upon and became part of everyday experience. "Anonymous" was often a slave woman who crooned lullabies to the babies she birthed and the babies she reared, who made up ditties at quilting and husking bees or while she planted in the fields and tended her garden, who created music in her capacity as midwife and healer, at funerals and dances and in church, who developed distinctive vendor calls as she sold her wares. "Anonymous" invented music to meet the occasion out of a communal pool of musical-religious traditions. Women and men stripped of their names passed on standards and tribal memory to those who came after.

It was in the years of elation, confusion and turmoil following the Civil War that jazz began to take shape. The war brought an end to slavery and to the isolation it imposed, which had prevented among blacks the free exchange of ideas that fertilizes art. With abolition came mobility, if not equality. Many black men wandered, looking for work or luck or new vistas, and music traveled with them. But black women, history tells us, were more likely to stay put and hunker down for new roots.[2] These were women who, as slaves, had carried double, even triple burdens. Not only did they work in the "big house" or in the fields—as cottonpickers, even as logrollers and lumberjacks—but they of course did their own housework, bore their children and cared for their men. After abolition they were hungry for stable family environments, and it was easier for them to find work as cooks, laundresses or maids than for black men to find employment. Although circumstances dictated that they were often the family breadwinners, they deferred to their men, especially in matters political. Above all else they devoted themselves to the hope of better lives for their children. Great were the physical and emotional demands upon them, and most found few opportunities and little time or energy for goals beyond survival. Even so, what must they have thought of the warning sounded by Sojourner Truth in the turbulent years of Reconstruction?

There is a great stir about colored men getting their rights, but not a word about the colored women; and if colored men get their rights, and not colored women theirs, you see the colored men will be masters over the women, and it will be just as bad as it was before.[3]

Some black women, homeless or manless, did wash up on various urban shores in those postwar years, there to work as laborers, entertainers or prostitutes, joining the "free" Creole women and light-skinned slaves who were routinely sold into prostitution or concubinage in cities like Louisville and New Orleans during the slave era and beyond. Only occasionally did these women rise above anonymity as entertainers. Historians refer, for example, to Mama Lou (or Mammy Lou), a "gnarled, black African"[4] who worked in the 1880s in a plush, well-known St. Louis brothel called Babe Connor's. Mama Lou was the brothel's greatest single asset, according to writer David Ewen. She "wore a costume that in a later year became identified with Aunt Jemima of pancake fame. . . . Mama Lou was big, fat, old and ugly—that is, until she opened her mouth to sing." She not only sang traditional spirituals and work songs for the delectation of white male patrons, but she wrote or, more likely, gave the definitive interpretation to at least two songs that became huge popular hits of the day and standard pieces of Americana. Of "Ta-ra-ra-boom-de-ray" Ewen says, "She made the song so much her own by her presentation of it that everybody identified it with her." And though songwriter Theodore Metz took credit for the smash hit "A Hot Time in the Old Town Tonight" in 1886, "it is more than probable that he helped himself to a melody he had heard Mama Lou sing in St. Louis." The same is probably true of "The Bully Song," or "The New Bully" (1895), and "Frankie and Johnny," for which other songwriters took the credit—and the royalties.[5] Scanty though the record is, Mama Lou emerges as one of the first of a dynasty of female improvisational singers.

But the most common musical sanctuary for black women, and their place of emotional release, was the local church. There, far from the randy enjoyments of the cabaret-cum-brothel, thousands of staid, hardworking women, in flowered hats and cloth coats, burst out of their chrysalises once or twice a week to become wild-toned butterflies of song. During slavery the church was often the only safe meeting place for black people. It was the place where highly codified (because dangerous) emotions were vented in song and witness. And its music has long provided a deep well from which musicians of all inclinations and instrumentation have drawn. Certainly the music of the black church developed the fine points of Afro-American call-and-response and encouraged the working out of rhythmic patterns, or "riffs"—elements that would later become central to jazz. The black church, it could almost be said, was the first jam session—and black women were always powerhouses in it. After hearing Sojourner Truth sing "There Is a Holy City," abolitionist Harriet Beecher Stowe wrote, "She seemed to impersonate the fervor of Ethiopia, wild, savage, hunted of all nations, but burning after God in her tropic heart and stretching her scarred hands towards the glory to be revealed."[6]

The church has indeed spawned mighty singers. Some, like Mahalia Jackson and Marian Anderson, became famous as gospel or classical singers; others, like Dinah Washington and Aretha Franklin, brought the tremendous gospel feel to worldly songs. Even strictly secular singers like Bessie Smith could whip up a religious fervor in the listener and create a nearly unbearable intensity of emotion. "The South had fabulous preachers and evangelists. Bessie did the same thing on stage," said guitarist Danny Barker. "She, in a sense, was like people like Billy Graham are today. She could bring about mass hypnotism."[7]

The black church, a European form of worship infused with African content, was not the only religious-spiritual source of black music where women were leaders. Many African beliefs and customs, such as the ring-shout, the call-and-response and spirit possession, survived among the slaves and were nurtured by numerous "fetish" religions of which whites were usually ignorant. According to one musicologist, anonymous slave women of New Orleans and environs were probably the most important transmitters and interpreters of the slave heritage, including music. Collectively they performed this function through matriarchal dominance of the fetish religions, above all vodun, more commonly known as "voodoo" or "hoodoo." While men served "aboveground" as preachers in the Afro-American churches, women held sway as "underground" priestesses.[8]

To a significant extent the songs of vodun concerned women, especially the "voodoo queens." The most influential and famous of these was the fabled Marie Laveau, who by 1830 had amassed considerable fortune and influence. (Other queens of voodoo also went by the name Marie Laveau, perhaps in the belief that it conferred a derivative kind of power.) The defiance, pride, posturing and boastfulness, and the vivid symbolism of these voodoo-queen songs—qualities that mark the later compositions of the blueswomen—are illustrated by the following lyric, originally sung in the Creole patois:

> *They think they frighten me*
> *Those people must be crazy*
> *They don't see their misfortune*
> *Or else they must be drunk.*

> *I—the Voodoo Queen*
> *With my lovely handkerchief*
> *Am not afraid of tomcat shrieks*
> *I drink serpent venom!*
> *I walk on pins*
> *I walk on needles*
> *I walk on gilded splinters*
> *I want to see what they can do!*
> *They think they have pride*
> *With their big malice*
> *But when they see a coffin*
> *They're as frightened as prairie birds.*
> *I'm going to put* gris-gris
> *All over their front steps*
> *And make them shake*
> *Until they stutter!*[9]

Outside the black subculture, in the larger society, public opportunities for women to perform music were extremely limited; it was mainly in the home that white women played and sang. By the late 1800s every home that could boasted a piano, a major source of entertainment in those pre-radio days, as well as a symbol of ease and refinement. Average musical tastes ran to thoughtful, dreamy, even treacly melodies, music that suited the ideal of the delicate, corseted female figure. As for the lyrics, they treated themes thought dear to the customers' hearts: the pure was glorified, and the wicked excoriated. After all, it was the little woman at home who bought and played the sheet music. Cigar-chomping men penned tender ditties in honor of Mother and Home—and a few women managed to cash in too.

Among them were songwriters like Hattie Starr, probably the first woman to successfully break into Tin Pan Alley, New York's production center for vaudeville and sentimental songs. Starr left her native South as a young woman in the early 1890s with a sheaf of music manuscripts under her arm. Arriving in New York, she was finally able to persuade singer Josephine Sabel to put some of these songs in her vaudeville act, and her "Little Alabama Coon" was a hit around 1893. Starr's success and persistence were more than matched by Carrie Jacobs Bond (1862-1946), an impoverished widow who built up her own music publishing house and produced her own concerts. "Just A-Wearyin' for You" (1901), "I Love You Truly" (1906) and "The End of a Perfect Day" (1909) sold by the carload and made her a rich woman. Dorothy Donnelly, Anna Caldwell O'Dea and Rida Johnson Young were also highly successful women songwriters who worked with the top men of the early (pre-Broadway) musical theater.* Though these women were in no sense involved with jazz music, their presence and success in the field of popular musical theater—which by the twenties would both inspire and be inspired by Afro-American music—presaged the greater role that women would soon play in the various strains of American music.

In retrospect it would seem that music should have been a fertile field of endeavor for women in late-nineteenth-century America. After all, most Americans at the time did not regard music as a manly occupation. What all-American boy would admit preferring Bach to baseball? Foreign men, or foreign-*seeming* men, were considered exceptions: they provided the "heavy" culture, taken like a dose of castor oil. As for black music, respectable people, both black and white, looked down on it, if they had any knowledge of it at all. But though the pursuit of "serious" and sentimental music was thought best left to foreigners on the concert stage and females at home, and the "jungly" sounds to the ex-slaves, women were not active as professional musicians for a simple reason: strong social conventions decreed that "nice" women did not work. They were not to demean themselves by handling money—i.e., playing for pay.

This stricture (which also prevailed in Europe and was the effective ruination of many a female career there) became almost a law of professional music during the latter part of the nineteenth century. Women classical players, even pianists, were typically regarded as box-office poison. The public, entrepreneurs claimed, just wouldn't accept women on the concert stage, unless they were opera singers. The American woman, like music itself, was thought best kept in the parlor. Amateur societies of all kinds existed and flourished, and exceptional talents did break the rule; but there it was, a sheer wall of social convention, attitude and custom to be scaled. Thus, budding female musical talents most often remained unformed, while skilled women musicians printed and performed unknown quantities of music for private consumption. Unappreciated beyond the confines of the family, they and their work remained anonymous.

But what about women who had no parlor piano to retreat to, women who were déclassé by virtue of skin tone or economic class or sometimes by choice? They would have to find ways to play for pay, and damn the consequences. So they did, especially in the new mass entertainment forms that were proliferating in the post–Civil War period.

---

*Isaac Goldberg, writing in *Tin Pan Alley*, mentions other early women tunesmiths, among them: Maude Nugent with "Sweet Rosie O'Grady"; Anita Owen with "Sweet Bunch of Daisies" and "Sweet Marie"; Clare Kummer with "Dearie"; Mary Earl with "Beautiful Ohio"; and Mable McKinley, Dolly Morse, Marion Gillespie, Kate Vaughan and Grace LeBoy (pp. 98–99). See also "Women Songwriters and Lyricists" in listing of "More Women in Jazz."

Foremost in popular entertainment were the minstrel shows, with bands consisting of fiddle, banjo, tambourine and clackers, also called bones. White minstrelsy flourished first, beginning roughly in the 1840s, and mainly based on a series of sketches featuring stock characters in blackface: old black men, idiotic black men, foolish black men—anything but sexy black men. After the Civil War these shows became increasingly lavish, with bigger and bigger production numbers. They also became somewhat less virulently or obviously racist; one suspects that white minstrels wanted to avoid competing with the real thing, since ex-slaves now began to form shows of their own. Women performers were banned from the white minstrel stage (though in time they were permitted to *attend* shows without fear for their reputations). But though women could not perform, a host of female characters played by men graced the stage: the desirable "yaller gal," or light-skinned Negro woman; the dark Mammy, who was wise and warm but harmless and sexually grotesque; the ethereal, cool, elegant white woman. And the female impersonators who played these parts became valued and respected players on the white minstrel stage.*

Restricted from playing the main stage, white women and blacks of both sexes responded in time-honored fashion: they formed troupes of their own. White all-woman troupes like Madame Rentz's Female Minstrels of San Francisco enjoyed a flurry of popularity toward the end of the century, and there were other examples. "Between 1870 and 1880," says one historian, "companies like the Ada Richmond Burlesquers and Ada Kennedy's African Blonde Minstrels became exceedingly popular."[10] These troupes included female banjo and bones players as well as comediennes, actresses and singers. Though popular due mostly to their enticing glimpses of legs in tights, the shows were full of music.

Meanwhile, male minstrels were advising the female members of their audiences to "keep the home fires burning" as feminists began to agitate for the vote and other rights. American pop songs of the late 1800s responded swiftly to these dangerous notions, and minstrelsy, a sort of live news commentary for the masses, spread the word:

> *When women's rights is stirred a bit*
> *De first reform she bitches on*
> *Is how she can wid least delay*
> *Just draw a pair of britches on.*[11]

---

*Notably Julian Eltinge. Interestingly, when women did begin to appear in latter-day minstrel and early burlesque shows (and later, most famously, in the Ziegfeld Follies), they were constantly being dressed up as men, mainly as sailors and soldiers, to show off their legs during this late Victorian period.

9

Unlike their sisters in white minstrelsy, black women got in on the ground floor of the black minstrel shows—for a few decades after the Civil War, one of the very few regular means of employment and upward mobility for entertainers of color. By the turn of the century black minstrelsy had developed more sophisticated shows, merging with tent shows, vaudeville and black musical comedy. In these shows and revues black performers were trained and exposed to music in every kind of city, burg and backwater. Thus, as entertainers and musicians, black women could become familiar firsthand with the development and permutations of black music.

This they did in large numbers, as musician-historian D. Antoinette Handy has shown in her impressively researched *Black Women in American Bands and Orchestras*. Working mostly from newspapers of the era, Handy unearthed the names of many of the black women musicians in the early minstrel, ragtime and vaudeville bands. Among them were a number of accomplished keyboardists:

> . . . Mrs. Henry Hart toured with her husband's Alabama Minstrels during the 1860s and '70s. Mrs. Theodore Finney played in her husband's popular Quadrille Band in Detroit during the 1880s. Lisetta Young, mother of famed tenor saxophonist Lester Young, toured with husband Billy Young's band during the first decade of this century, playing for small circus companies and tent shows. Another family unit touring in Louisiana at the same time was The Williams Ragtime Band, whose "Mistress of the Keyboard" was Lucy Williams.
> . . . Lewis Anderson ("Minstrel Rabbit") recalled that his mother played the accordion in The Muse Family Band during the early decades of this century in Franklin County, Virginia.[12]

Handy and historian Frank Driggs also mention pianist Isabelle Spiller and saxophonists Alice Calloway and May and Maydah Yorke, who played with the Musical Spillers, "a highly successful vaudeville team of the turn of the century."[13] White women in vaudeville bands were a somewhat rarer species, but a few did manage to land jobs; one of them was Buster Keaton's mother, Myra, often considered the first white woman to play saxophone professionally in America.[14]

The minstrel and vaudeville circuit was a hard training ground. Travel was constant, competition was stiff, money was short. Accommodations were poor or nonexistent for blacks in most of the proverbially hostile South, so that troupes acquired their own railroad cars when they could, using them to change, sleep and eat. Rural audiences were poor, unlettered, often drunk and demanding. It was humble, grinding work.[15] Yet a stable environment—

a home, if you like—for black music was forming in these postwar years. Black entertainment districts sprang up wherever the migrants went, places like Decatur Street in Atlanta, Beale Street in Memphis, the riverfront areas of St. Louis and Kansas City. These were crime-ridden areas, witness to drunken fights and shootings, haven to prostitution, gambling, drugs and guns.

But in these "districts" musical fires were fanned. Ragtime swept through the country in the early part of the twentieth century, spread by way of dancehalls, taverns, brothels and labor camps. Its lively, fresh energy fed a voracious public appetite. Though critics often lambasted it and confused it with its cousins, the blues and jazz, ragtime eventually settled sedately in the family parlor on sheet music and piano roll. Among the ragtime performers—and while the craze was on, everybody ragged—were a number of women: in Kansas City, Ragtime Kate Beckham and a very young Julia Lee, later a well-known pianist and singer; May Aufderheide, an Indianapolis pianist who composed "classic rags" in the early 1900s ("Dusty Rag," "Richmond Rag" and "Buzzer Rag"); Adeline Shepherd with "Pickles and Peppers"; and Muriel Pollock with "Rooster Rag." Sadie Koninsky scored with "Eli Green's Cakewalk," and Ida Emerson collaborated with Joseph E. Howard on a smash hit called "Hello, Ma Baby!" And it is May Irwin, says ragtime historian Sigmund Spaeth, who "will always be remembered as the real mother of ragtime in America; the song that did the trick was 'The Bully.' "[16] There were many other ragtime women, even abroad: in England, for example, a Madame Adami played piano on a 1913 recording of "College Rag." These songs appeared on piano rolls and later on early recordings.

"Ragging" the classics and pop songs—using that daring syncopation was a big part of the technique of the solo piano artists who played with flash and vigor in bawdy houses, ginmills, taverns and speakeasies, at rent parties and socials. Across the nation, these piano "professors" developed distinctive musical signatures and personal styles or idiosyncrasies in dress, behavior and speed of execution at the keyboard. Some wore diamonds in their teeth or on their cufflinks. The professors functioned in a playing atmosphere that was almost totally male—though it was difficult even for some men to work as piano players in the early part of the century. Eubie Blake relates how his strict, churchgoing mother threatened to beat him to a pulp when she discovered he was sneaking out to play in a neighborhood brothel (his good salary calmed her down).[17] We need only imagine how much more difficult it must have been for women piano players to gain employment.

Though ragtime and other early piano styles, notably stride and barrelhouse (all part of the melting pot of jazz), were also played at eminently respectable functions like picnics, boating parties and socials, it was the ginmills and whorehouses, with the steady employment and better money they could offer, that can be likened to a kind of musical school or laboratory where early musicians could exchange and work out musical ideas.* In such places a woman player was a true anomaly. Indeed, when women were employed in an entertainment capacity at the variety of nightspots that included instrumental music among the pleasures offered, it was rarely in positions other than prone. The problems that women players were up against in the early period of jazz are explored in the next chapter, which also profiles the lives of the few female performers who were able to break through the net of inhibiting factors and get down to the business of playing the music.

---

*New Orleans bassist Pops Foster confirms that many piano players in the Crescent City made their money working in whorehouses and says that some (most famously, Jelly Roll Morton) emulated the prosperous pimps of the district (*The Autobiography of Pops Foster*, p. 25n).

Chapter Two

FIRST LADIES OF EARLY JAZZ

*I don't know if it was rough or not. I was rough
right along with it.*

BILLIE PIERCE ON HER START
AS A PIANIST IN THE TWENTIES

New Orleans, in the late nineteenth and early twentieth centuries, was a great cosmopolitan shipping port that attracted people from all over the world and nurtured a rich admixture of French, Spanish, African and European music at funeral marches, fancy-dress balls, resort picnics, Mardi Gras and even the opera (the city had the first opera house in America and probably the first black orchestra). According to any definition, New Orleans was also the first great jazz center, and its hub was the Storyville vice district, though dance halls and theaters probably provided equal opportunities for the development of New Orleans jazz.

Legally cordoned off to prostitution, Storyville provided plenty of jobs for musicians; at its height it boasted nearly two hundred "houses of ill repute" and a plethora of saloons, bars and dancehalls. Piano professors, string trios and small bands held court in the lavishly appointed whorehouses that were world-famous for their elegance and their multiracial stocks of women. Cheek by jowl with the elegant houses were the wretched little shacks, or "cribs," where down-and-out whores and streetwalkers, often riddled with venereal disease and addicted to drugs, waited for customers.

Storyville was no place for the shy or sedate, or for proper bourgeois values. It was a place where men went to drink, gamble, drug and whore—to the accompaniment of music. Colorful characters abounded. Among them old-time trumpeter Bunk Johnson remembered a pianist named Mamie Desdoumes, "a blues-singing poor gal," he called her, "used to play pretty passable piano around them dance halls on Perdido Street." Jelly Roll Morton remembered Mamie too.

> ...the one blues I never can forget out of those early days happened to
> be played by a woman that lived next door to my godmother's in the
> Garden District. The name of this musician was Mamie Desdoumes.
> Two middle fingers of her right hand had been cut off, so she played
> the blues with only three fingers on her right hand. She only knew
> this one tune and she played it all day long....
>
> > *I stood on the corner, my feet was dripping wet,*
> > *I asked every man I met...*
> > *Can't give me a dollar, give me a lousy dime,*
> > *Just to feed that hungry man of mine.*
>
> Although I had heard them previously I guess it was Mamie first
> really sold me on the blues.

Bunk Johnson "played many a concert with [Mamie] singing those same blues. She was pretty good-looking—quite fair and with a *nice* head of hair. She was a hustlin' woman.... When Hattie Rogers or Lulu White [top madames] would put it out that Mamie was going to be singing at their place, the white men would turn out in bunches and them whores would clean up." Other "hustlin' women" also worked as musicians. Pianist and music publisher Spencer Williams mentioned a "house run by Miss Antonia Gonzales, who sang and played the cornet."[1]

Music was a natural part of life for the inhabitants of the Storyville district. Jelly Roll Morton described "the chippies in their little-girl dresses...standing in the crib doors singing the blues."[2] And Louis Armstrong, remembering his teenage years in New Orleans, recalled this advice from an older and wiser friend: "When you play the blues, [the whores] will call you sweet names and buy you drinks and give you tips."[3] The music was unrestrained and passionate, calling up all of experience. Early jazz recordings are permeated with this flavor, shot through with the sweat, pain and sadness of the lives of déclassé women working the streets and houses of the district.

But the spiritedness and beautiful ensemble playing of the early New Orleans jazz musicians carried no weight with respectable citizens. Never mind that jazz and blues music was a blood relative of sanctified sound: it was tainted, inextricably associated with all the undesirable aspects of life and therefore to be shunned. The godly and the upright dubbed it "devil music," especially the blues, which extemporized in its lyrics on all the unmentionables. Said Jelly Roll Morton, "Folks never had the idea they wanted a musician in the family. They always had it in their minds that a musician was a tramp, trying to duck work, with the exception of the French opera players which they patronized."[4] An anecdote recounted by New Orleans pianist Olivia Charlot, active during a slightly later era, speaks for many women who came from a more middle-class milieu:

> After I grew up and found out what was happening, I changed my mind [about jazz]. There wasn't much opportunity for me as a black person to be a concert pianist. Then I really began to go back to jazz. The first time I went out to play with a jazz band, my grandmother put up a big fuss. She said, "I think it's terrible. Those men are gonna disrespect you . . ." But I was married and I felt I could take care of myself.[5]

This linking of jazz with the seamy side of life—a pretty fair observation in many respects—had a deleterious effect on the potential careers of women jazz musicians, especially those who came from "good" homes.

But the stance of defensive isolation that early jazzwomen must have been forced to assume extended beyond bucking the attitudes and aspirations of their families. They also had to contend with the male musical brotherhood. Early jazz meant individual blowing in a group context, and the training, job referrals and recognition came from within the musical community. This fellowship, both a natural support system (though highly competitive) and a response to the economic difficulties of the profession, existed wherever jazz was played. An early jazzman, Warren "Baby" Dodds, viewed it this way:

> The musicians of those days were remarkable men. When the leader of an orchestra would hire a man, there was no jealousy in the gang. Everybody took him in as a brother. . . . They believed in harmony. If those men would happen to like you enough to pick you up, they would either make a musician out of you, or you wouldn't be any musician.[6]

Jazz writers frequently refer to the early jazzmen as a "clique" or "clan," and one holds the opinion that "mass misunderstanding [of the music] resulted in the development of a spirit of 'underground' comradeship among jazz musicians. It was a spirit that permitted a free exchange of ideas across traditionally forbidding economic, racial, musical, and geographic barriers, but it also bred clannishness and the tendency to set up a closed society-within-a-society."[7] Under such circumstances a woman musician attempting to break into jazz needed more than musical talent; she needed great self-confidence, a tough, no-nonsense attitude and the skills of a diplomat. For, to put it bluntly, she was outside the fraternity.

Of the handful of women who did manage to break into the early New Orleans jazz scene, most were piano players who mastered the strong, stomping piano accompaniment, often called "gutbucket," of the ensemble style. One of the most enduring and colorful of these musicians is Emma Barrett. Born in 1898 in New Orleans, she drew from the rich local musical atmosphere, listening as a little girl to the "guys who used to gather on the street corners at night with one or two guitars and sing some of the old tunes."[8] After practicing on her own, she gained experience by joining informal groups in her neighborhood. The party-going enthusiasm of New Orleanians of all classes insured the prosperity, or at least the existence, of all manner of orchestral and band units, and Barrett soon hooked up with one of the most popular, Papa Celestin's Original Tuxedo Orchestra. In 1923, on piano with Celestin and company, she had the distinction of being one of the very first women players in the music to be recorded.

Like many of the pioneer players, Barrett could not read music. But she was in steady demand, and throughout the twenties and thirties she played piano for a number of bands, developing her blunt, barrelhouse style, which has been described as a "pile-driver attack." She also toured outside New Orleans, mostly with Percy Humphrey's group. Initially dubbed "Sweet Emma," allegedly because of her "artistic" temperament, Barrett was nicknamed "The Bell Gal" because of her custom of wearing a red dress, red garters, red cap and jingling knee bells that shook as she played. Though she had a stroke in 1967, at which point she had been playing professionally for at least forty-five years, she continued to play throughout the seventies and into the eighties, a fixture at such New Orleans jazz centers as Preservation Hall. Largely unrecorded throughout the thirties and ensuing decades, she was fairly well documented on record during the revival of interest in New Orleans ensemble-style jazz in the sixties and seventies. Barrett died in 1982.

Papa Celestin also introduced New Orleans jazzwoman Jeanette Salvant Kimball to playing and recording activities.[9] Born in 1908 (or possibly 1910) in Pass Christian, Mississippi, Salvant began studying piano at the age of seven. She later credited her teacher, Mrs. Anna Stewart, with giving her an excellent foundation in classical and popular music. As a youngster, she played piano with a small string group at her local Catholic church and at school. In the mid-twenties, upon completion of high school, she joined Celestin's Tuxedo Orchestra in New Orleans after a sight-reading audition with the orchestra leader, who had heard of her talent through the grapevine. Salvant married fellow bandmember Narvin Kimball in 1929.

Celestin and his orchestra were significant as a leading society dance band that played at parties and at the elaborate black and white balls held separately during Carnival. In addition they traveled the South extensively, playing high-toned dances and balls. During the late twenties the group underwent a change in format, expanding from eight to fourteen pieces and changing from stock to special arrangements. Kimball remained with Celestin for many years, leaving in 1935 to raise her children. However, she continued to play locally, working with Herbert Leary's group for about five years, with a six-piece unit at the Dew Drop Inn for several years, and as a solo act. In 1953 she rejoined Celestin and stayed with his band (he died in 1954) well into the sixties, at the same time giving music instruction and playing piano and organ at her local church. Today, in the eighties, the piano of Jeanette Kimball—an "incredible right hand and striding left"[10]—continues to be a part of the jazz scene in New Orleans, and she is still an active presence in community affairs.

Pianist Billie Pierce (née Willie Madison Goodson) was another durable performer from the early days of New Orleans jazz.[11] She was born in Marianna, Florida, in 1907 and raised in Pensacola, but after 1929 she made the Crescent City her home. Pierce came from a large, music-loving family; her six sisters also played piano. She never learned to read music (she didn't have to, she said) but picked up the rudiments from her hymn-singing Baptist parents and quickly absorbed the music of the local bands and the New Orleans groups that traveled around the South in the teens. She and her sister Edna used to wait until their father went to bed and sneak out to hear the bands—often to find that another Goodson sister, Sadie, was holding down the piano chores. Billie recalled that "whenever a show at the Belmont Theater would get in a pinch for a piano player . . . the manager would send for a Goodson girl, not caring which one he got."[12] At about age ten, when Bessie Smith was playing Pensacola, Billie substituted as her accompanist for some two weeks. That singer remained her lifelong favorite.

By age fifteen Billie Goodson had left home for a life as a traveling performer, playing blues and what she called ragtime jazz. For the next seven or eight years, until the Depression hit, she worked all over the South. She first joined the all-black Mighty Wiggle Carnival Show, where she sang in the chorus, played the organ and sometimes danced. Then she hooked up with a succession of bands large and small, including Mack's Merrymakers in Florida, the Nighthawks Orchestra out of Birmingham, Alabama, the Joe

Jesse Orchestra, the Douglas Orchestra and Slim Hunter's Orchestra—bands whose instrumentation was like that of the New Orleans groups of the period: trumpet, trombone, banjo, drums, piano and bass. As a solo artist she usually worked house parties, shouting the blues and playing her ragtime piano. During those years as a teenager working on her own, the money was often good, she recalled, but the hours were long, with gigs often stretching from one night into the next. "I don't know if it was rough or not," she told an interviewer. "I was rough right along with it."[13]

The freewheeling young player first came to New Orleans to substitute for sister Sadie, also regarded as a fine pianist of the period (Sadie played with much of the best local talent, including Papa Celestin's orchestra, before settling in Detroit in her later years). In 1929, during a job with Buddy Petit's band on the *Madison*, a Lake Pontchartrain excursion steamer, Sadie

The Preservation Hall Jazz Band. LEFT TO RIGHT: George Lewis, De De Pierce, Billie Pierce, Cie Frazier, Louis Nelson, Narvin Kimball, Chester Zardis. *(Credit: William Ransom Hogan Jazz Archive, Tulane University Library)*

got sick and called on Billie to fill in. After that job Billie played in and around New Orleans for the next year. In 1930 she joined Alphonse Picou and his group at the Rialto nightclub for two years. Deciding to settle in New Orleans, Billie Goodson became part of the crowd of musicians working the waterfront clubs clustered around Decatur Street—rowdy work that paid $1.00 to $1.50 a night and involved numerous nightly floor shows. The tiny salary was augmented by tips, with "smutty" songs proving the most lucrative and popular.

In 1935 Billie married cornetist De De Pierce, who recalled getting his start in music when a female cousin who played in an "all-girl" band gave him a hand-me-down trumpet. Billie and De De teamed up to work at Luthjen's on and off for the next twenty-five years. During the thirties the Pierces also played Decatur Street joints and little French Quarter spots with colorful names like Kingfish's, Pig Pen's, The Cat and the Fiddle, and Popeye's. Together or separately, they worked with and knew all the local players, becoming fixtures in the city. Though both were plagued by ill health in the fifties, they made a remarkable comeback in the sixties with their brand of blues, boogie-woogie piano and jazz with a Creole flavor (as in De De's tune "Eh! La Bas"). Billie Pierce died in 1974 within a few months of De De's death.

Dolly Adams (née Dolly Marie Douroux), born in 1904, was another New Orleans–based veteran pianist who came from a musical family.[14] The Douroux family band, which included both her parents, began playing professionally in the 1880s; her father, Louis Douroux, was a trumpet player with well-known brass bands, and her mother played piano, violin and trumpet. At the age of seven Dolly began the formal study of piano, supplemented by instruction from her uncle Manuel Manetta, a noted local bandleader. At thirteen she joined Manetta's band, whose personnel occasionally included such talents as Kid Ory, the young Louis Armstrong and Joe "King" Oliver. Two years later Dolly joined Peter Bocage's Creole Serenaders, remaining with that group until she married in 1922. At sixteen she also formed and led her own group, which worked mostly as a pit band at the Othello Theatre, playing behind vaudeville acts and silent movies.

After her marriage Adams gave up music to raise her family—three sons who all became musicians themselves, and with whom she formed a group in 1937. The Dolly Adams Band went on to play for dances and fetes in New Orleans well into the late sixties, and Adams claimed that she was waiting for her grandchildren to be old enough to join the band too. Having begun as a Dixieland player, she made a stylistic concession to the times by introducing rock 'n' roll in later decades. Though primarily remembered as a pianist, Adams also played bass and drums according to some accounts.[15] She died in 1981.

On the whole, evidence of women playing instruments other than piano in the jazz of the teens and early twenties is hard to come by. Certainly there were some female players—De De Pierce's anonymous cousin and her fellow bandmembers, for example, or Lillian and Jamesetta Humphrey, daughters of trumpeter Jim Humphrey, who both took up the bass. Lillian became a professional musician on that instrument, and along with pianist Ida Rose, she later joined the twenty-two-piece Bloom Orchestra, one of a number of black symphonic groups that sprang up in various parts of the country in the nineteenth and early twentieth centuries. However, it is not recorded whether Lillian Humphrey played jazz. Irma Young, sister of later jazz great Lester, played saxophone in the Young family band, with her mother also on sax, Lester on tenor sax and brother Lee on drums. Reportedly it was Irma who taught the fundamentals of saxophone playing to the future "Pres."

But examples like Irma Young are scarce, and the general assumption has been that apart from pianists, the number of women instrumentalists active during the formative years of jazz was small indeed. As guitarist Danny Barker put it in his reminiscences of early New Orleans jazz and jazzmen:

Only a few women have become prominent playing piano and singing with jazz bands in New Orleans. This is probably related to the music being born and nurtured in its early years in the brass bands that marched up and down the streets of the city. Marching on the streets, especially with a heavy brass instrument, just wasn't considered appropriate behavior for girls. Even when the bands performed and used pianos (which was and still is the most common instrument taught to girls), many of the mothers just wouldn't let the girls join them.[16]

However, there is some research suggesting that this commonly held view may not tell the whole story. As noted earlier, D. Antoinette Handy has documented the extensive involvement of black women in jazz, vaudeville and classical music for at least the last century, and she mentions a number of female wind players from the early marching bands and jazz ensembles.[17] Handy's findings dovetail with the opinion expressed by Curtis D. Jerde, curator of the William Ransom Hogan Jazz Archive of Tulane University in New Orleans.[18] As a specialist in New Orleans jazz history, Jerde believes that black women, especially among the lower classes, participated as instrumentalists in the music that prefigured jazz—particularly in the popular brass and marching bands—much more widely than has been recognized. According to Jerde, it was not until the 1920s that the players became almost exclusively male, except on piano. Why, then, had the female players all but vanished by the second decade of this century? Jerde points to the increasing absorption of jazz into the American musical and entertainment mainstream, where women were acceptable as performers only in fairly circumscribed roles. If he is correct, unknown numbers of women instrumentalists passed from the scene just as New Orleans jazz was attracting national attention and their male counterparts were establishing a niche in jazz history.

In the early decades of the twentieth century, New Orleans jazz began to spread and interact with the music of other parts of the country. In the years before and during the First World War, Chicago in particular attracted huge

The Lester Young Family. STANDING LEFT TO RIGHT: Cousin Boots's wife, Lester's mother, Cousin Sport's wife; SEATED IN CHAIR: Lester's sister Irma; FRONT: Lester Young. *(Credit: Mary Young)*

numbers of black migrants to work in its factories and industries, and musicians from all over the South soon followed, finding jobs in the mushrooming cabarets, taxi dancehalls, roadhouses, theaters and ball-rooms, especially on the mostly black South Side. There was more money to be made in Chicago than in New Orleans, especially after the Feds closed Storyville down in 1917 as a war "security risk," and the Windy City became a focal point of employment and innovation for jazz musicians. It wasn't long before players of stature like the renowned Joe "King" Oliver moved up.

Soon after Oliver and other New Orleanians hit town, young white enthusiasts listened, learned and developed what is today called the "Chicago school," or "Dixieland." There is no evidence that women musicians participated in this music or played with its primary exponents, the Austin High Gang. As jazz writer Richard Hadlock describes the "gang," they were an "almost fanatic, exclusive inner clique. These men listened, practiced, worked, recorded, drank, and finally found fame together. They regarded themselves as a kind of musical family."[19] One of the few white women to make her mark on the Chicago music scene was bassist Thelma Terry, who did so as leader of a dance band called the Playboys, recorded by Columbia in 1928.

> Not only a remarkable musician in Chicago in the twenties, she would have been so anywhere at anytime, for while there were few enough girls in the band business, . . . the number of girl bass players could easily be counted on the fingers of one hand without the thumb. Dominating them all was diminutive, petite Thelma Terry, whose Playboys at one time included Gene Krupa. There were no women in the band at all.[20]

If the self-schooled, fine white jazz players maintained their all-male camaraderie, the same cannot be said for the black Chicago musicians of the period. Among them were some outstanding black women who devoted lifetimes to the profession of jazz.* The best known of these early jazzwomen, and one of the hardiest survivors, was Lil Hardin Armstrong, whose career began in and centered around Chicago, in company with famous expatriate New Orleans players.[21]

Born in Memphis in 1902, Hardin moved to Chicago with her mother in

---

*The results of the Chicago census for 1920–30 begin to suggest the extent of women's, especially black women's, involvement in music during the early years of jazz; in that reporting, 525 black men and 205 black women listed "musician" as their occupation (Leroy Ostransky, *Jazz City*, p. 88). With this hefty percentage of participation, black women must have played in bands of all types, as D.A. Handy's and Frank Driggs' research also indicates.

1918. Before long she had landed a job demonstrating sheet music at a State Street music store, a common selling technique of the era. "Oh, but Mother was indignant," she recalled. "The very idea, work! And, above all things, for only three dollars a week! 'I should say not, young lady,' she said."[22] For young Lil had studied piano from the time she entered school, playing marches, hymns and the classics, and two and a half years of music education at Nashville's Fisk University had further prepared her for a more ladylike career.

But Hardin's humble employment at the music store, where she became known as the "Jazz Wonder Child," proved to be a stepping-stone to a great career break. She soon received a raise, and then Mrs. Jones, who owned the store and was also a booking agent, sent her on an audition with the New Orleans Creole Jazz Band, which had just come to town and was working sans piano at a Chinese restaurant. Trying out for these self-schooled musicians, Hardin won the job. Though her formal skills, particularly her ability to notate music, came to be greatly appreciated later, her "proper" approach to playing at first caught the men off guard. "I asked for the music and were they ever surprised!" she remembered. "They politely told me that they didn't have any music and furthermore never used any. I then asked what key would the first number be in. I must have been speaking another language because the leader said, 'When you hear two knocks, just start playing.' "[23]

The job at the Chinese restaurant led to others on the burgeoning Chicago entertainment scene, at clubs like the Deluxe Cafe, the Dreamland, the Royal Gardens. As house pianist at the latter club, Hardin (whose mother continued to frown on her daughter's somewhat shady milieu and often waited to escort her home after gigs) came into contact with the increasing number of fine players from the South. By 1921 she had joined a top-ranked group led by the recently arrived King Oliver, and that year she traveled with the band to California for a six-month tour. Leaving San Francisco to return for a gig in Chicago at the Dreamland with violinist Mae Brady's band, she was replaced by pianist Bertha Gonsoulin, who remained with Oliver until late 1922. Lil then rejoined Oliver and stayed with him until 1924.

In 1922 the young Louis Armstrong was recruited by Oliver as his second trumpeter and came up from New Orleans to join the band. Louis and Lil married in 1924. Separated in the thirties, they divorced in 1938, but while they were together they formed a mutually beneficial musical partnership. As noted by their contemporary and fellow musician Preston Jackson, Lil was able to help Armstrong write down arrangements, a service she also performed for Oliver at a time when most bands still played from memory.[24] Recordings made by Oliver and company in 1923 for Gennett Records featured Lil's written arrangements, the first such instance in jazz. She also helped Louis learn to read music, but her chief contribution to his career was in encouraging him to leave Oliver in 1924 and go out on his own as the star soloist she knew he was.

Between 1925 and 1927 Lil Hardin was recorded with Armstrong and others on the now-classic Hot Five and Hot Seven discs, with composer credits on several numbers; two of her most famous tunes, "Struttin' with Some Barbecue" (with Louis) and "Brown Gal," are still popular today. Her playing on these recordings and on "The New Orleans Bootblacks" and "The Wanderers," 1926 dates for Columbia, displays the qualities that made her popular with the New Orleans musicians. "The thing that delighted Louis about Lil's piano when he first heard it," one writer notes, "was that

King Oliver's Creole Jazz Band. BOTTOM ROW, LEFT TO RIGHT: Baby Dodds, Harve Sutry, Joe Oliver, Johnny Dodds, Lil Hardin. STANDING LEFT TO RIGHT: Louis Armstrong, Bill Johnson. *(Credit: William Ransom Hogan Jazz Archive, Tulane University Library)*

she played all four beats . . . and thus she filled in a rhythm that New Orleans jazz had been using or implying almost from the beginning, and that Armstrong's ideas fully affirmed."[25] And Preston Jackson observed, "Lil never was a flash. She is a fine soloist and can lay those chords four beats to a measure and solid just like the doctor ordered. . . . When playing some of Louis Armstrong's records recorded by the Hot Five, notice the foundation. It will speak for itself."[26] Discussing the pianistic approach to jazz in twenties ensemble playing, another writer points out that "all the early pianists thought of the piano in terms of full, rich orchestral sounds. Lil Hardin, in the Hot Five and Seven recordings, played strictly rhythm and harmony, and even her brief solos clung to that concept."[27] Hardin herself, who cited Jelly Roll Morton's "heavy and strong" technique as the primary influence on her playing,[28] summed up her style colorfully and succinctly: "I beat out a background rhythm that put the Bechuana tribes of Africa to shame."[29]

During the late twenties and early thirties Hardin continued her formal studies, obtaining a teacher's diploma in music from the Chicago College of Music in 1928 and a postgraduate degree from the New York College of Music in 1929. She formed and led numerous groups during the thirties, including several all-male bands and two all-woman groups, one in New York around 1931 and one in Chicago in 1934. She performed frequently on live radio broadcasts and as pianist for various theatrical ventures, including *Hot Chocolates* and *Shuffle Along*. As house pianist for Decca Records in the late thirties, she was featured on a number of excellent small-band jazz dates. During the forties, fifties and sixties she recorded occasionally, appeared at clubs, mostly in the Chicago area, and continued to write music. By her own estimate, she composed some one hundred fifty pieces of music during her lifetime.

Lil Hardin Armstrong played her brand of hard-driving piano literally right up to the moment of her death: in 1971, at age sixty-nine, she died onstage while participating in a live television tribute to the late Louis Armstrong. In her long and many-sided career she provided inspiration and often playing opportunities for other aspiring jazzwomen, and her piano style defied the myth of the timid, lukewarm female touch. As she herself put it in describing her debut back in the teens, "I hit the piano so loud and hard, they all turned around to look at me."[30]

A pianist of equal strength, also much in evidence on the Chicago jazz scene by the twenties, was Lovie Austin (née Cora Calhoun), born in Chattanooga, Tennessee, in 1887.[31] Like Lil Hardin, Austin studied music formally, first at Roger Williams University in Nashville and then at Knoxville College. After a brief marriage to a Detroit moviehouse operator, Austin worked the vaudeville circuit as piano accompanist to her second husband, a performer. As leader of her Blues Serenaders she also managed and directed her own musical shows, including *Sunflower Girls* and *Lovie Austin's Revue*. Around 1926 she took the latter act to the Club Alabam, a black nightspot in New York, before concentrating her efforts in Chicago, where she lived and worked for the rest of her life.

During the mid- and late twenties, when the great black bands of countrywide fame were still recent phenomena—bands like Fletcher Henderson's and Duke Ellington's—Austin carved out a prestigious niche for herself as a leader of theater pit bands, most notably at the Monogram Theater, where all the great black performers played. Austin remained musical director of the Monogram for twenty years. The young Mary Lou Williams, soon to be famous for her own composing and piano playing, described the effect of seeing Austin on tour at a Pittsburgh theater:

> I remember seeing this great woman sitting in the pit and conducting a group of five or six men, her legs crossed, a cigarette in her mouth, playing the show with her left hand and writing music for the next act with her right. Wow! . . . My entire concept was based on the few times I was around Lovie Austin.[32]

Indeed, Austin was not only leader and pianist in the band; she wrote all the orchestrations for the theater groups. She did the same in her role as house recording pianist for Paramount Records, backing such singers as Ma Rainey, Ida Cox and Ethel Waters, and playing with musicians including Buster Bailey, Louis Armstrong, Kid Ory and Johnny Dodds. Alberta Hunter, with whom Austin shared composer credits on "Down Hearted Blues" (which Hunter recorded successfully, but which became a monster hit when sung by Bessie Smith), reminisced, "Lil Armstrong, she played a mighty blues. And don't ever forget Lovie Austin. She wrote and played a mess of blues. Lovie wrote 'Graveyard Blues' for Bessie Smith and made hundreds of those early records. And it was Lovie who helped me copyright my blues."[33] Austin, leading her Blues Serenaders, worked equally well with the famous blues singer Ida Cox, backing her on tour and on recordings.

In later years Lovie Austin's career and fortune waned as her style of music passed out of fashion. Complicated legalities kept her from enjoying any financial benefits from most of her reissued recordings and compositions. After working in a war plant during the Second World War, she became a dance-school pianist. She cut her last record in Chicago in 1961 and died there in 1972. Like Lil Hardin Armstrong's, her style of piano playing belied the stereotype of the "feminine touch." Hers was a powerful and rhythmic piano. Speaking of the instrumental number "Steppin' on the Blues," which she recorded in November 1924, one writer describes Austin's

Lil Hardin Amstrong. *(Credit: Bob Parent)*

percussive approach: "The two lead instruments [cornet and clarinet] are supported by the rocking piano of Lovie Austin, who pushes the beat along, filling in the bass parts, her right hand maintaining a steady flow of counter-melody."[34]

In addition to Lil Hardin Armstrong and Lovie Austin, Chicago boasted other good women jazz pianists in those early years. Irene Armstrong (also known under the surnames Eadey, Wilson and Kitchings) has been described as a "much-in-demand leader and player in Chicago's jumping jazz scene in the twenties."[35] She began her jazz career in her teens, working as a soloist and as leader of both small and large jazz groups, mostly in Chicago but in other Midwestern cities as well. One such group was a trio of women players called the Three Classy Misses, which included Dolly Jones, the first woman trumpet player to be recorded, and Kathryn Perry on violin and vocals. Irene Armstrong recorded "Love Me Mr. Strange Man" with Eloise Bennett in 1929. But after she married soon-to-be-famous pianist Teddy Wilson in the early 1930s, her own career came to an end. "I gave up performing," she said. "My mother-in-law disliked my working in public places alone, and Ted's career was more of a concern to me than my own."[36] She later wrote a number of outstanding songs, including "Ghost of Yesterday," "Some Other Spring" and "I'm Pulling Through," which were recorded by her close friend Billie Holiday and have become standards today.

Research discloses the presence of several other Chicago-based pianists during the twenties, including Mabel Horsey and Her Hot Five, who recorded in 1928, and Lil Hardaway Henderson, who played with Joe Oliver and company in 1924. Hardaway took over piano duties for Ma Rainey in 1926, when regular accompanist Thomas Dorsey became ill. She was popular in Windy City cabarets, recording as Diamond Lil and Her Gems of Rhythm. Pianist Georgia Corham, long featured with her Syncopators at the New Apex Cafe in Chicago, was also house pianist at the black-owned Black Swan Records, worked on the staff of W. C. Handy's music publishing firm and was the mother of guitarist John Collins.

Up from Alabama came the blind "sanctified" pianist-singer Arizona Dranes, who recorded for Okeh Records in Chicago between 1926 and 1928. Dranes had come to the attention of record producers through the praise of musicians who had heard her at gospel concerts in Birmingham and environs. Songwriter Alex Bradford described her effect: "She'd sing 'Thy Servant's Prayer' and crackers and niggers be shouting *everywhere*."[37] Dranes' rocking piano style clearly showed the connection between the black music of the church and of the world. "It is easy, listening to her play, to see the relationship between gospel, blues, and boogie-woogie as practiced by roving groups of pianists in most of the larger cities in the twenties and right up to World War II," notes one historian.[38] Dranes' small recording output made her Okeh's star gospel artist, but she was chronically ill and short of money, and sadly faded off the recording scene. Her influence was felt by at least one later gospel-jazz star, Rosetta Tharpe, whose style was shaped by Dranes' gritty whine, razor-sharp intensity and pure ragtime jazz piano.[39] Another early link between gospel and jazz was the churchy pianist Martha Belle Hall, also from Alabama, who gained the admiration of Duke Ellington with her interpretation of his "Sophisticated Lady."

While these and other women musicians were carving out careers in New Orleans and Chicago, women players were also emerging in the various pockets of jazz activity that sprang up around the country. On the East Coast, pianist-saxophonist-accordionist Ruby Mason led a theater pit band at the Orpheum in Newark, while Alma Lambert worked as a pianist-leader in the Princeton, New Jersey, area.[40] Washington, D.C., with a large and relatively prosperous black population that supported a variety of musical activities, was the home of two women pianists of note. Caroline Thornton, said musician Claude Hopkins, "could *really* play a piano. She worked in the pit at the Howard Theatre, and I used to go and sit in the pit and watch her play the acts. . . . and that's how I got my experience, through Caroline Thornton and also through Marie Lucas, another great pianist as well as a trombone player and arranger."[41] Gertie Wells was "the best piano player in Washington," according to her husband, Elmer Snowden. "She was tearing up Washington, and nobody could touch her band. I played in it until she got pregnant and then we had to give it up."[42]

New York, by the twenties, was on its way to becoming the nation's entertainment capital, and the black community in particular was in the midst of an intellectual and artistic flowering known as the Harlem Renaissance, which attracted many fine musicians. Among them were a number of women. Hallie Anderson, the organist at Harlem's Douglas Theatre, was well known as a leader of male and female dance bands in the late teens and twenties. Mattie Gilmore, a noted pianist of New York's early jazz period, played in the all-black New York Syncopated Orchestra led by Will Marion Cook. The above-mentioned Marie Lucas trained and developed orchestras for theaters in New York, Boston, Baltimore and Philadelphia. And at the popular Lincoln Theatre on West 135th Street in Harlem, Mazie Mullens held down the job as staff pianist and organist. It was there that a teenage Fats Waller came to refine his craft. "He was overwhelmed," says Waller's son, "by her vast knowledge of music and her ability to adapt any piece of music to the situation on the [silent picture] screen by changing tempo, rhythm, or harmonies. He moved down closer to Miss Mullens to watch and listen, and sat through the film staring at her flying fingers."[43]

Mullens was impressed with Waller, too; recognizing his seriousness and talent, she took him under her wing, taught him what she knew and let him sub for her. When she left the job, Waller became the Lincoln's regular organist.

Meanwhile, north of the border, Montreal-based pianist Vera Guilaroff paid homage to New Orleans in a 1926 recording of "Maple Leaf Rag." With fellow Canadian pianist Willie Eckstein, she formed a popular team called Les Vagabonds des Piano, which performed in Canada and England. Guilaroff also recorded and had her own radio shows for Canada's CBC. Known as the "Princess of Pianists," she was widely recognized as Canada's premier jazz pianist during the twenties and thirties.

A glance at activities elsewhere in the country, particularly in the Southwest and Midwest, shows numerous professional and semiprofessional band units that achieved reputations as "territory" bands (that is, they played regionally, not nationally). Such bands often included women players; indeed, many were family bands where boys and girls received equal attention and musical instruction. Aunts, uncles, cousins, parents, children—these latter-day minstrel-vaudeville touring troupes gave youngsters of both sexes training and experience on all types of instruments.

Among these groups was the much-respected Pettiford family band, which featured not only the great bassist Oscar but his sister Marjorie on saxophone. Formed in the twenties by Harry "Doc" Pettiford, a musician of mixed native American and black parentage, the band included his wife and their eleven children; Mrs. Pettiford taught theory and harmony. Oscar Pettiford later said of the group, "Musically, it was well in advance of most bands. We played mostly our own material; we only played some standards to please the squares."[44] Oscar's older sister Leontine played piano and doubled on the reed instruments, as well as providing most of the arrangements and teaching Oscar music theory. This, he recalled, was the only instruction he ever received; later he taught himself to play bass. He singled out his sister Marjorie (see Chapter 5, "Breaking the Taboos," for more on her) as "a real great saxophone player."[45]

The Hamptons were another black family band that worked around the same time as the Pettifords, primarily in the Midwest and Southwest, playing theaters, carnivals, weddings, dances, political affairs—functions of all kinds necessitating great familiarity with all types and tempos of music. The band, according to trombonist Slide Hampton, usually included fourteen pieces played by his four brothers, four sisters, the Hampton parents, plus various relatives and friends. By the forties this band was noted for its modern arrangements, often written by family members. The band subsequently broke up, and the various Hamptons went their separate ways.[46] A later musical Hampton is Slide's niece Paula, the drummer (see Chapter 5, "Breaking the Taboos").

The Texas-based Teagarden family, while not an organized band, gave siblings Jack, Charlie, Clois and Norma instruction and encouragement in equal doses. Jack, of course, later became a famous trombonist. Norma, on piano, went on to work with combos and bands (and often with Jack) in the Texas-Oklahoma area in the late twenties, thirties and forties. From 1944 to 1946 she played piano in Jack's big band, a unit that in 1945 included Mildred Shirley (Mrs. Lloyd Springer) on bass and vocals. Norma, who showed a liking for the work of Bix Beiderbecke, was a good, fast boogie stylist. In the late fifties she settled in San Francisco, where she continues to work locally and tour occasionally, as on a 1976 trip to Europe with a big band playing traditional (i.e., early) jazz.

Husband-and-wife teams also afforded many women in early jazz the opportunity to apprentice and perform. The young Mary Lou Williams, for example, married saxophonist John Williams before both joined what became Andy Kirk's Clouds of Joy band out of Kansas City. Mary Lou, who became the band's key soloist, writer and arranger, acknowledged the support and encouragement of John Williams on several occasions (see Chapter 4, "The Ladies at the Keyboard," for an extended discussion of Mary Lou Williams). Marge Coy, pianist and organist, teamed with her husband, drummer Gene Coy, and toured with his band, the Happy Black Aces, one of the most traveled of Texas bands, "playing a rambunctious two-beat style soon after the end of World War I. . . . [Marge] was the regular band pianist and was reported to play a style very much like that of Andy Kirk's Mary Lou Williams."[47] And certainly there have been many other well-known teams, from Lil Hardin and Louis Armstrong in the twenties to pianist Alice McLeod and saxophonist John Coltrane in the sixties. Such musical marriages have given many women performers entrée into the mostly male society of jazz.

It is to that society, and how women instrumentalists fared within it in the decades of growth and experimentation from the 1920s to the 1960s, that we turn next.

Part Two

WOMEN

INSTRUMENTALISTS

1920s — 1960s

Introduction

"MY SAX IS A SEX SYMBOL"*

In a study conducted by musicologists Susan Yank Porter and Harold F. Abeles in 1978, musicians and nonmusicians were asked to rate various musical instruments in terms of masculinity and femininity. The results were instructive, if hardly surprising. For both groups of participants the flute took highest marks as the most feminine instrument, followed by the violin and clarinet; the drums were perceived as most masculine, followed by the trombone and trumpet. In another study Porter and Abeles measured parents' views about the instruments they would choose for their children. Given a choice of eight instruments, mothers and fathers preferred the clarinet, flute and violin for their daughters, and the drums, trombone and trumpet for their sons. A test of attitudes among the public in general toward the "propriety" of various instruments for girls and boys reflected the same biases.[1]

Gender association in music goes further than the type-casting of instruments. Another survey of parents' career aspirations for their daughters showed that girls are most often steered toward careers in music as teachers, not as conductors, bandleaders or players.[2] And even within the music teaching profession, though the majority of elementary-school music teachers are women, the percentage slims as the grades get higher (and the positions more prestigious and the salaries fatter). At the top level of the

*In the words of Archie Shepp (quoted in Joachim Berendt, *The Jazz Book*, p. 233).

important university and professional posts women represent only a small minority.

Perhaps the most interesting study conducted by Porter and Abeles was their survey of attitudes among children themselves. Though very young children showed little difference in their selections of instruments, by the third grade "the girls' selections consistently moved toward traditionally 'feminine' instruments, with the difference between the sexes maximizing around third and fourth grade." The authors note that the way instruments are presented to children (for example, in a picture of the chubby boy "Tubby the Tuba")—that is, the extent to which existing gender associations are reinforced—profoundly influences the sex stereotyping of instruments for the potential players. They conclude that "sex-stereotyping of instruments may be diminished if care is taken when initially presenting the instrument, but as these gender associations exist outside the music class as well, consistent reinforcement seems necessary."[3]

Porter and Abeles did not specify the context in which they conducted their studies, but most respondents were probably thinking in terms of instruments in high school bands or classical orchestras, not jazz combos. We may conjecture that if they had asked specifically about jazz, their results would have been somewhat different, showing larger numbers of respondents rating most instruments, except piano and harp, as masculine. For jazz means improvisation, and the prevailing view, at least until recently, has been that instrumental improvisation means assertiveness means masculinity.

But where do such ideas come from? As with all forms of sexual stereotyping, this is a large question, and one that needs further exploration. Yet, though sex taboos regarding various instruments form one small part of complex historical and societal developments, some general patterns do seem to emerge. For one thing, there is a widespread notion that the larger the instrument is, and the deeper its sound, the more masculine it is[4]—and, as a corollary, the fewer the women who play it. As one writer said in a 1929 review of the Boston Women's Symphony Orchestra, under the baton of Ethel Leginska, "Women performers are not likely to attain masculine proficiencies with such unfeminine instruments as the double bass, French horns, trombones and tubas."[5] Many instruments, including the tuba, the contrabassoon and the acoustic bass, have apparently been played mostly by men because of their great weight and size. Then there is the phallic or sexual symbolism of certain instruments—the flute and drums in preliterate societies, for example, or the guitar in blues and rock music, or the saxophone and trumpet, which have been the most popular aggressive solo instruments in jazz.

In many cases the use to which an instrument is put provides at least a partial explanation for its association with one sex or the other. Thus the trumpet would appear to be the quintessential masculine horn; whether made of shell or bone or metal, its loud, carrying and even frightening reaches of sound have made it a leading instrument on battlefields and in the military. Retaining this militaristic-masculine significance, trumpets and cornets made perfect lead and "signifying" horns in the marching bands of early American popular music and in the New Orleans jazz ensembles that played exuberantly after funerals and at parades and fetes. In preliterate societies the power of the trumpet was almost tangible; anthropologists report that the mere sight of a horn was said to be fatal to women in some Amazon River tribes.[6]

The drums are an especially interesting case. Musicologist Francis Bebey says that in Africa the drums "are virtually a male prerogative." Most often symbolic of the female, they must be interpreted by men, with certain exceptions relating to the type of drum played and the manner of playing (i.e., with or without sticks).[7] (Apparently this symbolism transcends geographic and cultural boundaries: in 1941 Duke Ellington conceived and later cut an album titled *A Drum Is a Woman.**) Many African tribes use the drums in their fertility ceremonies and view them as the mouthpiece of the gods, a sacred medium of communication. It is said that in some tribes a woman who looks upon or even hears a drum during certain rites may be punished by death, for her glance is thought to "pollute" the instrument, rendering it powerless—which is to say, impotent.[8]

Stringed instruments, on the other hand, have long been associated with women. The harp especially has been a feminine symbol, at least partly because of its association with angelic—ladylike but sexless—qualities. The lute was played by women in ancient Egypt, the guitar in Europe, the musical bow in Mexico. In the Orient, and particularly in the Near East and India, stringed instruments have typically been played by women and have symbolized the passive female. In jazz, wherever a stringed instrument has played a more aggressive and percussive role, it seems to lose its passive connotation and become an acceptable vehicle for male players.

For instance, if stringed instruments have generally been deemed feminine, the guitar, in jazz, blues, rhythm-and-blues and rock, has become a male specialty—and often a macho one. According to one jazz writer, "Like the flute, the guitar is an archetypical instrument. . . . Psychologists have pointed to the phallic image of the flute and the similarity of the guitar to the

---

*On Columbia Records CL-951. "Duke thought then [in 1941] and still thinks of jazz," say the uncredited liner notes, "in terms of a woman, many women, and a drum, many drums. And so, the title of this work might well be 'Jazz Is a Drum Is a Woman.' " The notes go on to give a synopsis of Ellington's long piece, which includes "the transformation of 'an elaborately fabricated drum' into Madam Zajj. . . ."

female body." His prose heats up: "Like a lover, the guitarist must woo the body of his mistress, stroke and caress it, so that she not merely receives love, but also returns it.... The singer and his guitar symbolize the couple *per se*, symbolize love."[9]

Wherever there are strict ideas about what is "male" and "female" in a given society, instruments and music—even sound itself—may come to be typed by sex. Thus, in trying to make music fit gender stereotypes, one theory even has it that Mozart's sonatas and Chopin's concertos are "feminine," Beethoven's music is "masculine," and Tchaikovsky's music is "transsexual." Lest we dismiss such thinking as merely aberrant, we should note the frequency in music criticism of references to the "feminine" or "manly" sound of music and instruments. On this view, the *way* the two sexes play is supposed to be different, too—some critics feel, markedly so. In 1962 Harold C. Schonberg, music critic for the *New York Times*, asserted that "playing any instrument is a conflict in which the instrument must be dominated and—generally speaking—men are better dominators than women, if only by virtue of their size and strength."[10] And in 1979 Schonberg devoted a long article to an odd, tongue-in-cheek discussion of the alleged differences in male and female technique among classical pianists.[11] Virtuoso pianist José Iturbi held that "women are physically limited from attaining the standard of men, and are limited temperamentally besides."[12]* Such statements—and, indeed, much of the literature about women in music—seem to be based on the tired old assumption of the inferiority of the female sex. On this assumption, those women who are demonstrably superior can be conveniently ghettoized as exceptions, and we need hardly be surprised that the "female way" of playing instruments has been judged less forceful, less convincing, less sublime.

Perceptions of what is properly "male" and "female" in a given society tend to shape the gender associations of the various musical instruments and can even color the way musicians are heard. These largely unconscious attitudes have real effects on the choice of both instrument and type of career open to women in music. For example, in 1938 the eight hundred women instrumentalists who were members of Local 802 of the New York Musicians Union charged that the eighteen thousand male members had a virtual monopoly on professional work in New York City, with the result that the only women who could get jobs were the harpists, pianists and organists.[13] In other words, the women who played the traditionally acceptable "female" instruments.

*Iturbi apparently mellowed in later years; in 1973 he reportedly admitted that "his late sister Ampar...was always the better pianist" [Richard Lamparski, *Whatever Became of...?*, 5th series (New York: Crown, 1974), p. 67].

Though many musicians have never taken to heart the notion of a musical instrument "belonging" to one sex or the other, cultural assumptions about appropriate feminine behavior have worked against women's acceptance as instrumentalists for centuries in the Western world. For example, in 1528 Italian diplomat and philosopher Baldassare Castiglione wrote:

> Imagine with yourself what an unsightly matter it were to see a woman play upon a tabour or drum, or blow in a flute or trumpet, or any like instrument; and this is because the boisterousness of them doth both cover and take away that sweet mildness which setteth so forth every deed that a woman doeth.[14]

Jazz criticism, at a remove of over four centuries, has often conveyed much the same attitude; witness the comments of *New Yorker* jazz critic Whitney Balliett, who ventured in 1964 (in a piece about Mary Lou Williams, whom he praised as an "exception") that women have always, throughout jazz history, merely decorated instruments with strings—the piano, harp, vibraphone, and guitar. Balliett thought that women's peripheral and usually short-lived careers (as he saw them) were due to the female's lack of the physical equipment and poise neded to blow, beat, and slap instruments like the trumpet, bass, and drums.[15]

The notion that certain musical forms or instruments are "unfeminine" appears to be as old as music itself. Though a thorough investigation of the issue is beyond the scope of this book, a quick and necessarily abbreviated glance at the historical record suggests that women have always participated in music as instrumentalists but have done so within culturally imposed limitations that they transgressed at their peril.[16]

An immediate connection between womankind and music exists in language itself: the English word *music*, a feminine noun in the Romance languages, probably derives from the Greek *muse*, which designates any of the nine sister goddesses of ancient mythology who presided over learning and the creative arts. The first woman musician we know by name is Miriam, the timbrel-playing prophetess of Exodus 15:20. The greatest of the early Greek lyric poets, Sappho (fl. early sixth century B.C.), was also a musician; in her school for girls she gave instruction in the twin arts of which she was master. In Catholic hagiology the patron saint of music is Saint Cecilia, a Roman virgin martyr of the second or third century; paintings from the Renaissance depict her as a graceful woman summoning spiritual succor from her lute. Numerous ancient frescoes, artifacts and pottery designs, as well as countless specimens of later Western art, show women playing all manner of instruments. The visual examples vary from culture to culture:

musical bows in Southeast Africa; conch-shell trumpets in Crete; harps, lyres, double flutes and long-necked plucked instruments in the Near East, with particularly good Egyptian examples dating from around 1500 B.C. and showing girls receiving musical instruction.

Literary and historical sources also tell us of women's involvement in instrumental music around the world. Court records of ancient China, for example, describe a music conservatory patronized by the emperor himself and boasting over three thousand women musicians who performed for general entertainment and government ceremonies. At least some of these female music-making traditions survive in the Orient; the geishas of Japan and the courtesans of India preserve their ancient virtuosity on a variety of stringed instruments. Musical proficiency was also expected of the wives and courtesans of the Roman Empire, many of whom excelled on a large lyre called the cithara. Throughout the pre-Christian and early Christian periods of the Empire, female slaves sang and played for their masters' enjoyment, their value rising as their musical skills increased. And, of course, women of the peasant and laboring classes have always participated in folk music throughout the world.

In medieval France women troubadours composed verses of great eloquence and may also have performed them, possibly accompanying themselves on lute. The most richly inventive period of female music making in Europe began during the Renaissance, when, particularly in Italy, women in convents and orphanages established and directed their own ensembles (the convent often provided a safe and intellectually enriching haven for women during these centuries). Eighteenth-century Venice boasted a number of fine women's orchestras, with players drawn from the city's four music conservatories for orphaned girls. These conservatories enjoyed the support of such esteemed composers as Scarlatti and Vivaldi, who taught and composed for them. The women played both sacred and secular music, and their concerts were well attended by the general populace. But all the incidents mentioned would come to be viewed as exceptional for women in the light of their experience in Europe in subsequent centuries, during which a technical mastery of music was the prerogative of upper-class men, and the few upper-class women who became musically proficient were largely reduced to serving as patrons of male musicians. If they were permitted to exercise their own skills at all, they did so as amateurs, most notably during the eighteenth century, when the rustic instruments they favored—the bagpipes, hurdy-gurdy and lyre-guitar—dovetailed with the Rousseauean passion for pastoral simplicity. Professional status was rarely vouchsafed women musicians in Europe; even well into the nineteenth century, women who composed and played music were seldom accepted as the equals of men and often used male pseudonyms when publishing their compositions.*

In Africa, with its vast array of cultures and tribes, women have a long history as players of diverse musical instruments. Obviously any discussion of this topic presents a formidable challenge; even today there are an estimated fifteen hundred to two thousand different African tribal groups, and much research remains to be done. Again we can only skim.

One detailed study of music making in a specific African society was done by musicologist John Rublowsky.[17] He examined the highly organized and stratified West African kingdom of Dahomey, which by the eighteenth century had become one of the principal suppliers of the flourishing slave trade. Rublowsky found that the Dahomans had established guilds to train professional musicians as well as other craftsmen. Such guilds tended to be family affairs that apprenticed the aspiring player in preparation for a series of tough examinations on a variety of instruments, including flutes, trumpets, stringed instruments, xylophones and drums. Just possibly there were women musicians in these musical guilds, for eighteenth-century Dahoman women, unlike their European and American counterparts, were chiefly responsible for conducting the central economic affairs of the society, and they could vote, own property, serve as priestesses and fight as warriors. More probably, though, women were excluded from the music guilds as well as from the craft guilds. "Sculpture and music were arts open to anyone," Rublowsky observes, but his evidence suggests that "anyone" was a male child.[18] The probability of patrilineal musical instruction is supported by African musicologist J. H. Kwabena Nketia: "The transmission of roles from father to son is quite common.... specialization in musical instruments tends to run through families or households."[19]

However, female musicianship seems to have flourished in the large number of less stratified, more egalitarian African societies. According to Nketia, women in these simpler societies historically formed their own permanent associations specifically to make music. In many places they still do so; a recent documentary on Moslem women in Morocco, made by an all-woman crew, included footage of religious and social gatherings attended only by women and featuring all-female musical groups.[20] Women's dance bands and clubs usually performed for specific occasions such as female puberty rites, the healing of the sick, funerals and wakes, and sometimes

---

*Even in the vocal arena, traditionally more acceptable as an outlet for female musicianship, there was the phenomenon of the *castrati*, men whose artificially preserved high voices substituted for the female soprano in seventeenth- and eighteenth-century Italian liturgical music, women having been banned from participation.

court entertainments. Indeed, in most of rural Africa, music making was and is part of the fabric of everyday life rather than a specialized activity.

Though we can cite examples of women instrumentalists in various African societies—professional harp virtuosi in Uganda, fiddlers in Mali, the friction drummers of the Tuareg tribe, water drummers in East Africa, idiophone players in Ghana and Nigeria—it is not clear whether they constitute exceptions to the rule. It may be that in Africa, as in Europe, women musicians were more culturally acceptable as vocalists than as instrumentalists, but on the basis of existing research it is impossible to be sure.

Turning to the New World, we find that European attitudes largely persisted among the white population. Among blacks, though we find evidence of both patrilineal and matrilineal organization of transplanted musical activities, we cannot know to what extent African customs survived among and were transmitted by the first American slaves. Certainly the cultural interactions and borrowings were complex; musicologist Irene V. Jackson cites a popular bit of Afro-American oral history, adapted from English folklore, to illustrate her assertion that during the slave era "there were all kinds of taboos surrounding women in relation to music":

> *De whis'lin woman, and de crowin' hen,*
> *nevah comes to no good en'.*[21]

But some African attitudes and practices were doubtless passed along, particularly in the slave churches and the underground fetish religions. Evidence of such cultural transmissions is found in slave narratives, folk tales, popular myths and rhymes.[22] And the African influence on American slave instruments and music was also noted by white eyewitnesses, especially in letters from Southern plantation dwellers and in the accounts of foreign and American visitors to the South. Occasionally such testimonies to the direct African musical heritage make mention of women musicians. One observer, writing in 1819, described a gathering in Congo Square in New Orleans, which was then and remained for some time a famous center for slaves and freedmen to meet, make music and dance. Among other African-derived instruments, that nineteenth-century reporter mentioned "a calabash with a round hole in it, the hole studded with brass nails, which was beaten by a woman with two short sticks."[23] Was that anonymous woman drummer in New Orleans following an established tradition, or was she breaking a taboo?

If the evidence on this and other points is inconclusive, one thing is clear: throughout history, in Europe, Asia, Africa and America, often in spite of cultural restrictions on what and how they could play, women have participated in music as instrumentalists. Today's women instrumentalists have a long line of often anonymous foremothers to look to as they attempt to forge their careers.

The opinion surveys cited earlier prove that sex taboos regarding musical instruments and careers are alive and well in contemporary America. And these taboos may be even stronger in the male-defined jazz world than in other musical fields.* As we have already seen, there are many factors that have tended to inhibit women from participating fully and equally in jazz— among them the raunchy, even dangerous atmosphere in which some jazz was and is played; the general lack of encouragement from families and friends, especially in the status-conscious middle classes; the absence of accessible female role models; male reluctance to take women seriously as musicians; and male resistance due to the scarcity of jobs in a highly competitive field.

In carving out her career, the individual woman jazz player has frequently had to deal not only with such externally imposed conditions but also with more subtle attitudes and prejudices that she herself may have internalized to one degree or another. Such pieces in the puzzle of her self-image may have represented hindrances as real and powerful as the objective obstacles placed in her path. Speaking for themselves, many of the women instrumentalists quoted and interviewed in these pages discuss in a casual way their personal views about sex taboos in jazz. As individual artists they hold widely varying opinions as to how they have been affected by perceptions of the propriety of women playing certain instruments. Significantly, in many cases, one or both of their parents (or sometimes siblings, close relatives or teachers) were either musicians themselves or were unusually supportive of their playing ambitions. Those without supportive childhood authority figures often became rebels or so-called eccentrics.

By and large, critics and writers have skirted what one called the "thorny question of women in jazz,"[24] preferring to shroud the issue in silence.† Most who have broached the subject tend to the Balliett type of viewpoint; a few

---

*For evidence that things may be changing in the classical field, for example, see Paulette Weiss, "Women in Music," *Music Educators Journal* 65, no. 5 (January 1979). Weiss asserts that music has traditionally had "female ghettos" with clearly marked boundaries—primarily vocals, keyboards and strings. But, she points out, membership of women and minority players of all categories of instruments in U.S. classical orchestras has risen dramatically since about a third of those orchestras adopted "behind-the-screen" auditions in which the musician can be heard but not seen. Such attempts to circumvent prejudice and insure impartiality are all but unknown in the hiring practices of jazz orchestras and bands.

†British-born jazz promoter, critic and record producer Leonard Feather is one notable exception. Feather actively sought out, recorded and reviewed women players and singers in the forties and fifties; he is currently a spokesman at the annual Women's Jazz Festival in Kansas City.

have been apologists for women. But in spite of the evidence to the contrary, the long-held assumption in the jazz community has been—and is—that jazz is man's music. An anonymous jazz musician quoted by *Down Beat* in 1942 summed it up pretty well when he said, "Yeah, chicks is wunnerful, but they ain't nowhere on that playing kick."[25] This conviction as to the inherent maleness of the music is buttressed by the fact that jazz managers and decision makers—critics, record producers, promoters, et al.—are, almost to a man, men. (The extent to which women are working today in these jazz-related professions is explored in Part Four, "Equal Time.")

Taboos tend to lose their authority and their seemingly magical power when repeatedly and successfully defied. There were many women players who pioneered in this respect in the twenties and succeeding decades, paving the way for today's greater freedom. Part Two examines their careers. Chapter 3, "The Ladies in the Band," deals with the all-female bands; Chapter 4, "The Ladies at the Keyboard," is devoted to the large number of women players who made their mark as pianists; and Chapter 5, "Breaking the Taboos," discusses women who emerged as distinctive stylists on traditionally "unfeminine" instruments like trumpet, saxophone and drums.

Today, as notions of what constitutes "femaleness" and "maleness" are being subjected to reexamination, so are the gender associations of musical instruments, as one function of all that is perceived as sex-linked in our society. But it is not only our increasing open-mindedness that is replacing well-worn stereotypes; it is the increasing defiance of restrictive traditions by women players. Greater numbers of girls and women are now taking up the instruments and musical careers of their choice, and that is the most potent argument for equality in music generally and jazz in particular.

Chapter Three

THE LADIES IN THE BAND

---

*One more girl band is about all this country needs
to send it right back into the depths of the Depression.*

SATURDAY EVENING POST, 1936

The "women's group" idea is nothing new in American music; the women musicians who banded together in the 1970s and 1980s to form groups like Maiden Voyage, Alive! and the Jazz Sisters were following a tradition that can be traced back almost a century, to the first "Ladies' Orchestra," formed in Chelsea, Massachusetts, in 1884.[1] In minstrelsy there were all-woman troupes like Madame Rentz's Female Minstrels, and there were all-female instrumental groups like the Colored Female Brass Band, led by cornetist Viola Allen, which performed in and around Michigan in the late 1880s. In vaudeville Babe Egan's Hollywood Redheads was a popular group, sharing the circuits with many regionally based aggregations like the thirteen-piece Parisian Redheads out of Indiana. The Parisian Redheads, later known as the Bricktops, stayed together from around 1925 to at least 1930, headlining top theaters like the Palace in New York.[2] There were all-woman dance orchestras, too, like the untitled house band at the Atlantic Gardens on New York's Bowery in the late 1880s.[3] A Ladies Jazz Band played the Hippodrome in 1922, and the Ziegfeld Follies chorus girls, according to one writer, went beyond providing visual titillation: they "danced and played on such diverse instruments as the banjo, flute, xylophone, piccolo, trombone, cornet and snare drums."[4]

In New York Marie Lucas, trombonist, pianist and arranger, took the baton for the Lafayette Ladies' Orchestra around 1915 after the death of her father, Sam Lucas, who had served as bandleader. She solicited women players through newspaper ads around the East Coast, and her Ladies' Orchestra received good press notices. Lucas also trained all-male theater bands in the East. Guitarist-banjoist Elmer Snowden, who played in her Howard Theatre band in Washington, D.C., recalled that she recruited from as far away as Cuba. There she obtained the services of trombonist Juan Tizol, later a key member of Duke Ellington's orchestra.

As jazz developed, all-woman bands, as well as women leaders and players, emerged to play the music. Between 1914 and 1920 various all-female groups had long engagements at the Lafayette Theatre in New York, often under the direction of Marie Lucas. Lillian Adams and Her Deluxians, a five-piece women's group, broadcast from New York around 1926–27. Trumpeter Leora Meoux Henderson formed her first all-female band in

The Parisian Red Heads (later known as the Bricktops), 1927. *(Credit: Duncan P. Schiedt)*

1927. Advertised in the *New York Times* as "The Twelve Vampires—Twelve Girls Who Can Play Real Dance Music," Leora's ensemble appeared at well-known theaters and occasionally at the Roseland Ballroom, opposite husband Fletcher Henderson's orchestra. Lil Hardin Armstrong formed an all-woman swing unit in 1932 and held it together until 1936, at which time she switched to an all-male format. Lil's women musicians included Alma Scott, Hazel Scott's mother (who frequently led her own all-woman bands); lead trumpeter Leora Meoux Henderson; Dolly Jones on "hot" solo trumpet; and Mae Brady on violin (earlier Brady had fronted her own group in Chicago, a ten-piece mixed unit with Lil on piano from time to time). And, as mentioned earlier, pianist Irene Armstrong had her Three Classy Misses in Chicago in the thirties, with violinist Kathryn Perry and the excellent trumpet of Dolly Jones.[5] Recordings by these aggregations are all but nonexistent, so it is difficult to appraise the music they made.

The formation of all-woman bands and orchestras by both black and white players during the early years of jazz must be understood in part as a response to the difficulties of gaining access to the more established—that is, male—musical groups. Though, as we have seen, women did indeed participate in early jazz groups to an extent not generally recognized, they always formed a small percentage of the ranks of both the pedestrian, workaday bands and those that were artistically challenging. In this context women's groups served the practical purpose of giving players experience and a living wage in their profession, as well as providing the less tangible benefits of group acceptance.

On the negative side, women's bands faced the ever-present possibility of being dismissed by promoters, audiences and fellow musicians as novelty acts. When big bands became big business in the thirties and forties, every kind of gimmick was packaged as a band, and the music often suffered accordingly. For example, in 1941 a publicity shot in *Down Beat* magazine featured a group of six sets of identical (male) twins as the latest in combos. Given the popularity of female-as-sex-object as a promotional device in entertainment, the many serious and capable women musicians who formed all-woman groups were all too likely to be lumped together with the "all-girl" bands of the "Look, Ma, no hands" variety. A 1938 *Swing* magazine article testifies to the prevailing skepticism among listeners; it described the "hooting" and "scoffing" at the "all-girl gimmick" among "experts who were convinced of the impracticality of women insofar as popular dance music was concerned."[6]

For these reasons many women musicians resisted the women's band per se as a professional tactic. For example, clarinetist Ann Dupont, who was compared favorably by some writers to Artie Shaw, declared in 1939 that she was through with women's bands; she went on to lead an all-male band and managed to hold it together for several years. Just as many contemporary women musicians wish to be treated simply as musicians and do not make an issue of their sex, so did many of the women players of earlier eras. But whether they liked it or not, it *was* an issue, and an important reason for the scarcity of women in the established bands. The women players who eschewed the all-woman groups had few options; if their music remained "respectable," their careers quite often remained marginal.

If they thought about it at all, most bandleaders of the era were silent on the subject of hiring women—perhaps wisely so. Their classical counterparts have been more outspoken. In 1946 Sir Thomas Beecham, the English conductor who founded the London and Royal Philharmonics, asserted that "women in symphony orchestras constitute a disturbing element. If the ladies are ill-favored, the men do not want to play next to them, and if they are well-favored, the men can't."[7] Three decades later, in 1976, Zubin Mehta, then conductor of the Los Angeles Philharmonic, caused a flurry of protest when he explained that he didn't think women should be in orchestras because "they become men. Men treat them as equals; they even change their pants in front of them. I think it's terrible."[8] The attitude of Sir Georg Solti comes as something of an oasis in this storm of prejudice. "Players of either sex are good, bad, or mediocre," he wrote. "The argument that women players make a different or inferior sound is just not true. . . . I defy anyone to differentiate between 'male sound' and 'female sound.' "[9] Solti's opinion is emphatically not shared by big-band leader and jazz drummer Buddy Rich, who once barked, "I would never hire a chick for my band."[10] And he, along with many other jazz bandleaders, never did.

Many of the all-woman bands that came out of the Depression years represented an uneasy truce between making money and making music. Women bandleaders and players were picked for their physical assets as much as for their musicianship: hence the group billed as "The Band with a Bosom." A woman leader who attempted to buck this trend and succeed on her musical merits had her work cut out for her. Consider the career of Blanche Calloway, a well-known black singer and performer in the theaters and nightclubs of the twenties. She was reportedly passed over for younger brother Cab when Irving Mills' influential booking organization, which had promoted Duke Ellington and orchestra with great success, set about building another name band for the Cotton Club in Harlem. Blanche was left to cope with inferior bookings and chronic financial insecurity: "Blanche was an established star nearly ten years before anyone ever heard of her brother. . . . seemingly overnight she was being ignored in favor of Cab

Calloway. He had Irving Mills behind him and Irving Mills had the Cotton Club in his pocket."[11]

In 1931 Blanche fronted a band led by Charlie Gaines; later that year she fronted the Andy Kirk organization and then set about building her own band. Taking this band to Philadelphia, she built on the talents of such fine players as Ben Webster, Vic Dickerson, Cozy Cole and Clyde Hart; the latter contributed many arrangements to the band book. Calloway's band, with Blanche on vocals, played mostly swing music and traveled throughout the country. Drummer Cozy Cole reminisced about his tenure with Blanche Calloway and Her Joy Boys (which also recorded under the name of Fred Armstrong and His Syncopators), "I was with Blanche about two-and-a-half years. She was quite a girl, had a good personality and looked exactly like Cab.... for the time, we thought [the band] was great."[12] Around 1938, however, Blanche was forced to break up the band and declare bankruptcy. She went on to a varied career in music, first as a soloist, then working with a band at the Howard Theatre in Washington, D.C., later managing singer Ruth Brown and working as a disc jockey. But for all her talent and effort, she never achieved either the success of her brother Cab or the popularity of the all-female groups that were then capturing the public's fancy.

Around 1934 Irving Mills formed a theater band that was one of the very few examples of a large jazz-flavored unit truly integrated by sex. The Mills Cavalcade Orchestra was made up of free-lancers, and many of the women players later went on to work with all-woman swing units such as the Mills-backed Melodears. Female personnel included Althea Conley on trombone, Evelyn Pennah on tenor sax, Marie Carpenter on alto sax, Florence Dieman and Elvirah Rohl on trumpet, Gladys Mosier on piano and Henrietta Bouschard on violin. Though interest in this unique conglomeration was substantial, Mills inexplicably dropped the project after about six months.

But Mills was subsequently approached by a promoter named Alex Hyde, who had managed "all-girl" vaudeville bands, and late in 1934 Hyde organized one of the best-known all-woman big bands of the swing era, Ina Ray Hutton and the Melodears.[13] Ina Ray Hutton was the stage name of Odessa Cowan, a dancer and chorus girl born in Chicago in 1916. After a stint in the 1934 Ziegfeld Follies, the "Blonde Bombshell," as she became known, was appointed leader of the Melodears. This fifteen-piece band was made up of white women players (with perhaps a bit of fudging here and there—black and brown players were often passed off as "Oriental" or "Hindoo" in those segregated days). Ina Ray and the Melodears went on to great success, aided by the arrangements and bookings the Mills organization supplied. Throughout the last half of the thirties they traveled the nation and made recordings, film shorts and features, with Ina Ray waving her baton, hoofing and tap-dancing her way around the stage, sporting constant changes of costume (*Down Beat* reported in 1939 that her stage wardrobe included over four hundred gowns).

Gimmickry aside, the Melodears grew into a good swing band. As with most dance bands of any duration, the personnel naturally underwent many changes. In 1934 the band consisted of Kay Walsh, Estelle (or Estella) Slavin and Elvirah Rohl, trumpets; Ruth McMurray and Althea Heuman (probably Althea Conley), trombones; Ruth Bradley, Betty Sticht, Helen Ruth and Audrey Hall, reeds (saxophone and clarinet); Jerrine Hyde and Miriam Greenfield, piano; Helen Baker; guitar; Marie Lebz, bass; and Lil Singer, drums. Later notable players included pianists Gladys Mosier, Betty Roudebush, Ruth Lowe (who wrote the hit song "I'll Never Smile Again") and Marguerite Rivers, who also played bass; guitarist Marian Gange; reed players Evelyn Healm, Mildred Wilhelm and Nadine Friedman; the versatile Alyse Wills, formerly with the Chicago Women's Symphony and said to play twenty-five different instruments; and Virginia Mayers, who played trumpet, drums, saxophone, guitar and clarinet.

The Melodears made a number of film shorts, usually with a flimsy plot thrown in. These shorts generally followed a formula: the band played an instrumental number, followed with a novelty number and closed with another upbeat instrumental emphasizing ensemble work. *Swing, Hutton, Swing* (1937) is one such effort; the band does excellent section work on "Stardust" and "Susie Q" and has nice eight-bar solos by unidentified trombone, saxophone and clarinet players. The music, in fact, was good enough to prompt one jazz critic to insist that the sound track must have been dubbed by a male band. Other Melodears films include *Melodies and Models, Club Hutton* and *Feminine Rhythm;* Ina Ray Hutton also appeared in *The Big Broadcast of 1937* and *Ever Since Venus* (1944) and revived the "all-girl" film format in 1955 in *Girl Time*.[14]

When Ina Ray Hutton's all-woman band broke up around 1939, the bandleader continued to work, first with an all-male unit, then returning to her all-woman format in 1949 and appearing on local Los Angeles television during the early years of that medium. The Blonde Bombshell toned her act down, going from platinum to brunette, but she kept her firecracker personality. In 1956 she appeared with her band on an NBC national television show that just missed becoming a regular series; in 1960 she led a five-piece male group. Thereafter she retired from music and now lives in California as the wife of an industrial tool and electronics manufacturer.[15]

In a 1940 interview Ina Ray looked back on her career as leader of the Melodears.

I wanted to lead a band. It looked simple. Just waving a baton and waving——. You know. The boys liked it.

. . . We played the provinces. I guess I saw all the men in America out front. Some of them tried to get backstage—some sent mash notes. But I kept the sex in the saxophones. . . . There were a lot of laughs, and some tough breaks, too. One night in Flint we had a long haul to the next job. So we piled in the bus and started driving. It was wet out—both rain and drunks. A car hit us and the bus turned over. It was a mess. I had to crawl out a broken window. Then a woman asked me, "Are you Miss Hutton? I'd like your autograph."

Everything happened on one job in Nebraska. My wrist watch and bankroll were stolen. The girls lost their instruments. And a firecracker blew off a couple of my fingernails.[16]

Despite such occupational hazards, Ina Ray Hutton made a very respectable salary as star of the Melodears; she was even able to buy up Irving Mills' share in the band.

During the late thirties there were other all-female white big bands with reputations as good swing units, often playing on the same bill or in "battles" with male bands. Elinor and Her Smoothies featured Elinor Sten as pianist, accordionist and leader. A group called the Ingenues prospered under Louise Sorenson, who was praised by *Down Beat* in 1937: "[She] studied to be a trumpet player but can play every instrument in the band and has exceptional knowledge of harmony and how to handle orchestrating for a band with so much versatility. She has led bands under her own name and has traveled with bands on two world tours in 28 countries." *Down Beat* picked as outstanding bandmembers Alaskan Pat Haley on harp and Puerto Rican Frances Gorton, who played marimba and accordion but could, the reviewer said, play all the instruments.[17]

The most commercially successful of the white all-woman big bands utilized the glamorous-leader formula popularized by Ina Ray Hutton. Ada Leonard was a gorgeous frontwoman with a background in vaudeville. Her band, with above-average charts and good bookings, attracted some of the best young white jazzwomen of the early forties, women like trumpeter Norma Carson and violinist Ginger Smock, whose first professional gigs were with Leonard's band. For a time her group also included altoist Rosalyn (Roz) Cron, who played with an all-woman big band in Los Angeles in the late seventies and still free-lances. In the early fifties Ada Leonard starred on a Los Angeles television talent showcase.

Glamorous Rita Rio fronted another popular "all-girl" band before moving to Hollywood and becoming actress Donna Drake. In 1938 she responded to an anonymous *Down Beat* critic's rather brutal (and racist) attack on female musicianship with a published rebuttal that was well-meaning but is now interesting mainly for its period display of precious defensiveness. In an article entitled "Why Women Musicians Are Inferior" the critic had written, among other things, "Why is it that outside of a few sepia females the woman musician never was born capable of sending anyone further than the nearest exit? . . . You can forgive them for lacking guts in their playing but even women should be able to play with feeling and expression and *they never do it*." Rio countered that "feeling, tone and phrasing is a quality which girls alone are more likely to possess because of the aesthetic nature of their sex. I noticed girls, because of their feminine tendency, cooperate to make the rhythm section a united unit dependent on each other, rather than the masculine tendency to lead on his own instrument." Her closing argument is sweet, if weak: "Girls find a pleasing picture does not detract from good musicianship."[18]

The precision work of the all-woman swing bands was technically matched by the playing of several strictly commercial bands. One of these, the Hormel Girls' Caravan, was begun as a promotional device in 1946 and was still active in 1951. A drum-and-bugle corps that grew to a twenty-four-piece dance orchestra, the Caravan also spawned a combo that played jazz-inspired "Dixieland."[19] Another popular group was Phil Spitalny and His All-Girl Orchestra. Corny as its music may have been—what was then called "Mickey Mouse" music—Spitalny's orchestra lasted longer than any other all-female band, or than most bands of any kind, for that matter. Spitalny and company entertained and amused a substantial audience from 1934 to 1955.

Spitalny, a Russian émigré and a clarinet prodigy as a child, had led an all-male orchestra until Depression conditions forced him to disband it. Upon hearing "Evelyn and Her Magic Violin" at her debut recital (Evelyn Kaye Klein, a recent Juilliard graduate, and later Mrs. Phil Spitalny), the bandleader hit on the idea of forming an all-female orchestra. The idea was nothing new, of course, but Spitalny's approach was original at a time when bands were often slapped together overnight to cash in on the dance craze: having secured the "Magic Violin," he proceeded to scour the ranks of women players, reportedly auditioning at least a thousand before he found a group that satisfied him. Generally his players served long tenures with the band, no doubt because of the better-than-average money and the unusually liberal benefits, including paid vacations. Many of his musicians reportedly owned stock in the organization.

Playing light dance music, the Spitalny orchestra relied on band-members Evelyn Kaye, Velma Rooke (first trombone) and Rosa Linda (piano) for many of its arrangements. In its genre the band was immediately successful, winning awards and getting radio spots. According to *Swing*, Arturo Toscanini "was amazed at the precision and skill of these girls" and claimed that their radio show was his favorite. The same magazine enthused, "Spitalny proved that women could bring to dance music the famous feminine qualities of gentleness, good taste, charm and romance."[20] A hot band it was not.

"Famous feminine qualities" notwithstanding, a number of all-female big bands provided ample evidence that women could swing. As we have seen, some of these units were white, but more often they were made up of black women. The forties brought some integration of white and black players, but on the whole, racial integration was as rare among women's groups as among men's. Black bassist Lucille Dixon recalled that she could not get work with the dance band of a popular white leader; however, she did land a job as bassist for the Earl Hines Orchestra in the early forties.[21]

One of the earliest of the fine black all-woman jazz and dance bands was the Harlem Playgirls, organized in 1935 by Sylvester Rice. The Playgirls traveled around the country winning over skeptical audiences, as in a memorable engagement at the hard-rocking Savoy Ballroom in 1938. Among Playgirls personnel were trombonist Elizabeth King; Mary Shannin, Jean Ray Lee and Alice Proctor on trumpet; Marie Backstrom, who learned to play bass in one week; Pamela Moore on violin; Orvella Moore on piano; Lula Edge on saxophone; Jennie Byrd on drums; Ernestine "Tiny" Davis on second (solo) trumpet; and leaders Mayme Lacy and Babe Brisco. Lela Julius, who earlier had co-led a "jump" band with trombonist Edna Crump, stepped in as Playgirls leader in 1938. Many of these women later worked with the best-known of the black female bands, the International Sweethearts of Rhythm, and with groups like the Darlings of Rhythm orchestra, formed and led by Clarence Love after World War II.

The most famous of the women's bands began in a very humble way, and its story illustrates how female musicianship can flourish when given adequate support and attention. The International Sweethearts of Rhythm got its start as a fund-raising effort for the Piney Woods School in Mississippi. Piney Woods was a boarding school for poor and orphaned children—mostly blacks, but including other minorities—and was largely dependent on contributions for its survival. Laurence C. Jones, the school principal, was the driving force behind this all-girl band. After hearing Ina Ray Hutton and the Melodears, he decided to organize a similar group at the school to raise money by playing local dances and parties. "We had Mexicans, Chinese girls and others, so it was the *International* Sweethearts," emphasized Judy Bayron, an original member of the band. "Some of the girls were picked out of a marching band from the school."[22] But Laurence Jones was an indefatigable recruiter of teenage talent wherever it showed up, as Bayron's experience attests.

> I tagged along to the school with my sister Grace. We had met Mr. Jones in New York. He followed my sister home from her sax lesson. Finally, he came to the house—and his fly was open! My mother didn't speak English; she kept telling me in Spanish, "Will you get rid of this man?" Finally my sister calmed her down and told her who he was. My mother was so nervous. But he wanted us to move down to Piney Woods, for my father to teach there. But my father did not speak English and he told him, "It's going to be a little difficult for us to move down there!"

Then a sad twist of fate intervened in Jones' favor; the Bayron sisters' parents both died, and "finally, when we did become orphans, we did join the band. So at Piney Woods they said, 'What's empty in the band?' 'The guitar!' 'Give it to her.' I sat there for about six months just plucking on three strings. I didn't know the difference! Then there was an empty space in the trombone section, so they put me there."

Another bandmember was recruited in an equally unlikely manner. Evelyn McGee, who later married Sweethearts staff conductor-arranger Jesse Stone, recalled:

> I joined the band accidentally, through the band coming to Anderson, South Carolina, where I'm from. I was in my senior year of high school and the school asked the band to let me sing a song with them that particular night. The director, Mrs. Jones [Mrs. Rae Lee Jones, not related to Laurence Jones, had joined the band as manager-cum-traveling-housemistress], encouraged my mother to let me leave home that night. My mother came out on the porch with a lamp and said, "Who is it?" At that time, the Depression was just over in the South. My mother let me leave that night. We were extremely poor: I had a pasteboard box with all my things in it.

But the Sweethearts began to attract professional musicians as their appeal grew, and soon the band ventured far afield of Piney Woods, Mississippi, touring throughout the South, living and rehearsing on their bus. Willie Mae Lee Wong, who played baritone sax and served as band treasurer for many years, recalled those early days as follows:

> The original Sweethearts incorporated and we started out with a dollar a day for food and one dollar a week for pocket money—eight

dollars a week, and that continued for years. Then we got a substantial raise, to fifteen dollars a week. And when we ended up, we were making fifteen dollars a night for three nights . . . a week, which is forty-five dollars a week. But some of the professionals that were with the band, I understand they were making a hundred dollars, a hundred and fifty dollars a week.

Nor did the incorporated members of the Sweethearts of Rhythm profit from their later recordings and film work; in fact, they eventually discovered that all their savings, entrusted with Mrs. Jones over the years, had been lost through poor management.

Even so, band morale stayed high. The original players were, after all, only teenagers, and the band gave them a chance to travel and see much more of the world than they would otherwise have done. And they were being forged into a good, tight group. "We had a teacher that traveled with us on the bus as our tutor," said Wong. "And we rehearsed quite a bit. We were like a football team—we just turned pro. And we didn't really think about money—we just liked playing." Evelyn McGee Stone agreed: "We went on to what I would say were great heights, because I don't think any girls' band had the rhythm and the guidance we did to really get down!" The Sweethearts' few available recordings and films bear her out: this band swung.

The Sweethearts owed part of their success to the musicians who wrote and arranged for them. Bandmember Edna Williams, a fine solo trumpet player, was one of the first to do so. "She was very good," said Stone. "We played a lot of her arrangements in the early forties. Then we had Eddie Durham and Jesse Stone." Durham worked for the band after it broke with its founder, Dr. Jones, due to unspecified conflicts. (Jones then formed another all-female group called the Swinging Rays of Rhythm, which played extensively, mainly in the South.) After his departure the Sweethearts began afresh, fronted by the beautiful Anna Mae (or Anna May) Winburn. Winburn had been in Omaha, Nebraska, leading a band that included guitarist Charlie Christian for a time. This band, the Cotton Club Boys, was raided by Fletcher Henderson's orchestra in 1941, leaving Winburn stranded in Omaha. Thus she readily agreed to front the Sweethearts when she was approached. She debuted with the band at the Apollo Theatre.

Now the Sweethearts, with Winburn in front and Durham writing the arrangements, really began to attract attention. Durham tailored his "jump" tunes to the abilities of the players. "Knowing that there were few improvisers in the band [at that time], he wrote out solos for them that sounded as if they were improvised on the spot," notes one writer.[23] Jesse Stone succeeded Durham and further honed the band book. Maurice King began writing for the band in the mid-forties, when more experienced musicians had joined up, and he also added extensively to the Sweethearts' book. During the forties, thanks to its years of playing experience, the band achieved a polished sound and became known for its tight section work and rhythmic bounce.

The increasing excellence of the International Sweethearts of Rhythm attracted not only good professional black jazzwomen but also white players, who now wanted to work with this most prominent women's band. But integration brought the usual headaches; any obvious mixing of the races was virtually against the law in most of the South, where the band performed frequently. Alto player Roz Cron from Boston, formerly with the Ada Leonard band, was one of the first whites to join. "We didn't think of ourselves as white," she said. But the law did. "I had my night in jail in El Paso, Texas. Even though I was coached to say I was mixed, it didn't go over." Anna Mae Winburn recalled, "We had so many mixed girls, mulattas. And we had trouble from the cops about this." The familiar, hideous American comedy of trying to pass—as black, in this instance—worked sometimes, but "we couldn't paint their eyes," noted Winburn drily. "So we had quite a time—we did a lot to break down prejudice in the South." Winburn, Cron and their contemporaries were philosophical about racism because they felt they were doing something exciting and important in playing with the Sweethearts. "It was a ball," Cron concluded simply.

By the mid-forties the Sweethearts were playing the top spots—places like the Apollo and the Savoy Ballroom in New York—as well as roadhouses in the South. They traveled to Europe to entertain troops after the war, cut records and were featured in film shorts, including *That Man of Mine*, which starred Ruby Dee and had the Sweethearts playing the theme song. They appealed to audiences and fellow musicians alike. Bandleaders such as Jimmie Lunceford (whose style the Sweethearts emulated) and Earl Hines were enthusiastic about their bright, fresh sound. "You could put those girls behind a curtain and people would be convinced it was men playing," said Maurice King.[24]

At the end of 1948 the band, like so many others, broke up due to changing tastes and the economics of the postwar period. But for a decade the International Sweethearts of Rhythm garnered enthusiastic response from dance and jazz fans around the country, gave invaluable playing experience to scores of women musicians and showcased fine solo talents.*

*After 1948 personnel from the Sweethearts recombined under different names, and groups led by Winburn used the name "Sweethearts of Rhythm" into the fifties. Among the many players who passed through the ranks of the International Sweethearts of Rhythm from 1938 to 1948 were the following, in alphabetical order: Grace Bayron, saxophone; Judy Bayron, trombone; Pauline Braddy, drums; Viola (Vi) Burnside, tenor saxophone; Ina Belle Byrd, trombone; Rae

With groups like the Sweethearts and the Melodears achieving broad popular appeal in the United States, it wasn't long before the all-woman-band idea caught on in other countries as well. In Havana, Cuba, Concepción Castro led the all-female Anacoma Orchestra, and in Japan, Harumi Miyagama led a fourteen-piece swing band that appeared regularly at a Tokyo hotel ballroom. During the American occupation of Japan after World War II, an American woman, Sharon Rogers, formed a popular swing band in Osaka. Scholar S. Frederick Starr, author of *Red & Hot: The Fate of Jazz in the Soviet Union,* notes the existence in Russia of an all-woman jazz band, Zhen-Dzhaz, circa 1939.[25] And England had its fair share of female ensembles, though most of them, according to historian Frank Driggs, "were relegated to the provinces: The Rhythm Girls (Yorkshire), Gladys Wigginton (Newquay), The Boston Belles (Scarborough), Marie and Her Orchestra (Cardiff). A man named Don Rico was the Phil Spitalny of England in using an all-women string orchestra until 1936, when he changed over to brass and reeds (unfortunately considered male domain)."[26] In 1949 Blanche Coleman led an all-female European band to which reviewers responded positively, if with that flabbergasted tone they employed all too often when confronted by respectable female technique.

Englishwoman Ivy Benson, bandleader and alto saxophonist, deserves special mention. She managed to remain active in big-band music for more than thirty-five years, despite many obstacles. Having learned to play piano at an early age from her musician father, Benson moved on to clarinet, then to saxophone, and then to the usual problem—where to play. She joined a number of all-woman ensembles led by others but found the experience unsatisfactory. "All you had to do was toodle," she remembered. "Once upon a time it was almost laughable when one heard a girl attempt a jazz solo." Like many of her female contemporaries, she found better playing opportunities during the Second World War, when there was a shortage of males to fill band positions. After the war, in the face of what she termed "an unbroken struggle versus discrimination," Benson put together her own orchestra, composed entirely of women. Unrecorded for decades, she finally made her recording debut in 1976. Meanwhile she kept her band alive and playing, though often precariously. In an interview in the seventies, she catalogued the organizational and personal problems of running a big

---

Carter, trumpet; Roz Cron, alto saxophone; Ernestine "Tiny" Davis, trumpet; Lucille Dixon, bass; Amy Garrison, saxophone; Margaret Trump Gibson, bass; Ione and Irene Gresham, saxophone; Helen Jones, trombone; Roxanna Lucas, guitar; Marjorie (Marge) Pettiford, alto saxophone; Carline Ray, electric guitar and bass, vocals; Johnny Mae Rice, piano; Helen Saine, tenor and alto saxophone; Evelyn McGee Stone, vocals; Johnnie Mae (Tex) Stransbery, trumpet; Edna Williams, trumpet, vocals, arranger; Anna Mae Winburn, leader, vocals; and Willie Mae Lee Wong, baritone saxophone.

band—bandmembers running off with men, not paying adequate attention to their music, and so on—but concluded in high eccentric manner, "I've sacrificed two marriages. I sometimes ask myself, 'Why, for God's sake, do I do it?' I'm sure I'll die penniless. But I don't care."[27]

During the thirties many women were sanguine about the possibility of becoming truly integrated into America's bands and orchestras. Said one group of women musicians in 1936, "One fallacy about women in music has been...demolished by the women's orchestras: that women lack the necessary physical stamina to play...instruments such as the trumpet and trombone."[28] Because of the increase in women's musical activities during that decade, many seasoned players were available in the man-short years of the Second World War, and women hurried to fill the ranks of symphony orchestras, dance bands and, less frequently, jazz bands. During the war there was even a Marine Band composed entirely of women. But the benefits they gained proved to be short-lived; as a woman violinist predicted drily, "Come the peace and out we go. With 20,000 musicians and 2,000 jobs, how can it be otherwise?"[29]

By the late forties, with the disappearance of most of the large bands and the shift to small-group jazz, band opportunities were scarce for all musicians. Though some all-female combos survived through the fifties and sixties, the large all-woman groups dissolved. Not until the seventies, with the liberalization of attitudes and the resurgent popularity of jazz bands, was there a concerted effort to promote integration of the sexes in jazz, and a concurrent revival of the women's group idea.

Chapter Four

THE LADIES AT THE KEYBOARD

You've got to play, that's all. They don't think of you as a woman if you can really play.

MARY LOU WILLIAMS

The piano is one of the few instruments that seem more or less free of sex stereotypes. To the extent that it does carry unconscious gender associations, these associations deliver an ambiguous message. On the one hand, for example, Jelly Roll Morton recalled hesitating to take up piano for fear of being thought a "sissy";[1] on the other hand, though piano playing has historically been approved as a desirable feminine refinement, making a professional career of it was considered decidedly unladylike and was an option reserved largely for men. Nevertheless, as a fixture of many American households and most churches and schools, the piano was perhaps the most common form of popular entertainment until the mass media supplanted it, and so readily accessible that it has been the instrument of choice for a majority of women in both classical music and jazz.

It would be just about impossible to give a full treatment of all the good women jazz pianists who have come up since the twenties; such a project would take up an entire volume in itself. Neither can the piano's steadily expanding role in jazz music be discussed in detail, though the career of Mary Lou Williams, which is described at length below, offers a highly instructive

59

capsule history of changing piano styles from ragtime to swing to bop and beyond. Suffice it to say that the piano quickly became a vital rhythm accompaniment in early New Orleans ensemble jazz (as played by Lil Hardin Armstrong and Lovie Austin, among others) and continued in this role in groups large and small, as well as becoming an outstanding solo instrument. This chapter examines selected female exponents of diverse piano styles to give a portrait of the range and variety of their accomplishments.

As jazz developed during the twenties, its Afro-American components mingling with the mass-audience conventions of white popular music, the focal points of jazz activity became more geographically diffuse. New Orleans and Chicago continued to be important jazz and blues centers, of course, but from the twenties on, New York was in a special position; it had Tin Pan Alley, the theater, a burgeoning recording industry—and, hugely important, it had Harlem, a mecca for black talent. However, during the late twenties and early thirties, before New York's greatest creative jazz years, jazz also flourished in the Southwest and Midwest, above all in Kansas City, which for a time surpassed Chicago and New Orleans in job opportunities and stylistic inventiveness. Under the control of the Pendergast political machine, even as the Roaring Twenties slid into the Depression, Kansas City had plenty of money to spend on gambling, drinking and whoring. That meant plenty of jobs for musicians, who flocked to the city. Among them was the great Mary Lou Williams.

At the time of her death Mary Lou Williams was America's best-known and most revered jazzwoman. Throughout her career her femaleness was often treated by the critics like a hot potato to be juggled uncomfortably from hand to hand, or like a minor handicap—lameness, say—unfortunate but not disabling. "So fully has she made it that in discussing her work one almost forgets she's a woman," wrote Barry Ulanov in 1949, doubtless intending high praise.[2] "The fact that she is a woman has no bearing on Miss Williams' stature as an artist, but on the other hand, should not lead us to ignore or deny that her music has a delightfully feminine ambiance," said another writer.[3]

Mary Lou Williams herself, occupying the top echelon of jazz as a gifted composer, arranger and player fully versed in all styles and modes of the music, reflected in 1977, "I never thought about anything but the music inside of me. I guess what happened to me was really unusual for a woman, as during that time, a woman was supposed to stay home in the kitchen."[4] Few women have equaled her musical accomplishments, a fact that must have imposed a certain isolation along with the honor of being the "First

Lady of Jazz." But like most artists, she was used to feeling different and special. "Jazz is a self-taught art," she said, "and I was a loner."[5]

Mary Lou Williams (née Mary Scruggs, also known as Mary Elfrieda Winn and, when her mother remarried, as Mary Burleigh) was born in Atlanta, Georgia, in 1910. Her father left home around the time of her birth; she later recalled meeting him only once thereafter, years later when he surfaced briefly. When she was about four, she moved north to Pittsburgh with her musically inclined mother (whose remarriage not only gave her another name but also ten half-brothers and half-sisters). She recalled having begun to pick out tunes on the family piano as early as age three, and in Pittsburgh her indulgent stepfather encouraged her budding piano talent by giving her pocket money to play his favorites. Soon neighbors were inviting young Mary Lou to play at parties. "From the age of six until I was fourteen, I was all over the city playing. I became the 'little piano girl of East Liberty.' "[6] Even then her talent took her far, from the black neighborhoods to the homes of Pittsburgh's wealthy white elites, playing for families like the Mellons; at the same time, her stepfather often took her around with him to black theaters and clubs.

By the time she was in the fifth and sixth grades, the name and skill of little Mary Burleigh were also becoming known to the professional musicians who worked in and around the Midwest. McKinney's Cotton Pickers bandmember Chu Berry, for one, would often drop by her house and take her along to informal jam sessions where top jazz talent played. And she received some formal musical education from a Mrs. Alexander at Westinghouse Junior High School, where fellow Pittsburghers Billy Strayhorn, later Duke Ellington's staff arranger, and the soon-to-be great pianist Earl "Fatha" Hines also attended classes. (Earl Hines' first wife, "Baby" Hines, was an excellent local singer, Williams recalled.)

Clearly the "piano girl of East Liberty" was a prodigy. Had she been white, she quite conceivably would have become a classical concert pianist. But Mary Lou Williams was black, poor and in need of immediate employment. Partly in order to help support her family, she took her first job away from home in 1924 at age fourteen (some accounts have her on the road two years earlier). During her summer vacation that year, she worked as an accompanist on the local black vaudeville circuit, playing with a "home talent show" run by a man who liked to get inexperienced young girls drunk and take advantage of them. His plans were foiled in her case because a chorus girl, "one of the older girls of eighteen or so," became suspicious of the goings-on. By 1925, at fifteen, Mary Lou was on the road full-time, working with a small band that backed a comedian named Buzzin' Harris. Those early, green years with the circuses and carnies and traveling shows made for what Williams later termed simply "a terrible life."[7]

Despite the harsh conditions, the gifted young pianist kept her head and her spirits up. Her stint with Buzzin' Harris and company was not in vain, for she was soon befriended by John Williams, the band's baritone sax player, who often came to her aid and fought for her right to play piano; managers and performers were simply not accustomed to working with a woman player and would often refuse to do so unless cajoled. John Williams smoothed some of the rough edges of band life for the young Mary Lou, who married him in 1927.

That year the newlyweds settled briefly in Memphis, John's hometown, where Mary Lou occasionally played with small groups that sometimes included future bandleader Jimmie Lunceford and a woman named Bobby Jones, whom Mary Lou recalled as an excellent pianist. Late in 1927 John and Mary Lou headed for Oklahoma City, which had a lively musical scene, and within a year the nucleus of the big band for which Mary Lou Williams was to become key soloist, writer and arranger had been organized and was traveling in the Midwest and Southwest as a "territory" unit. The band, soon known as Andy Kirk's Twelve Clouds of Joy, played in roadhouses, dancehalls, saloons and such. Like other regionally based black bands of the pre-swing era in the late twenties (the best-known being the early Count Basie organization in Kansas City), the Clouds-to-be based their sound on "riff" arrangements, heavy doses of the blues and "jump" rhythms, though they also played more commercial, ephemerally popular songs. It was Mary Lou's writing that made the band superior in the "riff 'n' blues" format.

But in 1928 Mary Lou was not yet an official part of the Kirk outfit; instead, the future star who would be billed as "The Lady Who Swings the Band" took a job driving a hearse for an undertaker and often served as driver for the band as well. "I'd wait outside ballrooms in the car, and if things went bad and people weren't dancing, they would send somebody to get me and I'd go in and play 'Froggy Bottom' or some other boogie-woogie number—and things would jump."[8] She later reflected, "It may have been that they didn't want a woman in the band because women during that era were not really allowed to be in with a group of men. That made people scream and carry on, because they saw a woman that weighed about ninety pounds—to hear me play so heavy, like a man, that was something else."[9]

Around 1928 the newly formed Clouds decided to settle in Kansas City, with its bountiful opportunities for work, and there Mary Lou became a much-sought-after pianist. She later described the K.C. scene: "Now, at this time, which was still Prohibition, Kansas City was under Tom Pendergast's control. Most of the nightspots were run by the politicians and hoodlums, and the town was wide open for drinking, gambling and pretty much every form of vice. Naturally, work was plentiful for musicians, though some of the employers were tough people."[10]

In those days black and white musicians traveling the country by train often passed through Kansas City, a major railroad terminus. Many lingered for the feast of music the city offered, and Mary Lou played with the best of them: Ben Pollack and Jack Teagarden, Art Tatum, pianist-writer Tadd Dameron and the teenage Thelonious Monk, who came through town with a tent show. In the thirties the young Martha Raye, then a much-admired singer en route to Hollywood and a career in films, tarried long, entranced by the music. And there were the bands—among them, Count Basie's group on the way up—with great jazzmen taking part in innumerable after-hours "cutting contests." Mary Lou was much in demand at these jam sessions, which often lasted through the night and well into the day. "One night, around 4 a.m., I awoke hearing someone pecking on my screen. I opened the window on [tenor saxophonist] Ben Webster. He was saying, 'Get up, pussycat, we're jammin' and all the pianists are tired out now. [Coleman] Hawkins has got his shirt off and is still blowing.' "[11]

Mary Lou Williams with Andy Kirk's Twelve Clouds of Joy. *(Credit: Institute of Jazz Studies, Rutgers University)*

By 1931 Mary Lou Williams had "graduated," as she put it, "to composer, arranger and first-class chauffeur for the [Kirk] organization. I was not playing in the band but was doing their recordings for Brunswick and sometimes sitting in to try things I had written."[12] Her recording debut for Brunswick Records came in 1930, when the company called her to Chicago to record her compositions "Drag 'Em" and "Night Life"—for which, she said, she never received any compensation. That year Brunswick recording supervisor Jack Kapp insisted on using Mary Lou as band pianist on all Kirk dates. In late 1931 she finally became a full-fledged, full-time playing bandmember (initially as second pianist, but that didn't last long).

The evolution of Mary Lou Williams into a top-flight arranger and composer took place under the most rudimentary conditions—or rather, under her own steam, with a little help from her friends. "I could not set [my ideas] down on paper. I hadn't studied theory, but asked Kirk about chords and the voicing register [and] memorized what I wanted. That's how I started writing." Her first real effort, she found, "was beyond [the Clouds'] capabilities."[13] But she soon began supplying five or six arrangements a week, and at twenty-five she "was already the musical mastermind behind one of the nation's best swing bands."[14] Later she expanded her knowledge with the help of such excellent writer-arrangers as Don Redman and Edgar Sampson, and most of the best bandleaders of the swing era—Louis Armstrong, Earl Hines, Duke Ellington, Tommy Dorsey, Benny Goodman, Jimmie Lunceford—sought her out. Goodman, for whom she had done a very popular arrangement of her "Roll 'Em," tried to secure her exclusive services, but she refused, preferring to free-lance.

In 1936 a new arrangement of her early composition "Froggy Bottom," recorded for Decca, made both Williams and the Clouds hot. During this time she wrote music at what can only be described as an incredible pace. As she recalled her output, "In '36, the Kirk band traveled thousands of miles a week on one-nighters all through the South. By now I was writing for some half-dozen bands each week. As we were making perhaps five hundred miles per night, I used to write in the car by flashlight between engagements."[15] These prodigious feats of fresh writing brought her anywhere from three to fifteen dollars per arrangement. Worse, "I didn't know about copyrights and lost half my royalties."[16]

Gratifying as her success with the Kirk band must have been, the constant writing and arranging chores and the grind of road life began to wear Williams down. In addition she became increasingly dissatisfied with the musical constraints engendered—ironically—by the commercial success of the Clouds, which she more than anyone had helped make possible. A big draw by the late thirties, the Clouds of Joy now had to supply their audiences with recognizable hits and formulas. Boogie-woogie piano became the rage, and Mary Lou was a giant, with such tunes as the 1936 "Little Joe from Chicago." She began to feel more and more limited in her playing and in the adventurousness of her writing for the band. She held out until 1942, when she left the Clouds and divorced John Williams. Returning home to Pittsburgh, she formed a group that included the young local drummer Art Blakey. Shortly thereafter she married trumpeter Harold "Shorty" Baker, and together they joined Duke Ellington's band in 1943; there, as staff arranger for a period of about six months, she "arranged about fifteen things for orchestra," including the well-known "Trumpet No End."[17] But soon enough the restless composer moved on to a new phase of her career.

In the jazz world of New York during the forties, musicians were busily working out exciting, advanced approaches to playing, without reference to commercial considerations. By choice and by necessity, these musicians tended to form a community within a community, for "bop" was considered bewildering, threatening, even nonsensical by many of the older and more conservative ex-vaudeville, swing and dance-band players (as in Cab Calloway's famous remark that Dizzy Gillespie was playing "Chinese music"). But to Mary Lou Williams—the ex-carny piano player, swing-band star and boogie-woogie wonder—the modern music was a breath of fresh air. It took her back to the Kansas City days when she and her fellow musicians would often play among themselves what they called "zombie music," "frozen sounds." The more she experimented, the more she felt the rift between the demands of entertainment and her need to grow as a musician.

Many bop players became Mary Lou's close personal and musical associates during the forties, especially the horn players, fellow pianists Thelonious Monk and Bud Powell, and arranger Tadd Dameron. Her Harlem apartment was a gathering place for musicians to meet, talk and jam. Her own *Zodiac Suite,* twelve tone-poems on astrological themes, conceived as mood portraits of individual musicians, was one of the earliest modern jazz symphonic compositions. It was first performed in 1945, and then in 1946 at Town Hall in New York with the New York Philharmonic Orchestra, to great acclaim. Her short piece "In the Land of Oo-bla-dee," from the same period, is a delightful modern jazz composition.

Yet in spite of her interest and participation in the new music, Mary Lou was dismayed by the scarcity of opportunities to play what she wanted to play; as often as not, she was still called upon to be a "boogie-woogie mama." In 1952, like so many American jazz musicians then and now, she made a pilgrimage to Europe, where she was accorded greater respect by larger and more knowledgeable audiences. But she found that the market mentality prevailed abroad too, and finally, unwilling and unable to cater to its demands, she stopped playing completely in 1954. "I was bitter that nobody seemed to care about good music anymore. The club-owners only wanted music that sells good," she explained.[18]

Mary Lou retreated to the French countryside, and when she reemerged she was a changed woman. She gave herself over to constant prayer and converted to Roman Catholicism in 1957, after she had returned to New York. (Reportedly she chose that faith because the only place of worship that was continuously open in her neighborhood was a Catholic church.) Beginning in 1954, she also undertook a direct ministry to the "street people" of her community, especially down-and-out musicians ravaged by alcoholism, drug addiction and illness. Her apartment, always a haven for confreres, became a veritable rest home, fitted out with cots and a soup kitchen. To aid the rehabilitation of needy musicians, she established the Bel Canto Foundation and supported it by running a thrift shop and donating the profits from her own recently formed record company, Mary Records.

After her conversion, at the urging of fellow musicians and spiritual advisers, she began playing publicly again, appearing with Dizzy Gillespie's Orchestra at the Newport Jazz Festival, then taking on jobs at various top-ranked jazz rooms in the New York area. By the early sixties the compositions were flowing again, too. Like the later works of Duke Ellington, these pieces were primarily concerned with spiritual and religious themes. The lovely choral hymn "St. Martin de Porres" (named for the Black Christ of the Andes) was followed by three major masses, most famously the *Music for Peace* mass, which became known as *Mary Lou's Mass*. The celebratory, swinging suite, first commissioned by the Vatican in 1969, was rearranged for presentation by choreographer Alvin Ailey's dance company in 1971 and performed in 1975 and 1979 at St. Patrick's Cathedral in New York, as well as at many other churches.

Throughout the seventies, with Father Peter O'Brien, S.J., as her personal manager, Mary Lou Williams continued to play and to experiment with all aspects of the jazz literature. She had a long and notable engagement at the Cookery, the New York nightclub owned by her former Cafe Society employer, Barney Josephson. Her performance repertoire encompassed all the styles of jazz that she had lived through, making her a living repository of the music's history. In fact, as artist-in-residence at Duke University in North Carolina from 1977 until she was incapacitated in 1980, she included a "history of jazz" demonstration in her performances. Up until the end she showed her flexibility as a performer by concertizing with such diverse artists as swing-era clarinetist Benny Goodman and avant-garde pianist Cecil Taylor.

The Mary Lou Williams of the seventies wooed the listener with her polished, seasoned playing, characterized by a rock-steady rhythmic pulse and a deft, rolling attack on the keyboard—a smooth but driving swing combined with often delicate and always melodic ideas. Though illness slowed her down in her last years, she remained active up to the final days of her life. When she died of cancer of the spine in May 1981, her passing brought eulogies from all over the world. One memorable event was the June 1981 Tribute to Mary Lou Williams at New York's Town Hall, with pianists Barbara Carroll, Hazel Scott and Rose Murphy and a big band conducted by trombonist-arranger Melba Liston performing Williams' compositions and arrangements from the thirties to the seventies.

A master of her craft as well as an inspired artist, Mary Lou Williams had this to say about being a woman in jazz.

> You've got to play, that's all. They don't think of you as a woman if you can really play. I think some girls have an inferiority complex about it and this may hold them back. If they have talent, the men will be glad to help them along. [And] working with men, you get to think like a man when you play. You automatically become strong, though this doesn't mean you're not feminine.[19]

Looking back on the early days in Kansas City, Mary Lou Williams remembered "three girl pianists apart from myself. One was Julia Lee, who took little part in the [jam] sessions. Another I recall only as Oceola; the third was known as Countess Margaret."[20]

Pianist-singer Julia Lee had a long career as a popular Kansas City performer. Born into a musical family in 1902 or 1903, she took piano lessons and sang with her violinist father's string group as a child. She began her professional career at about age fourteen, when she joined her brother George E. Lee's Singing Novelty Orchestra, remaining until the mid-thirties. Julia Lee worked as a soloist in Kansas City clubs for the next twenty years, playing in a vigorous barrelhouse and boogie style and becoming well known for her double-entendre song lyrics ("Snatch and Grab It," "Gotta Gimme Watcha Got," "Do You Want It?"), many of which she wrote herself. In the forties she cut a number of popular sides for Capitol that illustrated her style of K.C. bounce piano, and in 1948 she was a guest performer at the presidential inauguration of fellow Missourian Harry Truman. Julia Lee died in 1958.

Little is known of the woman whom Mary Lou Williams remembered as "Oceola," but Countess Margaret, the other "girl pianist," was a Kansas City performer who showed great promise. Known as "Countess" or "Queenie," Margaret Johnson was born in 1919 and by the age of fifteen was leading her own band. During her teens she also worked with Harlan Leonard's territory band and often jammed with Lester Young, who was then approaching stardom in Count Basie's orchestra in Kansas City. According to Mary Lou Williams, Johnson "was a friend of Lester Young, and when I was sick for a time, Andy Kirk sent for her to take my place. The tour got her, I fear, for she died of t.b. before she had done very much, though I hear she was quite good."[21] Margaret Johnson died in 1939, at the age of twenty. Her recorded work, limited to one session, "reveals a mature style (derived from Basie), an assured manner and a clean technique,"[22] according to one writer.

Other women pianists mentioned by musicians and historians of the Kansas City jazz heyday include Nellie Britt, Lee Etta Smith, Fay "Oregon" Jones, Edith Griffin, Essie May, Vivian Jones and ragtime stylist Nancy Trance. Charlotte Mansfield, who worked as a small-band and solo pianist in many Kansas City nightspots, had a husky, gravelly voice and a bottom-blues piano style. Pianist Lillian Lane worked with Jesse Price's group during the thirties. Somewhat later, from the forties until her death in 1977, the very popular pianist Bettye Miller worked in and around Kansas City as a soloist and with her husband, bassist Milt Abel.*

Elsewhere around the country there were plenty of other women plying the keyboards, and often singing too; vocals were practically obligatory for most "girl piano players" of the thirties and forties. "I didn't consider myself much of a singer," said Nellie Lutcher, "but they kept after me, so I sang."[23] As we will see later, singing has been one of the principal means of legitimizing a woman's presence on the bandstand. Thus, whether by choice or by necessity, many talented women pianists (as well as other instrumentalists) also made their mark as vocalists, "singing for their supper" in the harshly competitive jazz-as-entertainment business.

Una Mae Carlisle (1918–1956) was one such player, a swing-style pianist who, according to one commentator, built her career mostly around her vocal work, "and yet, as a protégée of Fats Waller in the mid-thirties, she couldn't help but develop a strong piano style, for that was what Waller played."[24] Born in Xenia, Ohio, the part-Indian, part-black performer got off to an early start, singing publicly at the age of three and studying the piano as a child. When she was in her teens, in the early thirties, this "exceptionally gifted pianist" came to the attention of Fats Waller.[25]

As a member of Waller's troupe, Carlisle (or, as Fats called her, "Sister Gizzard-hip") learned much from the master, forming a crush on him in the process. In 1934, her musical allegiance intact but the romance over, she

---

*These Kansas City women are typical of the many women jazz or jazz-oriented pianists who achieved long-term popularity locally and regionally. For example, in 1939 *Down Beat* lauded pianist Lynne Belle Stapp of Oklahoma City as "the female Peck Kelly" (Kelly was a famous but reclusive early white jazz pianist from Texas). The careers of these women of local reputation, often fine players, lie beyond the scope of this book, but they offer fertile ground for further research.

went to New York and auditioned as a dancer at the Cotton Club; she got the job but promptly quit, determined to stick to her music. After working for a while as a copyist and occasional arranger, she landed a job with the *Blackbirds* revue, which went to Europe in 1938. And once overseas, she landed a recording date in England for producer Leonard Feather, had numerous club dates and did film work in France, operated her own club briefly in Montmartre and studied harmony at the Sorbonne.

The idyll ended as World War II engulfed the Continent, and Carlisle returned to the States in 1940. The following year she had great success with two of her compositions, "Walkin' by the River" and "I See a Million People," which she recorded for Bluebird Records; other Carlisle songs include "Where the River Meets the Sea," "Glory Day," "You're on Your Own" and "Who Kisses Who"—a small sampling of the five hundred or more tunes she estimated she had written by 1952. She was also a popular nightclub performer and had her own radio shows in the late forties and early fifties. When ill health forced her to retire in 1954, she returned to her hometown and died two years later, at the age of thirty-eight.

Cleo Patra Brown, another popular entertainer of the thirties and forties, has been described as "a kind of off hand slyly stylized and intimate singer-pianist, related stylistically to Nellie Lutcher and Rose Murphy."[26] In Chicago in the thirties she recorded "It's a Heavenly Thing," a tune that according to Lutcher, "sort of started a trend for girl piano players and vocalists"[27]—namely, the emphasis on sly, coy or somewhat risqué humor backed by boogie-woogie piano.

Cleo Brown was born in Meridian, Mississippi, in 1909. The daughter of a Baptist minister, she began taking piano lessons at age four, becoming accompanist for her father's church choir as a youngster. When she was ten her family moved north to Chicago, and she continued her piano studies, landing her first professional job at fourteen with a traveling orchestra. Along with pianist Virginia Hayes, Brown was credited with contributing to the distinctive Chicago boogie-woogie sound in the twenties—well before it became a craze. Her brother was a close friend of barrelhouse pianist Pinetop Smith, and in 1935 Cleo Brown created a variation of "Pinetop's Boogie Woogie" that went far to establish her fame and made her the rage of Chicago. In the forties Brown moved to California, where her recordings achieved new popularity during the latter part of that decade. Plagued by poor health, she retired from professional playing in the fifties.

Rose Murphy, with whom Cleo Brown is often compared, was a very popular performing and recording artist of the forties and early fifties. Born in Xenia, Ohio, in 1913, she got an early start as a pianist and was performing publicly by age seven.[28] Murphy was billed as the "Chi-Chi [or "Chee-Chee"] Girl" and was known for her novelty vocals. Like Brown and

Nellie Lutcher, she cultivated a very mannered style aimed at entertainment—what Frank Driggs calls a "highly rhythmic kind of near-jazz,"[29] a strongly stated foundation lightened by a floating melody line and superstylized vocals. In the 1970s she returned to the limelight, playing at such clubs as New York's Cookery in a style that had developed considerably. In the eighties Rose Murphy continues to perform her sprightly songs.

Nellie Lutcher's story follows a pattern common to many women musicians of this period: the early flowering of musical talent in the black child of the South; encouragement by a family member or teacher in school or church; recognition by older musicians, often by a jazz luminary who adopts the young player; the apprentice career and subsequent independence of the developing musician; and finally, gravitation to a more commercial sound, often funny, fluffy, silly or risqué, and nearly always with vocals. The drift to a more salable sound has always presented a strong temptation to the jazz performer, perhaps especially to the woman pianist.

Lutcher was born in Louisiana in 1912 (some sources, including Lutcher, say 1915) and grew up in the Lake Charles–Baton Rouge area. Her musical gifts flourished at an early age in the rich musical atmosphere of her home. Her father, Isaac Lutcher, was a bass player who worked locally with such players as Bunk Johnson, and he taught his daughter to play the guitar, violin and mandolin. Her mother played piano, and young Nellie, by the time she was eight or nine, was following suit at the local Baptist Sunday school, studying music with a church matron. Nellie's father played in the Imperial Jazz Band, a local New Orleans–style jazz-oriented orchestra, and Nellie was soon inducted—a development decried by the Baptist piano teacher. "I think it's awful for that little girl playing jazz music," she warned Nellie's mother. "She's going to hell."[30]

Undeterred by such dire threats, Lutcher not only kept on playing in the band but also filled in from time to time for absent accompanists in the sin-filled tent and medicine shows that passed through Lake Charles; once, at age twelve, she subbed for Ma Rainey's pianist. By sixteen she was on the road full-time as pianist with the Southern Rhythm Boys, a big band of fifteen to seventeen pieces. Like Mary Lou Williams, she wanted to be an arranger, and she made her first efforts in that direction with the Rhythm Boys in the early thirties, while still in her teens. Usually, she recalled, the pay for her arrangements came in the form of a percentage of the proceeds from the door.

Road life for a black woman musician in the twenties bristled with unpleasantness, especially in Texas and the deep South, where Lutcher's band route took her on a string of one-nighters. Aside from potentially dangerous harassment by a drunken clientele, Lutcher found that the biggest problem was to secure lodgings. If there were no accommodations for blacks in a given locale, "you just wouldn't sleep or maybe you'd just have to stay in the car until somebody arranged a place. There was no such thing as going to a hotel"[31] (a state of affairs that lasted well into the fifties for black artists traveling in the South; see the Clora Bryant profile in Part Five).

In 1935, a seasoned veteran of the road at age twenty-three, Lutcher settled in Los Angeles, where work was plentiful, if poorly paid. It took another decade or so before she hit it big. But meanwhile she became part of the local music scene. She worked steadily at the Club Alabam on Central Avenue, L.A.'s largest and most popular black entertainment spot, and when the club closed for the night she was a fixture of after-hours and breakfast jam sessions. After she married in 1947, her home became a gathering place for musicians to play and party, among them Nat "King" Cole, Art Tatum and Lottie Moser, a woman Lutcher singled out as a "marvelous pianist."[32]

For her paying gigs, Lutcher learned to tailor her music to commercial exigencies: the small-club solo pianist in those days relied on the "kitty," meaning that a tiny salary was augmented by tips from pleased customers. Following the example of Cleo Brown and Nat Cole, fine pianists who had much success when they shifted their emphasis to popular singing, she began to concentrate on developing her entertaining vocal style. And she wrote tunes steadily, among them her hit records "Real Gone Guy" and "Hurry On Down," as well as "Under a Blanket of Blue," "The Object of My Affections," "Lake Charles Boogie," "Chi-Chi-Chi-Chicago," "Sally Walker" and "Fine Brown Frame." But for most of the forties a recording contract eluded her; instead, like many other artists, she made several one-shot recordings for small labels and received only a flat fee—that is, no royalties. "The way it was at that time," she explained, "you usually ended up owing the record company."[33]

Lutcher's big break came in 1947 when she appeared as a volunteer performer at a March of Dimes benefit in L.A. By then she had a loyal and appreciative local following but was mainly limited to playing small club dates, working as an intermission act and so on. Her March of Dimes performance proved pivotal; Capitol Records producer Dave Dexter was present and was so impressed with her that he immediately signed her on. A wise decision: her first Capitol recording, "Hurry On Down," backed by "The Lady's in Love with You," was a huge hit.

With big bookings and a high salary, Nellie Lutcher remained a popular performer into the fifties, when she retired from music and became a successful real estate agent. Her effervescent voice and subtly inflected phrasing, combined with her slightly risqué humor, were enhanced by a piano style that, like Rose Murphy's, both flowed and lifted the melody with a pleasant, swinging effect. In the seventies Lutcher reemerged, playing a long engagement at the Cookery in New York in 1980.

The postwar period saw the rise of a number of fine female pianists, most of them based in New York. Among them was singer, pianist and vibraphonist Dardanelle Breckenridge, known simply as Dardanelle. Her swinging, relaxed style brought her to the attention of the jazz community in the early forties and won her high praise. Art Tatum, the great pianist whom she emulated, nominated her as best new vibraphonist in the 1945 *Esquire* Jazz Poll, and vibraphonist Lionel Hampton chose her as the best new pianist of that year. By the late forties Dardanelle was leading a popular trio that appeared frequently at the Hickory House on Fifty-second Street in New York, and her future as a musician seemed secure. In the fifties, though, she went off the scene, moving to Chicago to concentrate on raising a family. To the delight of jazz lovers, she began to play and record again in the late seventies. Jazz critic Gary Giddins describes her effect on him: "Here's this sweet, grandmotherly southern belle who seats herself with practiced poise, smiles demurely and then *cooks*. I had forgotten how much drive she has on her instrument."[34] She accompanies her playing with softly styled, intimate vocals.

Hazel Scott was born in Trinidad in 1920 but lived in the States from 1924 on. A child prodigy, she made her professional debut at the age of five and later studied at the Juilliard School. In her early teens she played with the American Creolians, an all-female orchestra led by her mother, Alma Scott, who played a variety of instruments and also worked with Lil Hardin Armstrong's all-female orchestra. At sixteen Hazel Scott had her own radio show, and by eighteen she was fronting a band, singing popular songs in several languages and writing most of her own arrangements and some original material, including her theme, "A Swingy Serenade." Her trademark became "swinging the classics," and she entertained at clubs such as Cafe Society Uptown and Downtown, where she was a popular fixture from 1939 to 1945 with a repertoire that mixed classics, blues and boogie. Her eclectic and fluent style showed the influence of such pianists as Art Tatum and Earl Hines. Her star status was more firmly fixed by a short-lived marriage to the controversial Harlem preacher and congressman Adam Clayton Powell, Jr. Hazel Scott continued to perform successfully in New York clubs in the following decades, with a 1957–59 sojourn in France. Shortly before she died of cancer in 1981, she appeared as a featured performer at a tribute to the late Mary Lou Williams.

Like Hazel Scott, Dorothy Donegan cultivated a boogie-woogie and "swing the classics" style during the forties. Relying on specialty numbers and a truly virtuosic technique—often relayed in "show-biz" routines bordering on slapstick—she won a big audience. This extremely gifted pianist was born in Chicago in 1924 and studied the instrument formally from the age of eight. She began as a church organist and became a player in cocktail lounges before making her mark at top clubs and appearing in films. Though Donegan plays well in any style and remains a popular draw in the eighties, many jazz lovers feel that her emphasis on superheated visual antics and technical tricks detracts from her artistry.

The same period during which Scott, Donegan and company dazzled also witnessed the emergence of a new crop of women pianists whose playing departed from the supper-club singer-entertainer tradition, with its reliance on novelty vocals or boogie-woogie mixed with Beethoven. These women were attracted to the jazz of the era, now known as bop, which derived much of its impetus from the frustration of many musicians with styles and clichés that boxed them into the role of "entertainer." Foremost among those who

Hazel Scott. *(Credit: Bob Parent)*

broke with the past was Mary Lou Williams, who lent her majestic presence to modern jazz happenings. But there were other women pianists who followed suit, and several became cogent players with distinctive styles. In a further departure from the past, a larger proportion of them were white, and some were non-Americans.

Marian McPartland, one good example of such artistry, is today well-established on the jazz scene as performer, recording artist and producer of some of her own albums. Born Marian Margaret Turner in 1920, she began studying music in a genteel fashion in her native England. She was groomed for a career as a concert pianist at London's Guild Hall School of Music, where she studied piano, violin, harmony and composition. But the budding teenage jazz player braved official and parental disapproval to listen to the recorded sound of pianists such as Teddy Wilson and Art Tatum. At the Guild Hall, she recalled, "jazz was taboo, but we managed to have jam sessions occasionally."[35]

In 1937, at the ripe age of seventeen, Marian came out of her jazz closet and took a vaudeville job as a piano accompanist. By the time World War II broke out she was entertaining troops in the British version of the USO, working mostly as accompanist and jam session organizer. A significant outcome of this work was her 1944 meeting with Dixieland trumpeter Jimmy McPartland, who was stationed in Britain. Initially the jazzman wasn't thrilled about playing with a British lady pianist, but something must have gone right, for in 1945 they were married (later divorced, they remained on good terms). At war's end they moved to the States and jumped into the music scene, struggling along in time-honored fashion. "If you become a musician, Margaret, you'll marry a musician and live in an attic," Marian's mother had predicted. "And that's exactly what happened," McPartland told an interviewer.[36]

During the late forties and early fifties Marian McPartland worked with her husband's Dixieland groups, but she also got into modern jazz and was especially influenced by the long, flowing lines with which Bud Powell built his solos. "I knew very little then about the distinctions between styles and hadn't fallen into any set pattern myself," she explained.[37] Encouraged by her husband, she moved deeper into the new musical arena of bop, forming trios with which she worked regularly at such New York clubs as the Hickory House (1952–60), the London House and later the Cafe Carlyle, where she still plays today. Articulate and well-informed, Marian McPartland has become a familiar presence in the jazz community, appearing frequently on radio and television, her byline adorning occasional articles in newspapers and magazines (including a rave for Mary Lou Williams in *Down Beat* in 1964). With the rise of interest in women in jazz, she has emerged as one of the most active spokeswomen and historians.

McPartland's technique evolved steadily throughout the fifties, sixties and seventies. Some critics had complained that the earlier McPartland did not really swing, that she was too swift and stiff, and many felt that she tended to overplay. But the critical consensus is that she has now overcome these tendencies. An indefatigable worker, McPartland is also notable for her vast and well-chosen repertoire. She entertains with polished elegance and swings with rigorous chordal improvisations (as in a fine recent album, *Solo Concert at Haverford*).

McPartland has described her own evolution of attitude about being a woman in jazz in several interviews. In 1973 she told Whitney Balliett:

> When I started out, I had the wish, the need, to compete with men. But I don't feel that way anymore. I take pride in being a woman.[38]

What she said in 1959 about the qualities she most admires in a woman player stands as a fair description of McPartland herself: "I want a woman pianist who plays like a woman, with the warmth, sensitivity, feeling, perception and all the womanly virtues, plus a little masculine saltiness in humor, surprise and accent."[39]

Another persuasive piano stylist of the postwar period was Barbara Carroll (née Coppersmith). Born in Massachusetts in 1925, she studied piano from the age of five and attended the New England Conservatory of Music. Like McPartland, Carroll showed an early preference for jazz over the classics, and while McPartland was entertaining troops in Britain during the war, Carroll took her female trio to camp shows for U.S. soldiers stationed in New England. By the late forties she was regularly visiting New York and Philadelphia so she could absorb and play modern jazz. Like most young pianists at the time, she was heavily influenced by Bud Powell and Art Tatum, and she became known as a polished, melodic pianist. A 1947 *Down Beat* review had nothing but praise for her "gal's trio": "Fans flocking to hear Dizzy at the Downbeat club have been getting ample bonus kicks from the Barbara Carroll trio, the club's relief unit."[40] Her sophisticated repertoire, application of delicate tone colors and light but insistent swing helped her become a top-ranked performer on the supper-club circuit.

During the sixties Barbara Carroll stopped playing professionally to concentrate on raising her daughter (she was widowed in the fifties) but resumed her career in the seventies with recordings and concerts, including solo performances at the Newport Jazz Festival in 1979 and at the Town Hall tribute to Mary Lou Williams in 1981. Some thirty years ago she alluded in an interview to the occupational hazards of being a woman in jazz: "At the beginning, I used to be dragged when people would give me that 'She's good for a girl' routine. But I think now they're starting to listen to me as a pianist first."[41]

Lorraine Geller (née Walsh) was another well-regarded white pianist who emerged in the forties. Born in 1928, she had her first important jazz gig (1949–52) with former Sweethearts of Rhythm leader Anna Mae Winburn in a combo that included young tenor saxophonist Willene Barton. She then worked and recorded with husband Herb Geller's quartet and in 1957 accompanied popular song stylist Kay Starr. She died in 1958, only thirty years old. She is remembered for her delicate melodic phrasing.

Beryl Booker, born in 1924, became active on the New York jazz scene in the late forties. A hard-swinging, self-taught black pianist from Philadelphia, she never learned to read music. She was much in demand as a wailing piano player and worked with bassist Slam Stewart in a trio intermittently from 1946 to 1951. That year she joined vocalist Dinah Washington as accompanist, backing her until 1953 and rejoining her in 1959 for another stint. As a leader Booker played in various clubs, including the Embers in New York in the mid-fifties. In 1954 she took an all-woman trio (with Bonnie Wetzel on bass and Elaine Leighton on drums) to Europe on tour, recording with the trio and with tenor saxophonist Don Byas in Paris. In the seventies Booker continued to play and record with small groups. She died in 1980.

Another black pianist and vibraphonist is Terry Pollard, who enjoyed an excellent reputation in the jazz world during the fifties. Pollard was born in Detroit in 1931; like Booker, she was a self-taught player and began by imitating her pianist father. She became a paid musician quite casually by sitting in with the band at her high school graduation dance when the pianist failed to show up; after the gig she was offered his job. From the late forties to the late fifties Pollard worked and recorded with a number of groups, notably with the popular vibraphonist Terry Gibbs from 1953 to 1957. Back in Detroit that year, she formed her own trio to play locally, turning down professional opportunities outside Detroit in order to remain with her husband and family. A recording Pollard made around this time with fellow Detroiter Dorothy Ashby caused one jazz critic to rate her as "one of the best in the country on piano."[42] Her hard-swinging, soulful, witty piano stylings would doubtless have made her a name jazz artist had she not chosen to stay in the Motor City.

Jutta (or Utta) Hipp, born in Leipzig, Germany, in 1925, studied painting before turning to jazz piano in the forties. Prior to and during the Second World War she played in jam sessions at the Leipzig Hot Club, one of many local clubs that served as important forums for jazz in Europe before the American occupation. Fleeing from the Russian invasion of her city, Hipp went to Munich and began performing and recording there; from 1953 to 1955 she had her own quintet in Frankfurt. In 1955 Jutta Hipp moved to New York, where her playing, inspired by pianist Lennie Tristano, won her a ready following and important jobs, including dates at the Hickory House. By the late fifties, however, Hipp's style had become increasingly diffuse, and despite the earlier enthusiasm of listeners and critics about her future as a jazz pianist, she gradually dropped away from music.

A recent article on the dying art of the jazz organ duly mentioned all the hard-driving male exponents of this first cousin of the piano but failed to mention Shirley Scott.[43] Scott was born in 1934 and first studied piano in her hometown of Philadelphia. She took up the trumpet in high school before settling on organ in 1955. The following year she displayed her peppery, hard-swinging, blues-rooted style to good effect with tenor saxophonist Eddie "Lockjaw" Davis and his group, remaining with Davis until 1960. She

The Beryl Booker Trio. *(Credit: Bob Parent)*

then left to form her own group and soon joined forces with tenor saxophonist Stanley Turrentine; their musical (and marital) partnership broke up in 1971. Since 1974 she has frequently toured with her group, featuring tenor saxophonist Harold Vick. A prolific recording artist, she is also a crowd-pleasing performer with a raft of technique. As one critic noted, she is known for "shifting stops and mixing tone colors, an arsenal of organ effects."[44]

Along with many other female keyboardists, the women discussed in this chapter enriched the jazz world with their playing abilities and their diverse styles. That there has been such a number of fine jazzwomen on the piano comes as no surprise, for, as noted at the outset of this chapter, it is an easily accessible instrument that is multifunctional, eminently respectable and relatively uncluttered by gender associations. Though some female jazz pianists became "supper-club" or "cocktail-lounge" entertainers, the many strong, swinging women players belie the myth of an inherently "feminine" way of playing. The truth is that the ivories have been tickled daintily by men, pounded forcefully by women and vice versa. As Marian McPartland put it, "Some think because you play with any strength or solid feeling, you play like a man. There are a lot of men who play with a light, delicate touch, and I think they'd be upset if you said they played like a woman. You play the way you are."[45]

Chapter Five

BREAKING THE TABOOS

When I was in my teens, I went with some friends to hear
Woody Herman's band, and there, in the trumpet section,
was a woman. We looked at Billie Rogers as if she had three
heads and marveled that she could even finish a chorus.

NAT HENTOFF, 1979

When vibraphonist Marjorie Hyams looked back on her tenure with Woody Herman's First Herd in 1944–45, she assessed her position as a bandmember as follows:

> In a sense, you weren't really looked upon as a musician, especially in clubs. There was more interest in what you were going to wear or how your hair was fixed—they just wanted you to look attractive, ultra-feminine, largely because you were doing something they didn't consider feminine. Most of the time I just fought it and didn't listen to them. [One of the ways she fought it was to insist on wearing a band uniform instead of a dress.] Only in retrospect, when you start looking back and analyzing, you can see the obstacles that were put in front of you. I just thought at the time that I was too young to handle it, but now I see that it was really rampant chauvinism.[1]

Most women jazz players did not experience such difficulties in working with the established big bands, for the simple reason that the better bands, like those of Count Basie, Duke Ellington and Stan Kenton, along with scores of lesser groups, rarely or never hired women players. The big-band route to a career in jazz was largely closed to women reed, brass and rhythm players, unless they joined one of the all-female groups that flourished during the swing and dance-band era. Those women who did play key roles in the male big bands were usually vocalists or occasionally pianists, arrangers and writers (Mary Lou Williams with Andy Kirk's Clouds of Joy band is the most outstanding example). Still, a considerable number of women instrumentalists managed against heavy odds to carve out careers for themselves as jazz musicians, bringing dignity and professionalism to a field of entertainment that often responded with shabby treatment or amused paternalism—if it responded at all. Some of the women discussed in this chapter worked primarily in all-female contexts, others were able to break into the male bands, but all were talented players, and many developed distinctive styles and solo capabilities.

For example, there were several noteworthy women trumpet players. Leora Meoux Henderson (who doubled on saxophone) was born in Louisville, Kentucky, in the 1890s. Classically trained, she began playing trumpet professionally with the Musical Spillers, a famous black vaudeville group that also included Isabelle Spiller on tenor sax, doubling on alto, baritone and trumpet. Leora Meoux settled in New York City, where she played extensively in theater bands as well as vaudeville during the late teens, notably in the pit band of the popular Lafayette Theatre for about a decade, often as leader of her all-woman Vampires band. She also played with Lil Hardin Armstrong's All-Girl Orchestra in the early thirties and with the Negro Women's Orchestra and Civic Association. Known primarily as a straight (that is, nonsoloing) lead player, Meoux credited Louis Armstrong with helping her learn to play jazz.

Meoux knew Armstrong through his short but historic association with bandleader Fletcher Henderson, whom she married in 1924—the act for which she is most often remembered by jazz historians. She met her future partner while playing a riverboat dance date in the early twenties, she on trumpet, he on piano (at the time she was married to trumpeter Russell Smith). After her marriage to Henderson she contributed in various ways to his organization, helping with arrangements, often serving as road manager, sometimes subbing on second trumpet and sax (especially in 1931–32) and occasionally recording with the band (even, one expert believes, doing some solo work—a rare phenomenon at that time for any woman player).[2] In later life she faithfully nursed Henderson through a long illness until his death in 1952, surviving him by six years.

Dolly Jones, also known as Dolly Jones Armenra and Dolly Hutchinson, was a trumpet player and cornetist who came from a musical family; her mother, Dyer Jones, was a powerful trumpeter of the pre-Armstrong days. Based in Chicago, Dolly toured with Ma Rainey's band in 1925 and recorded with trombonist Al Wynn's group in 1926, worked with Lil Hardin Armstrong's all-female group in the early thirties, and around 1932 led her own group, the Twelve Spirits of Rhythm, which received excellent press.[3] Pianist Irene Armstrong used Jones in her group in Chicago and had high praise for her playing: "She didn't play high, but had imagination and a great sound and beat. Like Lady Day, she had a natural ear."[4] That the attractive and photogenic Dolly Jones was an excellent mid-range solo trumpeter is confirmed by her work in an all-black film short called *Swing*, made in 1937.[5] Eventually leaving Chicago, Jones settled in the Philadelphia area, where she continued to play into the early seventies.

Valaida Snow, born in Chattanooga, Tennessee, about 1900, was the most famous female trumpet player and one of the best-known jazzwomen to emerge in the pre-swing era. She became a star in the American black community in the twenties and then an even bigger star in Europe, where she found more opportunities to perform. Snow's fame was due as much to her showmanship as to her playing abilities. By all reports she was a charismatic bandleader and entertainer—to the detriment, some felt, of her potential as a musician. "I always liked her trumpet playing," said Mary Lou Williams. "She was hitting those high C's just like Louis Armstrong. She would have been a great trumpet player if she had dropped the singing and concentrated on the trumpet."[6]

Valaida Snow was born into a show-biz family that included sisters Lavaida and Alvaida; her mother, a music teacher and entertainer, taught her to play several instruments. Around 1920 she began her career in Philadelphia and Atlantic City nightspots, making her New York debut at Barron Wilkin's popular Harlem cabaret in 1922. From there she had rapid success. Her skills as a performer were varied and impressive: as player, singer, dancer and/or bandleader, she participated in a number of black musical revues that sparkled in the twenties, notably *Chocolate Dandies* and *Will Masten's Revue*.

In 1926 Snow began what would be a twenty-year world commute as a performer. From 1926 to 1928, in the Far East, she headlined a show that included Jack Carter's band, dancing, singing, playing the trumpet and fronting the band. Back in America in 1928, she resumed her work in shows and nightclubs, mostly out of Chicago. She toured Russia, the Middle East and Europe in 1929 and led a group that included pianist Earl Hines at the Grand Terrace Ballroom in Chicago in 1933. In 1933 she also cut her first record and joined Hines' orchestra for a year's touring. In London she conducted the *Blackbirds of 1934* show band. During the thirties she made a number of film shorts in Los Angeles and abroad, appearing in the United

States in *Take It from Me* and *Irresistible You,* and in France in *L'Alibi* (1936) and *Pièges* (1939), also released as *Snares* and *Personal Column.*

Valaida Snow was beautiful, bursting with energy and talent. Entertainer Bobby Short remembered the five-foot-tall trumpet star as a glamorous success symbol. "Fabled Valaida Snow," he called her, "who traveled in an orchid-colored Mercedes-Benz, dressed in an orchid suit, her pet monkey rigged out in an orchid jacket and cap, with the chauffeur in orchid as well."[7] But though Snow was a star in America and had more work than many musicians, including headlining the Apollo Theatre in 1936, that year she opted to settle in Europe. Based primarily in Paris and Scandinavia, she found greater playing and recording opportunities and worked with various bands all over Europe, cutting more than forty titles during the late thirties. She became known abroad as "Queen of the Trumpet" and "Little Louis."

But the good years came to an end for Snow abruptly when, around 1940, she was caught in Scandinavia during the Nazi occupation and interned there.* Released in 1941 or later, she returned to the States in unstable health and was nursed by producer Earle Edwards, whom she subsequently married (she had previously been married to dancer Ananias Berry). Snow began performing again in 1943, fronting a band at the Apollo Theatre, but though she continued to star at theaters and clubs around the country into the fifties, her singing and playing became more commercial and she soloed less, never quite recapturing the prowess of her past (as evidenced by her recordings from the forties and fifties). In 1956, soon after playing an engagement at the Palace Theatre in New York, she died of a cerebral hemorrhage.

Another woman player who created a stir during the thirties was tenor saxophonist L'Ana Webster (later Hyams), one of the first white women jazz players to be featured as a soloist with a big band. She joined trombonist Mike Riley's band in 1937, and *Down Beat* reported that her fine work there caused a "sensation" during performances at such clubs as the Onyx in Chicago. She recorded with Riley's band in 1938, taking the tenor sax solos, and *Down Beat* again raved, writing that "she amazed fellow musicians by her talent and her arranging ability."[8] Webster, who also played alto sax and

---

*Conflicting reports have circulated about various aspects of Valaida Snow's life, including her birthdate, given in different sources as 1900, 1905 and 1909, and particularly concerning her experience during the early forties while in Scandinavia. She is variously said to have been placed under house arrest in Sweden or in Denmark, to have been confined in a concentration camp for one, two, or three years, and to have lost so much weight that she was down to sixty-eight pounds at the time of her release (or escape). As a black, she was undoubtedly the target of Nazi abuse, but I have been unable to establish the facts about her European tribulations during the Second World War. For differing accounts, see D. Antoinette Handy, *Black Women in American Bands and Orchestras,* p. 132; John Chilton, *Who's Who of Jazz,* p. 383; and Harrison Smith, "Valaida's Gone," *Record Review,* May–June 1956.

Valaida Snow. *(Credit: Duncan P. Schiedt)*

clarinet, married pianist Mike Hyams, brother of vibist Marjorie Hyams. Her style was characterized by one writer as owing an "obvious debt to Lester Young; she projects a gentle, pliant image."[9] Interviewed in the 1970s, she expressed a sentiment shared by numerous other serious women jazz players of the swing era: "One thing you've got to remember is that there simply weren't that many good female musicians around then. So many . . . were so bad—and had given all of us something of a bad name. After I played with a group I'd have no trouble—but I always had to prove myself first."[10]

Tenor player Viola (Vi) Burnside was held in high regard among black saxophonists, with her vigorous, swinging, melodic style in the tradition of tenormen like Ben Webster, Coleman Hawkins and Don Byas. As a high school classmate of future tenor great Sonny Rollins, she was quickly recognized as a musician with potential and became a major female talent when she began playing professionally. Burnside was featured as a soloist with the Harlem Playgirls in the mid-thirties and then with the International Sweethearts of Rhythm until the mid-forties. A crowd-pleaser as well as a respected jazz player, she continued her career well into the fifties as a leader, settling finally in Washington, D.C., where she led small groups and orchestras and was an active member of the local musicians' union. Burnside was a pioneering woman jazz player whose influence on other women musicians was considerable (see the Willene Barton profile in Part Five for one assessment of Burnside's impact).

By the forties the trickle of women players with solo capabilities had become a small but steady stream feeding the jazz river on trumpet, saxophone, trombone, bass, drums, guitar and harp. Among others, trombonist Melba Liston had begun to make her mark both as a talented player and as an arranger by the middle of that decade (see the Melba Liston profile in Part Five). And there was the excellent trumpeter Billie Rogers, whose style was informed by swing-era master Roy Eldridge's, and who inspired such consternation in young Nat Hentoff and his friends.

Billie Rogers was born in 1919. While attending the University of Montana, she played in a campus big band led by her brother and then went on to work in vaudeville and dance-band contexts. As part of the trumpet section of Woody Herman's band from 1941 to 1943, Rogers was often a featured soloist on trumpet and vocals. After leaving Herman, she settled in California and led an all-male big band with her manager-husband, Jack Archer. The band played a four-month engagement in New York before breaking up. In 1945 Rogers joined an orchestra led by Jerry Wald. She went on to form groups of her own, working with them well into the fifties.

Ernestine "Tiny" Davis, who became known as a powerhouse trumpeter, was born in 1907 in Memphis and began her professional career in the Midwest. Starting in St. Louis, she worked for a time out of Kansas City before settling in Chicago, where she has been based for several decades. Like Vi Burnside, Davis—known as "Tiny" because of her short stature and wide girth—joined the Harlem Playgirls in the mid-thirties, moving to the International Sweethearts of Rhythm around 1939 for an eight-year tenure as a featured soloist and sometime vocalist. In 1947 Davis organized her own all-female group, a six-piece combo called the Hell-Divers, which stayed together for about six years, traveling extensively. The Hell-Divers was made up of former music students from Prairie View College in Texas who had been part of a college orchestra called the Co-Eds. Under the guidance of Louis Armstrong's manager, Joe Glaser, the group debuted at the Blue Note Club in Chicago to much fanfare and became Decca Records' first all-female recording artists.

A versatile entertainer-musician, Tiny Davis has also shown a penchant for humorous antics and novelty numbers. A publicity release for the Hell-Divers described her as follows: "She plays trumpet, slaps a guitar, beats conga drums, thumps a tambourine, sings vocals and finds time to wave a baton over her six girls." Among the "girls" was alto sax player Bert Etta "Birdie" Davis, who joined singer Dinah Washington's backup band during the fifties. Washington dubbed her "Ladybird" and gave her a role as featured soloist. By the seventies Ladybird had settled in San Antonio, Texas, where she continued to play her horn in local jazz and gospel contexts. Fellow Hell-Divers included Maurine Smith on piano, Helen Cole on drums, Margaret Backstrom on tenor saxophone and Eileen Chance on bass. In the seventies Tiny Davis' group was still performing in Chicago as a trio or quartet, with her daughter Dorothy on piano and bass, and veteran Helen Cole on drums.

In the forties the technically advanced style of jazz known as bop attracted some female instrumental adherents. Trumpeter Norma Carson, born in Portland, Oregon, in 1922, was a hard-blowing player of the modern school originated by such musicians as Dizzy Gillespie and Fats Navarro. Carson began playing trumpet during the thirties, at the age of twelve; her father was a trumpet player, and she and a sister followed suit. After graduating from high school, she landed her first professional job with Ada Leonard's all-woman big band. She then joined the International Sweethearts of Rhythm, and when that band broke up she became a member of a small group formed by tenorwoman Vi Burnside in the late forties. In 1951 Norma Carson spoke pointedly about the disadvantages of being a woman player:

> I've never found it an advantage to be a girl. If a trumpet player is wanted for a job and somebody suggests me, they'll say "What, a chick?" and put me down without even hearing me.... I don't want to be a girl musician. I just want to be a musician.[11]

A Leonard Feather–produced album called *Cats vs. Chicks*, which pitted women against men jazz players, shows Carson holding her own against trumpeter Clark Terry. During the fifties she settled in Philadelphia, where she continued to work locally.

Another trumpeter who really swung was Edna Williams, who played with a bright, bubbly tone and also sang, played accordion and other instruments, arranged and wrote music. Respected as a fine, lyrical soloist, Williams both played and arranged for the International Sweethearts of Rhythm. After leaving that band in the mid-forties, she cut her first record with a featured solo spot in a small group. Soon thereafter, her untimely death cut short a promising career. Jean Starr, another alumna of the Sweethearts trumpet section, played with the Jimmie Lunceford Orchestra, and with Benny Carter's orchestra in 1944–45. And Clora Bryant, a native of Texas, settled in California during the forties, carving out a reputation there as a bop trumpeter of the Dizzy Gillespie school (see the Clora Bryant profile in Part Five).

Among the bop-oriented saxophone players who came up in the forties was Californian Elvira (Vi) Redd, also known under her married name, Goldberg. Redd's career was guided by her great-aunt, Mrs. Alma Hightower, who helped many young, talented black teenagers in the Los Angeles area in the forties, including trombonist Melba Liston. And Redd was surrounded by musicians at home, too: her father, Alton Redd, was a veteran New Orleans-style drummer, her brother was a percussionist, and she married drummer Richie Goldberg.

Vi Redd began to be recorded as a leader in the sixties, winning increasing attention from the press and the jazz public in ensuing years. Known primarily for her work on alto, she also plays soprano sax and sings. Her blues-drenched, sweet-and-sour, preaching horn style has led some critics to compare her to the great Charlie Parker, the fount of bebop alto. Redd has gigged with such top-ranked players as Max Roach, Roland Kirk and Dizzy Gillespie, and she has toured extensively as a leader in Europe, Africa (including with Count Basie's orchestra in 1968) and Japan. For many of her years as a jazz altoist she also worked as a teacher in the California public school system. In the early sixties Leonard Feather wondered whether "the honor of becoming the first major horn woman in jazz history may well fall to the talented and indomitable Mrs. Goldberg." Not likely, he cautioned, unless "a lot of people . . . divest themselves of a long outmoded prejudice and realize that emancipation [of women] is with us."[12]

Other notable women sax players who emerged during the forties include tenor saxophonists Willene Barton, whose first important professional job was with ex-Sweetheart personnel (see the Willene Barton interview in Part Five), and Elsie Smith. Smith, who doubled on clarinet, joined Barton in a combo during the mid-fifties. She was said by colleagues to read like lightning. Born in Louisiana in 1932, she was based in Los Angeles during the late forties and early fifties. She joined Lionel Hampton's Orchestra in 1952-53, worked with Fred Skinner's Band in 1953-54 and then became a free-lancer. Rejoining Hampton in 1956, Smith was recorded with his orchestra in 1958.

The English tenor saxophonist Kathleen Stobart is well known in the European jazz community for her full, rich, lyrical sound. She joined Humphrey Lyttleton's Band in England in the fifties as featured soloist and also worked during that decade with her own group, billed on recordings as Kathleen Stobart and Her Orchestra. Technically an outstanding player, she has kept up with new developments in the music and has continued to be professionally active abroad, with occasional visits to America.

Besides the horn players, many other women instrumentalists performed in jazz contexts during the forties and fifties. Marjorie (Margie) Hyams, vibraphonist, pianist and writer-arranger, was said to have been discovered by bandleader Woody Herman when he chanced to hear her playing in an Atlantic City club. Reportedly he urged Hyams to get her own band together, but she opted to play in his orchestra instead. Vibes, of course, was a popular instrument during the swing era, as played by such men as Red Norvo and Lionel Hampton, and Hyams was compared favorably with these musicians during her 1944-45 tenure with Woody Herman. Although she gained widespread recognition as a member of the Herman band, she was unhappy about the scant opportunity to stretch out and really play in that kind of large-group context. In 1945 she left Herman and formed her own trio, which stayed together until 1948. During those years she received enthusiastic press, as at a 1947 Carnegie Hall concert as part of a trio led by pianist Mary Lou Williams, with June Rotenberg on bass. Hyams garnered even more attention when she joined George Shearing's very popular combo in 1949, remaining until 1950 and cutting some jazz hits, such as "September in the Rain." In 1950 the career of Margie Hyams, which had catapulted the young musician to an enviable position within a very few years, came to an abrupt halt when she opted to leave music for marriage.

Jazz and jazz-influenced harp was explored by several women musicians. Adele Girard was classically trained—her father was concertmaster for composer Victor Herbert, and her mother was an opera singer—but teamed with husband Joe Marsala, the trumpet player, she was billed as a "swing" harpist during the thirties. She played the Fifty-second Street clubs, recorded with Marsala and made several film shorts, one of which included her "Harp Boogie." Daphne Hellman and Corky Hale (née Hecht) experimented a bit later with a jazz approach to the instrument. Hellman continues to play into the eighties, based in New York, as does Hale, who is also proficient on piano, flute, and vocals. Hale made her recording debut on the West Coast around 1954, then worked with dance bands such as Harry James' and as accompanist to various singers, including Mel Torme in 1956 and Billie Holiday in 1957. Based in New York in the eighties, she concertizes in Europe as well as the States.

The most important of the women jazz harpists is Dorothy Ashby, who achieved subtle versatility on the traditionally cumbersome instrument; her guitarlike electrified harp voicings, interpolated with traditional harp-playing techniques, led some listeners to compare her with jazz guitarist Wes Montgomery. Ashby began, however, as a pianist in her native Detroit; her father, a guitarist, taught her harmony, and she went on to advanced studies in piano, harp and vocal technique at Wayne State University in the early fifties. During that decade she began to focus primarily on the jazz harp, working in and around Detroit and the East during the fifties and sixties with such players as Louis Armstrong and Woody Herman, and with her own trios. She also hosted a local jazz radio show, wrote a book about modern harmony for harp and piano, wrote tunes and won attention from the jazz community with a series of recordings begun in 1961. She continued to be active on the Detroit music scene in ensuing years. In the seventies she moved to California and established herself as a studio musician.

A few women have turned their attentions to the jazz violin. As mentioned earlier, violinist Kathryn Perry worked with pianist-songwriter Irene Armstrong in Chicago during the thirties, and violinist Mae Brady led groups and played in that city in the teens and twenties. Perry later married pianist Earl Hines. Violinist Emma "Ginger" Smock led one of the first all-female jazz combos to perform on television. This group, which appeared on a local California station in 1951, also included trumpeter Clora Bryant, pianist Jackie Glenn, bassist Ann Glasco, drummer Matty Watson and sometimes guitarist Willie Lee Terrell. Ginger Smock was classically trained as a youngster and aimed for a concert career. But after she began listening to jazz fiddlers like Joe Venuti, Stuff Smith and Eddie South, she became interested in improvisation and made the switch to jazz in her late teens. In an interview in 1951 she voiced the oft-heard complaint of women players: "It's hard for a girl to get anywhere in the musical profession, and for a girl jazz musician, it's even harder. We have to face the fact that a lot of people think there's something sort of—well, unladylike about a girl jazz musician."[13]

Like Ginger Smock, Bonnie Wetzel was a classically trained violinist who started out with a classical career in mind. Born in Vancouver, Washington, in 1926, Wetzel became oriented to jazz in her teens. When her high school band needed a bass player, she forsook the violin and took up that instrument to fill the slot. Upon graduation, along with classmate

Norma Carson, she joined Ada Leonard's all-woman big band and toured with it for about two years. She then became part of a trio led by former Melodears guitarist Marian Gange. In 1949 she met and married trumpeter Ray Wetzel, and together they joined Tommy Dorsey's band. Shortly thereafter, Ray Wetzel was killed in a car accident and Bonnie decided to leave the band and settle in New York. She worked as an active free-lancer during the early fifties, playing with such notable musicians as trumpeters Red Rodney and Roy Eldridge, as well as with Beryl Booker's all-woman combo, Soft Winds, which toured Europe and America in 1953–54. Bonnie Wetzel's bass was much in demand during these years and can be heard on several recordings, especially in all-woman combinations. She died of cancer in 1965.

Vivien Garry was a California bassist who played an active role in West Coast jazz during the forties. Garry, then married to guitarist Avrid Garrison, has been described as "a catalyst in many jam sessions in the L.A. area throughout the forties.... She wanted to be on top of all the developments in music and formed different groups to work in clubs there."[14] Her steady timekeeping and "bounce" can be heard on a number of recordings made during the period.

On the East Coast, electric bassist Carline Ray is a veteran performer who has been much in evidence since the late seventies in groups led by Melba Liston and by pianist Nina Sheldon, and with the Universal Jazz Coalition. She remembers her first gig as a "taxi dancehall date" in 1941, while still a student at the Juilliard School of Music. By 1946 she had joined the Sweethearts of Rhythm as rhythm guitarist and vocalist; in 1948 she joined Erskine Hawkins' band as vocalist and played the black theater circuit. Winning a scholarship in vocal music, she enrolled in the Manhattan School of Music and got her master's in 1956. In the fifties she formed a trio with former Sweethearts Edna Smith and Pauline Braddy Williams, going on to work with locally based big bands on Fender bass, usually as the only female member. From 1969 to 1979 she played with the Skitch Henderson big band and toured extensively. Ever calm on and off the bandstand, Ray says, "I never felt strange about being a woman in music. I enjoy what I'm doing, and I'm all business. We're musicians first. As for being women, that's incidental. Have confidence in what you do and know your limitations—and be all business." She admits, however, that "after thirty-five years, I *am* tired of wearing gowns on the bandstand."[15]

Another woman bassist to emerge in the forties was Lucille Dixon, who has been active in both classical and jazz music. From 1943 to 1945 Dixon worked with the Earl Hines Orchestra. She then formed her own Lucille Dixon Orchestra, which played from 1946 to 1960, mostly at the Savannah Club in New York. During those years Dixon's personnel included many outstanding musicians, among them Taft Jordan on trumpet, Buddy Tate on saxophone, Tyree Glenn and George Matthews on trombone, and Sonny Payne and Bill Smith on drums. During the sixties Dixon expanded her career, working as principal bassist with the Boston Women's Symphony Orchestra in 1964–65. In 1965 she became manager of the Symphony of the New World, an orchestra formed to showcase and promote the talents of minority musicians in classical music. Dixon continues to work as a free-lance jazz player, and in the summer of 1981 she appeared in the Kool Jazz Festival's premiere concert featuring women players.

Of the several women jazz guitarists to develop during the forties, the indisputable "first lady" is Mary Osborne, who followed the style set by Charlie Christian on that instrument (see the Mary Osborne profile in Part Five). Osborne was preceded by another "first lady," blues guitarist Memphis Minnie, who played, sang and wrote in the country blues idiom from the twenties through the fifties.

Memphis Minnie, also known as Minnie Douglas and Minnie Fowler (matters are further complicated by the sometime addition of husbands' surnames—she had three, all musicians: Casey Bill Weldon, whom she married in the twenties; Kansas Joe McCoy, from 1929 to 1935; and Ernest Lawlar, from 1939 to about 1961), was born around the turn of the century in Algiers, Louisiana. As with Valaida Snow and many other pioneer women musicians, her birthdate is subject to question and is variously given as 1896, 1897, 1900 and 1902.[16] Minnie's father gave her a banjo when she was a child, and by the time she was in her teens she had gained a local following as a Memphis guitar player and blues singer. Some accounts of her early life say she ran away from home and joined the circus for a stretch, but in any event she was back in Memphis in 1929, because a Columbia Records talent scout discovered her there, playing in a Beale Street barber shop. Her recording debut for Columbia followed soon after in New York, where she waxed some excellent duets on guitar with husband Kansas Joe McCoy. (Her later colleague, blues guitarist Big Bill Broonzy, gives the year of her debut on records as 1928, the record company as Columbia-owned Vocalion, and the song as "Bumble Bee."[17])

In 1930 Minnie and Joe McCoy went north to Chicago. There she became a well-known local spokeswoman, attuned as she was to the chronic hardships of life for poor blacks, further aggravated by the Depression. She became a fixture at South Side blues clubs such as Ruby Lee Gatewood's Tavern, where she held forth at "Blue Monday" parties, remaining popular until she moved back down to Memphis in the mid-fifties in poor health. She spent the last years of her life in a nursing home and died in 1963.

Memphis Minnie had a fine sense of the dramatic; in her blues shouting, she croaked, moaned, cracked and twisted her voice judiciously. Her vocal talent was matched by a superb improvisatory blues technique on guitar. As one writer put it, she "seemed to be able to pick sounds from all around Memphis and integrate them into her playing, [which makes] her one of the most satisfying country blues players, male or female."[18] Among her compositions and/or hit recordings are "Tricks Ain't Walkin No More" (about poverty and depression at the street level), "Bumble Bee Blues," "Queen Bee," "What's the Matter with the Mill?," "After While Blues," "North Memphis Blues," "Have You Seen My Man Tonight?," "Looking the World Over" and, perhaps her favorite, "Me and My Chauffeur Blues."*

Memphis Minnie was no stranger to the resistance encountered by so many women instrumentalists in blues and jazz. In his autobiography Big Bill Broonzy relates a colorful anecdote about the reception the then-unknown Minnie got at a Chicago club in 1933:

Me and Memphis Minnie played the first contest between blues singers that was ever given in the USA....

Everybody was saying:

"Is that man going to play against that poor little weaker woman? He should be ashamed because any man should beat a woman playing a guitar."...

...So this white man comes... to me and says:

"Bill, is this thing going to be done fair?"

"Yes, sir," I said. "We have the three best blues singers and players for judges."

"Who are they?" he asked.

"Sleepy John Estes, Tampa Red and Richard Jones."

"Well, they know the blues," he said. "It's OK then. I just wanted it done fair because all the people are saying they know you can play better than Minnie."

"I don't know about that," I said to him, "but I'm gonna try to win those two bottles so I can get in a corner and drink until I get enough."...

So I sang "Just A Dream" and they liked it very much. Then I sang "Make My Getaway" and I got down off the stand.

Tampa Red called Memphis Minnie to the stand and everybody

---

*Other women blues and blues-folk-rock guitarists to follow her style include Bonnie Jefferson, born in Arkansas and now settled in San Diego; Vanzula Carter Hunter; Jessie Mae Hemphill, a popular figure at blues festivals around Mississippi in the seventies and eighties; Etta Baker, an Appalachian picker; Elisabeth Cotten, a popular folk guitarist who wrote "Freight Train"; and contemporary rock performers Bonnie Raitt and Terry Garthwaite, who play blues-influenced guitar.

got quiet. She first sang "Me and My Chauffeur" and the house rocked for twenty minutes, then she sang "Looking the World Over."

John Estes and Richard Jones went to the stand, picked Minnie up and carried her around in the hall until her husband saw them, got up and told them: "Put her down, she can walk."

He was jealous of any man. So Memphis Minnie won two bottles.[19]

Several women jazz drummers were active during the forties and fifties. Pauline Braddy served throughout the forties as anchorwoman on the traps with the International Sweethearts of Rhythm. Pola Roberts first studied piano and then bongos as a youngster in Pittsburgh; her interest in percussion was sparked by a musician uncle. She went on to work with organist-bassist Gloria Coleman in the fifties, later moving to New York and joining the Jazz Maidens, a quintet of women led by Melba Liston in the late fifties. Roberts rejoined Gloria Coleman's combo and recorded with her in the early sixties. Known for her good technique, she has said she was primarily influenced and encouraged by drummers Philly Joe Jones and Art Blakey.

Another drummer influenced by a musician uncle was Paula Hampton, niece of trombonist Slide Hampton. By the sixties she had emerged as a talented player, and she has since been active in the New York area. Among other groups, she has played with the Jazz Sisters, an all-woman outfit led by pianist Jill McManus in the seventies; Celebration, an all-woman quintet led by singer Evelyn Blakey, daughter of drummer Art Blakey; and the Sights and Sounds Revue. Drummer Elaine Leighton, a high school classmate of tenorman Stan Getz and trumpeter Shorty Rogers, backed singing duo Jackie and Roy in 1945–50, then worked with ex–Sweethearts of Rhythm personnel in a combo led by Anna Mae Winburn in 1953. She joined Beryl Booker's trio, Soft Winds, later that year and remained until 1954. From 1957 to 1959 she led her own combo at the Page Three Club in New York. Drummer Dottie Dodgion got her start in the later forties in the San Francisco Bay area as a singer. She then studied with Charles Mingus and went on to work extensively in both large and small group contexts (see the Dottie Dodgion profile in Part Five).

These women—and many others—played jazz during the decades when to be a woman in jazz was to be truly an exception. Their presence, against often formidable odds, constitutes a rebuttal to an argument that has been prevalent in one form or another for centuries. Boiled down, this argument holds that women cannot and should not play most instruments. Though the jazzwomen seldom attracted serious attention from writers, reviewers, club owners and record producers, they could and did play; some made it nationally and internationally despite the obstacles, while many more established good reputations on a local or regional level. Sadly, many faded out *after* they had become established, so that their careers were truncated or else information on their later years is scarce or nonexistent.

But their presence, for however short a time, carries a powerful message today, as it did then. They were trailblazers in the art and business of jazz as serious music and entertainment. Yes, a woman *can* play jazz, their music announced. Yes, she can play the trumpet, the saxophone, the drums. She can be free to choose what and how she will play. As musicians, these jazzwomen are part of the history of jazz, and their stories help to complete our understanding of the music's past. As pioneers and role models, they are harbingers of a brighter future for jazzwomen to come.

Part Three

WOMEN

VOCALISTS

1920s – 1960s

Introduction

VOICE AS INSTRUMENT

Probably the first singers to utilize the improvisatory techniques that would develop, centuries later, into what is loosely called jazz singing were Africans. Many ethnomusicologists regard the African griots, improvising troubadours who functioned as a kind of musical town crier/gossip, as forerunners of Afro-American vocal technique (these singers still practice their art today, and some, women like Konde Kuyate of Guinea and Miriam Makeba of the Xhosa tribe in South Africa, have become famous beyond their homelands). The African vocal tradition is an ancient and fertile one. As Ghanaian music scholar Francis Bebey says, "Vocal music is truly the essence of African musical art. . . . [A] prime motive of instrumentalists is to reconstruct spoken or sung language."[1]

Thus the voice was not only the first instrument, giving birth to song, but it was a major inspiration for players. And this intimate connection between voice and instrument, so apparent in African music, carried over into the Afro-American vocal tradition. In sound production and style, the black players and singers who brought their music with them to America had a mutual influence on one another, an intimate interrelationship that runs through black sacred and secular music and can be heard in the earliest recordings of blues and jazz. The singers, predominantly women, who participated in early ensemble jazz were part of what can be regarded as a dialogue between vocalist and player. The black female singers of the twenties and thirties, later to be identified as a group under the somewhat misleading label "classic blues" artists, used their song material (mostly but not entirely blues) as clay with which to mold a music akin to that of the players. Early recordings show numerous instances of singers striving for instrumental sounds, using growls and slurs in the manner of a trombone or trumpet. Bessie Smith is an outstanding example, and many others, scarcely known today, also tried for hornlike effects, among them Adelaide Hall with Duke Ellington; Gladys Bentley, a famous cabaret performer who growled and scatted briefly like a trumpet on a 1928 recording of "How Much Can I Stand?"; and blues singer Mary Dixon, scatting on "You Can't Sleep in My Bed" in 1929.

The goal of players and singers in the Afro-American musical tradition is the ever more perfect expression of the inner voice—their own individual sound. And just as an important tool in the jazz player's arsenal of technique is imitation of the human voice, with its seemingly endless capacity for sound production—cries, growls, moans, slurs, shouts, whispers, wails—so do jazz singers work to develop as improvisers in large part by copying instruments. The creative cycle of jazz music embraces both the singer as player, with an instrumental approach to vocalizing, and the player as singer, with a vocalizing approach to playing. To say that a singer wails like a horn or that a player sings on the horn is a mark of high praise in jazz. Many horn players have profited from listening to vocal improvisers, and "great jazz singers improvise as horns might, often using lyrics as vehicles to transport their rhythmic fancies. Their voices approach the tonal qualities of horns, and the development of jazz vocal styles is closely aligned with the dominance of certain instruments within the music."[2] When the music is really cooking, jazz player and jazz vocalist carry on a running exchange that blurs the distinction between the sources of their sound.

Such an approach to song is of course quite different from the classical European approach. As American black music was evolving during the eighteenth and nineteenth centuries, whites tended to react to it with bewilderment, distaste or ridicule and often dismissed what they heard as weird, wild, even disgusting. Though some whites were moved by the sonorities and rhythms of black music, especially in spirituals, the prevailing white view was that black singers displayed "unseemly" emotion and broke the rules of "proper" singing, breathing when and where they liked, chopping words up in their phrasing, slurring or straining as they saw fit. Even in the 1920s a singer like Bessie Smith was considered "crude" and "loud" by many listeners. And after Mahalia Jackson became world-famous, the story goes, she was almost persuaded to study with a classical voice teacher. Happily she did not, as such alien standards would doubtless have made her self-conscious and detracted from her natural gift.

But in spite of the fact that early improvising black singers were often misjudged and misunderstood, as time went on many listeners and performers became excited by the expressive possibilities of black vocal music (Al Jolson and Sophie Tucker are famous examples of white performers who copied and learned from Afro-American song technique in the early part of the century). In the words of one critic, "Jazz liberated [the singer] from the precise pitches and more or less arithmetically calculated rhythms of European music, permitting him [or her] to order the words within a phrase in a manner closer to the natural melody and the natural rhythm of speech."[3]

The one big difference between players and singers is, of course, that singers deal with words as well as music. Jazz freed singers to improvise on both, and the way they have chosen to handle the lyric, or text, of a song has varied greatly. Conservatives have argued for a strict, close reading of the text, while radicals have often done away with words entirely. Between these two extremes, most jazz-influenced singers have aimed in their treatment of the lyric for an emotional impact that somehow resolves the inherent tension between words and music. The manner of this resolution has been one of the most creative—and most disputed—aspects of the craft of jazz singing and has led to the emergence of various stylistic "schools." Many singers have found a satisfying balance in a careful yet individualistic approach to the structure of the song, combined with solo space at the "break" to stretch out and scat.

Most of the so-called blues singers of the twenties, trained in those pre-microphone days in vaudeville, tent shows, revues and so on, were quite precise in their stage diction and gave full value to their song lyrics. Perhaps the prime example is Ethel Waters, who sang blues material early in her career but developed into a sophisticated singer of popular song with a jazz approach. The style she had perfected by the thirties nicely illustrates the difference between straight and jazz-based pop singing. With a fairly direct reading of the lyric, she manipulated tone, timbre and rhythm to give her delivery a permeating jazz flavor. Unfamiliar with such techniques, straight pop singers of her era could not hope to equal the subtleness and suppleness of her sound. Later pop-jazz singers followed Waters' lead in the idiom, developing further subtleties in the manipulation of rhythm, phrasing, shading and emphasis.

Another approach was brilliantly advanced by Waters' contemporary Bessie Smith. Though billed as the "Empress of the Blues," Smith has come to be regarded as the first important woman jazz singer. Especially through her mastery of time, so essential to an effective jazz performance, she succeeded in conveying deep intensity of feeling and multiple meanings in her material. "Bessie's way . . . was to restrict the range of a song to no more than five or six notes and to construct her phrases so economically that a change in direction of just one note could have a startling dramatic or emotive effect," wrote bandleader Humphrey Lyttleton. She had an "unerring rhythmic instinct based, like Louis Armstrong's, on an underlying rhythm of twelve eighth notes (or four quaver triplets) to the bar," and she used "improvisation in its fullest sense on the melody of a song to express a deeper meaning than that of the words on their own."[4] Thus Smith, along with Armstrong, is generally considered one of the giants of Afro-American vocal music during the twenties. She took the folk blues idiom and imbued it with sophisticated technique. As Richard Hadlock says, "Like the best instrumentalists, Bessie Smith could fashion a compelling solo from the absolute minimum of musical raw material and, again like most jazzmen, was frequently forced to do just that.... In her work, instrumentalists recognized the sort of individuality they tried to express on their own horns and strings."[5]

In the decades following Smith, Waters and company, many improvising singers developed the reading of the song's text into a fine art as well as a popular one. The trend (assisted by the introduction of the microphone) was to refine the often declamatory style in phrasing of the blues period, as Billie Holiday did so superbly in the thirties and after. But in short order there arose another crop of singers who paid less attention to the lyric and aimed more at improvising off the melody and harmonic changes of the tune (claiming, often with justification, that the words to most songs were unworthy of attention anyway). For these singers, trying more deliberately for a hornlike sound, the words often seemed an encumbrance to the music, especially when taken at a fast tempo. Scatting—what one writer calls "free improvisation on syllables, often nonsensical"[6]—provided the solution.

Jazz scatting in an extended way was first recorded by Louis Armstrong, who spluttered "nonsense syllables," to the delight of listeners, when he forgot the words to the song he was singing. At its best, scatting draws a direct line between the singer and the music and creates high musical exhilaration, especially when balanced by careful handling of the lyric at other points in the song. Outstanding female practitioners of this art within an art include such individualists as Ella Fitzgerald, Sarah Vaughan, Sheila Jordan, Betty Carter and Anita O'Day. Though there are jazz singers who have never or only rarely scatted (Billie Holiday did not), and though the ability to scat by no means completely defines the good jazz singer, the trend has been toward more ambitious and sustained scatting among emerging jazz singers of recent years. For scat singing is one of the principal means by which a singer can exhibit and explore her vocal-instrument technique as a horn player might.

The strands of the Afro-American vocal tradition continue to overlap and borrow from one another, and it is impossible to draw strict lines of demarcation that would once and for all separate what is "jazz singing" from what is not. Jazz is always in flux and is periodically refreshed, as when older styles like the classic blues of the twenties enjoy a new vogue, or when new approaches or different media emerge, like Brazilian popular song styles and electronic music. (At least as often, many feel, the music is "polluted" by gimmicks and devices from the commercial music world, as nearly all attempts to create jazz-rock "fusion" seem to bear out.) But though the boundaries containing jazz country for singers are in dispute, that country becomes more densely and heterogeneously populated as time goes by. There are improvisatory singers of all kinds—those who target their delivery strictly for supper clubs and "saloons," those who sing only slow-tempo ballads, those who sprinkle their "soul" liberally with jazz feeling. Some only scat; others are revered in the hermetic world of gospel and would not wish to sing "worldly" jazz. Still others were trained for opera.

What unites these singers and often proves more important than their differences in material and emphasis is the tradition of Afro-American music, and specifically of singing. Good improvising jazz singers walk tightropes, perform balancing acts, swallow fire. In plainer words, they take risks in their craft that the singer of pop tunes or opera cannot. Their safety net is the rhythm that underpins their aural arabesques. Whether backed by a trio or just a piano or winging it alone, these singers share a sure inner pulse; without it, they are like the emperor without his clothes. Often understated or even unstated, this sense of time makes the difference between a stiff, metronomic reading of a tune and one that flows and propels a song forward without rushing it. Today the improvising jazz, blues, gospel or pop singer can claim a wealth of technique that her predecessors formulated and elaborated from African roots grafted to European harmonic and melodic elements. In her search for her own sound, she uses this arsenal in her manipulation of time, in her phrasing of the lyric, in her scatting, in her treatment of the chord structure and, just as important, in her gift for dramatic interpretation, which can render the same song funny, angry, witty or sad.

In the final analysis, regardless of their backgrounds and artistic choices, all the women who have striven for self-expression in the exacting discipline of improvisatory singing have contributed to the music we call jazz. Part Three examines the careers of some of these singers who made their mark in the decades from the classic blues era through the swing era and bop to the emergence of the avant-garde and free experimentalism in the sixties (the latter area is discussed more fully in Chapter 9, "The Contemporary Scene"). Chapter 6 deals with the women who perfected the art of blues singing as a vehicle of personal expression, often to the accompaniment of the top jazz players of the day. Some of them stuck to the rural country blues idiom, backed by more rustic instruments, but they and their urban counterparts were the foremothers of the increasingly sophisticated jazz singers to come. Chapter 7 assesses the contributions of the "canaries," the "girl singers" who appeared with the big bands of the swing era. Though so often slighted as a type, many of these women were good at their craft, and some used the time they spent with the bands to advance the art of jazz singing. Chapter 8 testifies to the diversity and inventiveness of improvisatory singing by examining in detail female vocalists working in a variety of more modern jazz and jazz-based vocal styles.

Chapter Six

THE BLUESWOMEN

[Blues means] what milk does to a baby. Blues is what the
spirit is to a minister. We sing the blues because our hearts
have been hurt, our souls have been disturbed. But when you
sing the blues, let it be classy.

ALBERTA HUNTER, 1977

The blues, like all folk music, spread by word of mouth. As it grew in popularity, it came to be written down and somewhat standardized—in 1912, for example, W. C. Handy published "Memphis Blues," and in 1914 "St. Louis Blues"—but it remained essentially a personal commentary, tailored to suit the individual singer, and rough at the edges. The blues eventually became famous, of course, and lucrative for at least some of its practitioners, but not without a struggle. In form and content, it long remained in disfavor with the churchgoing black working class and the aspiring black middle class. The whites who ran record companies knew little of the blues' huge potential market, and the press ignored it until late in life, for the white press did not report black events and the black press tended to cater to bourgeois tastes. Until the blues became popular, just about the only black music on record was religious in nature: such material as revival shouts recorded as early as 1902 and spirituals recorded by groups like the Fisk Jubilee Singers.

But the blues put black music on the map in 1920, when a persistent black composer and promoter named Perry Bradford finally persuaded Fred Hagar of the General Phonograph Company to wax a black artist on Okeh Records—Mamie Smith, a fairly obscure vaudeville singer. Mamie debuted with "That Thing Called Love"/"You Can't Keep a Good Man Down," not strictly blues, but bluesy pop vocals. Sales were good enough to convince Okeh to record Mamie Smith again, this time on the more genuine blues tunes "Crazy Blues"/"It's Right Here for You," which also featured tenor saxophonist Coleman Hawkins in his recording debut.

Reportedly selling a then-incredible seventy-five thousand copies in the first month of its release, and eventually nearly three million, "Crazy Blues" made Smith an instant star and opened the floodgates to other black artists. Record scouts combed the South and found a great reservoir of talented blueswomen and bluesmen; hundreds of women were recorded, all aiming for their own "Crazy Blues." Most sang a more sophisticated, smoother version of the rougher-hewn country blues (also called "folk" or "rural" blues, and usually sung by men). The repertoire of these "classic blues" singers, as they later became known, often included "torchers," pop songs from Tin Pan Alley, and show tunes from vaudeville and the musical theater as well as blues. Unlike their country sisters, they usually sang to the accompaniment of jazz players. This teaming of blues vocals with jazz accompaniment aided the black singers of the twenties in developing the distinctive jazz-influenced vocal styles that can be heard on the records of the period. And the new recording surge also opened up a big market for the spirituals and gospel, the kissing cousins of "devil's music," as blues and jazz were often labeled.

From roughly 1920 to 1933, until the depths of the Depression brought everything to a halt, the blues reigned in the marketplace of black music, and the women who sang the blues ruled with it. Queens and empresses were made—women like Bessie Smith, Ma Rainey, Ida Cox, Sippie Wallace, "Chippie" Hill, Gladys Bentley, Alberta Hunter, Lucille Hegamin, Ethel Waters, Victoria Spivey, Edith Wilson and many more, now forgotten, like Mattie Hite and Mae Alix, top club acts of the period. Often these were fast-falling stars, women who knew fame and glamour one day and obscurity and poverty the next. Some were prolific songwriters, and though they dealt with the standard lovesick-woman-as-victim motif, many of their titles pointed to other concerns: "Penitentiary Bound Blues," "Black Dog Blues," "Fire and Thunder Blues," "Evil Mama Blues," "Death Sting Me Blues." The lyrics to these songs, often startlingly uninhibited, were disparaged as "gutbucket," "low-down," "lower-class"; the singers themselves were also criticized, and a strong personality like Bessie Smith was considered coarse and ill-mannered. Respectable folk shuddered and blushed, but black record buyers and a growing number of knowledgeable whites bought millions of their records.

. . .

The first of the great women blues singers was Ma Rainey, often called "Mother of the Blues." It has been claimed that this minstrel performer was first attracted to the blues around 1903 by a strange, poignant tune sung by an unidentified young girl; whether or not this anecdote is true, road life as a traveling singer certainly provided her with ample exposure to the blues.[1] In any case, when Ma Rainey did take up the blues in performance around the turn of the century, she began the mass popularization of this black folk idiom that lies at the heart of jazz. Deep South in her identity, Ma sang, and in many cases wrote, blues songs that were rooted in the Southern black experience. She rarely toured north of Virginia, and it was only after the commercial success of the blues that she worked out of Chicago. Ma Rainey sang about what she knew; very often that meant lonely, troubled, violent women. She gained a reputation as a spokeswoman and racial heroine among Southern blacks because she understood her mostly rural, poor audience perfectly and played her role, with its possibilities for escape into glamour, to the hilt.

No one would deny that Rainey was not physically attractive (one contemporary called her "ugly-attractive"[2]) but though she had her prima donna side, her pride and her temper, hers was a generous nature packaged in glitter and dazzle. Fellow singer Victoria Spivey loved the image and artistry of Ma Rainey, especially her skill with double-entendre lyrics:

> Oh Lord, don't say anything about Ma. All her gold hanging around her tight. Ma was a mess. Ain't nobody in the world ever yet been able to holler "Hey Bo Weevil" like her. Not like Ma. Nobody. I've heard them try to, but they can't do it. "Hey Bo Weevil." All right. 'Cos bo weevil he was eating up everything down South. That worm would eat up all the food and everything. And she holler "Hey Bo Weevil you been gone a long time." Now there was two *meanings* to that. I was such a smart little hip chicken, I knew just which bo weevil she was talking about. Oh I was clever![3]

Poet Sterling Brown loved Ma's delivery:

> She wouldn't have to sing any words; she would moan, and the audience would moan with her. She had them in the palm of her hand. I heard Bessie Smith also, but Ma Rainey was the greatest mistress of an audience. Bessie was the greatest blues singer, but Ma

really *knew* these people; she was a person of the folk; she was very simple and direct.[4]

Ma Rainey was born in 1886. At a tender age she took to the road as a singer with traveling shows, at least in part to escape the poverty of her environment. Born Gertrude Pridgett, she acquired her name when she married Pa Rainey at eighteen; for a time in the mid-teens they were billed in a song-and-dance act with the Tolliver Circus as "Rainey & Rainey Assassinators of the Blues." Later their Rabbit Foot Minstrels became a vehicle for Ma's powerful blues delivery. After the record companies started to sign black artists, she became Paramount's biggest-selling star of the twenties, though she was thirty-eight years old and a seasoned trouper when "discovered" by the talent scouts. Significantly for the future of black singing styles, Rainey took Bessie Smith, ten years her junior, under her wing as part of her act for a period between 1913 and 1916. Although in later years Smith did not always like to acknowledge her musical debt to Rainey, she doubtless absorbed a great deal from the more experienced older singer.

In her peak recording years Rainey cut sides with such jazz artists as Louis Armstrong, Coleman Hawkins and Fletcher Henderson, yet she always retained her rural, down-home style and feel. In all she cut ninety-some records, the last in 1928. She continued to perform during the thirties and then retired to the home she had built in the South. Comfortably off in her later years, she owned two theaters and remained active in community affairs. She died in 1939, just as critics and collectors were becoming aware of her contribution.

One star who really lived up to the title of blues queen during the Roaring Twenties was the fabulous Ida Cox. A vaudeville artist as well as a blues singer, she produced and headlined lavish shows during the twenties, commanding a top salary and attracting good musicians, among them pianist Lovie Austin and her group, the Blues Serenaders. Cox wrote much original material, including "Wild Women Don't Have the Blues," "Fogyism" (about superstition), "Western Union Blues" (about the rejected woman) and "Tree Top Tall Papa" (about the unfaithful lover). Like many others, she had her morbid side, which expressed itself in songs like "Coffin Blues" and "Bone Orchard Blues."

After the crash of 1929–30, which put most of the black women singers out of work, Cox retired temporarily to the large home she had built for herself in Tennessee. A resilient performer, she later returned to work the black theater circuits, but she had only a few more record dates after her heyday in the twenties, including one with Hot Lips Page, James P. Johnson and J. C. Higginbotham, all top jazzmen, in 1939; one with trumpeter Henry

"Red" Allen in 1940 (that date featured another grim Cox composition, "Last Mile Blues," about going to the electric chair); and a final session with Coleman Hawkins in 1961 at age seventy-two. By then, sadly, her voice was just about gone. Ida Cox died in 1967.

Lucille Hegamin was another classic blues singer with a varied repertoire that also included vaudeville and pop material. Like many of the twenties blueswomen, she faded away once her fling with fame was over, but it was a good fling. Hegamin was the second black woman singer to record: "Jazz Me Blues"/"Everybody's Blues," for Arto Records and Black Swan in November 1920. Born Lucille Nelson in Macon, Georgia, in 1894 or 1897, she started singing as a youngster in her church choir but received no formal musical training. She called herself a cabaret artist and was billed as the "Georgia Peach" when she went to Chicago in 1914. There she sang everything from blues to popular songs in a jazz style, in a voice described as "clear and rich, with...perfect diction and jazz feeling....With all the music-hall overtones, she was still an extremely good singer of jazz-based blues."[5]

The year 1919 found Hegamin in New York City, where, with her Blue Flame Syncopators, she recorded "Jazz Me Blues" and "Arkansas Blues," issued in 1921. She worked the New York clubs and was featured in the Cotton Club revue of 1925. Recalling her performing days, she later said, "You really had to wail for there were no mikes. It's much easier today, but then you just *had* to have a voice—there was no faking."[6] In all Hegamin recorded over forty sides, many for Cameo, including the hit song "He May Be Your Man, but He Comes to See Me Sometimes." She also toured with several shows, including the road company of the hit revue *Shuffle Along*. Many years later, in the sixties, fellow blues singer Victoria Spivey found Lucille Hegamin living obscurely in Harlem. The sides Hegamin cut at that time for Spivey's record company, plus a few cuts for Prestige-Bluesville, broke a silence of nearly forty years. But she was an old woman by then and died soon after, in 1970.

Vaudeville and the theater provided a route for many other black singers who contributed to the blues craze. Rosa Henderson (1896–1968), one of the most popular, used her strong, sweet voice to advantage on nearly one hundred records between 1923 and 1931, including the noteworthy "Penitentiary Bound Blues" and "Back Wood Blues." Cleo, or Cleothus, Gibson capitalized on her resemblance to Bessie Smith to boost her career, recording the erotic "I've Got Ford Movements in My Hips" and "Nothing but the Blues" before she faded off the scene. Vaudevillian Mary Mack sang the blues from time to time, and her colleague Viola McCoy, accompanied by Fletcher Henderson bandmembers, showed promise on "If Your Good Man Quits You, Don't Wear No Black" and other songs during her short recording career (1927–30). Katherine Henderson, niece of blues singer Eva Taylor, tried the blues as well, but a more skilled Henderson was Edmonia, who recorded with Lovie Austin, Tommy Ladnier and Jelly Roll Morton.

And Bessie and Mamie were not the only Smiths to belt the blues of the era. Clara and Trixie Smith (unrelated) were blueswomen known for their renditions of double-entendre, erotic and jazz-backed material. Clara had a particular ability to interpret provocative songs and by the mid-twenties had developed into a good blues singer; her "Nobody Knows How I Feel Dis Mornin' " and "Shipwrecked Blues," with Louis Armstrong accompanying, are collector's items, as are her duets with Bessie Smith in 1923 and in 1925. Her "Whip It to a Jelly" and "Jelly Look What You Done Done," moaned in a low, sultry voice, exemplify the frank expression of human and sexual experience often found on the "race records" of the period. Very little is known about Clara Smith's life; she was born in the South, probably in South Carolina, at the end of the nineteenth century, had a career marked by increasing facility in her art, and died in 1935, forgotten. Trixie Smith's story is even sketchier. Her reputation rests on a 1925 recording with the ubiquitous Armstrong, "The World's Jazz Crazy and So Am I"/"Railroad Man Blues," and on a 1938 session with Charlie Shavers and Sidney Bechet, "Freight Train Blues." She died in 1943.[7]

The state of Texas, in earlier decades as now, supplied many blues and jazz artists with a distinctive, characteristically hard-edged and aggressive sound. Sippie Wallace, the "Texas Nightingale," is the best known of the women singers from the Lone Star State. Born in Houston in 1899 under the name Beulah Thomas, she came from a musical family. She moved to New York in 1923 and toured for many years on the TOBA circuit, singing and playing the piano (TOBA, the Theater Owners Booking Association, was a black entertainment agency whose initials were also said to stand for "Tough On Black Artists"[8]). Wallace's "Morning Dove Blues," with King Oliver accompanying on cornet, exhibited her lyric grace. After she had been away from the music scene for many years, the redoubtable Victoria Spivey located her in Detroit in the sixties. Wallace subsequently toured Europe and often teamed with slide guitarist and singer Bonnie Raitt in the seventies. At Kool Jazz Festival concerts in 1980 and 1981 she was a featured singer.

Another Texan was Maggie Jones, also born in 1899. Her moaning voice was recorded on Columbia, Pathé/Perfect, Black Swan and Paramount (often under the name of Fae Barnes). Her recording of "North Bound Blues" was notable for its candid treatment of living conditions for Southern blacks, and her "Good Time Flat Blues," with Louis Armstrong, was equally explicit. But Jones never hit it big, and after 1930 she seems to have faded off the scene. Fellow Texan Mary Dixon recorded for Vocalion and Columbia in 1928 and 1929, doing memorable versions of "Black Dog

Blues" and "Fire and Thunder Blues." In Dallas in 1928, in the moaning style favored by many Southwestern singers, Hattie Burleson cut "Sadie's Servant Room Blues," a simple yet shrewd commentary on life belowstairs. Other Texas blueswomen include Moanin' Bernice Edwards, Bessie Tucker, Lillian Glinn, known especially for her "Shake It Down," and Monette Moore, who worked and recorded in the twenties with Charlie Johnson's Paradise Orchestra in New York.

One of the finer blues singers hailed from Charleston, South Carolina. Bertha "Chippie" Hill was born in 1900 or 1905 into a family of sixteen children. At the age of thirteen she moved to New York City, where she quickly got herself a booking at Leroy's, a club that featured the young Ethel Waters. Hill began as a dancer but added singing for the extra money it paid. After moving to Chicago, she entered a local talent contest and won first prize—a recording date with Louis Armstrong for Okeh. The two cut "Georgia Man" and "Pratt City Blues" in 1925. She went on tour, including a stint with Ma Rainey, and became known for her tough, unsentimental delivery of such songs as "Black Market Blues." In the late twenties Chippie Hill dropped out of show business for a number of years. But in 1946 she did a recording date for Circle Records, with Lovie Austin on piano, and after a triumphant appearance at the Paris Jazz Festival in 1948 her comeback seemed assured. Tragically, she was killed shortly afterwards in a car accident.

Memphis, Tennessee, has been home to a number of fine blueswomen, many in the country blues tradition usually associated with male artists. These women had a rougher sound and sang mostly blues rather than vaudeville or pop material, using traditional folk-blues instrumentation (guitar, harp, banjo, etc.) rather than jazz accompaniment. Besides the excellent blues guitarist, singer and composer Memphis Minnie, already discussed as an instrumentalist, there was Laura Dukes, known as "Little Bit," who sang, danced and played the ukelele from the thirties through the fifties, retaining a loyal local and regional following into the seventies, when she sang and strummed with Son Smith's band. Other Memphis blues singers include Hattie Hart, Mattie Delaney, Madelyn James and Jenny Pope, all of whom recorded in the late twenties and the thirties for labels such as Brunswick and Vocalion.

The Memphis women had their counterparts throughout the South, Southwest and Midwest. Outstanding among them was Lucille Bogan from Birmingham, Alabama. Bogan, also known as Bessie Jackson, was one of the first black women to record and write songs with explicit sexual imagery; she often chose to sing about prostitution. Her recording career, mainly for Okeh and Brunswick, spanned the years 1923 to 1937. She is best remembered for "Sloppy Drunk Blues," "Black Angel Blues" and "Tricks Ain't Walkin'

No More" (Memphis Minnie also recorded a memorable version of "Tricks").

Midwestern practitioners of rough-hewn blues include St. Louisans Louise Johnson, Alice Moore and Mary Williams Johnson. The latter wrote some noteworthy songs, such as "Black Man Blues" and "Baby Please Don't Go." "Mary Johnson Blues" and some of her other songs told of her love, marriage and breakup with blues guitarist Lonnie Johnson; sung in a quiet, moaning style with simple directness, they appealed to the country blues record buyers of the region. From Kansas City came blueswoman Ada Brown, who cut "Evil Mama Blues" in 1923 with the Bennie Moten band (which would provide many of the personnel for the later Count Basie Orchestra). After her appearance in the film *Stormy Weather* (1943) singing "That Ain't Right" with Fats Waller, Ada Brown faded off the scene. Bandleader Moten's sister, Etta, was known as "The Brown Thrush of Song" and appeared in several films. Two durable performers who stuck to the old-time blues approach and material throughout their long careers were Philadelphian Princess White (1881–1976) and Chicago-based Mama Yancey, born in 1896. Long married to pianist Jimmy Yancey, "father of boogie-woogie," Mama Yancey still performs occasionally, as at the 1981 Kool Jazz Festival in New York City.

New Orleans spawned several fine black women singers (not all of them blues artists) during the period of great ensemble jazz in that city. Among them were "Blue Lu" Barker, born about 1914, wife of guitarist Danny Barker; Esther Bigeou (1895–1936), who was known as "The Creole Songbird"; and Ann Cook (1888–1962), who sustained a popular local reputation. Lizzie Miles (1895–1963) got her blues and what she called "gombo French" (or black Creole) tunes right out of her own neighborhood. She recalled that as a little girl of six or seven, she began singing with a band run jointly by Kid Ory and King Oliver. She married in her teens but left home and husband to join the circus, singing with the sideshow band; later she played Chicago and New York clubs. During the Depression, like so many of her sister artists, she had to abandon music as a profession and for many years supported herself as a housemaid and barmaid. In the fifties Miles made a comeback during a revival of interest in New Orleans–style jazz and blues, remaining popular until her death in the sixties.[9]

There were many other good vocalists of the twenties about whom information is almost totally lacking. Martha Copeland recorded over thirty 78s, including Victoria Spivey's composition "Black Snake Blues." Sara Martin was popular during that decade; among her better-known recordings is "Death Sting Me Blues" with King Oliver. Eliza (or Liza) Brown recorded duets with the equally obscure Ann Johnson. Virginia Liston recorded briefly from 1923 to 1926, and Margaret Johnson did at least one recording with soprano saxophonist Sidney Bechet. Gladys Bentley, a popular Harlem entertainer and male impersonator, specialized in risqué songs, as did Mattie Hite. Hannah Sylvester was another singer of the period, unearthed by Victoria Spivey and recorded again in the sixties.

Happily, there were black women singers who remained in show business during the lean years and turned their talents in new directions—radio, the theater, movies and later television. A few made comebacks as singers, notably Edith Wilson (née Goodall), who died in 1981. A stage performer as well as a recording artist, Wilson was the first black woman singer to record for a major label—"Nervous Blues" for Columbia in 1921 with Johnny Dunn's Jazz Hounds. Blues writer Derrick Stewart-Baxter said of her, "Amid all the refinement and histrionics there is hidden deep down in the roots of blues, another Edith Wilson, a jazz singer, who can shout out a song with feeling and conviction."[10] This she did, for example, on her version of Lucille Hegamin's "He May Be Your Man."

Born into a musical family in Louisville, Kentucky, Wilson wanted to go on the stage from the time she was a little girl. In the early twenties she appeared at the Cotton Club with Duke Ellington and his orchestra, starred in a *Blackbirds* revue and in *Hot Chocolates* with Louis Armstrong and Fats Waller (Waller's song "Black and Blue" was written specifically for her) and toured Europe several times. During the Depression, her versatility stood her well. She sang with numerous bands, including Ellington's, Cab Calloway's, Benny Carter's and Jimmie Lunceford's, and she also played the part of Kingfish's mother-in-law on the *Amos 'n' Andy* radio show and took the part of Aunt Jemima for Quaker Oats. In addition she was a prolific songwriter; at the time of her death in 1981, there were reportedly stacks of compositions piled up in her Chicago home. Her last major appearance was at a Tribute to Black Broadway, 1900–1945, at New York's Town Hall in 1980.

Among the enduring performers in the blues tradition, Victoria "Queen" Spivey is outstanding as both a promoter and an object of the blues revival that has flourished since the sixties. During the twenties Spivey sang, wrote songs and played piano, organ and ukelele. In her native Texas she played with legendary bluesman Blind Lemon Jefferson around Houston and Galveston. Around 1926 she made her first recording, of her own "Black Snake Blues"; "T.B. Blues," in 1927, was another characteristically realistic song, concerning that dread disease of poverty, and sung in a tough, hard-edged voice; her "How Do You Do It That Way," recorded with a six-piece band that included Louis Armstrong, dealt sharply with loneliness. By 1929 Spivey was at the peak of her popularity. That year she starred in King Vidor's all-black musical film, *Hallelujah*, and headlined the Hunter's Serenaders, a band with which she continued to work into the Depression. In the forties she performed on the road in *Hellzapoppin'* and married dancer Billy Adams, with whom she continued to entertain until the early fifties.

In the sixties Victoria Spivey successfully co-produced a series of reissues and new blues and jazz records by Lucille Hegamin, Hannah Sylvester, Alberta Hunter and others. Continuing to write songs that reflected what she saw around her, Spivey made trenchant, searing musical statements: on alcoholism and drug addiction in "From Broadway to Seventh Avenue," on sadism in "Black Belt," on suicide in "Brooklyn Blues." As Stewart-Baxter said, "She is cynical at times, sordid too, but these are genuine songs."[11] Spivey, who died in 1976, remained active to the end.

The comeback of singer Alberta Hunter was one of the most successful within the blues and jazz world during the seventies. In 1977, after a hiatus of twenty-odd years, Hunter resumed her performing career and won immediate acclaim both from old fans and from new generations of listeners. At the time, by her own reckoning, she was eighty-two; in 1983, at eighty-eight, she was still performing regularly and was working on her autobiography.

Like so many of the blueswomen of the twenties, Hunter was born poor (in Memphis, in 1895), left home at an early age and was without formal musical training. Hunter's mother worked as a maid in Memphis, and her daughter followed in her footsteps, earning, she later calculated, six dollars a week plus board as a cleaning girl. When she learned that she could make more money in Chicago, she headed for the big city without hesitation—and without her mother's knowledge. "I had fifteen cents when I ran away from home on an eight-year-old-child's bus pass. Where I was going, I didn't know," she recalled.[12] In Chicago she ran into a friend from home, and this fortunate coincidence provided her with a place to stay. At first she earned her keep by peeling potatoes and washing dishes, but show business soon beckoned; in borrowed dresses, young Alberta began to make the rounds of Chicago's many black nightspots.[13] Still in her early teens, she finally landed a job at a dive called Dago Frank's, where, as she put it, "the sportin' gals hung out."[14] She made it her business to learn a new song every night, from piano rolls or from other performers, and she quickly worked her way up the club circuit. By 1919 she was a featured performer at the Dreamland Cafe, the best of the city's black cabarets, with Lil Hardin Armstrong often accompanying her. Counting tips, she was now making several hundred dollars a week, a far cry from her humble salary as a maid. Hunter also recorded extensively during this period with artists like Eubie Blake, Fats Waller and Louis Armstrong, often singing her own songs.

In the early twenties Hunter moved to New York and got a big break almost immediately, replacing Bessie Smith in a Broadway show called *How Come*, which ran for a year. Soon thereafter Smith chose Hunter's "Down Hearted Blues" for her Columbia recording debut, which eventually sold an

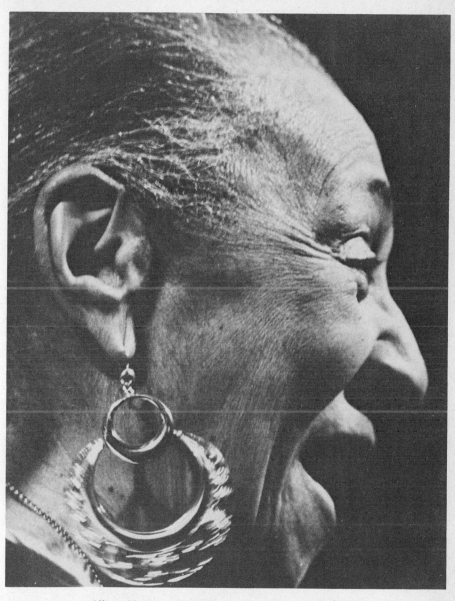

Alberta Hunter. *(Credit: Barney Josephson, The Cookery)*

estimated one million copies—"And I'm still collecting the royalties,"
Hunter said proudly in 1978. "I'm too slick to let 'em cheat me outta that."[15]
As the twenties rolled on, Hunter went from success to success. She toured
the top clubs in America and then went to Europe, performing in *Showboat*
with Paul Robeson in London, and becoming a top cabaret star in Paris and
a favorite of the international smart set. She headlined the international
vaudeville circuit in the thirties, appeared with Ethel Waters in *Mamba's
Daughters* in 1939, toured the world extensively for the USO in the mid-
forties and continued to perform into the fifties. In 1954, upon the death of
her mother, Hunter abruptly abandoned her musical career and became a
practical nurse. In 1977—by her own account, having not so much as
hummed a tune in the bathtub for more than twenty years—she was coaxed
out of retirement by her former Cafe Society employer, Barney Josephson,
who booked her for a long and successful engagement at his present New
York club, the Cookery. She still performs there regularly and records
periodically for Columbia.

Today Alberta Hunter's delivery is as strong and sure as ever, her lower
register especially forceful. Her sweet-and-sour voice is suffused with a
wonderful blend of churchy fervor and consummate technical sophistica-
tion. At the same time, her way of communicating feelings is direct and
simple, utterly devoid of histrionics. She has the superlative diction of the
accomplished singers of her era, as well as a finely developed ability to
convey double meanings. In the twenties her white contemporaries studied
her performances closely: Al Jolson loved her interpretation of "St. Louis
Blues," and Sophie Tucker was particularly fond of Hunter's own "A Good
Man Is Hard to Find." For many listeners the Hunter trademark became
"heartbreak" songs, but she tartly dismissed any connection between those
woebegone lyrics and her own experience: "I never did have the blues about
no man in my entire life! Even if I got sad, I'd never let them know it."[16]
(Though Hunter was married briefly, to Williard Townsend, the couple
soon separated. She has since remained single.)

Alberta Hunter is an outstanding example of an independent, self-
directed woman whose strength rests on resilience, faith and discipline. Even
after music had reclaimed her, she continued to live simply, dress in
comfortable clothes, visit her old nursing patients—and defy pat generaliza-
tions. "I call her the Grand Old Lady of the blues," says Barney Josephson,
"for she *is* grand. She has never put red to her lips nor tasted any liquor, not
wine, not beer. When she sang in Paris boites where they expected the singers
to sit with the customers and drink, she never did. And just because she wrote
the blues doesn't mean any man ever treated her that way. No man ever
could."[17]

Hunter continues to deliver her unique repertoire of refined ballads and gutbucket blues, fists characteristically planted on her hips or fingers slicing the air as she emphasizes a point with upraised arm. In performance she is always vital and fresh, spinning the inimitable spell of the great cabaret artists of the twenties. As interpreted by Alberta Hunter, the blues becomes a medium capable of directness or delicacy, saltiness or sadness. "The blues?" she has said. "Why the blues are part of me—almost religious. Like a chant. The blues are like spirituals, almost sacred. When we sing blues, we're singin' out our hearts, . . . our feelings."[18] But in the best blues tradition the sacred is inextricably mingled with the profane. At the close of a recent Cookery set Hunter announced that she was going to sing "I've Got a Mind to Ramble," an old classic. "Now, children," she warned her audience, "I'm goin' way down in the gutter and get those blues. Some people take a ballad and sing it real slow and say it's the blues. Don't believe 'em. *I'm* gonna sing some blues—so help me!"[19]

In the seventies Columbia Records reissued five double-album recordings of the biggest-selling and most famous of the blues singers, the woman who stands above all others in the idiom. But in the twenties "The Empress," Bessie Smith, had a tough time breaking into the lucrative new recording field. In 1920, already well established as a performer, she went north and tried to get a record date. To no avail. One story has it that she failed a test with Black Swan Records because she interrupted a song with "Hold on, let me spit!" and the president of the company immediately ended the audition.[20] Finally, about three years later, she won a hearing at Columbia from a newly installed producer named Frank Walker, who knew her associate Clarence Williams. Columbia was ailing at the time—in fact, almost bankrupt. Walker decided to take a chance on a Bessie Smith session, and the gamble paid off. "Down Hearted Blues" (backed by "Gulf Coast Blues") was a huge smash, putting Columbia and Smith in the money. Bessie Smith had arrived in a big way. Her concert audience was already huge and surpassed Ma Rainey's, encompassing as it did both rural Southern blacks and urban Northern blacks as well as some white theatergoers; but records really catapulted her to fame. In the six months after her recording debut in February 1923, she made eighteen more sides; eventually she was to make a total of one hundred eighty.

With the possible exception of Ethel Waters, Bessie Smith was without peer among women singers in the Afro-American tradition of her era. As many observers have pointed out, Smith was the most important black singer in terms of bridging the gap between country blues and the more sophisticated blues-based style called classic blues. Country blues she knew from childhood, when she sang for change in her hometown of Chattanooga, Tennessee, a stop on the minstrel circuit. Her urbanity, more in keeping with changing conditions for blacks moving in great numbers to

Northern cities, was expressed not only in refashioned lyrics but in the jazz-inspired phrasing and timing she brought to her interpretations. This sophisticated approach to singing the blues made her, in the opinion of many, the first of the great women jazz singers. Billie Holiday, the great jazz singer of the next generation, listened to Bessie and to Louis Armstrong as a young girl, later citing them as her two main vocal influences.

Though shunned by status-conscious and "respectable" blacks, Smith was an important presence in the black community and among Harlem's chic white pleasure-seekers of the Roaring Twenties. At five nine and nearly two hundred pounds (Columbia Records impresario John Hammond qualified her weight as more muscle than fat), she was a large-scale beauty and an intensely magnetic, not to say rambunctious, personality on stage and off. Where Ida Cox, Alberta Hunter and company were stars, Bessie Smith became *the* star. She spent her money freely, loved to party and eat and drink—and drink caused her plenty of problems, as she herself acknowledged in songs like "Me and My Gin" and "Gin House Blues." She had many lovers, male and female, and acquired a husband upon whom she lavished gifts. She was especially renowned during those high-flying Prohibition years, 1923 to 1928, the years in which she left her main musical mark.

She was much more than a glamorous figure, of course; stories of her righteous anger when roused are legion. One tells of some Ku Klux Klanners who came to the tent show she was working—to collapse the tent and disrupt the show. Smith assembled a group of prop boys to stop the robed Klanners, but the boys ran away in fear. She then went up to the men alone, put a hand on her hip, cursed and hollered, "I'll get the whole damn tent out here if I have to. You just pick up them sheets and run!" Yelling on, she drove them off the grounds. Then she walked over to the prop boys and laid into them: "And as for you, you ain't nothin' but a bunch of sissies."[21]

There was a dark side to her nature; anxiety and turmoil plagued her, even at the height of her success. And with the onset of the Depression, the high-rolling days were ending for her, as they were for most people. Record sales plummeted, and even more significantly, the advent of radio and the "talkies" was creating a demand for another kind of singing, more intimate, confidential and soothing: the blues were becoming passé. From 1930 to 1933 Smith went unrecorded. Her troubled marriage ended. During the mid-thirties she attempted to rebuild her fabulous career, working clubs again, eager to record and willing to sing more commercial material. Trying for a comeback, she recorded some vaudeville-pop songs with a black and white swing band—an exercise that, if not entirely successful (and many listeners felt it was not), did suggest a new direction for her musical career.

It is futile, though fascinating, to speculate on what might have been;

futile because in 1937 Bessie Smith died in a fatal car accident at the age of forty-two. The facts surrounding this accident and the treatment—or lack of treatment—Smith subsequently received are still debated.[22] It is certainly significant, as John Hammond has pointed out, that her death, like her life, was remarked only by the black press. The white press and the white public were largely ignorant of her existence.

But jazz musicians, black and white, were anything but ignorant of Smith's great talent; she recorded with a vast number of notable contemporaries. Musicians from Louis Armstrong to Bix Beiderbecke to Billie Holiday were inspired and influenced by Bessie Smith. Within the framework of the popular twelve-bar blues pattern or, less frequently, the eight-bar and sixteen-bar patterns, she was a master. Her attack and control were fully developed, and admirers rhapsodized on her musicianship. "Her voice was an instrument and she gave fresh value to almost every note she sang, bending it to her will," said one listener. "At times she would slide down on her top notes, dropping them down an octave. Her suspension and timing was amazing, and her habit of dragging over a word or syllable into the next bar was copied by many others."[23] She also had a highly developed sense of time and could move her phrases around the beat effortlessly—an ability so vital to the swing feel that later generations of jazz singers would elaborate. Her heavy, beautiful contralto, which has been aptly described as "cast-iron," could fill even a large hall with ease in those pre-microphone days.

It was her way of moving her commanding vocal instrument that influenced singers and players, both then and later. One enthusiast suggested that she would have made a marvelous opera diva. Certainly, though untrained in the European sense, hers was a voice thoroughly schooled through apprentice years in tent shows and stage shows; her singing helped to define an emerging art form that possessed its own resources of theatricality, passion and thorough control, especially rhythmically. Those who saw her perform caught the influence of the Afro-American church in her movements, in the fervor of her vocal style. (Though no one could have been more secular than she in her private life, Bessie reportedly always tried to get to church on Sunday.) Smith's singing combined elements of spirituals and nascent gospel, the rural blues of Ma Rainey and the music of the tent-show and black vaudeville circuits. Above all she was blessed with instinctive and impeccable musicianship. If Ma Rainey took the blues from the back room and put them on stage, Bessie Smith raised the blues to an art form and pointed the way forward for jazz singing.

In evaluating the contributions of the black women blues singers of this period, it is important to emphasize the extent to which their repertoire was limited by economic considerations: the market dictated that they sing blues or music in a quasi-blues format for an almost exclusively black audience, under the heading of "race records." With few exceptions, black women singers were marketed as blues singers. Bessie Smith, as noted, ventured outside the genre, especially in her last recordings; Mamie Smith, though billed as a blues artist, was more a contemporary pop singer. But in the twenties, one singer who could and did sing the blues also established herself as an interpreter of American popular song and won an audience, white as well as black, for her efforts. With a clear, rich voice and polished diction, Ethel Waters sang a repertoire that included pop and show tunes, many of which became standards. It was she who introduced Harold Arlen's great "Stormy Weather"; she was also the first to sing "St. Louis Blues," and she made "Dinah" a hit in 1925, when she replaced the great Florence Mills as headliner at the Plantation Club. As one writer describes it, "In introducing and popularizing the song 'Dinah' she rephrased it, using syncopation and rubato extensively, adding a synthetic 'hot' touch through her use of occasional growling tones, and paved the way for the use of Tin Pan Alley material by every jazz vocalist in later years."[24]

This innovative singer, billed as "Sweet Mama Stringbean" when she was a youngster on the TOBA circuit, was born in 1900 or 1902 in what she described as a tough interracial area in the town of Chester, Pennsylvania. Show business offered her a way out, and Waters was able to get her career under way as a teenager in New York after World War I. She worked with Fletcher Henderson for Black Swan Records and in 1921 recorded a successful version of "Down Home Blues." Meanwhile she prodded Henderson, well on his way to becoming one of the most outstanding bandleaders of the twenties, to get "jazzier" in his piano playing, recommending that he study with piano giant James P. Johnson.

A powerful actress and a volatile personality, Waters enjoyed the esteem of top-ranked jazz musicians and was a favorite with the public. Cornetist Jimmy McPartland remembered, "We [Bix Beiderbecke and the 'Austin High Gang'] liked Bessie Smith very much too, but Waters had more polish.... She phrased so wonderfully, the natural quality of her voice was so fine, and she sang the way she felt."[25] For many, Ethel Waters ranks right up with Bessie Smith; they and the other women singers of the twenties are perhaps best seen not as blues singers but as artists improvising with the material given to them at the time. Individually and as a group, they made a formidable contribution to jazz and to the popular singing of their day.

As the reader will have noted, many of the early blueswomen ended their days in obscurity and poverty. Mamie Smith, the singer who started it all with the smash hit "Crazy Blues," had a decade of fame and fortune before the Depression left her out of work, and though she tried a comeback in 1940, at about age fifty-seven, she died penniless six years later and was buried in an unmarked grave. And how many more who are only footnotes to musical history today never even had a hit record or a taste of glamour? Writer Barry Ulanov describes the majority of the black vocalists as "rarely comfortable financially. They sang for gin and rent money and their masterpieces appeared on the so-called 'race' labels of record companies. Few reached the tiny affluence which would have given them a fair life."[26] Jobs for them were usually one-nighters, with a slow crawl up to the better-class cabarets if they were lucky. They paid their dues in the flourishing underworld of Prohibition speakeasies and taverns. Pearl Bailey, then a young cabaret singer in a Pennsylvania mining town, conveys the seedy reality of these joints in her autobiography:

> When [the pimps] found out you were a nice girl only out to do show business, they respected you. . . . Now, the girl singers did "ups." "Ups" meant going from table to table singing the same song. Sometimes the customers put money on the table and you took it off. No, my sweet, not with your hands but with your thighs. You pulled up your dress to a certain height and grabbed the money off the table. Some of you may recall the small dimes and how hard they were to snatch off.[27]

Or, as Alberta Hunter recalled about her stint at the Dreamland Cafe in Chicago with King Oliver's band, "Singers then would go around from table to table singin' to each table, hustlin' dollars in tips."[28]

Many of these women were destroyed or diminished in the fast-moving scene, but others, like Pearl Bailey and Alberta Hunter and Ethel Waters, were able to develop their talent in the close, bruising atmosphere. These largely self-schooled singers shook off the dust of their humble, sometimes sordid beginnings and went on to live rich, full lives. The stars, like Mamie Smith, Ida Cox, Ma Rainey and Bessie Smith, lived lavishly and spent ostentatiously, conducting themselves with the distinctive flash and abandon of the Jazz Age. A heroine of the people, the blues singer would present herself as a symbol of success, in *all* her finery. Ma Rainey kept a trunk deep with money and sported a heavy gold necklace with matching gold earrings. Wearing beaded headbands, waving giant ostrich fans and blowing kisses, she would emerge onstage from a huge box made to look like a phonograph.[29] Inevitably, stars who followed outdid Rainey, and her gold necklaces came to seem like trinkets next to some of their outfits. Remembering Ida Cox, Victoria Spivey gave an idea of the standard of glamour: "What a dresser she was. . . . Seven hundred to fifteen hundred dollars was nothing for a petticoat, and I'm not lying. For a head-piece she wore crowns, jewels and feathers. Those jewels were not fakes, they were *real!* . . . Her show was big—there was nothing she missed. She had everything. She had sixteen chorus girls kickin' them up."[30] In those Scott-and-Zelda years, the singers' private lives sometimes rivaled the latest Hollywood scandals, and alcohol and drugs often helped fell the star faster.

Yet it was the blueswoman who held and molded the power of the word in black music. Her public did more than adore her: they respected her. Though she might be rejected by polite society, to the people who came to hear her "tell it like it is" she was a kind of preacher, a priestess. The tent, the tabletop, the stage, the darkened, smoke-filled nightspot—these were her forums. If she was good, she could raise up power and display her strength and allure as a black person, and as a woman. Through her music, she and her nodding, commenting audience found a way to uplift themselves, as well as to vent their anger, laugh at fate and bemoan bad fortune. If she often lived out her bizarrest fantasies in life, in song she preached the gospel of reality and of dignity wrung from the circumstances at hand. She painted her canvas with the deep, bruised colors of pain and suffering, the bright points of anger and joy, the sassy shades of her independent disposition. She moaned and she whined, she shrieked, growled, bellowed, accused and consoled.

The values of deep emotional intensity communicated by the blueswomen were passed along to successive generations of powerful black singers, from Ma Rainey to Bessie Smith to Billie Holiday to Abbey Lincoln, Aretha Franklin, Betty Carter and many more, and they deeply influenced white jazz singers too. In an America where the black woman was too often the "slave of slaves," the women who sang the blues founded a tradition of vindication and release, and established their dignity. Like their piano-playing sisters throughout the land, they proclaimed themselves free agents and tried to live up to the name. Corsets off, hair bobbed, gin at the hip and fingers snapping, they sang their freedom.

Chapter Seven

THE "CANARIES"

Ask any ten bandleaders as to their pet headache...
nine will answer "girl vocalists."...[But] you can't
deny that a beautiful girl in front of a mike looks
pretty good to the paying males.

SWING MAGAZINE, 1938

Looking back at the movies and music of the thirties, it seems like America was always dancing—Fred Astaire and Ginger Rogers elegant on the screen, and the general population twirling and swaying on dance floors in hotel ballrooms, restaurants, roadhouses, cabarets, halls and nightclubs, always to the sound of a big band. In fact, it sometimes seems that America danced its way right through—and out of—the Depression. Dancing to live bands had been picking up steam as a form of popular recreation since the twenties, when older folks waltzed and foxtrotted to "sweet," syrupy society bands and flappers Charlestoned and black-bottomed to "hot," jazz-influenced bands. By the thirties dance bands were a major source of entertainment, a craze that peaked during the Second World War, spawning ever more athletic routines like the jitterbug.

To feed this national pastime, which quickly became big business, a seemingly endless number of bands, players, leaders and gimmicks sprouted everywhere. Money-minded promoters styled their products along the assembly-line approach. The goal for a neophyte band was to get a local radio show and the exposure that went with it. At the time, advertisers sponsored whole shows instead of buying spots, and the entertainers would often be named after the sponsor—the Gold Dust Twins or the Ipana Troubadours, for example. So the bands vied for sponsorship, and if one caught on, a nationwide radio hookup might result in fame and steady work. Some first-rate bands got their start this way, notably the great Count Basie orchestra out of Kansas City in 1934.

To strengthen a band's commercial appeal, it became almost mandatory to have a female vocalist. Count Basie's band was an exception initially, but on the advice of music entrepreneurs (especially John Hammond of Columbia Records) Basie enlisted the services of Billie Holiday and then of Helen Humes.[1] As a general rule, the female vocalist's appearance was at least as important as her singing, if not more so, for it was she who provided the visual and emotional link between the audience and the bandstand.[2] She must look appealing according to her type—sexy or smoldering or kittenish or girl-next-door, in billowy gown or tight sheath, hair piled up à la femme fatale or falling softly about her face. And *all* that makeup. Universally called the "girl singer" (and, for variety, "chirper," "torcher," "crooner," "warbler" or "canary"), she was like a singing cheerleader for the team behind her in uniform. As in the traditionally male-dominated games of basketball and football, the team took care of business—in this case, the musical business—while the vocal pom-pom girl stood supportively and decoratively on the sidelines. Her musical chores were usually limited to singing the thirty-two bars of the melody's refrain between the band's section arrangements and instrumental solos. Almost always she was the lone woman in the band, conspicuous in her party clothes against a field of serious, suited males.

One historian of the big-band era has attempted to analyze the often precarious status of these women. "A single girl among a pack of men certainly had her problems," he says. Among them he mentions several that are not unfamiliar to working women today, including the sometimes lascivious employer, the array of libidos and egos of the male crew, and the lower status, reflected in lower pay, of most female vocalists. The writer goes on to discuss various strategies for coping with this inferior, loner status. "Some girls tried very hard to be one of the boys, an attitude that was often resented. Others protected themselves with a pronounced air of independence, which might have been a good defense maneuver but also produced much loneliness. Still others tried the extra-feminine approach, which sometimes resulted in the capture of one man for good."[3] Such "captures" were many, as women singers naturally tended to form relationships with musicians who had similar tastes and interests. Yet coping with everyday sexual and emotional pressures must have been difficult indeed for many singers.

Onstage the female vocalist may have looked glamorous, yet her life on the road with the band was anything but. As for any itinerant troupe, conditions were difficult—constant travel, irregular meals and rest—and worse, of course, for black performers, with the second-class treatment they so often received. Not surprisingly, the average woman band singer during the swing era received less pay per week than the average band instrumentalist. For example, a trade magazine of the period noted that the average female vocalist made from fifty to seventy-five dollars a week, of which she paid ten dollars for hotels, twelve to fifteen for meals, five to the hairdresser, and one to three for miscellaneous expenses.[4] Under such conditions, and in most cases without union protection, she was vulnerable if her employer expected her to perform certain extramusical duties.*

But a more usual cause of complaint for the female vocalist was the mundane hassle of maintaining a wardrobe. Usually she had to pay for her dressy attire (Helen Humes, for instance, remembered her delight at finding a thrift shop where she could purchase the elegant gowns she needed at prices befitting her salary as a starting singer). The singer also had to see to it that her clothes always looked clean and well-pressed—no small accomplishment in the cramped and hurried world of one-nighters that made up the general band schedule. A few women did rebel: singer Anita O'Day created a stir in the forties by insisting on wearing a uniform as part of Gene Krupa's band, and Marjorie Hyams, vibraphonist with Woody Herman's band in the forties, did the same. But wearing a band uniform was too far-out for the majority of women singers.

If the status was uneasy, the pay generally low and the conditions often arduous, why did so many women want to sing with big bands? For the fact is that there was a seemingly limitless supply of aspiring "girl singers." First of all, band singing was a job, which meant a lot during the Depression. And it was a job that carried a certain aura of prestige and glamour with it. More

*According to George Simon, "Unestablished vocalists were generally paid less than the musicians in the band. One reason: they had no union to protect them" (*The Big Bands*, p. 33). Union organizing of big-band singers of both sexes occurred largely through the efforts of the American Guild of Variety Artists (AGVA), officially established in 1948. AGVA grew out of the American Federation of Artists (AFA), which began organizing at about the same time as Actors Equity did in the twenties. Through most of the swing era AFA was open to singers; in addition, the Musicians Union did and does represent singers who also play an instrument, even if only a percussive accessory like the tambourine. Debra Brodlie, organizing consultant for AGVA, told me in June 1981 that she could find no instances of sex discrimination suits brought by women singers against bands or bandleaders in the thirties and forties. Though abuses certainly took place, legal action concerning sex prejudice came more slowly than did efforts to improve job conditions, especially wages and benefits. Such job-related efforts did occur frequently in the forties, said Brodlie, with resultant boycotts of nightclubs and the like.

important, ambitious singers, both female and male, often hoped that with luck, looks and persistence they could achieve success beyond the spotlight of the bandstand. And some did go on to become actresses or big solo stars—singers like Rosemary Clooney, Doris Day, Dale Evans, Harriet Hilliard and Lena Horne, to mention several. By the end of World War II, when social and economic conditions were contributing to the demise of the big bands, many singers had become as big a draw as the bands themselves and often outlived them in the public's memory.

But the majority of the female singers (like most of the bands themselves) *were* easily forgettable, synthetic products foisted on the audience by an entertainment industry as nervously competitive then as it is today. Players complained about the singers' lack of preparedness, often with cause, and *Down Beat*, a trade paper for band and jazz musicians during the thirties and forties, stated that "chirpers [are] always looked down on by musicians as unhip dress extras."[5] In another *Down Beat* article, "The Gal Yippers Have No Place in Our Jazz Bands," the author argued that white women singers had no opportunity to absorb jazz and were therefore incapable of being anything but sex symbols.[6] *Swing* magazine tellingly summed up the prevailing attitude:

> Ask any ten bandleaders as to their pet headache. . . . nine will answer "girl vocalists." . . . Yes, girl vocalists are a nuisance. Too many of them are beautiful, and can't sing. Those who have talent are usually gobbled up by the movies or shrewd promoters who exploit them. . . . [But] no matter what stand you take, you can't deny that a beautiful girl in front of a mike looks pretty good to the paying males.[7]

Most bandleaders neither expected nor encouraged musical expertise from their singers. And though it is unfair to condemn the "chirpers" for performing the role assigned to them, the fact remains that most contributed little to vocal music except a pretty face.

Nevertheless, amidst the promotional hoopla of the swing and dance-band craze, when many groups and singers strove for an easily commercial sound, just about every woman singer who would later be important in vocal jazz served time in the bands. Indeed, women in jazz have been given their meatiest roles to date as singers in bands geared to producing good music. For women, the business and practical concessions that bands had to confront cut both ways. The fact was that a pleasant physical presence *and* a good voice could be strong selling points on the bandstand, as Count Basie quickly realized. Furthermore, a knowledgeable singer, unlike an equally skilled woman instrumentalist, ruffled no feathers about the propriety of her role, posed no threat to male players by way of increased competition for jobs, and did not disturb the status quo by invading what was regarded as male musical turf. No, indeed: a woman singer with intelligent ears could be a real plus for a band.

Thus, despite the general disdain for the "canaries," the male big bands not only supplied good "straight" pop singers but were one of the main routes of participation for women in jazz. Certain prescient bandleaders and musicians saw the value of adding the human voice to instrumentation, and by providing a steady working climate for their singers, they had much to do with the development of vocal jazz. As early as the twenties, Duke Ellington utilized the voice as a component of his orchestral texture by featuring Adelaide Hall (most famously, singing her wordless trumpetlike vocalise on "Creole Love Call," recorded in 1927). Hall went on to become a well-known performer in Europe, settling in London. Ivie Anderson (1904-1949), who first sang with the Earl Hines band in 1930, moved to the Ellington orchestra in 1931 and had the longest tenure of any Ellington singer, staying until 1942. Born in Oklahoma and educated in a convent school in California, she had studied vocal music formally and worked in shows and revues, notably *Shuffle Along*. She was possibly the first black woman singer to work with a white band—the Anson Weeks Orchestra in 1928—but it was with Ellington that she became well-known. He "voiced" her strong, almost metallic sound so that it meshed with the other instruments, and many memorable Anderson songs with the band resulted, including "Rocks in My Bed," "Oh Babe, Maybe Someday," "It Was a Sad Night in Harlem," "I'm Checking Out, Goombye," "It Don't Mean a Thing (If It Ain't Got That Swing)" and "I Got It Bad and That Ain't Good." She also appeared in the Marx Brothers film *A Day at the Races* in 1937. Anderson was succeeded in the Ellington orchestra by many fine singers, including Betty Roche, Joya Sherrill, Kay Davis and Marie Ellington (no relation to Duke).

In the mid-thirties the vocal possibilities of rhythmic, melodic and dynamic shading and variations, though suggested and beautifully illustrated by such forerunners as Ethel Waters and Bessie Smith, were still hazily perceived by most singers. They relied almost entirely on the *words* to convey the song's message; the vocal devices in jazz singing that plumb the emotional depths and ranges of a song were largely unexplored territory. It took singers like Mildred Bailey, Lee Wiley, Billie Holiday, Ella Fitzgerald and Helen Humes to show how a melody and lyric could be mined vocally, much as horn players were doing instrumentally. These singers, too, served valuable time with the big bands.

Among the vocalists of jazz who sang with swing, dance and big bands, Billie Holiday is one of the most highly regarded. She was, as mentioned, the first "girl singer" to join the Basie band, in 1937, soon after it hit big in the East. In that band, she maintained a close musical relationship with her male confreres, especially with the great tenor saxophonist Lester Young. Due to contractual problems, Billie Holiday could not record with the Basie band during her stay. Only two sides, taken from a radio broadcast and reissued by Columbia, provide accessible documentation of her work with Basie, but those who heard them in concert acclaimed the partnership. Prior to her Basie days Holiday also worked with Teddy Wilson and his studio orchestra, and after Basie, with Artie Shaw's band on the road, recording some wonderful sides with both; "Any Old Time" is among her outstanding recordings with Shaw. After 1940 Holiday went out as a solo artist (her career and her contribution to jazz singing are discussed at length in the next chapter).

Mildred Bailey (née Mildred Rinker) was a large woman with a smallish, lovely voice. Born in 1907 in Tekoa, Washington, she learned native American music from her part-Cherokee mother, was playing piano in a local movie theater by the age of sixteen, and then worked in theatrical revues. Most critics agree that she was the first nonblack female singer to really understand jazz, though not the first to attempt it. Sophie Tucker, billed as "The Last of the Red Hot Mamas," listened closely to the black female singers of the teens and twenties and even toured with jazz accompaniment from 1917 to 1921, and there were other white vaudeville and stage performers who appreciated and imitated the vitality of black song styles, among them Blossom Seeley, Belle Baker and Dolly Kay. But Mildred Bailey didn't copy: she was an innovator.

Bailey began to sing in the big time with Paul Whiteman's orchestra in 1929. Her brother, singer Al Rinker, and his pal Bing Crosby were members of Whiteman's Rhythm Boys, a vocal group, and they urged Whiteman to hire her, which he did after hearing her demo record. Initially she encountered resistance from jazz audiences. One listener who later became a Bailey fan explains, "It was an era when white bands were patterning themselves after Negro orchestras, and white performers were getting rich singing classic Negro material by aping colored performers who had originated it. But [Bailey] never made a song that didn't have her name on it indelibly, though she was startlingly free from gimmicks. . . . Songs that she introduced, records that she made, had an alarming habit of turning up as somebody else's hits."[8]

Bailey's phrasing, superb diction and warm, tender tone more than compensated for an instrument of limited range, and she became known for the way she tenderly caressed and gently rocked her material. She was "The Rockin' Chair Lady," after a bluesy song she first recorded with Whiteman and then with Red Norvo in the thirties. Her special forte was interpreting the better pop tunes of the day, but she could sing the blues as well. "When she sang the blues she was never a white woman trying to sound like a Negro blues singer. . . . They are her blues, and she felt them deeply."[9] Great singers in the Afro-American idiom recognized this; she counted Bessie Smith among her friends (they liked to get together and cook—food).

In 1934 Mildred Bailey left Paul Whiteman's band and formed her own with husband Red Norvo, vibraphonist. Her singing, and what witnesses called an electric stage presence, helped keep the band alive in an era that favored the frantic in music over the subtle. Billed as "Mr. and Mrs. Swing," Bailey and Norvo concentrated on a tasteful, musicianly approach, and though their avoidance of gimmickry narrowed their audience, they were critically praised. In 1938 *Down Beat* spoke for the jazz "purists" when it declared, "You mention Mildred Bailey and you've disposed of the entire lot of whites [singers]."[10] Such a sweeping statement was, of course, a disservice to several excellent white singers, but it accurately reflects Bailey's standing at the time in white jazz circles.

But by 1939 Bailey and Norvo found they had to break up the band—and the marriage. Bailey went out as a single until her death in 1951, never finding the broad popular acceptance she felt she merited, never quite getting a hit record on the order of, say, Ella Fitzgerald's "A-Tisket, A-Tasket." She continued to sing wonderfully and to introduce many fine songs, but the dark side of her sensitive nature also became more evident in time. Some who knew her have suggested that the lack of real commercial success combined with her emotional problems to embitter and isolate her. One writer speculates that "she wanted to be the [slender] person who went with the voice . . . the inner person she constantly projected as she sang."[11] Certainly whatever psychological problems she may have had were pointed up by her overeating, which eventually endangered her health. When her heart gave out in 1951, she was close to being broke and had cut herself off from most of her friends.

Yet it is this woman who is remembered, while most of the commercially successful singers of the era are now forgotten. Bailey left a stamp on the swing era with her fresh-voiced approach to popular song, her tasteful, self-trained pliancy. By all reports, she just couldn't stand to sing in an uncongenial atmosphere—it had to swing! And during her career she sang with the best, musicians like trumpeter Roy Eldridge, clarinetist Benny Goodman, tenor saxophonist Coleman Hawkins, pianist Mary Lou Williams and many, many more. Indeed she was one of the premier jazz singers of her era, with a true understanding of vocal jazz in a big-band context.

Unlike Mildred Bailey, Ella Fitzgerald, who followed her by several years, became both a great jazz singer and a household name. She began by having to contend with the glamorous "canary" image and soon transcended it completely. Fitzgerald was born in Newport News, Virginia, in 1918 and soon settled in Yonkers, New York, close to New York City.

Orphaned at fifteen, she indulged in typical teenage dreams of fame. Though she was (and is) extremely shy and retiring, her dreams were soon to be realized a hundred times over. "Connee Boswell influenced me more than any other singer, but I really wanted to be a dancer," she later recalled. She entered her first amateur talent contest intending to dance, but she changed her mind and sang instead, and "they booed me off."[12] Fortunately for music lovers, she tried another amateur contest, again singing. This time she made a stunning impression with her rendition of "Judy." In short order she was introduced to bandleader Fletcher Henderson, who said he'd call and didn't, and to bandleader Chick Webb, who said he wasn't interested in girl singers. But neither man had heard her, so some enthusiastic listeners arranged for a Webb "audition." Somehow she was smuggled into his dressing room, where she duly sang for him and won him over. Now he had to convince his manager. "Listen to the voice," he said according to legend, "don't *look* at her."[13] And another convert was made, for the big, awkward teenager sang with bell-like vocal clarity, was always in tune, had great rhythm. Soon after she auditioned for Webb, Ella Fitzgerald was singing at the Savoy Ballroom, the most swinging dance palace in New York. The year was 1935. She was seventeen years old.

Her association with Chick Webb proved mutually beneficial. Though crippled by tuberculosis of the spine, Webb was a marvelous, energy-packed drummer and spirit; he guided her developing talent, becoming both her musical and legal guardian. As one writer described it, "Her appearance was certainly not in her favor. She was a big girl and knew nothing about how to dress. . . . but Chick determined to have her, even bought her dresses—and in two weeks, she was the hit of the Savoy. Ella was then living at an orphanage—Chick became her legal guardian and devoted a lot of time to her."[14]

Recordings soon followed. For Decca she shone on "I'll Chase the Blues Away," "Sing Me a Swing Song and Let Me Dance," "A Little Bit Later On," "Tain't What You Do, It's the Way That You Do It" (with bits of scat), "If You Can't Sing It, You'll Have to Swing It" and other tunes that put both Ella and the Webb organization at the top among dance-band lovers. Her voice had the "little-girl" quality that was part of the period's singing style, a quality that in her case always seemed to come from a fresh, ever-youthful spirit. Her swing version of "A-Tisket, A-Tasket," to which she wrote lyrics (with Al Freeman), was a popular smash, as were "Flat Foot Floogie" and "My Last Affair." (As a songwriter she also contributed "Oh, but I Do," recorded in 1945 by Nat "King" Cole, and a lyric to Duke Ellington's "In a Mellotone.") When Chick Webb died in 1939, Ella Fitzgerald became, at twenty-one, the nominal leader (and the draw) of the Webb band and remained so until 1941, respected as an equal by the players in the orchestra.

Though fame came to her early, Ella never stopped working on her instrument. In the forties, as bop developed, she became a solo artist and honed her improvisational skills. Her scatting was (and is) a revelation; her renditions of "Lady Be Good," "Flying Home" and "How High the Moon" are classics. In the late forties, when impresario-producer Norman Granz took over personal management of her career, Ella Fitzgerald began to interpret top-shelf popular material, immortalizing the works of Cole Porter, Rodgers and Hart, Gershwin, Ellington and Irving Berlin in a superb series of "Songbook" albums. On standards, show tunes and ballads, she is wonderfully warm, with exquisite phrasing, a perfect ear and that dollop of melancholy that gives body to her easy, sometimes jaunty, often honeyed delivery. The Fitzgerald persona communicates as pure and humble, and most of her peers rate her as their favorite singer. Indeed, any accounting of the ongoing musical career of Ella Fitzgerald inevitably ends in tribute to the would-be dancer who became a delightful star of the swing era as a teenager, developed into a superb, swinging interpreter of popular American song literature and continues to perform and refine her artistry to this day.

Among other fine vocalists who emerged in the thirties was Connee Boswell, who was born in 1907 (or 1912, depending on the source) and died in 1976. Strictly speaking, Boswell was not a big-band singer, but she did record with a number of big bands, including those of the Dorsey brothers, Benny Goodman and Don Redman. She and her sisters, Martha and Helvetia (Vet), were so much a part of the sound of the swing era that they are included here, especially as they greatly influenced other women band singers. Connee Boswell was an innovative vocal talent on several fronts. She and her sisters had an unusually broad education in music in their native New Orleans. All three played for a time with the New Orleans Philharmonic Orchestra, Connee mastering cello, piano, saxophone and trombone. She also sang, wrote and arranged music from an early age and was first recorded in 1925, in her teens.

The Boswell sisters left classical music to form a vocal and instrumental trio, and their unique harmonizing on Connee's witty settings of popular tunes made them a quick national hit, especially after they appeared at New York's Paramount Theater in 1931. The sisters toured and recorded extensively from 1931 to 1935, when Martha and Vet left the group to marry and raise families. The success of the trio was primarily due to Connee's imaginative concepts: instead of the on-the-beat barbershop style of close harmony that was then current, the Boswells established a swinging, jazz-influenced vocal sound that became popular all over the world and set the precedent for later, more commercially successful trios, notably the Andrews Sisters.

A victim of polio as a child, Connee Boswell was confined all her life to a wheelchair, but she had a long and happy marriage as well as a successful career as a soloist from the mid-thirties until the sixties. She was popular on radio, records, theater tours and films (among them *The Big Broadcast, Moulin Rouge, Artists and Models, Syncopation* and *Kiss the Boys Goodbye*). Among Connee's hit tunes were "Martha," "Bob White," "Whispers in the Dark" and "Heebie Jeebies," which became the title of an off-Broadway musical tribute to the Boswells staged in 1981. Reissued recordings document the fresh voicings, good musicianship and irrepressible high spirits of this original musical talent.

Lee Wiley was born in Oklahoma in 1915 and, like Mildred Bailey, was of part native-American descent. A superb, smoky-voiced singer, she began working professionally as a teenager. During the thirties, Wiley sang, mostly on radio, with such groups as Paul Whiteman's orchestra and the society band of Leo Reisman. In the late thirties and early forties, she did outstanding work with the Eddie Condon group. Wiley wrote tunes as well, notably "Got the South in My Soul" in 1932 and "Anytime, Anyday, Anywhere" in 1933 (with Victor Young). Like Fitzgerald, she made a series of recordings of the works of leading American popular composers. After she married pianist Jess Stacy in 1943 (they divorced in the late forties), the two followed in the footsteps of Bailey and Norvo and formed a big band that had a brief life in the mid-forties. Wiley then went out as a solo artist, often working with top-rated jazz musicians in big-band contexts. She died in 1975.

Lena Horne, Ella Fitzgerald's contemporary, was not the instant vocal star that Ella was. She started out as a showgirl at the Cotton Club, then landed a singing job with Noble Sissle's orchestra in 1935, at age eighteen. She was hired more for her looks than for her musical talents, which were then—by all reports including her own—fairly undeveloped. But with Sissle (best known for the hit show *Shuffle Along*, with Eubie Blake) and especially with Charlie Barnet's band in 1941, Lena Horne blossomed into much more than "window-dressing" as her rare dramatic gift began to surface in her singing. As a soloist in ensuing years, she worked closely with her musician husband, Lennie Hayton, and her expressive abilities and control of her instrument continued to develop remarkably. She is not given to hornlike phrasing, and aside from Mildred Bailey, she takes her main inspiration from pianists like Teddy Wilson, not from other vocalists. "I love the piano. I think it's the perfect instrument for a singer to learn from," she said in an interview.[15] She draws from the best popular music for her repertoire and is renowned for her interpretations of such songs as "Can't Help Loving That Man," "Stormy Weather," "The Lady Is a Tramp" and, more recently, the consummately rendered "Watch What Happens." By 1981, when she opened her one-woman Broadway show, *Lena Horne: The Lady and Her Music*, she had won universal recognition as a top-ranked singer beyond categorization.

Such singers as Bailey, Fitzgerald, Boswell, Wiley, Horne and Holiday cultivated a sound that was markedly different from that of the previous generation of popular singers, in part because they were closely exposed to big-band music and jazz in their years of apprenticeship. Their lighter, more confidential and subtle style of singing was also made possible by technical innovations—the introduction of the microphone in live performance, along with the spread of radio as the primary entertainment medium. Amplification was especially suited to the art of such innovators as Billie

Lee Wiley. *(Credit: Bob Parent)*

Holiday and Lee Wiley, for whom belting a song would have meant vocal ruin but who could and did swing superbly.

In addition to Holiday, Fitzgerald and other greats of the era, notable vocalists were trained in the many big bands that incorporated and/or elaborated upon the lessons of the masters. Among these were bands led by men like Artie Shaw, Benny Goodman, Jimmie Lunceford, the Dorsey brothers and Stan Kenton, many of whose vocalists developed followings of their own. Though they did not make their mark as jazz stylists, they deserve mention as good popular singers and active contributors to the music of the big-band era.

One such singer was Helen O'Connell, born in 1920. O'Connell sang with the Jimmy Dorsey orchestra from 1939 to 1943 and was a huge favorite with audiences. Her intimately styled ballads and "torchers" and her swinging duets with fellow Dorseyite Bob Eberly—tunes such as "Amapola," "Green Eyes," "Yours," "Tangerine"—were big hits. O'Connell also appeared in several movies, including *The Fabulous Dorseys* in 1947. O'Connell's contemporary, Helen Forrest, was born in the teens and sang during the swing era with the bands of Artie Shaw, Benny Goodman and Harry James. She is widely considered one of the best of the big-band singers. At one point she shared vocal honors in Shaw's band with Billie Holiday and benefited from Holiday's encouragement and advice. Forrest's warm, musically knowledgeable style was well showcased in ballad arrangements; with Harry James, several good examples are her versions of "Skylark," "I Cried for You," "I Had the Craziest Dream" and "But Not for Me." In an interview Forrest credited Harry James with aiding her development as a singer: "Harry . . . gave me the right sort of arrangements and setting that fit a singer. It wasn't just a matter of my getting up, singing a chorus, and sitting down again."[16]

Four other fine big-band singers were Jo Stafford, Martha Tilton, Helen Ward and Kay Starr. Stafford, born in 1920, became well-known with the Tommy Dorsey band. In the late thirties she joined the Pied Pipers vocal group, which worked with Dorsey as a quartet around 1940. She went on to a career as a soloist, her theme song being "Smoke Dreams"; other hit songs of the fifties included "You Belong to Me" and "Shrimp Boats." Martha Tilton, born in 1918, sang with Benny Goodman from 1937 to 1939, after a stint with Jimmy Dorsey's band. Typically described in the trade papers as a "cute little blonde," she had hit singles with "And the Angels Sing" (1939) and "I'll Walk Alone" (1943). She also appeared in a number of movies, including *Sunny* (1941), *Strictly in the Groove* (1942), *Crime, Inc.* (1945) and *The Benny Goodman Story* (1956). Helen Ward, born in 1916, was considered one of the quintessential band singers of the swing era and gigged with numerous bands, notably with Benny Goodman from 1934 to 1936.

Among her tunes were "Goodie Goodie," "It's Been So Long" and "You Turned the Tables on Me." In 1979 she recorded her first album in twenty-five years and made appearances at New York clubs. Kay Starr, born in 1922, began her career as a country singer in Memphis. In the late thirties she served in groups led by Joe Venuti, Bob Crosby and Glenn Miller, and in the forties she worked with Venuti again and with Charlie Barnet. Starr also appeared in movies, notably in *Make Believe Ballroom* (1949) and *When You're Smiling* (1950).

June Richmond (1915–1962) was a good pop singer and blues belter. She sang with the Les Hite band in 1937, and with the Jimmy Dorsey orchestra and the Cab Calloway band in 1938, but her most notable job was with Andy Kirk's Twelve Clouds of Joy from 1939 to 1943. She appeared in a Broadway show entitled *Are You With It?* (1945) and in several films before moving to France in the late forties. Maxine Sullivan was another black singer who worked with both white and black bands. Born in 1911, she is still professionally active today. She began singing with her uncle's band, the Red Hot Peppers, in her native Pennsylvania—then, as now, occasionally playing flugelhorn and valve trombone as well as singing. Sullivan established her ultra-cool, relaxed but swinging song style with such recordings as "Gone with the Wind" (1938) and "Loch Lomond." After making these swing hits with Claude Thornhill's band and touring with Benny Carter's band in 1941, she began a long tenure as vocalist with bassist John Kirby (then her husband) and his group at top-ranked rooms and clubs, notably the Onyx Club in New York. Among the songs associated with Maxine Sullivan and her inimitably calm delivery are "Annie Laurie," "If I Had a Ribbon Bow," "A Brown Bird Singing," "Blue Skies" and "A Hundred Years from Today." In addition to being a very popular swing era singer, Sullivan appeared in several movies, including *Going Places* (1938) and *St. Louis Blues* (1958), in the musical *Swingin' the Dream* (1939) and in the play *Take a Giant Step* (1953). After her successes of the thirties and forties Sullivan became a nurse and went on to found and actively participate in a Bronx-based cultural center called The House That Jazz Built.

A number of jazz or jazz-influenced singers who began working professionally with big bands in the forties, at the tail end of the era, later went out on their own and are now solo stylists. Not content to concentrate on the pleasant treatment of pop themes and romantic ballads, these budding jazz talents saw themselves as vocal musicians—as had Mildred Bailey, Ella Fitzgerald, Billie Holiday, Helen Humes (see the Helen Humes profile in Part Five) and Lee Wiley in the thirties. Anita O'Day is one outstanding example of such a singer, and of the more modern (that is, bop) musical approach that jazz vocalists of the forties were beginning to develop. O'Day's work with Gene Krupa's band and Stan Kenton's orchestra gained her a reputation among swing era critics as an iconoclast. She was certainly one of the first white female singers among the crowd of "chirpers" to apply new instrumental innovations to her craft, and many who were at first put off by her hornlike approach became converts. "Whereas most band singers had projected a very feminine or at least a cute girl image, Anita came out strictly as a hip jazz musician," one writer noted.[17]

O'Day's vocal style started a trend among other young singers and particularly influenced her successors in Stan Kenton's organization, June Christy and Chris Connor. Christy replaced her in Kenton's band in 1945 and had a big hit with "Tampico" before going on to a career as a soloist. Connor, who shared O'Day's taste for spirited, swinging numbers, came to national attention with Kenton in 1952–53. Before joining him she had worked with trombonist Bob Brookmeyer's combo in Kansas City in the forties and with a vocal group in Claude Thornhill's big band in New York in 1949. In the seventies, her voice more mature and surer in intonation, Connor made a well-received comeback.

Peggy Lee's springboard to a long and successful career as a solo performing star was her stint with Benny Goodman's band from 1941 to 1943. Lee credits big bands with giving her invaluable practical experience, with teaching "the importance of interplay with musicians. We had to work close to the arrangement. . . . like all band singers, I learned to do the best with what they gave me. I will say this: I learned more about music from the men I worked with in bands than I've learned anywhere else. They taught me discipline and the value of rehearsing and how to train."[18]

Another top-ranked solo vocalist who got her professional start working with big bands was Dinah Washington. Coming from a background in church gospel singing, Washington joined Lionel Hampton's band in 1943 by way of word-of-mouth praise from such musicians as Fats Waller, who had heard her sub for Billie Holiday at Chicago's Down Beat Room in 1942 (while working as a ladies' room attendant there). "She got up [at her audition] and sang 'Evil Gal Blues,' and boy, she broke it up!" recalled bandleader Hampton. "Her real name was Ruth Jones, but I asked her if she would mind if I changed it." "I don't care what you call me, as long as you give me a job!" she reportedly answered.[19]*

Hampton changed another singer's name a few years later, in 1948. Eighteen-year-old Lillie Mae Jones became Betty Carter, and during her two-year stay with Hampton's band her identification with the new jazz, and especially her scat singing, helped modernize its sound. "Most of the female

*Impresario Leonard Feather, the composer of "Evil Gal Blues," points out, though, that Dinah Washington couldn't have sung "Evil Gal" at her audition for Hampton because he hadn't written the song yet. He also says that it was Dinah's manager, Joe Glaser, not Hamp himself, who gave her her new name.[20]

singers could swing," she said in an interview three decades later. "We could play the horns but we just didn't dig into it like men and you had to dig into it like men in order to compete.... I figure the men have the horns. I think that most men felt that jazz was a strong, man's art and since songs portrayed love and sweetness that women are more capable of dealing with that."[21]

The young Sarah Vaughan joined the Earl Hines Orchestra in 1943 as vocalist and second pianist, gaining valuable experience before moving to Billy Eckstine's modern band in 1944. Both bands were stocked with many highly gifted bop players, notably Charlie Parker and Dizzy Gillespie. According to George Simon, "To this day Sarah Vaughan...credits [her band experience] for much of her musical development."[22] Vaughan's contemporary, singer Carmen McRae, began a slower climb to the top by serving briefly in the bands of Benny Carter, Mercer Ellington and Count Basie during the same era.

As is clear from the examples of Anita O'Day, Peggy Lee, Dinah Washington, Betty Carter, Sarah Vaughan and Carmen McRae (all discussed at greater length in the next chapter), working in the big bands gave many young female singers the opportunity to be much more than "canaries" or "window dressing." Under the right conditions the relationship between singer, bandleader and player could be and often was mutually beneficial. Female band vocalists, performing constantly, had to learn how to project a song under all types of conditions. Often they went without proper rest— hard enough on any musician, and murder on the vocal chords. Since "danceability" was stressed over "singability," they frequently had to sing at tempos and in keys inhospitable to their range and equipment. But where the leader took the possibilities of the human voice seriously, singers became an adjunct to the brass, wind and reed instruments and were encouraged to blow, particularly at the end of the swing era, when bop was emerging.

As the big-band era wound down in the late forties, opportunities for singers to apprentice with bands dwindled. Few large organizations could afford to maintain themselves, and promoters saw the advantages of small-band combinations, which cost less and were geared to the innovations then under way in the music. In the 1970s, with the rekindling of interest in the big bands, some of the "girl singers" of the thirties and forties began to appear publicly and record after a long hiatus; many—like Rosemary Clooney, Chris Connor, Helen Humes and Helen Ward—sounded better than ever. But by and large, big-band singing, with all its abuses, limitations and charms, is a vanished art, and the "canaries," in their high heels, low-cut gowns and gaudy makeup, are a set piece of the romanticized past.

Chapter Eight

THE JAZZ SINGERS

---

*I hate straight singing. I have to change a tune to
my own way of doing it.*
                                    BILLIE HOLIDAY

*If a jazz singer is what I am at the roots—amen.
But being typed is a form of death.*
                                    CARMEN McRAE

*I want to make music. That is, use my voice like
an instrument.*
                                    ANITA O'DAY

" . . . [t]hen suddenly she is there, and everybody knows, and they crane their heads backward to see her, since she has come in [to the nightclub] by the street entrance like anyone else. Or, not like anyone else at all: she is more beautiful, more shining, holding her face forward like a flower, bright-eyed and smiling, high yellow cheekbones, white teeth and cream-white gardenia at her ear."[1] Thus does Alice Adams describe Billie Holiday in her recent novel, *Listening to Billie*. In *The Heart of a Woman*, Maya Angelou, who met Holiday shortly before her death, describes a very different woman, sans gardenia—"a lonely sick woman, with a waterfront mouth. . . ."[2] Adams writes of the charismatic star riding high on fame in the thirties, Angelou of the embittered, toughened woman at the end of her career.

Billie Holiday: singer, artist, myth, heroine, victim. Before her, jazz singing was generally regarded by musicians and listeners alike as an offshoot of playing. Most people thought of Bessie Smith as a blues singer, and Louis Armstrong's vocals were viewed as an entertaining adjunct to his trumpet playing. But with Holiday and with the times—the thirties—jazz singing began to come into its own. Splendid stylists like Ethel Waters, Mildred Bailey, the young Ella Fitzgerald and Helen Humes were emerging, with hip phrasing, clear, lightish voices, bouncy rhythm, an often girlish quality. But Billie Holiday—with her raspy-edged voice, her bittersweet reading of lyrics, her ability to communicate so intimately and intensely, and her unerring ability to swing—was something new. Such were her personality and her gift that she could lay out feelings in a way seldom equaled in jazz singing before or since.

Though she had her detractors (famously Ethel Waters, who reportedly snapped that Holiday's voice "sounded like her feet hurt her"), one mark of her excellence was her complete acceptance by and close musical rapport with her peers, the jazz musicians. Billie Holiday, crowned "Lady Day" by tenor saxophonist Lester Young, the "Pres," loved to trade choruses, phrase like a horn. "I don't think I'm singing," she explained. "I feel like I'm playing a horn. . . . What comes out is what I feel." She said she was aiming for "Bessie's big sound and Pops' [Louis Armstrong's] feeling."[3] Her "big sound" came through not so much as volume but as penetration, a kind of keening intensity that split the air. The feeling seems all her own. Early on in her recordings she displayed vulnerability and a peculiar dash of naiveté; in later years her delivery grew both rawer and heavier, drenched with world-weariness and an often caustic saltiness. Without doubt her troubled life and her addictions to heroin and alcohol took their toll artistically.

Billie Holiday, born Eleanora Fagan in Baltimore in 1915, was the daughter of Sadie Fagan and guitarist Clarence Holiday, who served time with McKinney's Cotton Pickers and Fletcher Henderson's big band. As a child she was shunted from relative to relative. According to her autobiography, she was sent to a home for "wayward girls" after a neighbor attempted to rape her when she was ten.[4] Significantly, she spent the happiest part of her childhood doing cleaning work for a neighborhood whorehouse madame who let her sit and listen on the Victrola to her idols, Louis Armstrong and Bessie Smith. At the age of fifteen, in 1928, she moved with her mother to Harlem, where she was put in a boardinghouse that functioned as a brothel. There she became a prostitute for a time. But by 1932 she was reunited with her mother, and her career as a professional singer began casually enough soon afterwards when she landed a job in a local Harlem nightspot called the Log Cabin Club. There, she recalled, the salary was eighteen dollars a week plus tips for singing from midnight to 3:00 A.M. every night.

Holiday's singing was quickly appreciated by many in her audience, if not always by the club owners. Columbia Records impresario John Hammond, one of the first whites to acclaim her (and to record her, in 1933 with clarinetist Benny Goodman), mentions in his autobiography that her musicianly inventiveness was well developed from the start: "She had an uncanny ear, an excellent memory for lyrics, and she sang with an exquisite sense of phrasing."[5] Her need to improvise cost her jobs, though, since club owners tended to frown on any deviation from straight singing. But the Holiday residence, where her mother ran a restaurant cum social club, became a home away from home for many jazz people, and Billie went to jam sessions and cutting contests as frequently as players did. Her close musical and personal friendship with the great Lester Young dated from this period.

By 1937 Billie Holiday was established enough to land a job with the Count Basie orchestra, then new to national fame. She stayed with the band for about a year, leaving to sing with Artie Shaw's unit in 1938—and finding road conditions for a black woman as difficult with a white band as with a black band. Her appearances with Basie and Shaw, along with her previous recordings with pianist Teddy Wilson and orchestra (1935), brought her nationwide attention and praise. She was becoming a star. When she was offered a steady job in New York at Cafe Society Downtown starting at seventy-five dollars a week, she consolidated her fame among the sophisticated nightclub set. There was no other singer with the appeal, personal as well as musical, of Lady Day. After staying at Cafe Society for about two years, she went on to star as a featured solo artist at top clubs around the country, recording steadily and upping her salary considerably, to a thousand dollars a week and more. She was glamorous, beautiful, adored; her impeccable musicianship made her an inspiration to other singers. Said Carmen McRae, "In her visualization of song, and in her aura, she was to me, then a young hopeful, a combination of idol, alter ego, and mentor."[6]

Despite her success she was unhappy, increasingly so, and gained notoriety along with her fame. By the early forties Holiday was addicted to heroin, and not always reliable or reasonable. Some club owners wouldn't risk hiring her anymore. The pushers were part of her entourage, and she was often tailed by narcotics agents. In 1946 she made an attempt to detoxify in a hospital, but she was arrested on a drug charge in 1947 and sent to prison. Upon release she went back to New York City and tried to work, but she was denied a cabaret card, the police-issued permit then needed by entertainers in order to work in New York clubs. She did some illegal club dates, appeared at a Carnegie Hall concert, temporarily triumphant, and then went out of town to work. She and her second husband, Louis McKay, were busted for drugs in 1956. By then Holiday had begun to drink heavily— the age-old "cure" of drug addicts—and her health declined rapidly. She made her last public appearance in May 1959 and was then hospitalized; while in the hospital, she was again arrested for possession of narcotics, a questionable charge this time around. But her fight was over. Ill and wasted, her voice broken, she died in July of that year.

But Billie Holiday's immense musicianship stayed with her to the end; as tired as her voice became, the feelings never ceased to flow in song—almost unbearably so at times during those last ravaged years. An intuitive artist who made any tune, pop, blues or standard, her own, she was a musician among musicians, never a "girl singer" fronting the band. She was also a composer and wrote a number of songs that became classics alongside her interpretations of standards. Her "God Bless the Child," with lyrics by Arthur Herzog, is said to have been inspired by her grandmother. It is her most famous song, and one of our most moving musical statements about the "haves" and "have-nots." With Herzog she wrote another moving ballad, "Don't Explain," and the swinging, blues-inspired "Fine and Mellow." Her "Billie's Blues" is a self-portrait of a troubled but proud woman.

Many people have seen Holiday as a sacrificial brown beauty, a haunting victim-symbol, but some who knew her thought that the addictions that populated her life with pushers and police were inevitable, that she was too sensitive not to have been destroyed. Certainly her story raises some hard questions, chief among them: Could the America of her era have allowed a black woman of such sensuality and sensitivity to achieve success *and* wholeness? Lena Horne, another singer from the thirties who became a symbol of idealized black womanhood, poses this question as a kind of running theme throughout her autobiography. Horne says in effect that while it is indeed possible for a black woman to win through, she must also tote up the personal psychic and emotional costs in a society where racism and sexism exact enormous energies from the black woman artist.[7] Carmen McRae, upon whom Billie Holiday made such a deep impression as a woman and singer, once analyzed her this way: "Singing is the only place she can express herself the way she'd like to be all the time. The only way she's happy is through a song. I don't think she expressed herself as she would want to when you meet her in person. The only time she's at ease and at rest with herself is when she sings."[8]

The standard Billie Holiday set as a jazz singer was one of implicit, sure and unrelenting swing—the essential sense of time or pulse upon which the jazz interpreter relies to fashion a statement. Her diction and phrasing, underpinned by this often implied rhythmic drive, cast ever-changing light and shadow on the lyrics of a song, revealing ever new layers of meaning. Her control and careful craftsmanship suffused her songs with unparalleled emotional breadth and depth, and her recorded legacy remains a standard for jazz singers and players everywhere.

In 1943 an unknown teenage singer stood on the stage of Harlem's Apollo Theater, that testing ground of new black talent where Ella Fitzgerald had debuted a decade or so before. Sarah Vaughan, whose splendid vocal equipment and expert musicianship would soon thrill audiences and spawn scores of imitators, was there, she later said, on a dare from friends in New Jersey. But the unprepossessing nineteen-year-old (early in her career some observers described her as "toothy," "scrawny," "plain," "unglamorous") brought to her Apollo performance—which, with her rendition of "Body and Soul," was a triumph—a solid background in music.

Born in Newark, New Jersey, in 1924, Sarah Vaughan was steeped in music from an early age, both at home, where her father, a carpenter by trade, played the guitar, and at church (Mount Zion Baptist), where her mother sang in the choir. She began studying piano at age seven and was a church vocal soloist and organist by twelve. In her teens she played the piano at the Newark Arts High School and sang informally at parties. "While I was playing piano in the school band," she told an interviewer, "I learned to take music apart and analyze the notes and put it back together again. By doing this, I learned to sing differently from all the other singers."[9] Though she was geared by her religiously oriented parents toward a career in church or concert music, jazz was in her blood. By the early forties, "I thought Bird and Diz were the end. . . . At that time I was singing more off key than on. I think their playing influenced my singing. Horns always influenced me more than voices. . . . as soon as I hear an arrangement, I get ideas, kind of like blowing a horn. I guess I never sing a tune the same way twice."[10]

Both Ella Fitzgerald and Billy Eckstine, then singing with Earl Hines, came to Vaughan's aid after her Apollo appearance; Fitzgerald cautioned her to be careful about agents and managers, and Eckstine recommended that Hines hire her as co-vocalist for his big band. Within weeks Sarah Vaughan was working with Hines as vocalist and second pianist, alongside many of her player idols. Her lovely voice, supple and true in pitch, immediately pleased her fellow musicians, and her instinctive harmonic sense dovetailed with the explorations of the new crop of instrumentalists soon to be called bop players. With her willingness to dare improvisatory feats, she was quickly hailed as the vocal counterpart of these innovators. A superb addition to the Hines band, she went with Eckstine when he left Hines to form his own modern jazz big band. She then sang with bassist John Kirby's popular group. By 1946 she had established herself as a solo artist, working up from intermission pianist and singer at Cafe Society Downtown to headliner of that and other New York clubs.

As Vaughan recorded, she began to place high in the polls. Her debut recording was done for Continental Records in 1944; by 1947 she had a number of popular tunes out. Her version of "The Lord's Prayer" on Musicraft was praised by Marian Anderson, another of its interpreters. To the delight of audiences—and possibly to the despair of fellow singers—her phrasing, intonation, range and inventive powers blossomed. By the fifties she was a major attraction worldwide and had a recording contract with Columbia (a sinecure that she, like most top-ranked jazz and jazz-oriented singers, has often lacked since).

Yet "The Divine One," or "Sassy," has had detractors, too. During the fifties she had a big pop hit with "Brokenhearted Melody" and irked some jazz purists by successfully recording both pop and jazz (on Mercury and its jazz label, EmArcy). Other critics have pointed to what they regard as a loss of emotional depth or impact, the sacrifice of textual meaning to her inimitable aural gymnastics. Indeed, Vaughan's process of maturation could be compared to the harnessing of a waterfall: the darts and swoops from top to bottom register, the profusion of cascading embellishments, have in the past seemed to some hearers too much of a good thing. But Vaughan has displayed greater control of her gift, especially since the seventies. As critic John S. Wilson put it, the "soaring highs and incredibly full lows now flow in a smooth, imaginatively directed manner instead of the swooping ululations that once billowed through her singing."[11] On the other hand, many fans have always maintained that she could do no wrong, delighting in the rich cornucopia offered by Vaughan the ceaseless improviser. Whatever their stance on her past performance, nearly all listeners agree that her voice has continued to improve with time. Like good wood, her lower register has deepened and richened in color over the years; her middle register is faultlessly lyrical; her higher register—she characteristically shifts into effortless falsetto—is true and pure. Through years of strenuous work under conditions that would fell an opera diva, Vaughan's singing has only gotten better, more extended in range and less prodigal in technique.

One can only wonder as to the still-unexplored possibilities of this marvelous voice. In 1947 Vaughan mentioned that she wanted to do a concert and a recording of spirituals, and she has often expressed the wish that someone would write an opera for her. In recent years she has added Brazilian music to her repertoire. Her interpretations of many standards endure: wonderful versions of "You're Blasé," "If You Could See Me Now," "I Cover the Waterfront," "Body and Soul," "Tenderly," "Everything I Have Is Yours," "I'll Remember April," "Easy Living," "I Remember Clifford," "Here's That Rainy Day," "Misty," "Don't Blame Me" and more recently "Send in the Clowns." Today, in the eighties, Sarah Vaughan's beautiful voice, excellent scat singing, impeccable rhythmic sense and butter-melting ballad work continue to thrill audiences.

A firmly established contemporary of Sarah Vaughan is Carmen McRae, born in Brooklyn, New York, in 1922. McRae studied piano and music from an early age, winning scholarships for advanced piano study. But her career as a musician took a detour after high school, when she opted for a job as a government clerical worker in Washington, D.C. By 1943, though, she was back in her native New York, flirting with show business, working in an office by day, playing piano and singing in local clubs by night. During a gig as a chorus girl in Atlantic City, McRae was encouraged by fellow entertainers to quit straddling the fence and go for broke as a performer.

For a while it looked like she might not make it. Club work was slow in coming for the song stylist who is today, for many, the definitive jazz-based singer. During the forties and fifties, while she was paying her dues, McRae was immersed in music, taking inspiration both from Billie Holiday and from the modern jazz then being born. In the forties she was married to the great drummer Kenny Clarke for a time and worked briefly with the bands of Benny Carter, Count Basie and Mercer Ellington. In the late forties she found steady employment in Chicago to sustain her, and in the early fifties she returned to New York, working as intermission pianist at Minton's, the Harlem jazz club. Finally, by 1954, word was out: Carmen McRae was the latest "discovery" when she won the "new star" vocalist award in *Down Beat* that year. She dropped the piano to concentrate on singing and began the long trek through record-company land. Like Vaughan and Fitzgerald, she recorded pop tunes as well as jazz and built a following with sophisticated, spicy interpretations of such songs as "Guess Who I Saw Today," "I'm Always Drunk in San Francisco," "For Once in My Life," "Alfie" and other standards.

As a teenager McRae had copied Billie Holiday as closely as possible, and Lady Day even recorded one of McRae's compositions, "Dream of Life," in 1939. Years later McRae dedicated an album of songs associated with Holiday to her late idol (no imitation, this time, but a tribute). Many listeners feel that McRae has inherited the Holiday gift for portrayal, the ability to make each song a dramatic statement, with the lyric the story line. McRae believes in giving full value to the text of a song, a talent she honed in the fifties during her years as an intermission singer-pianist. As she has said, "No matter what song I sing the lyrics have to be meaningful and believable—unless, of course, you're doing up-tempo tunes. Then nobody listens to the words. They're too busy keeping time to the rhythm."[12]

Like her contemporaries, Carmen McRae characteristically works with a trio that functions as the rhythmical underpinning so important for the improvising singer. In the eighties she brings to her performance a voice burnished to a glow, a polished and highly disciplined manner and a surer intonation. The concentrated emotion she gives a song, her superb control and use of well-marked pauses for dramatic effect, her faultless diction and way of italicizing the lyric—these are the fruits of her long years of apprenticeship. McRae once called Ella Fitzgerald "the epitome of jazz feeling and the popular song welded together. With her, the transition from jazz to the commercial context wasn't only smooth, it was artistic."[13] She might have been speaking of herself, for she too melds jazz feeling with the popular repertoire, and makes an art of it.

Like Billie Holiday, Anita O'Day had a childhood of poverty and disruption, and an adulthood scarred by addiction to drugs. But O'Day has survived heroin, jail and illness and has kept on singing.[14] Though her voice was described in the forties as "scratchy" and "small" and her intonation has been faulted, she made her mark with the authority of her improvisations. Then, as now, her strong suit—what caused listeners to sit up and pay attention—was her intuitive, rhythmical approach and her willingness to take chances with phrasing and time. As Nat Hentoff noted, "She improvises cross-accents much as a jazz drummer does. Her alterations in tempo, with constantly fresh approaches to phrasing, renew old chestnuts and glean new meaning in standards."[15] Her sly, hip manner and husky tone also contributed to her appeal and influence.

Anita O'Day was born in Chicago in 1919 into a poor family. She came to performing early and quite unromantically: in her mid-teens, during the Depression, she spent two years working as a professional walkathon contestant. At nineteen she was working in the kind of nightclub best described as a "joint," often as a singing waitress; in 1939, at twenty, she got her first important job singing with a combo at the Off Beat Club, a jazz room, where her natural musicianship and swinging approach quickly gained her a good reputation among musicians. She cited Billie Holiday, Mildred Bailey and Martha Raye as early influences on her vocal style.

In 1941 O'Day joined the big band of drummer Gene Krupa, who had become a star with Benny Goodman before going out on his own. In 1944–45 she moved to Stan Kenton's band and nationwide exposure, rejoining Krupa briefly in 1945 and later appearing in *The Gene Krupa Story* (1959). Hit recordings like "Let Me Off Uptown" (with trumpeter Roy Eldridge), "That's What You Think" and "Thanks for the Boogie Ride," all with Krupa's band, and "And Her Tears Flowed Like Wine," with Kenton's band, made her many jazz fans' favorite "girl singer." But that wasn't enough for the lady who wanted to wail, and she went out as a single artist. In big bands, she complained, "there's no real singing. You're handed arrangements; everything is planned for you and you just do your part."[16] Billie Holiday had expressed similar feelings, but in general, for a singer to consider herself a musician first required a level of self-esteem rare among women singers of that era.

Anita O'Day continued to perform and record extensively, though her personal life suffered many disruptions: heroin addiction, arrests, incarceration, overdoses and even heart failure in the late sixties, which finally led her to quit drugs cold-turkey. In the seventies, here and especially in Japan, where she enjoys great popularity, she made a comeback and reestablished herself as one of the outstanding jazz singers. Her swinging inventiveness and fresh phrasing have been showcased on tunes many associate with her, including "Sweet Georgia Brown," "Tea for Two," "Honeysuckle Rose," "A Nightingale Sang in Berkley Square," "Blue Moon" and the samba "Wave."

Betty Carter's physical stance during a performance can be likened to that of a runner waiting for the starting gun. As she moves about the stage, she reminds us how physical singing can be. Her approach to her music is so fervent and fierce that it often overwhelms the first-time listener; to my mind, no jazz singer comes closer to the intensity of black gospel music than Betty Carter. Everything about her goes toward making her one of the great singers of jazz—the body English, the superlative, almost compulsive need to improvise on the changes of a tune, the intense emotional response to the music. Carter puts her personal stamp on the music, whether standards or little-known tunes. She sweats for her audience. "If you're sitting in that audience ready to fight me from the very beginning, I'm going to have a hard time getting to you," she has allowed. "But if you've got a heart at all, I'm going to get it."[17]

But for all that, Carter worked for decades without recognition, not to speak of the fame and fortune accorded many other singers. To her the explanation is simple: "I'm not *supposed* to have a hit record. I've always been a *jazz singer*. It takes time to develop, and the record companies just aren't going to *stand* for it. When jazz becomes popular, it's like all music today: produced, controlled, computerized."[18]

Carter was born in Flint, Michigan, in 1930. She began singing jazz as a teenager and soon gravitated to the heavy musical action in Detroit, dabbling in jazz singing by age sixteen. The music quickly became her mission, in spite of discouragement from her family: "They were such religious people that they didn't believe that singing in bars and things like that was good for the soul, and they thought I was committing a real sin by going into the field of show business."[19] While she was apprenticing, bebop was exploding onto the jazz scene, and Carter sat in at many jam sessions, earning the nickname "Betty Bebop." After winning a local amateur contest she landed a job singing with vibraphonist Lionel Hampton's big band in 1948 and soon began learning to write some of her own arrangements. Carter and the bandleader had an uneasy professional relationship, as she later recalled wryly:

Hamp used to ask me which band I liked better, his or Dizzy's [Gillespie had just formed his supercharged big band, staffed by the most modern innovators of the time]. I would say Dizzy's and he'd fire me. Gladys Hampton [Lionel's wife, who managed his large orchestra for many years] loved my work and had a funny feeling that I might do something. Every time he'd fire me, she'd rehire me. He fired me seven times and I stayed with the band two and a half years, struggling; but I don't regret it, because Hamp provided me with a training ground. I went everywhere and I was young and I was doing my little thing and I was scatting. I was learning.[20]

Today widely considered the premier scat singer, Carter developed her unique style in response to what contemporary instrumentalists were doing and, to a much less significant degree, in response to what other singers were doing. And this was true for most of the jazz singers then apprenticing: the sound of the horn, and especially the saxophone, had an overwhelming impact on vocal jazz concept and approach. Carter's essays into wordless vocalise in the late forties and fifties paralleled the pioneering work of her player idols, especially alto saxophonist Charlie Parker. "Scat singing is good training," she once said. "It trains your ear to be in tune and to hear different changes."[21]

At first Carter was unsure of her direction:

I started out not really knowing what I had going for me. I didn't know whether I had the right voice. Sarah Vaughan had been on the scene a couple of minutes and there was a "Sarah Vaughan voice." Billie Holiday had had a concept of jazz, but here was this beautiful voice coming on the scene. Right away we knew that with that voice there was no way of stopping her.[22]

But Betty Carter soon learned to exploit what was most effective in her own equipment. As one writer says in describing her early recorded work:

> The decision—whether or not conscious—to develop her husky, widely spread timbral quality is one example of the astute musical decisions Carter made. Another is her move to lower keys. . . . When she sings in a comfortably low key, she achieves an admirable regularity of timbre throughout her range. . . . Betty's musical decisions (especially about pitch and timing) are made with an assurance and musicality that for most musicians comes only after many years of work. She can . . . swallow, bend or fade a note with ease, and her complete control makes her deviations from traditional interpretations a success.[23]

Carter's detractors claim that the lyric of a tune nearly disappears in some of her rapid-fire treatments, as in her version of "My Favorite Things," taken at breakneck tempo. To this criticism—one that is leveled at many singers who like to scat a lot, among them Anita O'Day—Carter replies that when she thinks the words of a song are negligible, she won't hesitate to sacrifice them to the music.

During the fifties Betty Carter often worked in shows and revues with blues and r&b artists like Muddy Waters, Sonny Terry and Brownie McGee, Brook Benton, the Coasters and the Flamingos.

> The audience reaction was always dynamite, so that told me that I was doing the right thing musically. So did the few club owners across the country who liked my work too, who kept booking me into their clubs whether they made any money or not. I had a club owner in Philadelphia who kept me alive for years by doing that because he liked my work. He figured everybody had to like it one day or the other.[24]

She achieved a milestone in her career when she worked with Ray Charles as an added attraction on a theater tour. That stern perfectionist made her his musical associate, and from 1960 to 1963 Carter and Charles worked together, producing a memorable 1961 recording that has long been out of print. Her main musical influences continued to be saxophonists like Charlie Parker and Sonny Rollins, with whom she toured Japan in 1963. If she was not yet well-known in the sixties, she was honing what she calls "my bebop act." Along the way she married and had two sons (about her private life, she has said, "I'm doing that independent thing [and] males are afraid of that"[25]). Carter agrees with the many jazz musicians who have characterized the sixties as the nadir in terms of opportunities to perform. As she pointed out, the "free" or "avant-garde" jazz of that decade appealed to a mostly white audience, while soul music became the commercially acceptable sound for blacks.

But her time was coming. Underrecorded during the fifties and sixties, in 1971 she formed her own record company, Bet-Car Productions, on which she has produced a number of albums. By the midpoint of that decade, jazz had shown that it was far from moribund, and Betty Carter's audience had grown to the point where she became an important attraction. In 1978 she took her place alongside Ella Fitzgerald and Sarah Vaughan at a triumphant Newport Jazz Festival concert. And in the eighties her unswerving devotion to jazz singing and her virtuoso scatting have become a model for other singers to study and emulate. Among many songs bearing the distinctive Carter stamp are "Wagon Wheels," "My Favorite Things" (she does it in fast four-four time though it was written as a waltz), Thelonious Monk's "Round About Midnight" (which she does, in turnabout fashion, as a waltz) and intense readings of such ballads and medium-tempo songs as "Girl Talk," Cole Porter's "Most Gentlemen Don't Like Love" and her composition "I Can't Help It."

Betty Carter's sound is so hornlike as to crumble the distinction between vocal and nonvocal jazz. As much as any gifted instrumentalist, Carter has expanded the possibilities of the art of improvisation. In concert she carefully builds her delivery of superfast up-tempo tunes, medium-tempo standards and ballads, pouring herself out on stage like a fine actress or athlete. By the end of the set Betty Carter usually has her audience on its feet. The performance over, the intense body still, she stands at rest, spent like a runner after the race.

The big-band singers and the formulators of vocal jazz influenced many later singers who are not easily pigeonholed or neatly classified. Among them is Annie Ross, one of several white singers who established reputations within modern jazz circles. Born into an English music-hall family in 1930, she was transplanted to New York as a youngster and subsequently won an MGM film contract by way of a talent show. She appeared in some *Our Gang* comedies and as Judy Garland's sister in *Presenting Lily Mars* (1942) before turning to a singing career in her teens.

In the late fifties vocalists Jon Hendricks and Dave Lambert were scouting for a woman singer to complete their ambitious new jazz trio, someone with a pliant, swinging sound who could hit the high notes easily. They were greatly impressed by Ross, especially by her 1952 version of

"Twisted" (her lyric written to Wardell Gray's saxophone solo—"My analyst told me that I was right out of my head . . . "—since recorded by Joni Mitchell, Bette Midler and Mark Murphy). Joining Lambert and Hendricks in 1958, Ross met the challenge of duplicating trumpet and saxophone solos with her witty readings and her "ability to simulate instrumental sounds, extraordinary both in concept and execution, . . . helped enormously by her range, which is twice that of the average jazz singer."[26] Lambert, Hendricks and Ross scored a big success with their debut recording, "Sing a Song of Basie." Hendricks later lauded Ross' ability, especially as a lyricist; she also contributed words to "Farmer's Market" and "Jackie," solos by trumpeter Art Farmer and pianist Hampton Hawes respectively. "We begged her for more lyrics," said Jon Hendricks, himself a highly regarded lyricist. "But Annie wasn't having any of it—she just didn't feel she was as good as I was. We pleaded—we told her 'Twisted' was brilliant. But she just wouldn't write more."[27]

With Lambert, Hendricks and Ross, Annie Ross achieved an unusual degree of popularity for a jazz singer. But in 1962, due to health problems, she was forced to leave the group during a European tour (she was replaced by Ceylonese-born Yolande Bavan; Anne Marie Moss also did a stint with the trio, which disbanded in 1964). Ross settled in London, where she ran her own jazz club called Annie's Room and undertook a number of acting assignments. She has since continued to act, sing and write songs, including "Annie's Lament" (a ballad), "The Time Is Right," "Straight on 'Til Morning" and "Alfie Darling." Occasional appearances in America have demonstrated her versatility in handling pop and theatrical material as well as jazz.

Like Annie Ross, Morgana King is an actress (most famously in *The Godfather*) as well as a popular singer with a jazz background. Born in Pleasantville, New York, in 1930, King began to train for a career as an opera singer but dropped out to pursue jazz singing. Beginning in the late forties, she immersed herself in the jazz scene, working with small groups until she had become a top supper-club attraction in the sixties. King is associated with a hip pop sound, as in her recordings of "A Taste of Honey" and "Corcovado," but when she wants to be she is a good jazz improviser and scat singer. She creates an eerie effect in her scatting as she moves around in a kind of vocal highwire act at the dizzily high top of her enormous range. Few singers can reach those high notes, let alone scat there.

Carol Sloane, another highly regarded white jazz stylist, has a warm, rich, slightly husky voice, excellent intonation and innate musicianship. Jon Hendricks recalled that she once subbed for Annie Ross on a day's notice and sang the difficult and challenging parts superbly. A Rhode Island native born in 1937, Sloane began singing with a local dance band in Providence as a teenager. She then worked with local trios, in musical comedy and with the Les and Larry Elgart Orchestra (1958–60) before making a well-received debut at the Newport Jazz Festival in 1961. In the eighties she is more in evidence than she was in the seventies, performing frequently on the East Coast, as at the Kool (formerly Newport) Jazz Festival in 1981.

The black singer and pianist Shirley Horn, born in 1934 in Washington, D.C., is still a well-kept secret for most jazz fans. She studied music privately and then at Howard University before coming to the attention of musicians like trumpeter Miles Davis, who promoted her swinging sound. Since the sixties she has recorded and worked fairly extensively on the East Coast from her base in Washington, where she enjoys an excellent reputation. Recent recordings give further evidence of her talent.

A more famous singer-pianist from Washington, D.C., is Roberta Flack, who was born in North Carolina in 1940 and moved at an early age to the nation's capital. Her blend of jazz, soul and pop helped make her a superstar in the seventies. Classically trained, she received several prizes for her piano renditions and at fifteen won a music scholarship to Howard University. After graduating at age nineteen, she began teaching and performed as piano accompanist to opera singers. But in 1965 Flack shifted her interest from European classical to Afro-American music and decided to pursue a career as a solo performer. By 1970 she had garnered considerable attention and praise, both for her singing and for her compositions and arrangements. One writer described her as "a totally unique personality with a supreme gift of communication. Roberta Flack sounds like nobody else, and sounds like she meant to stay that way."[28] Enthralling as a performer, she has had a string of hits including "The First Time Ever I Saw Your Face," "Killing Me Softly with His Song," "Reverend Lee," Bob Dylan's "Just Like a Woman," Les McCann's "Compared to What" and "Where Is the Love" (with Donny Hathaway).

A number of women song stylists associated with jazz specialize in sophisticated ballad standards, often drawn from the American musical theater, sung slowly or at mid-tempo and usually performed in an intimate setting. The doyenne of such singers is veteran Mabel Mercer, who built her legendary career of more than sixty years by interpreting little-known musical gems. A theatrical background contributed to her superbly articulated, subtly inflected and idiosyncratic song style. Of mixed black and white parentage, Mercer was born in England in 1900. Her family were show folk, and after a brief convent education she took to the stage as a dancer in vaudeville. In the thirties she won praise for her singing during a lengthy engagement at the Paris club run by expatriate American performer Ada Smith, known as Bricktop. In 1938 Mercer settled down in America (except for a brief move to the Bahamas) and became a venerated fixture at a series of small, chic New York rooms, performing regularly through the seventies. As late as 1982, at age eighty-two, she was still making occasional appearances. For many listeners Mabel Mercer is an acquired taste, but one that can rapidly become a habit. Popular and jazz singers of all stripes (notably Frank Sinatra and Bobby Short) have long adored her and have acknowledged her influence.

Singer Blossom Dearie (also a pianist and composer) was born in East Durham, New York, in 1926. She first came to attention in her teens as part of the Blue Flames, the vocal group with Woody Herman's big band during the forties. From the Blue Flames she went to the Blue Rays, who handled the vocals for the Alvino Rey band. In Paris in 1952 she formed and wrote arrangements for the Blue Stars, a vocal group that included Annie Ross for a time. The Stars had a hit that year with "Lullaby of Birdland." Returning to the States in 1956, Dearie established herself as a solo singer-pianist in small, intimate clubs—the setting that best serves her sweetish and fragile-sounding voice. But Dearie combines a small vocal instrument with large-scale musical acumen. Though she often perches at the line where hip becomes precious, when she digs in and discreetly swings she shows that there is a touch of metal hidden in the velvet glove, belying the notion that fragility means lack of power. She has gained a place in many jazz lovers' affections with her delivery and choice of material, including many of her own songs: "I'm Shadowing You," with lyrics by Johnny Mercer; "Hey, John," an amusing ditty she wrote after meeting John Lennon ("Look at me digging you digging me"); "Sweet Georgie Fame," which pianist George Shearing recorded successfully in Britain; "Long Daddy Green (The Almighty Dollar)"; "I Like You, You're Nice," a sweetly wistful come-on (also recorded superbly by Irene Kral); and many more. In the eighties Blossom Dearie continues to issue albums on her own Daffodil Records.

Peggy Lee (née Norma Egstrom) is, like Blossom Dearie, a talented songwriter as well as a singer. Born in North Dakota in 1922, she sang on a local radio station in Fargo in her teens. After establishing herself as a vocalist of note with Benny Goodman and his orchestra (1941–43), she went on to a career as a solo artist. She wrote a string of hits, mostly in the forties, many with then-husband and former Goodman guitarist Dave Barbour. These include "You Was Right, Baby," "It's a Good Day," "Mañana," "What More Can a Woman Do" and "I Don't Know Enough About You." She also co-wrote several movie songs, including the score to Walt Disney's *Lady and the Tramp*, and collaborated with Duke Ellington on "Goin' Fishing" and with Cy Coleman on "Then Was Then and Now Is Now." A meticulous performer, Peggy Lee is associated with effortless-sounding, impeccably phrased, relaxed readings of popular songs with jazz inflections. Especially during the fifties (as on recordings like "Black Coffee" for Decca and on pairings with pianist George Shearing) she had an easy, intimate and earthy delivery. Lee is also a poet, painter and actress, notably in *The Jazz Singer* and *Pete Kelly's Blues*. Today she continues to perform in her deceptively easy, laid-back style.

The fine ballad work of the late Irene Kral, who died in 1978, graced only a slim number of recordings. Sister of Roy Kral (of the singing duo Jackie and Roy), this Chicago-based singer was born in 1932. Kral worked with local vocal groups and bands as a teenager and then joined Woody Herman's and Maynard Ferguson's big bands as vocalist before settling in Los Angeles in the late fifties. In 1974 Kral teamed with pianist Alan Broadbent, and their partnership produced exquisitely rendered, delicate ballads. Irene Kral had a lovely, resonant voice with a discreet vibrato, flawless diction and intonation, and a slight, attractive nasality and shaping of phrases that resembled Carmen McRae's (but where McRae's readings tend to the astringent, Kral's melt like butter). She was a master of quiet understatement and good taste.

Teddi King (1929–1977) was born in Boston. After high school she won a vocal contest sponsored by Dinah Shore and traveled for a year singing for the USO and the American Theatre Wing. She studied classical singing and jazz piano, then apprenticed with various bands, joining George Shearing's quintet in 1952–53. Subsequently, as a solo performer, she played numerous jazz rooms and worked in Las Vegas. A warm, velvety sound coupled with great care in her handling of lyrics made her a favorite among fans of the ballad.

Vocalist Helen Merrill (née Helen Milcetic) conveys her own brand of discreet swing through a rather small instrument that projects well at all parts of her range. Like Lee Wiley before her, Merrill has a quality of smokiness, a sexy, sighing sound that wraps around the listener like a light fog. Her delivery is especially suited to ballads, where wistfulness can be so appealing, but she also becomes a belter on up-tempo tunes. Born in New York in 1930, Merrill began singing professionally in 1946; by 1952 she was a vocalist with the Earl Hines big band, along with Etta Jones. But the big-band days were essentially over, and she went on to work with small groups for the rest of the fifties, cutting a number of fine albums, some with arranger-pianist Gil Evans. In 1959 Merrill moved to Europe for a three-year stay; 1967 found her in Japan, where she lived until 1972, building a successful career, cutting numerous albums for Victor and producing others for Trio Records. Since she returned to the States, Merrill has become a major club attraction. For many listeners, ballads remain her forte.

A few female singers have made their mark as members of jazz vocal groups. In the fifties and early sixties, the most influential of these groups was Lambert, Hendricks and Ross, already discussed in connection with Annie Ross. In the late seventies, after the death of Dave Lambert, Jon

Hendricks formed Hendricks, Hendricks and Hendricks, a family affair, with his wife, Judith, performing the trumpet high-note chores originally done by Annie Ross. The Hendricks' daughters are also associated with this popular performance group in the eighties.

Since the forties the husband-and-wife vocal team Jackie and Roy has been delighting fans with sophisticated, tightly professional duets grounded in the jazz idiom. Jackie Cain began to sing publicly at age five. In the forties she worked in Chicago with local groups and joined Charlie Ventura's Bop for the People combo. There she met the skillful arranger-pianist Roy Kral, later to become her husband. Ventura's group was a popular attraction because of its bop lines sung in unison, with and without lyrics, a device Cain and Kral continued when they went out as a duo. Jackie and Roy have had an active, durable career marked by excellent choice of material, fine arrangements, a polished approach and the crystal-clear, pliant soprano of Jackie Cain.

A number of important female vocalists who got their start in gospel come under the umbrella of jazz singing as an individualized improvisatory art and have directly or indirectly brought gospel song techniques to jazz singing. Historically, women who sang gospel music were mostly poor women, culture bearers and music makers who remained anonymous beyond the black church. Even today gospel is almost a subculture unto itself, with well-defined rules of vocal comportment. It has remained rooted in the black church, and it is mainly the province of women. As one musicologist observes, "The urban Black folk church [is] an institution which is largely sustained and comprised by Black women (attendance at any Black folk church will bear this out). Singing groups in Black folk churches are comprised largely of women."[29]

The example par excellence of a stalwart "godly" singer whose church music became familiar to the world at large is the great Mahalia Jackson (1911–1972), born in New Orleans and immersed from an early age in the music of that city. She compares favorably with her early major singing influence, Bessie Smith, in sheer vocal power, expressiveness and gorgeous bluesiness. But the devoutly religious Jackson got her tremendous bounce, or lift, from "sanctified" shouting rather than from the worldly blues. Mahalia Jackson moved to Chicago as a young woman and rose from cleaning lady and church singer to the heights of artistic and financial success, concertizing around the world. For many years her pianist was the excellent accompanist Mildred Falls. Her recording of "Move On Up a Little Higher" (1945) sold more than a million copies. She occasionally teamed with jazz musicians, as in a memorable 1958 concert with Duke Ellington and his orchestra, where she performed his "Come Sunday," his arrangement of the Twenty-third Psalm, and a vocal tribute to Louis Armstrong.

Jackson's great gift and tremendous success with the secular audience were unprecedented in gospel music, but others made good careers as gospel-influenced singers in a jazz vein (recall pianist-singer Arizona Dranes in the twenties). Accompanying herself on guitar, Sister Rosetta Tharpe (1915–1973) was a well-known figure on the gospel circuit. In 1938 she appeared at a landmark concert, From Spirituals to Swing, at Carnegie Hall in New York, and that year she became well known singing in a Cotton Club revue with Cab Calloway's band. She performed later with Lucky Millinder's orchestra and as a soloist at Cafe Society and other rooms. Two of her hits in the forties were "That's All" and "Shout, Sister, Shout." Lil Green (1919–1954) was another popular singer who had a gospel background. Jailed for killing a man in a roadhouse brawl, she sang at the prison church services and later popularized a blues-cum-gospel style with a hit record, "Romance in the Dark." She had another recording success with "Knockin' Myself Out"/"Why Don't You Do Right?" Green was based in Chicago and worked mostly in the Midwest as a popular nightclub attraction, often accompanied by blues guitarist Big Bill Broonzy.

When she emerged in the forties, the superb stylist Dinah Washington (1924–1963) was the outstanding vocal proponent of the union of gospel's lofty, soaring lilt with the earthy, salty quality of the blues. Born Ruth Jones in Tuscaloosa, Alabama, she moved to Chicago as a child and became immersed in musical activities at St. Luke's Baptist Church on the South Side. By the age of eleven she was singing and playing the piano at St. Luke's; then, with her mother, she formed a singing team that toured black churches in recital. She served St. Luke's as church choir director, soloist and pianist until 1942, when she left to sing "worldly" music at local nightspots. Gospel had given her the foundations of her style as a jazz-pop singer, a sharply declamatory enunciation and a rich, bluesy phrasing. Like several other black women singers discussed in these pages, she began her climb to secular success by winning an amateur talent contest, at the Regal Theater in Chicago. In 1943 Ruth Jones joined Lionel Hampton's band, and she soon recorded: four Feather songs, including the hits "Evil Gal Blues" and "Salty Papa Blues," in a combo of Hampton sidemen, with the vibist-leader on some selections.

With her gospel approach to secular song, Washington remained a top "soul" singer on the scene throughout her life, though she cut plenty of jazz sides as well as r&b and commercial numbers; two of her big hits were "What a Difference a Day Makes" and "Unforgettable." A riveting personality came through all her material, and her phrasing remained confident, intimate and conversational in the best Afro-American manner. Her personal life rivaled Bessie Smith's and Billie Holiday's for tumultuousness: like them, she had a famous temper. She married seven times, got into various legal scrapes and finally died at age thirty-nine, probably from an overdose of pills and alcohol. Her sensuous, easy delivery, salty declamatory phrasing and innate mastery of rhythm inspired many singers who followed. The cry or "tear" in her voice can be heard in singers Esther Phillips, Ruth Brown, Gloria Lynne and La Vern Baker. Today the popular jazz-influenced singer Nancy Wilson is her closest stylistic adherent, and the talented Ernestine Anderson, who has built a fine reputation abroad, also shows an affinity.

Dinah Washington's successor as queen of gospel-blues-soul flavored with jazz phrasing is unquestionably the powerfully equipped Aretha Franklin, who cut an early album called *Unforgettable* in tribute to Washington. Franklin was born in Memphis in 1942. Her mother left the family when she was six, and young Aretha and her four siblings were raised by her preacher father and saturated with the music of the black church. At the age of fourteen Aretha was singing with her father's well-known traveling gospel caravan shows. By 1956 she was making her first recordings as a gospel singer, influenced and inspired by the great gospel singer Clara Ward.[30] Franklin remained faithful to church music throughout the fifties, but at eighteen, in 1960, she was persuaded to record soul and pop material as well as gospel, probably following the example of Ray Charles, whose recent admixture of the two idioms had been most successful.

Aretha Franklin was no overnight sensation as a "worldly" singer, however. She was underutilized by her record company, Columbia, and she took the usual club route, singing show tunes and ballads. But after she switched to Atlantic Records she hit her stride, and from 1967 on she recorded hit after powerful soul hit, her preacherlike exhortations meshing with the new movement toward black pride and community. Suddenly she was the most successful black woman singer in America, and like her great predecessors, she became a powerful symbol as well as singer. "The blues had been transfigured by anger and pride," observed one writer. Aretha was "earth mother exhorting, preacher woman denouncing, militant demanding, forgotten woman wailing."[31]

As time went on, a streak of trouble ran through the mounting success story. Franklin's performances were sometimes marred by temperament and conflict. Her personal problems were aired, and it seemed clear that she suffered psychologically. And as gospel writer Tony Heilbut speculates, "Perhaps the pop idiom seldom provides sufficient inspiration for her.... Happy or sad, Aretha is a gospel child."[32] For many fans, her early gospel recordings and later material like the album *Amazing Grace* (with the Southern California Community Choir, directed by the Reverend James Cleveland) represent her highest achievements to date. At her best, Aretha Franklin stands firmly in the black female vocalist tradition, where the holy and the high have so often mingled with the earthy and profane, enriching the technique and the art of jazz singing.

Several other excellent singers have deep roots in the black church. One is Chicago-born Lorez Alexandria, who sang spirituals and gospel in Midwestern churches as a girl, touring for some eleven years with a Baptist *a capella* singing group. But when she made her career switch to popular music, Alexandria consciously avoided the use of gospel-soul mannerisms. In her style gospel is rather a subtle coloration in phrasing. She has a light, casual-seeming delivery, an adventurous melodicism and a rich, throaty tone.

> I tried actually to divorce myself from singing with religious overtones or aspects.... Maybe it's because I had this kind of background. The Gospelizing or use of so-called "soul" singing—that sort of thing—has become very large in the business. [But] I'm not a shouter and I'm not a Gospel singer. I wasn't a Gospel singer when I was singing in the church. I can't yell; I can't do this other thing. But I was effective.... Anybody can sing spiritually without being labeled a Gospel singer.[33]

Alexandria worked with the Ramsey Lewis trio in 1958 and has been based on the West Coast since 1961. She has cut several fine albums.

Dakota Staton is a veteran jazz and pop singer based on the East Coast. Her exuberant style, including a good scatting technique, owes much to her contemporary Sarah Vaughan, as well as to gospel-derived soul mannerisms. Born in Pittsburgh in 1932, Staton sang professionally with her sisters before going out as a single. Her appearance at a jam session at Harlem's Baby Grand jazz club in 1954 helped land her a record contract with Capitol the following year, and she cut a big-selling album, *The Late, Late Show*. Staton favors time-tested rousers like "Broadway," a song long associated with her. With her smooth, practiced delivery and pliant, hornlike phrasing, she is popular in Europe (she went to England in 1965 and remained for several years) as well as in America, where she has been active since the seventies.

Singer, pianist and composer Nina Simone (born Eunice Waymon in 1933) brings a gospel intensity to her brand of secular preaching. She found her surest role as an activist in the black civil rights movement, scoring big from 1959 into the sixties with such songs as her "Mississippi Goddamn." Her fervor and vinegary sound are counterbalanced by solid formal training at the Juilliard School of Music in New York and the Curtis Institute in Philadelphia, where she also taught piano for a few years. Simone has often turned for songwriting inspiration to the words of black poets, as with her music to Paul Dunbar's "Compensation" and Langston Hughes' "The Backlash Blues" and "To Be Young, Gifted and Black." Her own "Four Women" is a starkly drawn portrait of the stereotypical roles assigned to black women in America, a sharp line-drawing of social realities.

Abbey Lincoln (formerly Gaby Lee and since 1975 known as Aminata Moseka) is distinguished as a singer, actress (*Nothing But a Man, For the Love of Ivy*), songwriter and symbol of black pride. Born in Chicago in 1930, she began her professional career as a nightclub singer during the fifties. She was successful at the Moulin Rouge in Los Angeles in the mid-fifties as much for her attractiveness as for her vocalizing, and an early recording for Liberty also exploited her physical charms. Titled *Abbey Lincoln's Affair . . . A Story of a Girl in Love*, it displayed her sprawled on a floor in a tight gown, and the liner notes pondered her anatomical rather than vocal attributes. But she was in very attractive voice, too, backed by an orchestra directed by Benny Carter.

Lincoln soon left the world of low-necked gowns and commercialization behind. By the early sixties, with such important musicians as Thelonious Monk, pianist Mal Waldron and her then-husband, drummer Max Roach, she collaborated as writer and/or singer on recordings that were searing statements of black reality and consciousness. Notable among these were *We Insist! Freedom Now Suite* (1960), followed by the 1961 *Straight Ahead* (" . . . to nowhere"), which also featured "Retribution" ("Let the retribution match the contribution") and the roots-conscious "African Lady." By the late seventies Lincoln's compositions and material (as in the *People in Me* album) evinced less of the bitterness and coiled-up, near-claustrophobic rage of the past, with more relaxed communication of her feelings of dignity as a black woman and artist.

For many listeners Abbey Lincoln's singing recalls the emotive abilities of Billie Holiday. She has a rather grainy vocal texture, a sweet-and-sour delivery and a broad emotional range, from scathing to buoyantly joyful. And she has studied African music and vocal techniques, using clicks, calls and growls for dramatic effect, as in "I Know Why the Caged Bird Sings." Her phrasing tends to the percussive. In her performing she is especially attentive to the content of her material, seeing herself as part of a tradition of singers like Billie Holiday and Bessie Smith, who addressed the economic and social realities of black life in America. Like these predecessors, Lincoln stands in the forefront of jazz singers who go to the heart of the matter.

The influence of American jazz singing techniques extends around the world, and a number of non-American improvising singers have developed into distinctive stylists in their own right. In Britain singer-actress Cleo

Laine is celebrated for her nimble voice, amazing, supple range and dramatic gift. A stellar performer today, she made her professional singing debut in London in 1952, when she auditioned for and won a spot with the John Dankworth Seven. Several years later she married saxophonist Dankworth and formed a musical partnership with him, making a name for herself in Europe as a *grande dame* of popular and jazz-influenced song. In performance she employs jazz shadings and a variety of moods in brilliant dramatic exploitation of her material. Laine waited some twenty years, until the early seventies, before appearing in America, where she repeated her European triumph at a spectacular concert at Lincoln Center in New York.

There are several established Scandinavian vocalists of note. Alice Babs, a very popular Swedish singer born in 1924, is also active in European television and films. Characterized by an ethereally pure sound and a big range, her voice graced Duke Ellington's Second Sacred Concert, in performance and on record. Monica Zetterlund, another Swede, was born in 1937 and began singing professionally with her parents' band at the age of fourteen (her father was a tenor saxophonist, her mother a bassist). She has gigged extensively throughout Europe and especially in Scandinavia. Norwegian Karin Krog, a versatile performer, is also active in television jazz programming and conducting workshops. She has recorded or worked with several American jazz artists, notably with the Don Ellis orchestra and the Clare Fischer trio (around 1967).

Among Latin American singers, Brazilian Astrud Gilberto has been well known since her vocal contribution to "The Girl from Ipanema" (1962), recorded with tenor saxophonist Stan Getz and composed by João Gilberto, then her husband. The record sold over twenty-seven million copies and made bossa nova and Astrud Gilberto hugely popular around the world. This success came casually: she was asked to sing the lyric to "Ipanema" as an afterthought during the recording session. Though not a jazz singer, she is a stylist who phrases and inflects with a jazz flavor. Since the late seventies, after a period as a housewife in suburban Philadelphia, Gilberto has been appearing in clubs again, often with young guitarist Emily Remler. Another established Brazilian singer hugely popular in her country but known only to aficionados in America was the excellent and versatile Elis Regina, who improvised in the Afro-Brazilian tradition. Her career was tragically cut short in 1982, when she died at age thirty-six.

The contributions of the many veteran and emerging singers who have worked under the dictates of the Afro-American aesthetic are rich in scope and musical inventiveness. For all their diversity of style, training, race, class and era, the improvising singers are sister artists who have made a lasting impression on their public. And they are the most abundant crop of women in jazz to date.

But will the harvest of fine vocal improvisers inspired by the jazz tradition continue to be replenished? Some practitioners of the craft are less than optimistic about the future of jazz singing, and since they are on the firing line of the music, so to speak, their comments are worthy of close attention. Says Carmen McRae:

> There's plenty of work out there—at least for the established singers. Ella, Sarah, Peggy Lee, Mel Torme, Joe Williams are working all the time. And I certainly can't complain. There's a lot of work for the name singers. But I'm pessimistic about the outlets for those who need it, the young unknown singers. Where are they gonna learn their craft? Where are they gonna pay their dues? I'm also pessimistic about the future of jazz singing. That is, jazz singing as *we* know it. It's a disappearing art. The young, upcoming singers aren't singing pure jazz. At least I don't hear them.[34]

Betty Carter puts it even more forcefully:

> You could be an individual in those days [the forties, when she was apprenticing], but today you either have to sound like somebody or almost sound like somebody. Black people have to sing the gospel sound or close to it. The white people have to sound like Linda Ronstadt or somebody else in that whole circle, so they're in trouble. So here we are in a world where everybody is like everybody else and we're not getting any real musicians; the musicianship level is down. . . . Everybody wants to be a star today. We were brought up in this business to be an individual. If you check it out you'll notice that there are no duplicates in black music—there's only one Dizzy, only one Miles, one Monk, one Sarah Vaughan, one Ella Fitzgerald. . . . [Today] we don't have a whole field of young musicians who want to really learn about the whole spectrum of music and not vamp themselves into a hole.[35]

And Sheila Jordan (see the profile of Jordan in Part Five) speculates on possible reasons for the perceived lack of young black jazz singers:

> It seems to me that today there are a lot more young singers comin' up that are white that are interested in jazz than black singers. I find a lot of young black musicians coming up not really that interested in

playing jazz, and most of the young black singers. Maybe they don't want to struggle with it, maybe they want to make money and they want to be out there working consistently. And maybe they don't have the devotion to the music that people had before them, like Betty Carter. But this would be the time for them to sing jazz! Because it would be much easier for a young black singer today than it would have been twenty, thirty, even ten years ago.[36]

In spite of these grave reservations, there are plenty of young and not-so-young singers around the country who are working where and how they can to develop as improvising singers (some of them are discussed in Chapter 9, "The Contemporary Scene"). Many study with private teachers, with established singers and players, in the courses increasingly offered as part of college and university curricula, or in workshops, clinics, choirs and showcases at clubs. It is as true today as it was at the turn of the century, when Ma Rainey first took to the stage, that the singer in the improvising tradition needs single-mindedness, patience and dedication as well as technique. It may not be clear what the new developments in this tradition will be, but perhaps that's part of what improvising is all about.

Part Four

EQUAL TIME:

BEYOND

FRATERNITY,

TOWARD

COMMUNITY

1960s–1980s

Chapter Nine

THE CONTEMPORARY SCENE

*Now, more than ever, female musicians have
a greater sense of self, and improvisation has
become the personal idiom of their artistry.*
REGINA WEINREICH, 1978

This chapter surveys women's participation in the contemporary jazz scene as players, leaders, composers, singers, producers and managers. The jazzwomen who have emerged since the sixties exhibit great diversity in style and concept. Some of them have utilized the growing network of women's organizations and festivals and have played in all-female combinations, others have participated in male-female groups, and a small but growing number have been active in traditionally all-male jazz bastions. Where possible, I have included their views on the situation of women in jazz today along with a discussion of their musical achievements.

As in the past, the piano leads as the instrument chosen most frequently by female jazz players. And, in the tradition of Mary Lou Williams, many contemporary women pianists are active composers and orchestrators as well as performers. Two important figures who have won international attention, especially since the seventies, are Carla Bley (see the profile of Bley in

Toshiko Akiyoshi. *(Credit: Bob Parent)*

Part Five) and Toshiko Akiyoshi. Both place high each year in jazz polls here and abroad as composers and big-band leaders.

Toshiko Akiyoshi's involvement with jazz began with her exposure as a teenager to the music that flooded her native Japan along with the American Occupation after World War II. Akiyoshi was born in 1929 into a comfortably-off Japanese family living in Manchuria. At the urging of her father, himself a practitioner of the Noh drama, she and her three sisters took lessons in ballet, Japanese traditional dancing and piano. "I dropped the dancing and the ballet right away," she later recalled, "but I loved the piano. But it was all classical music. I didn't know a thing about jazz, and in fact, didn't like it at all."[1] During the thirties and throughout World War II, Manchuria became a battleground for contending Japanese, Soviet and Chinese forces, and in 1947, as the Chinese Communists were consolidating their control of the region, the Akiyoshi family left, returning to Japan with only the clothes on their backs.

Postwar Japan, then as now, offered a good and inexpensive education in jazz by way of numerous student coffeehouses stocked with jukeboxes and records. Young Toshiko soon fell under the spell of jazz and was particularly impressed when she heard a friend's collection of 78s by pianist Teddy Wilson. She became part of the jazz scene in Tokyo, first working as a dance-band accompanist. "I didn't know the chord names or anything," she said later.[2] But that didn't interfere with her growing popularity; by 1952 she was established with her own band and plenty of engagements. Then she began to feel the need for further study—and exposure to the music on its native ground. A 1953 recording she made in Tokyo for entrepreneur Norman Granz, along with recommendations from American artists such as pianist Oscar Peterson, eventually won her a full scholarship to study in America at the Berklee College of Music in Boston. After she came to the United States in 1956, word spread that she was a keyboardist and composer of promise—all things considered, that is: as she told Leonard Feather, in those first years in America "I dealt with both racial and sexual prejudice. I played clubs and TV wearing a kimono, because people were amazed to see an Oriental woman playing jazz."[3]

Akiyoshi, then greatly influenced by pianist Bud Powell, completed her studies at Berklee and married saxophonist Charlie Mariano in 1959. During most of the sixties, in New York and Japan, she worked in a small group context, often with bassist Charles Mingus. In 1967 she debuted as composer-conductor at Town Hall in New York in a concert that included original solo, trio and big-band compositions. In 1969 (having divorced Mariano, with whom she had a daughter) she married saxophonist-flutist Lew Tabackin and formed a quartet with him. When Tabackin was called to Los Angeles to work in the *Tonight Show* band, the two set about forming a jazz orchestra that soon became one of the most interesting and exciting big bands around. Begun in 1973 as a rehearsal band to showcase Akiyoshi's compositions and allow for jazz improvisation within a tightly organized, challenging ensemble context, the Akiyoshi-Tabackin big band became her instrument, with Tabackin playing Billy Strayhorn to her Duke Ellington. In the ensuing decade she has composed, arranged and conducted a whole library of music that reflects her musical vision.

At first, one writer says, there was "a tremendous amount of skepticism about a Japanese woman writing for a jazz band in Los Angeles."[4] Akiyoshi addressed this "problem" in an interview: "Being female I think you have a little difficulty because you're seen as taking a man's job. Maybe now it's much better than before.... when we formed the band it was a new experience for the musicians to rehearse under a woman. I had to think that aspect through very carefully. I think that emotionally a man still has a hard time taking orders from a woman."[5] Bandmember Mike Price, a trumpet player, was in the group from 1973 to 1983, when the leaders decided to transfer from Los Angeles to New York. He pointed out that the experience of working with a woman boss was not only new but refreshing,

> both on the level of her commitment, in a field where that isn't always so, and also her being a woman. From the very beginning of rehearsals in 1973, it was very obvious that this was a person who's very committed to music and very serious about bringing about a real, viable musical entity. And this is something that's been intact in her through all the time I've been in the band. And it's also important that she and Lew did this essentially as a team effort. It was more equality among musicians, rather than "Now we're going to include a woman."[6]

Elsewhere, Akiyoshi has discussed her position both as a non-American and as a woman in jazz:

> Competition wasn't as tough [in Japan] as in the United States, so I could rise to the top quicker.... There was less female competition in Japan. Whenever women competed in a man's world in the United States, they didn't succeed. Those that did, became separated from the mainstream and wound up as piano players in the more sophisticated, high class clubs, such as the East Side Club or the Hickory House in New York. A few, such as Marian McPartland, did succeed.[7]

The Akiyoshi-Tabackin band performed and recorded successfully in Japan in the mid-seventies before receiving similar attention in the States.

"There was tremendous interest in the band from the beginning by the Japanese public," said Price, "and also she had been recording for Japanese companies throughout her career, so it was a very logical step to record the band there."[8] The album *Long Yellow Road*, cut in 1974, was well received in Japan, and *Kogun*, which followed in 1975, became a jazz hit there. Meanwhile, after building an audience on the West Coast, the band made its first East Coast tour in 1977, playing the Newport Jazz Festival. That year also saw the first U.S. releases. In 1981, having left a major label to form their own record company (Ascent), Akiyoshi and Tabackin continued to keep their sixteen-piece band together with weekly rehearsals and world tours, winning consistent critical praise and numerous awards—a considerable achievement considering that it is no small feat to keep *any* big band together at a time when transportation costs alone are approaching the prohibitive. Their move to the East Coast was marked in the jazz world by a concert at the 1983 Kool Jazz Festival.

As Carla Bley looks both to her European roots and to the Afro-American tradition in composing for her big band, so does Akiyoshi draw on her Oriental identity in her music. "I came to think that being Japanese was not a negative aspect [in the jazz world]. Rather it was a positive aspect in that I could draw something from my own culture and perhaps return to the jazz tradition something that might make it a little bit richer than before."[9] Many of her compositions, what she terms her "programmatic" music, portray and elucidate the Japanese experience. The composition "Kogun" is described by Price as

> inspired by a news story about a Japanese soldier who was found in the jungles in the Philippines in about 1974. He was finally talked into surrendering—in a war that had finished some thirty years before! And Toshiko was very moved by the sense of tragedy which had occurred in this man's life, that he had spent his whole life adhering to a cause or military organization in which he believed, and all the productive years of his life were wasted out of a sense of duty and honor to himself and his country. It was a dramatic event, with somewhat of the sense of futility about it. All these very complicated feelings are intertwined in this composition.[10]

The composition "Tales of a Courtesan," from the album of the same name, is described by Akiyoshi as inspired by the Japanese courtesans of the Edo era. "At that time women weren't supposed to be educated, but these courtesans were trained and educated because they had to entertain high-cultured men. So these women were far above the women of their culture, yet at the same time they were slaves. Escape was punishable by death. They were leading a luxurious life, but their basic human rights were completely denied. This contrast to me was something very unique.''[11] And the suite "Minamata," on the *Insights* album, concerns the sad fate of a small village in Japan "where a chemical company built a plant. The village became a big city and people thought that was tremendous progress for them. But the plant's waste went into the ocean, fish ate the waste, people ate the fish and got mercury poisoning. And it affected not just one generation, but the next as well. This story is told through the music.''[12]

Akiyoshi also borrows from her cultural past by including traditional Japanese instruments and folk-song elements in many of her works. For example, the pieces "Sumie" (the Japanese word for a style of brush painting) and "Hen-Pecked Old Man" (a character in a folktale) utilize traditional themes and the sounds of the susumi drummers, whose playing is punctuated by deep guttural emissions. "These folk-song sounds are more obvious to the Japanese than to us," pointed out Mike Price. "Our appreciation is more related directly to the sound of the music itself, because we're hearing those sounds for the first time.''[13]

A major factor in the unique and easily recognizable sound of the band is Akiyoshi's approach to voicing harmonies. As Peter Rothbart observes, "Many contemporary writers use a more horizontal or linear writing approach . . . (voicing the accented or stressed notes vertically, then simply writing melody notes to link the pitches together). Akiyoshi prefers to voice each note vertically, no matter how fast it goes by. This way [she says], 'if it is played slowly, there will still be a beautiful line.' . . . Her works often change meter several times, . . . her accents are often unusually placed, . . . her forms are often quite extended.''[14] Another Akiyoshi characteristic is her unusual accentuation of the woodwinds in support of Tabackin, the band's principal soloist.

When conducting, Akiyoshi impresses with a firm demeanor that is fully concentrated on eliciting the sounds she wants from the sixteen pieces before her. A meticulous craftswoman, she communicates precisely, using her whole body to speak for her. Observing rehearsals, I watched her work with the band: she would often hunch over or move to stand taut against a wall, stilled in the act of listening. As a pianist she has begun playing and recording more frequently in recent years with small groups; with her band she concentrates more on her position as leader and composer than as soloist. When she does solo, she demonstrates impeccable technique and a broad grasp of the styles of jazz ranging from Jelly Roll Morton interpretations through ferociously paced Bud Powell–inspired bop to her own highly articulate and passionately engaged originals.

A number of other women have built successful careers as jazz key-boardists since the sixties. Patti Bown, a colorful and forceful player with a technique strongly rooted in gospel and blues, is today an established performer on the East Coast. Born in Seattle, Washington, in 1931, she began as a classical pianist but soon switched to jazz. She settled in New York in the mid-fifties and joined the band of fellow Seattleite Quincy Jones in 1960. She is a frequent solo performer, and her original compositions have been recorded by Jones' orchestra as well as by Count Basie and his orchestra, J. J. Johnson, Melba Liston and others. She has also composed and performed for theatrical productions.

Alice McLeod Coltrane was born in Detroit in 1937 and studied music theory, harmony and organ as a child. In 1959, in her early twenties, she studied in Europe with expatriate pianist Bud Powell, remaining a "disciple" upon her return to the States in the early sixties. She then worked with such musicians as tenor saxophonists Johnny Griffin and Lucky Thompson, spending a year on the road with vibraphonist Terry Gibbs in 1962–63 (she had been preceded in that capacity by fellow Detroiter Terry Pollard). McLeod came to prominence after she met the great tenor saxophonist John Coltrane in the mid-sixties. They married, had three sons and formed a union that was artistic as well as romantic. Alice became an adherent of modal pianist McCoy Tyner, a seminal member of John Coltrane's important quartet, and she replaced Tyner as the group's pianist from 1966 until John's death in 1967.

After she met John Coltrane, Alice's music was increasingly informed by her personal spiritual quest. She traveled to India, where she studied Eastern thought, became a Hindu and adopted a new name, Turiya Apaina. Already proficient on organ as well as piano, she took up the harp next, using it to achieve tranquilizing and meditative effects. Her recordings and concerts from 1968 on, accompanied by such players as Archie Shepp, Pharoah Sanders, Ornette Coleman and many others, often featured her playing percussive instruments such as the tambourine and wind chimes. Since that time her music can be said to have been subsumed in or subordinated to her spiritual quest, and her concert appearances and recordings have dwindled. She has stated her musical goals clearly: "I would like to play music according to the ideals set forth by John and continue to let a cosmic principle of the aspect of spirituality be the underlying reality behind the music as he had."[15]

Valerie Capers, composer, arranger and conductor as well as pianist, has performed and conducted numerous engagements, including a date at Carnegie Hall in the late seventies. Blinded at age six by a viral infection, she went on to win a scholarship to the Juilliard School of Music and received a classical background there. But her brother urged her to explore jazz too: "He talked about the responsibility of a black woman to get involved with jazz," she told an interviewer. "But now I'm a pianist—no label. And in my writing, I'm not concerned with any particular style....If you have the musical background and some idea of the emotional impact the music should have, the musical style will hang together."[16] Capers' most notable composition to date is a two-and-a-half-hour Christmas cantata entitled "Sing About Love," which blends a variety of jazz styles with traditional European forms and gospel singing by a twenty-voice choir backed by a twenty-two-piece orchestra and piano. Capers writes in Braille, after which the music must be transferred to the regular notes of the staff. This, she says, is "very tedious, but you just accept it."[17]

The black pianist, organist and composer Amina Claudine Myers was based in Chicago during the sixties and most of the seventies, where she was one of the few women musicians involved with an influential collective called the Association for the Advancement of Creative Musicians (AACM). She also worked with tenor saxophonist Gene Ammons' group for several years. Myers' playing embraces an eclectic mix—strong doses of gospel-barrelhouse-blues as well as the rumble and crash of modern atonality, stride piano meshing with spirituals, then yielding to avant-garde "free" playing of a characteristic, nervous intensity. In 1979 Myers performed her "Improvisational Suite for Chorus, Pipe Organ and Percussion" with a nineteen-piece ensemble; many of her other compositions concentrate on *a capella* choral voicings with piano accompaniment. She is now based in New York and also performs in Europe.

There are several other fine players who fall within the loose category of the experimental or avant-garde. Among them is Jessica Williams, who has been based in San Francisco since 1978. By the eighties Williams had made a name for herself on the West Coast as a pianist of note. Born in Baltimore in 1948, she began piano studies as a child and entered the Peabody Conservatory of Music at age nine. There she was recognized and encouraged as an improviser rather than as a classical interpreter. After some seven years at the conservatory, she began gigging as an organist with local jazz groups around the East Coast. She then headed west, where she quickly established herself on the Bay area scene as a soloist and leader of the eleven-piece Liberation Orchestra. A follower of psychiatrist-philosopher Wilhelm Reich, Williams mused to an interviewer about her passion for piano: "Maybe it's a mission and maybe it's just a pastime. Maybe it's a hobby. Maybe it's a mental disease. But it's certainly not a business, and I'm not approaching it that way. I'm approaching it as how much music I can get on this planet before I stop playing."[18]

Another pianist of formidable technique and devotion to her art is Joanne Brackeen, who has garnered increasing critical recognition since the seventies. A former Californian now living in New York, Brackeen treads the slippery path of jazz improvisation with an unusual degree of serenity. Her playing is informed by a passionate, relentlessly exploratory harmonic approach and ceaseless rhythmic complexity, and her high level of technical expertise is matched by her intense concentration.

Brackeen, born in California in 1938, is a largely self-taught musician. As a child she picked out solos on the piano by copying them note for note from her parents' records. By the time she was a teenager her direction as a jazz improviser was clearly set; having won a scholarship to the Los Angeles Conservatory of Music, she left the school after just three days, explaining that she wasn't interested in the classical training it offered. Instead she began to sit in at local clubs, where she was able to learn from such top jazzmen as saxophonists Dexter Gordon and Harold Land. And she continued to copy solos, especially Charlie Parker's (she claims to have thoroughly learned Parker, Bud Powell and later John Coltrane by this method).

In 1960 Joanne married saxophonist Charles Brackeen and left the playing scene for a while (they've since split up). "When I got married, making sure my children had a mother during their younger years was what mattered most to me. [She had four in rapid succession.] I still played and wrote music, and that was enough. It wasn't until we moved to New York in 1965 that I began to appear in public again."[19] By 1969 she was in prestigious playing company, securing a job with Art Blakey and the Jazz Messengers. There she remained for three years, the only woman player to hold down a job with the Messengers for any significant period. She landed the position by a bold act of self-assertion: "I heard Blakey's group in a club. The piano player was just sitting there, but he wasn't playing. He didn't know where they were in the tune. So I went up on the bandstand and started playing. After I finished I thought it was pretty strange for me to do this, but that must have been how I got the job."[20]

Brackeen played with saxophonist Joe Henderson's group from 1972 to 1975, when she joined saxophonist Stan Getz. This last job won her growing recognition through increased international exposure in performance and on recordings. Brackeen stayed with Getz's group until 1977 and then began a career as a solo performer with a commitment to playing her own compositions. As a solo artist Brackeen has performed extensively, often appearing with virtuoso bassist Eddie Gomez. She has also recorded frequently and won many awards. An uncompromising individualist, she disturbs some listeners and electrifies others. "It's hard to believe those delicate arms and hands can get that strength out of the piano," observes her manager, Helen Keane. "And she has the kind of courage to do *her* material. The real heavyweights in the music compliment her for this. They say, 'Yes, that's what you *must* do. We need something new, we need variety, we need to be excited by something.' "[21]

One senses in Brackeen an unswerving commitment to patient, long-range nurturance of her art. "It seems to me that everything you do, no matter how you feel about it, is the preparation for what comes later," she has said. "I don't know what it's like *not* to have confidence in what you're doing."[22] Her views on the position of women in jazz today mirror the sentiments of the late Mary Lou Williams, who also responded to questions about women in jazz by stressing the requirements of the music. "If I want a bass player, I want a player at Eddie Gomez's level. What woman can I call?" Brackeen asks.

> If a woman wants to be fine and bother to develop the music . . . it has to be at the same level that men have taken it to. She can't come fifty years later and be fifty years behind—and let me tell you that they *are*—most of them are. You'll hear them playing the notes but you will not hear the feeling, the flow, the maturity, the spirituality, the thing that you hear from the man. It's not because they're women, it's because they haven't developed. . . . They may think that because they have a little of it, they can see further than they can and they actually think they're great. And they are *good*, some of them are very good, but there's no Charlie Parker on the saxophone, there's no Art Blakey on the drums, there's no Stan Getz on the saxophone . . . [23]

Yet Brackeen sees great possibilities for women jazz players in the future: "I think that women want to and will bother to and there are a lot who are on the path if they just get that . . . human spirit. . . . I think that if anybody—a woman or a man—plays and expresses certain qualities of the human spirit, then he or she will be heard and recognized."[24] Her criteria for great jazz playing aim for that rarefied air—thinly populated by either sex—where the musician not only works to develop the highest possible level of technical facility but is also concerned with expressing the reaches of feeling that ultimately separate the technician from the artist.

Among other talented women pianists on the scene today are Nina Sheldon in New York and Jean Cheatham in California. Sheldon was born in California but has been based in New York since the sixties. She studied at the Juilliard School and is a performer, composer, singer and lecturer. After apprenticing with numerous players, including saxophonists Sonny Stitt and George Coleman, she led the house trio at the Village Gate jazz club from 1974 to 1977. Sheldon then formed and led the all-woman combo Aerial (1979–80), and she continues to be a popular performer at East Coast clubs. Her playing is characterized by layers of airy runs built by her right hand while her left hand feeds firm, rhythmic chords. She is also noted for her witty, melodic compositions. Jean Evans Cheatham, with her husband, trombonist James Cheatham, has been based in San Diego since the late seventies. She is an active presence on the local jazz scene, serving as president of the Lower California Jazz Society, conducting weekly jam sessions at local clubs and continuing to compose, arrange and perform in a variety of contexts, including for television and documentary films. Her playing is crisp and swinging, stylistically indebted to such pianists as Count Basie and Teddy Wilson.

Vibraphonist Vera Auer is one of the few women currently active on this instrument. Born in Vienna, Austria, she studied classical music before turning to jazz and the vibes in the fifties. In Europe she worked with such players as guitarist Attila Zoller and pianist Joe Zawinul, recording for several labels. After emigrating to the United States in 1961 and obtaining a scholarship to John Lewis' School of Jazz in Lenox, Massachusetts, she went on to form her own groups and performed on the East Coast with diverse musicians, including trumpeter Ted Curson and pianist Mal Waldron.

Numerous women players other than pianists have also emerged since the sixties. Eclectic in style and philosophy, these women musicians have been growing in number to such an extent, especially since the seventies, that space permits only a selective survey.

Among the group of talented women saxophonists is Jane Ira Bloom, based in New York since 1977 and now in her twenties. Primarily a soprano saxophonist, she began on alto and also plays flute and other reeds, including the nagaswaram, an Indian horn. Bloom is an active free-lancer who has won attention here and abroad for her original concepts as both leader and player. She often works with singer Jay Clayton and her group, and she has produced two albums featuring her own compositions.

Born in Massachusetts, Bloom studied music as a child. After high school she attended the Berklee College of Music, then went to Yale for graduate work in composition and harmony. In New York she continued her studies in harmonics and technique with saxophonist George Coleman. Noted for her clear tone and flowing lines, Bloom explained her evolution in an interview: "I went through a period listening to Charlie Parker and Phil Woods, wanting nothing but to play like them and think as fast as they could. And God, how I tried! But somehow it never came out that way. It just wasn't natural to me. I always go back to Miles [Davis], his way of condensing ideas, getting to the heart of the matter." Her approach to writing music is impressionistic: "When you get dry musically, you look out at other things. I like painting, theater, dancing. I have tunes entitled

'Smog,' 'Shrub,' 'Desert.' These titles are not necessarily descriptive, just gestures and images, translated into music."[25] As to being a woman in jazz, Bloom says:

> As a kid I was oblivious to being a woman jazz player. I was just determined to be as good as I could be. As I got out of the comfortable, non-threatening environment of school, I never encountered the negative vibes in the playing world because such people would never hire me anyway. When I go out to play in New York, I'm just like everybody else: on constant trial because the availability of work is so small.... I want to keep playing and recording: it's as simple as that. It's hard, slow work.... it's happening very slowly and I'm trying to be patient.[26]

Jean Fineberg is another reed player and active free-lancer based in New York. As a child she wanted to play clarinet, but her mother told her it would give her buck teeth, so she took up the flute and later the alto.[27] In her thirties she apprenticed first on the rock and pop scene as a reed player with the all-woman rock band Isis and with Laura Nyro and David Bowie. She then studied jazz technique in the excellent program at the University of Indiana. With trumpeter Ellen Seeling, she formed Deuce, a combo made up of men and women, which often performs in New York clubs with a versatile repertoire of jazz and jazz-rock, much of it original. In 1981 Fineberg was a featured performer at a concert of women instrumentalists at the Kool Jazz Festival.

California-based Fostina Dixon, whose main horn is the baritone saxophone (she also plays alto, flute, clarinet and bass clarinet), sings and leads her own sextet, Collage, in the Los Angeles area. Like Jane Ira Bloom, she is in her twenties and studied at the Berklee College in Boston. In New York for a year (1980–81), she gigged with musicians such as Melba Liston, Slide Hampton and Frank Foster and played in a quartet called Folks with woodwind player Steve Coleman and others. In the late seventies she settled in Los Angeles, where she played in big bands led by Leslie Drayton and Gerald Wilson, free-lanced as a studio musician and put together Collage, which derives its name from the eclectic range of music the group handles— "Blues, straight-ahead four-four, funk and jazz-funk," Dixon enumerates.[28]

As a young black woman playing jazz, Dixon has the following observations on the contemporary jazz scene: "There still is some active discouragement of you if you're a woman—not as much, but psychologically, there is still some." And in her view, the rites of passage into the aggressively competitive "inner circle" of one's male peers can be difficult: "Guys can still try to belittle you, make it seem like you don't have it together. So being a minority, you have to be noticeably better or they're not going to accredit you. If you're an okay player, then you're 'all right for a girl.' So you have to be an exceptional all-round player." Like most of the emerging women, Dixon seeks out playing opportunities in the mainstream, mostly male circles, but she sees the idea of women musicians banding together as positive reinforcement. "We women need to support each other because of the suppression, but to keep in mind that it's only to help us. A lot of the older ladies are hard. They're mentally bitter because they were forced, at a certain point, to become one of the fellows. . . . Today, a lot of times, unless ladies create their own space, they're not gonna be seen."[29]

Another musician who came to attention during the sixties and seventies is trumpeter Barbara Donald, who also sings and plays saxophone, trombone and piano. Donald was born in Minnesota in 1942 and moved to California in 1956. She studied horn and voice in Los Angeles, took to the road at age eighteen with various rock groups and then led her own jazz-oriented groups before settling again in Los Angeles. A fine straight-ahead player with strong technique and a lilting, melodic sound, she was also one of the few women to take an important part, both as a player and on recordings, in the avant-garde or experimental jazz scene in the sixties. During this period she participated in many musical experiments on the East and West Coasts with her then-husband, saxophonist Sonny Simmons. In the seventies, quoting Donald indirectly, Leonard Feather reported, "She's still struggling to become accepted as a woman artist, and fighting this planet's low conception of music."[30] In the eighties Donald lives in Washington, leading her own group Unity, and performing with the Seattle Composers and Improvisers Orchestra.

Trumpeter and flugelhornist Ellen Seeling is a versatile player in her thirties who has been co-leader of the combo Deuce with saxophonist Jean Fineberg since the late seventies. A Wisconsin native, Seeling was the first woman to graduate from the University of Indiana's jazz program in the seventies, taking a master's in music under the direction of David Baker. After gigging with various rock and pop groups, she settled in New York as a free-lancer. Besides her jazz work, she is a Latin player and was part of the all-woman salsa orchestra Latin Fever, with Fineberg and others.

Janice Robinson, another active New York–based player, was born in Pennsylvania in 1951. She achieves a big, full-toned sound on her trombone. Among her many musical credits since the seventies is her work in the Thad Jones–Mel Lewis Orchestra (1974) and in Clark Terry's Big Bad Band and the Gil Evans Orchestra (1976). She was the only female member of the Collective Black Artists Ensemble, serving as leader of its trombone section. In the seventies she also co-led a quintet with Sharon Freeman, a French-horn player, pianist, composer and arranger who has won numerous awards and grants. Robinson now leads her own quintet, which has included such players as bassist Buster Williams and Ron Bridgewater on saxophone. She dismissed the "women's problem" in a 1981 interview: "Some people have told me that I'd never make it as a jazz musician because I'm a woman instrumentalist—a trombonist.... [But] I don't find it harder finding gigs than my male counterparts.... Discipline and hard work doesn't have a gender."[31]

Guitarist Emily Remler hails from New Jersey. By 1981, at the age of twenty-three, she had gone far to establish herself as a versatile free-lancer in New York and was working frequent club dates, often with Brazilian singer Astrud Gilberto. Remler taught herself folk and then rock guitar before studying at the Berklee College in Boston. In her late teens she moved to New Orleans, where she apprenticed with show, rock and jazz bands; with her excellent reading skills, she was much in demand in that city. Eventually she came to the attention of guitarist Herb Ellis, who recommended her for a gig at the Concord Jazz Festival in California. Out of that date came a recording contract with Concord Records, a remarkable achievement for a young player.

The young guitarist and composer Monnette Sudler apprenticed in Philadelphia and New York with saxophonist Byard Lancaster, drummer Sonny Murray, saxophonist Sam Rivers and the Sounds of Liberation Orchestra in the seventies. Her own compositions are featured on records released since the latter part of the decade. In her music Sudler tends to the meditative and reflective, playing in the octaves style first formulated by Wes Montgomery.

Teenage drummer Terri Lyne Carrington already has an impressive résumé as a player, having won praise from such luminaries as the late Roland Kirk, trumpeter Clark Terry and drummers Max Roach and Buddy Rich. Carrington began studying with jazz drummer Keith Copeland at the age of ten. On the basis of a performance with pianist Oscar Peterson in 1976, at age eleven, she was the youngest performer ever to win a scholarship to the Berklee College of Music. Born into a musical family, Carrington was encouraged to switch from alto saxophone to the traps when she lost her front teeth at age seven. In 1978 she said that she didn't want to be "just a drummer" and that she intended to write and arrange as well as play.[32]

Electric bassist Carol Kaye became established in Los Angeles as a successful studio musician in the sixties and seventies. Her father was a trombonist, her mother a pianist. Kaye began guitar lessons at age thirteen, and within a year she had progressed enough to teach guitar herself. As a teenager in the late fifties, she played in various jazz combos in the Los Angeles area, switching to the electric bass in the sixties. During these

Carol Kaye. *(Credit: Marilyn Cross)*

apprentice years, the "chick with a pick," as she was described, worked a day job as a technical typist. She soon established a popular music school and a music publishing company, wrote several widely used books about bass playing and produced a number of records. Kaye went on to do hundreds of studio sessions, playing bass on pop dates and film scores and in many of the orchestras backing Ray Charles. She also continued to work in jazz contexts with pianist Hampton Hawes, drummer Spider Webb (her husband) and trumpeter Clora Bryant. This excellent player, who has been praised for her "full, clear sound and exceptional technique,"[33] moved to Colorado in the eighties. In an interview mid-career, she had this to say about her experience as a studio musician: "They [the male players] did their best to break me, because they don't believe in women, but I proved to them that I could play my instrument. I stuck up for myself, but in a nice way, without destroying the man's ego. Once I established my playing abilities, it was easy. I was no longer a female oddity. I was a musician, commanding $70,000 a year."[34]

Since the sixties interest in the blues has been building, and the vitality of the tradition is once again evident on the contemporary scene. Several blues singers who first emerged after the classic era found newly enthusiastic audiences, and a fresh crop of blues singers arose to carry on where they left off.

One of the greatest of later women blues singers was Big Maybelle Smith (1924–1972). Born in Jackson, Tennessee, she began as a church singer and later toured with a revue that included the International Sweethearts of Rhythm. She also sang with Tiny Bradshaw's orchestra before becoming a solo artist. A superlative blues shouter with a gritty powerhouse of a voice, she made an impact on audiences geared to rock in the sixties. Big Mama Thornton, born in 1925, is another great. In 1939, at the age of fourteen, she went on the road as part of the *Hot Harlem Revue* out of Atlanta, Georgia, as a singer, dancer and comedienne (thus following in the footsteps of Bessie Smith, who began the same way in the teens of the century). Thornton later settled in Houston, Texas. She had her first hit record in 1951 with "Let Your Tears Fall, Baby," toured with the Johnny Otis Show in the fifties and in 1953 was the first to record "Hound Dog," later immortalized by Elvis Presley. In 1980 Thornton participated in a Newport Jazz Festival tribute to blueswomen, sporting a thirties-style double-breasted suit, ten-gallon cowboy hat, cane and harmonica.

At the same concert Chicago blueswoman Koko Taylor appeared with her group, presenting the contemporary electric blues sound of the Windy City. Taylor moved up to Chicago from her native Memphis in the fifties, developing her hard-edged style in the thriving South Side blues scene. Claiming fellow Tennessean Memphis Minnie as an important early inspiration, Taylor recorded her own brand of funky, realistic material in the sixties and has worked steadily since. Like Memphis Minnie, Taylor writes much of her own material, and her songs include paeans to female pride and braggadoccio in a tradition that goes back to the New Orleans voodoo queens. Following in the footsteps of some later New Orleans women, Irma Thomas emerged in the seventies as a notable singer in the tradition of Lizzie Miles and other New Orleans jazz-flavored blues singers. Other contemporary black blueswomen include Georgia-born Carrie Smith, singer-actress Linda Hopkins and Olive Brown, all torchbearers of the Bessie Smith tradition.

Lastly, there is the work of a number of white women singers directly inspired by the blues. Best known is the late Janis Joplin, the Texas-born rock star who paid musical and emotional allegiance to Big Mama Thornton and especially to Bessie Smith. Blues-influenced singer and slide guitarist Bonnie Raitt counts the indefatigable Sippie Wallace among her many influences and often tours with her. Detroit-born Barbara Dane was an active presence in the sixties as a political activist and blues singer; one of her notable compositions is "Working Class Woman." Jean "Jazzie Jeanie" Kittrell, from Birmingham, Alabama, has written blues songs including "I'm a One Man Woman But I Never Found My Man," and Carol Ann Leigh is a noteworthy San Francisco–based blues singer and pianist. Abroad, JoAnn Kelly is a popular British blues singer and guitarist influenced by Memphis Minnie, and Ottilie Patterson is an Irish-born blues stylist.

The jazz singers who emerged in the sixties and seventies followed varied stylistic paths, just as their sister instrumentalists did. In the past twenty-odd years there have been both refinements of existing techniques of improvisatory singing and many new experiments, both acoustically and electronically. Working within the avant-garde (or "free" or "experimental") movement in modern jazz, several singers followed a route that forsook harmony, or changes, as well as the established rhythmic frameworks. Though this experimental music remains a minority movement within jazz, one that delights some listeners and confuses or bores others, advocates of the avant-garde argue that it is simply one more extension of the art of improvising. Certainly, in their search for something new, the experimental vocalists have created an often provocative sound.

One of the best-known vocal experimenters is Jeanne Lee. Born in New York in 1939, she came from a family where music was important. Her father was a classical singer who also sang spirituals, so she was exposed to European and Afro-American music as she grew up. As a teenager Lee sang with a female r&b vocal group and with a band, won an Apollo Theatre amateur talent contest, took piano lessons and played piano in her junior high school band. By the early sixties she was singing with pianist Ran Blake and had signed a record contract with RCA. But the contract was soon dropped; apparently Lee's musical concept was too avant-garde for the corporate music structure.

Lee was undeterred. "Why duplicate what other singers were doing beautifully?" she said recently. "I would like to attain that sense of reality that Abbey Lincoln has. I like Billie Holiday for the same reason. I admire Carmen McRae, Betty Carter and Sarah Vaughan because they are really technically precise—but Abbey and Billie have that added dimension of the humanity coming through the technique."[35] Lee, who has performed with such different stylists as Roland Kirk, Cecil Taylor and John Cage, often utilizes what she calls "sound poems." "The word is your thirty-two bars," she explains. "You state your word and then you start to improvise according to your knowledge, your craft, your feeling, to make emotional musical sense."[36]

What Lee calls "translation of energy" may best explain her approach to music and to sound itself. For her this means "making your own words, making sounds, being a cloud, being a vibration, being a voice, many voices. The [free-form] instrumentalists are doing the same thing—finding new ways of working through their horns."[37] Frequently gigging in Europe with pianist-vibraphonist Gunter Hempel since the seventies, she has employed dance, poetry, film and video in performance, and she often seeks audience participation. When she succeeds in injecting her type of emotional catharsis (what she calls "seeing it through") via an art stripped of artifice, Lee can communicate powerfully and elicit a rare degree of gut response from the listener. A calm, thoughtful figure, she strives to create a music that preserves and articulates psychic needs and dangers at a time when many feel that technology has nearly outdistanced humanistic values. She has long been a student of anthropology and dance, myth and ritual, and has focused on the work of Carl Jung. She tends to vocalize from the bottom of her register but plays upon her whole range, emitting sounds that one can imagine as cries of love or of giving birth or of mourning.

A contemporary of Jeanne Lee is New York–based singer Jay Clayton, active since the sixties both as an experimentalist and as a singer capable of working within traditional jazz settings. Clayton is particularly adept at hornlike lines (as in "Blow Through Your Mind," a recording by the group Unity). "I feel like a horn player," she says. "When I identify as a horn, I want to identify as a musician. There are a lot of musical lines a horn does that I can sing. Miles Davis always sounded vocal to me."[38] Clayton performs frequently as leader of her own group and with other combos on the East Coast.

Other vocal experimentalists on the current scene include Linda Sharrock, Dee Dee Bridgewater and Rita Warford. Sharrock, now in her early thirties, began her studies as an artist, but after taking music theory with Giuseppe Logan she changed direction. She toured with flutist Herbie Mann, worked with Pharaoh Sanders and then teamed musically and maritally with guitarist Sonny Sharrock, working mostly in Europe since 1973. In the eighties Linda Sharrock occasionally records in America. Dee Dee Bridgewater, born in 1950, sang in an experimental vein in the early seventies, showcasing her pliant voice, for example, in a recorded extemporization with bassist Reggie Workman. She joined the Thad Jones–Mel Lewis big band for a stint from 1972 to 1974, after which she developed a career as a pop singer. Chicago-based singer Rita Warford participated in the avant-garde Association for the Advancement of Creative Music in the seventies. She continues to teach and perform in Chicago, and in 1980 she staged a tribute to female jazz vocalists there.

In addition to the avant-garde singers, a number of promising talents have emerged since the sixties to forge personal styles more closely aligned to mainstream jazz. Janet Lawson, based in New York, served a long apprenticeship in the sixties and seventies, gigging with many established players before forming her own quartet at the end of the decade. Her style is geared to a total instrumental vocal approach; like Jay Clayton, she considers the voice another kind of horn. A singer of wide range, Lawson is intensely committed to scat singing and has studied bop harmony with saxophonist Warne Marsh, a Lennie Tristano disciple. A contemporary of Lawson's is Nancy King, born in Eugene, Oregon, in 1940. As a teenager she sang around San Francisco in supper clubs and lounges, worked in Las Vegas, went on the road with what she termed a "sophisticated funk" band and then turned to the challenge of jazz singing. She is a skillful improviser with a husky voice, excellent intonation and bright, trumpetlike phrasing. Carol Fredette is another fine veteran now based in New York. Like King, she spent years on the road as a pop singer in the better supper clubs. With her lovely, supple instrument and instinctive musicality, she is especially outstanding for her treatment of American and Brazilian ballads. Singer Dianne Reeves was born in Denver and is presently based in Los Angeles. Now in her mid-twenties, she combines studio work in California with a job as vocalist in a jazz-rock band. Clark Terry featured Reeves as his band vocalist at the 1979 Wichita Jazz Festival, and she appeared at the 1980

Women's Jazz Festival, where her range, powerful emotive ability and versatility led many listeners to predict an important future for her as a jazz singer.

A number of foreign-born improvising singers have developed their talents since the sixties, among them Briton Norma Winstone, who works in free-form as well as more traditional jazz contexts. A popular presence on the European jazz scene, she cites as major influences Frank Sinatra, Ella

Dianne Reeves. *(Credit: Marilyn Cross)*

Fitzgerald and Carmen McRae. Winstone has worked with the Edge of Time group and frequently since 1977 with Azimuth, which includes her husband, John Taylor, and trumpeter Kenny Wheeler. Urszula Dudziak, born in Poland in 1943, came to the United States in 1974 with husband Michal Urbaniak, an electric violinist with whom she had been performing since the mid-sixties. Dudziak makes use of electronic devices such as the echoplex and ring modulator for percussive, nonverbal vocal effects. Her singing can scrape the stratosphere, yet she manages to keep a clean, clear execution and excellent intonation in her ethereal excursions. She has won a substantial audience in America.

Several Brazilian improvisers have established themselves here since the sixties, and one of the most popular is Flora Purim, born in 1942. Purim moved to New York in 1967 with husband Airto, the percussionist, and was heard with Stan Getz's group as his featured singer in 1968. She later worked with Gil Evans' band (1971) and joined pianist Chick Corea's Return to Forever for a time, gaining a wide popular audience. Her soaring, wordless vocalise, based on a sensual Brazilian delivery and often utilizing the echoplex, is one example of the fusion of Brazilian popular music with American jazz and rock. Singer, pianist and composer Tania Maria represents another outstanding blending of Brazilian music with American jazz. Born in 1948, she studied classical piano as a child but became interested in popular music as a teenager. After studying to be a lawyer, she opted for a career in music in 1970 and made several records in Brazil. But, she pointed out, "I was a woman in a macho culture. A woman is supposed to serve a man, not do something he can do."[39] In 1974 she moved to Paris, where she headlined a Brazilian club and made several more albums. Her American recording debut came in 1981. A fresh, unique stylist with a cascading flow of melodic invention, Tania Maria improvises piano lines in unison with her wordless vocals—double-barreled scatting with strong rhythmic and melodic appeal. Another exciting Brazilian improviser is Angela Soares, a young singer who began working in Rio de Janeiro nightclubs in her mid-teens and moved to New York in the late seventies. An exuberant performer in the melodic-percussive Brazilian vein, she has been influenced by Sarah Vaughan and by her late compatriot Elis Regina.

All-female combinations playing all types of music have flourished for at least the last century in America, and it should come as no surprise that the resurgent feminism of the last decade has given rise to a whole new crop of all-female or predominantly female jazz units. Among the better "lab" bands to come out of colleges, for example, is the Yes M.A.A.M. (Musicians Ain't Always Men) big band from North Texas State University, with seventeen women and four men. In 1976 trumpeter Clark Terry put together his All-Girl Big Band for the Wichita Jazz Festival, and the Los Angeles–based big band Maiden Voyage (see the profile of bandleader Ann Patterson in Part Five) has been playing to enthusiastic audiences since the late seventies. In New York in 1982, saxophonist Kit McClure put a fifteen-piece all-woman band under her name. The band features original jazz-rock fusion as well as traditional swing arrangements.

A number of these recent all-woman groups originated on the East Coast. In the seventies gospel-style vocalist Evelyn Blakey, daughter of drummer Art Blakey, led an all-female group called Celebration, which included the talented drummer Paula Hampton among its members. Another New York–based unit active in the late seventies was the Jazz Sisters, led by pianist Jill McManus, with Janice Robinson on trombone, Lynn Milano on bass, Jean Davis on trumpet, Willene Barton on tenor sax and Paula Hampton on drums. The Sisters played jazz, jazz-rock and blues material in East Coast clubs. Aerial, a quintet led by pianist Nina Sheldon, with Carline Ray on bass, Barbara Merjan on drums, Barbara London on flute and Jane Ira Bloom on reeds, was featured at the Women's Jazz Festival in 1979 and was the first all-woman group to appear at the Newport Jazz Festival, that same year. Melba Liston and Company, led by the noted trombonist-arranger, began as an all-woman septet in the late seventies, providing exposure for a number of women players, including Carline Ray, Janice Robinson, Dottie Dodgion on drums and Erica Lindsay on tenor sax (see the profiles of Liston and Dodgion in Part Five). Liston's group became a mixed ensemble in 1981. New York also boasted an all-woman salsa orchestra, Latin Fever, which included Jean Fineberg on reeds, Ellen Seeling on trumpet and Nydia "Liberty" Mata on percussion.

Elsewhere in the country, numerous groups featuring women have formed since the seventies. These include Airhart in Missouri, Second Hand Rose in Ithaca, New York, Bougainvillea in Boston, and Thornebird, led by trumpeter Edwina Thorne, also in Boston. Sojourner is an ensemble of black women players out of Chicago and Detroit. In 1981 its personnel included leader Shanta Nurullah on sitar and bass; Elretta Dodds on clarinet, bass clarinet and tenor sax; Aisha Hill on congas; Gerry Moore on drums; Kari Patrice Nessoma on flute and harp; Chavunduka Sevanhu on percussion and vocals; Rita Warford on vocals and percussion; and Sherri Weathersby on bass and percussion. The five-piece group Quintess and the sextet Satin Dolls play mainstream jazz in Los Angeles, while the San Francisco area boasts several all-woman groups, including a combo led by pianist Mary Watkins. In Europe the avant-garde eight-piece Feminist Improvising Group features free-form pianist Irene Schweizer, and in Sweden there is

Melba Liston. *(Credit: Marilyn Cross)*

Salamander, an avant-garde quintet featuring female saxophonists and pianist.

One group that has attracted a good deal of attention in the feminist community and among many jazz listeners is the West Coast–based ensemble Alive!, consisting of classically trained bassist and cellist Suzanne Vincenza, percussionist Carolyn Brandy (who uses congas and a variety of other percussive instruments), drummer Barbara Borden, pianist Janet Small, vocalist rhiannon (spelled with a small *r*) and manager Barbara Edwards. Functioning as a leaderless collective, Alive! presents jazz-influenced music with a strong Latin rhythm component. The group communicates its feminist-humanist philosophy in original compositions and in its relaxed, warm manner. Its music, which features individual soloing in a jazz context, draws on eclectic sources. The song "City Life" mirrors the harshly abrasive, fast-moving urban reality; "There's No Separation," a piece written by former Alive! pianist Julie Homi, is a mature love song; the group's interpretation of "Wild Women Don't Have the Blues," as sung by rhiannon, transforms Ida Cox's song into liberated woman's rallying cry; and in "Spirit Healer" they exhort their hearers to find their own strength.

In performance Alive! can have a powerful effect on their audience. "There's a spiritual thing that happens," says Carolyn Brandy. "We are very honest about that: there is a definite connection. More often than not we leave people on their feet, applauding, full of joy." Adds rhiannon, "We are really shooting at a pretty broad audience. Women, for sure, but our music is for jazz audiences, too. Maybe a good way to put it is it's for the 'alternative culture' audience."[40] Collectivist, feminist, serious about the music—these commitments, increasingly evident in groups formed by women like the members of Alive!, present interesting possibilities for change in the jazz world of the future.

Chapter Ten

BUILDING A SUPPORT SYSTEM

*My mother took me to the Apollo Theatre to see
the Sweethearts of Rhythm, and I thought, "Oh,
boy, those girls can do it—I can too."*
WILLENE BARTON, TENOR SAXOPHONIST

In recent years activities aimed at retrieving the history of women's
participation in all types of music in all eras have increased markedly, so that
in the eighties there are a variety of scholarly and musical organizations that
publish books and articles, hold conferences and solidify support systems for
women musicians and researchers. Both here and abroad, conferences and
music festivals have been organized since the seventies to feature women
performers. Among the most popular is the Michigan Women's Music
Festival, held each August in Hesperia. Several contemporary jazzwomen
have participated in that festival's broad offering of music by women,
including pianist Julie Homi, the combo Deuce and pianist Mary Watkins.
Regionally based festivals have been mounted in the San Francisco area and
the Midwest. Chicago's week-long Bessie to Billie to Now Festival in April
1981 presented a nonet called Black Women Make Music, singer Flora Purim
with percussionist Airto, a group of jazzwomen playing traditional New
Orleans ensemble jazz, and tributes to Chicago blueswomen featuring Edith
Wilson and Mama Yancey. In Europe the 1979 Festival of Women in Music
held in Rome, Italy, featured many American and European jazzwomen.

In New York the Universal Jazz Coalition (UJC), directed by jazz and arts administrator Cobi Narita, has sponsored and showcased women in jazz since the late seventies at numerous workshops, lectures, tributes and jam sessions. The New York Women's Jazz Festival, now an annual event with scores of well-attended musical happenings, began as the Universal Jazz Coalition Salute to Women. Its purpose, Narita explained, was simple:

> I had always felt that women jazz musicians did not get the attention as artists that they should. Club owners will always pick a male leader for a band. And the male leader, with an opportunity to choose among equally qualified musicians, will pick men rather than women. I felt that women needed something like that Kansas City festival [the Women's Jazz Festival] in New York to give them an opportunity to show that they can play.[1]

The UJC also mounted an important concert in tribute to the recently deceased Mary Lou Williams in June 1981. Many of the arrangements Williams had written since the thirties for the big bands of Count Basie, Jimmie Lunceford, Andy Kirk and others were performed by a big band under trombonist-arranger Melba Liston, and some of Williams' compositions were interpreted by pianists Barbara Carroll, Hazel Scott and Rose Murphy. There were also excerpts from a documentary on Williams by filmmaker Joanne Burke. The Universal Jazz Coalition continues to offer year-round concerts and workshops for women singers and players, also serving as a valuable link between players and the public.

Among other noteworthy activities are events promoted by women's music historian Cathy Lee in Boston at the nonprofit loft workspace called Studio Red Top. Lee's purpose is "to promote appreciation of the enduring contributions women have made to jazz business and art, both presently and historically."[2] Since the seventies Studio Red Top has been a center for workshops, music-appreciation classes and programs on women in jazz. One such event featured producers Rosetta Reitz and Geri Hamlin on "Self-Producing a Record Album" and also included Reitz's film and lecture presentation "Mean Mothers: Independent Women's Blues." Through her extensive studies of pioneering singers in blues and jazz, Reitz attempts to encourage a fresh view of these great female artists, as heroic foremothers rather than as passive victims of the inferior status of their sex. Her approach has led some jazz and blues writers to criticize her as a revisionist historian who brushes over the inescapable facts of powerlessness in the blueswomen's lives, but Reitz has succeeded in revealing and making accessible these performers' defiant, independent side through reissues of their recordings on her Rosetta Records, and at several Kool Jazz Festival concerts. Reitz is one of several writers and researchers to publicize women in jazz. Among others who deserve credit are Cathy Lee, D. Antoinette Handy, Marian McPartland, Frank Driggs, Chris Albertson, Derrick Stewart-Baxter, Leonard Feather, Pauline Rivelli, Ann Charters, Harriet Janis, Helen Oakley Dance, Hettie Jones, Caroline Johnson, Sally Placksin, and disc jockeys Audry Wells in the Bay area and Ruth Royal in Kansas City. British photojournalist Valerie Wilmer and American photographers Deborah Feingold and Marilyn Cross have provided visual documentation, and fashion photographer Barbara Bordnick produced a stunning series of color portraits of several women jazz performers for *American Photographer* (September 1978). And the list of woman writers, photographers, etc., has kept right on growing.

Historically, very few women have been involved in a significant way in the business aspect of jazz music. In the thirties Helen Oakley, who later married swing writer Stanley Dance, was hired as a record producer by entrepreneur Irving Mills for his Variety Records. At Brunswick-ABC she oversaw production of small-band jazz dates for such players as Johnny Hodges, Chu Berry and other Ellingtonians. Bess Berman was a co-owner of Apollo Records in the forties, and Harriet Janis co-produced traditional blues and jazz for Circle Records. Elaine Lorillard was one of the prime movers and original producers of the Newport Jazz Festival back in 1954. More recently, however, an increasing number of women have turned their attention to the business end of jazz. Several established their own labels, among them Victoria Spivey (Spivey/Queen Vee Records) in the sixties and Rosetta Reitz (Rosetta Records) in the seventies, and there is an increasing trend for artists to produce their own records (Carla Bley, Toshiko Akiyoshi and Betty Carter, for example). Maxcene Adams is executive director of the Wichita Jazz Festival in Kansas each year; Ann Sneed produces concerts here and abroad; Harriet Choice is a Chicago producer who mounted a concert of blues and jazz performers from that city at the 1981 Kool Jazz Festival. Ethnomusicologist Verna Gillis manages and produces a diverse selection of contemporary music at Soundscape, a New York club. In 1968 Helen Keane collaborated with producer Claude Nobs on the first Montreux Jazz Festival, which featured pianist Bill Evans. Keane is now a top-ranked manager and record producer (see the Helen Keane profile in Part Five). Other women managers include Martha Glaser, who served the late pianist Erroll Garner for many years; Maxine Gregg, whose roster includes saxophonist Dexter Gordon and trumpeter Woody Shaw; Barbara Laurence, a manager and publicist of solid reputation in New York; and Laraine Goodman in Berkeley, who currently concentrates on the promotion and management of women jazz performers.

The parent organization for women in jazz is the nonprofit Women's Jazz Festival, Inc. (WJF), out of Kansas City, Missouri, which has held annual concerts, workshops, jam sessions and lectures every March since 1978, attracting hundreds of players—well-known, emerging and totally unknown musicians from around the country, Canada and abroad. Festival co-producers Carol Comer and Dianne Gregg described the purpose of the festival in a 1979 interview: "Women who are still intimidated by the macho, hairy-chested male with his open shirt and his saxophone, with having to compete with that—philosophically and politically as well as musically—can look up other women and get together with them to play. They can start that way and build support and confidence: *then* they can go out."[3] The festival's *National Directory of Female Jazz Performers*, published yearly, lists by state the names, addresses and professional résumés of women performers to facilitate network building (in New York, the Universal Jazz Coalition publishes a directory of women performers for that city).

The Kansas City organization seeks out emerging young players through scholarship and combo contests, and its concerts feature unknowns as well as stars. In 1979 I watched a seemingly endless stream of aspiring women players mount one of three stages set aside for continuous jam sessions in the mall of the Kansas City Crown Center Hotel, the festival headquarters. There were women of every size, shape, color and age group, and a goodly number of men. One enthusiast, a fiftyish black female tenor player from a small town in Texas, told me she had heard about the festival from friends and decided to make her way north by Greyhound to check it out. She eventually got her chance and played a rousing blues in the hard-edged Texas r&b style. Among the well-known women who have participated in previous festivals are Carla Bley and her band, the Toshiko Akiyoshi–Lew Tabackin big band, and pianists Joanne Brackeen, Marian McPartland and Mary Lou Williams, who performed her *Mary Lou's Mass* at a Kansas City church. Vocalists Betty Carter, Urszula Dudziak, Flora Purim, Ernestine Anderson, Carmen McRae, Janet Lawson and Cleo Laine have concertized at the festival, as have organist Shirley Scott, bassist Carol Kaye, trombonist Melba Liston and the all-woman Maiden Voyage big band.

According to Dianne Gregg, this important organization came about as a fluke inspiration, the product of idle conversation with WJF co-founder Carol Comer.

We were driving back from the Wichita Jazz Festival on the Kansas Turnpike, which is very long and very boring, discussing the festival. We felt very badly that Kansas City, one of the homes of jazz, did not have a festival comparable in stature to the Wichita festival. And Carol was saying, "You know, there were no women featured at the festival this year. And really not to any extent before that." We felt very badly about that, both being involved with the music in different

ways [Comer as a vocalist and journalist, Gregg as a disc jockey]. So
we were lamenting the fact that there were no women featured, and
wasn't that a shame and how come there never are anyhow. And we
started talking about the other jazz festivals in the world and how they
very rarely featured women. So Carol said, "I have a really radical
idea—why don't *we* have a women's jazz festival?"

"We both laughed," Comer added.[4]

In the jazz world at large, such an idea *was* long in coming: not until
1981, for example, was there a concert showcasing women players at the Kool
(formerly Newport) Jazz Festival. Reportedly pianist Marian McPartland
approached festival producer George Wein about such a concert in 1975, but
he turned the idea down. By 1980, however, the climate had changed enough
so that Rosetta Reitz's concert featuring women in blues could be mounted.
Reitz co-produced "The Blues Is a Woman" at Newport in 1980 and again at
Kool in 1981, when she also co-produced "Women Blow Their Own Horns."
In 1982, singer Sylvia Sims mounted a Kool Jazz tribute to women
songwriters. In large measure, the successful reception of Comer and Gregg's
brainchild paved the way for such later activities.

"Oh, the idea of a women's jazz festival was funny," continued Gregg.
"We chuckled about that for a long time—several times. But the turnpike's
long and *very* boring. By the time we got close to Kansas City, we thought it
wasn't a radical idea at all—it was a good idea. So we said, 'Let's do it.' "[5] The
seed that sprouted that night grew remarkably fast. Local jazz fans joined
with Comer and Gregg and began fund-raising efforts; the National
Endowment for the Arts came through with a generous grant; the media
provided extensive coverage; and musicians, notably Marian McPartland,
received the idea enthusiastically.

As a clearinghouse for the promotion of women in jazz, the festival also
provides an opportunity for diverse groups to meet and exchange ideas each
year. As Comer sees it, the WJF brings together "feminists who don't know
much about jazz and who come together because it's a women's jazz festival,
and the jazz fans—they learn about the women in jazz. They're coming from
two different sides and they meet us in the middle."[6] Perhaps most
important, the festival is a forum for aspiring jazzwomen and holds out the
promise of a better future. As Dianne Gregg says, "You have to create a
market for these women musicians first. You have to prove yourself first.
Then come the goodies, the recording contracts." And in Comer's words:

You're building your audience for the future, you're giving role
models, and you're generating respect for women. There are aspiring
young female instrumentalists out there now who heretofore have not

had any role models. A trombone player who says, "I want to play like Bill Watrous" now can say "Janice Robinson" or "Melba Liston," for crying out loud. And that's so important.

We always say that one of our main goals is that we want to become obsolete. We *want* to go out of business! Ultimately, women should be just as integral a part of the jazz music scene as they are becoming in any other field or occupation. It may take a hundred years before that's a reality, but women *are* as good—and as bad—as men. So the sooner we can go out of business the better. Then we'll just do a jazz festival.[7]

Despite lingering prejudices, the growing number of talented women pursuing careers in jazz bodes well for the integration of women into the mainstream of the music on all fronts. Meanwhile the array of activities promoting their participation is so lively and diverse that we can enjoy the journey almost as much as the destination.

Part Five

PROFILES

In the following pages, profiles of ten women involved in jazz emerge from interviews and biographical research. I wanted to let women players, singers, composers, bandleaders and, in one case, an artists' manager and record producer, speak for themselves. Besides the obvious differences among these jazzwomen—differences of age, race, experience and education—I hope the individualism that jazz encourages has been clearly distilled as well. Their opinions are their own, and often vary widely, as you'll see. One or two uncomfortable "home truths" emerge, as do some controversial notions about women—and men. The interviews took place on the dates given below.

Willene Barton   *May 18, 1981*

Carla Bley   *August 14, 1979*

Clora Bryant   *March 11, 1981*

Dottie Dodgion   *November 16, 1980*

Helen Humes   *October 24, 1980*

Sheila Jordan   *November 28, 1980*

Helen Keane   *May 8, 1981*

Melba Liston   *July 4, 1979*

Mary Osborne   *March 15, 1981*

Ann Patterson   *March 4, 1979*

WILLENE BARTON

Tenor Saxophonist

"They say I play gruff—you know, hard. Well, that's how the men played. Now you see women play hard too. With these women now, how would you tell the difference about if it's a woman or a man, with somebody like that who can play so hard?"

When Willene Barton appeared onstage at a concert one evening in the spring of 1981, the lone "lady sax player" evoked strong disapproval from at least one male member of the audience, seated immediately behind me. "Women ain't supposed to play no horn!" he huffed loudly; there was a nervous titter from some who heard him. Barton raised her horn to her lips and, unperturbed, strolled into one of her favorite songs. She built "Pennies from Heaven" from a slow walk to a rousing, near-ecstatic climax in the carefully constructed manner of the swing-style tenor player, urging her ideas on with dipping and swaying movements of her instrument. And there were no more complaints from the audience.

More common at a Barton performance is a kind of family pride, for many of her contemporaries (she is in her fifties but won't divulge her exact age) who have listened to her since the 1940s in clubs around the boroughs of New York are often in attendance. "She bought her mama a house with that horn," confided an older man during the Women Blow Their Own Horns concert at the Kool Jazz Festival on July 4, 1981. Nearby another listener, a young woman who said she was studying the baritone sax, showed interested bystanders a copy of Barton's sole album to date, *The Feminine Sax*. "My daddy told me to be sure and get Willene's autograph on it," she said.

Willene Barton was born in Georgia, and her interest in music was sparked there. "I came to New York when I was ten, but when I was a kid in Georgia, I had seen somebody teach himself how to play, and that influenced me to learn. At that time, remember, all the bands were either made or broken by the tenor player. It was all saxophone players. You had a *lot* of them. In my family I had an uncle who played—clarinet. But my mother thought, 'Well, it's nice you can play, but why don't you go get yourself a job?' " Barton's face widens in a grin. "Later on, when I first went on the road with Anna Mae Winburn and I was getting ninety dollars a week, my mother, who was making about forty dollars a week, kind of changed about *that*."

Barton was largely self-taught on her instrument. As she describes it, "I didn't go to any conservatory or anything like that. When I came out of high school—Manhattan High—I studied with some people privately. And then I came into the city and studied with a man named Walter Thomas. I also had some help from Eddie Durham. He had an all-girl group called the Darlings of Rhythm and spent a lot of time with women musicians. So he took me under his wing, and I used to follow him around and watch him work."

While still in high school, the budding saxophonist had gone to several concerts that significantly strengthened her desire to play. "At that time the Sweethearts of Rhythm were going, and my mother took me to the Apollo Theatre to see them several times. And I was star-struck. I thought, 'Oh, boy, those girls can do it—I can too.' " Indeed, her role model was a tenor player she could immediately identify with. "When I visited Harlem and saw these girls play, I just couldn't get over that. The one in particular who was extraordinarily good was Vi Burnside [featured soloist with the Sweethearts]. She opened the door for the rest of us. When I saw Vi, I said, 'Well, that was just great.' Let me tell you, she shook the place *up!*" Barton was also impressed by a woman named Peggy Becheers. "She was with the Sweethearts of Rhythm and is one of the finest tenor players I ever heard, male or female. She was the lead tenor player and later the second tenor, or solo player. She never had much to say to anybody, but she always called me 'Youngblood.' Some years later I saw her in California, and she told me in this funny way she had, 'You just keep on playin', just *keep on playin'!*

"I guess about three years after I saw the Sweethearts [circa 1948] somebody had me go to the Apollo Theatre and meet the band's director, Maurice King. He auditioned me for the band at the Theresa Hotel. And he said to me, 'You're not ready now, but you *will* be, and someday you're going to be exceptionally good.' "

Although Willene Barton never played with the International Sweethearts of Rhythm per se—the band had broken up by the time she started her professional career—she did play with many ex-Sweetheart members in new combinations. "In 1951 I started off, and by 1952 I got a real nice job with Anna Mae Winburn [former Sweethearts leader]. She formed her own group that year which was a twelve-piece band for a particular show tour, a revue that starred Peg Leg Bates, with dancers and the whole thing. I played fourth tenor. The second tenor did all the solo work, of course, but I got to solo a bit."

The fact that Winburn's unit consisted entirely of women was a big selling point. "You never had to be without a job when these women's bands were going. And you see, when I was coming up there weren't *that* many women players, so they'd say, 'Well, she doesn't know much, but we'll take her.' For example, in the early fifties I had no experience playing nightclubs. I hadn't even figured out what to do with the blues or what to do with something with thirty-two bars. Everything was wrong! But as bad as I was musically, what I did *sold*, which is why they kept me in the band. Whatever I did, it went over big with the people, as wrong as it was. And what's so difficult today for a lot of musicians, male and female, is that they have no place like that to learn. I was on the road for months and months at a time, which meant I played every single night. And I was in a band with true professionals who could turn me on to what was right and what was wrong, and they did."

Still young and green, Barton soon encountered the test of mettle that lies at the heart of jazz playing: the "cutting contest." It is the classic confrontation, where the new bids to replace the old, where an experienced player faces a novice onstage and demonstrates in front of an audience the standards the inexperienced player must master to become a peer. The cutting contest is generally thought of as a quintessentially male event, but as Barton unfolds her story, it becomes part of women's jazz history too.

"After the Sweethearts broke up, every manager, everybody in New York, was after Vi Burnside, so she easily got herself a group and traveled all over. I have never seen a woman command that much attention as far as a horn is concerned. I mean, she showed up in every big city in America. She made her debut at a club called the Baby Grand in Harlem, and I understand that you couldn't get near the door. It was like that at every club she went to with her band. Well, this particular time she was in Cleveland, and she was *queen* of the show, of course. In those days everybody came to see what the tenor player was made of. So then I came into town with Anna Mae and a smaller group she had broken down after the tour we made. We had trumpet, tenor, rhythm and Anna Mae herself on vocals. And everybody in town said to me, 'Oh, you gotta play with Vi Burnside.'

"I think it was the first weekend we were there that she came down to our club, the Ebony Lounge. And the place was packed. Now, I had a brand-new instrument, all pretty and shiny. So Vi asked if she could borrow my horn. I said sure. And she got up there and she turned the place *out*. She played every note that was supposed to be in everything! So I knew that that was it. The next week I went over to see her at *her* club, a place called Gleason's. When the people saw me, they demanded that *I* play, so she gave me *her* horn. And when I left there they put so much money in the bell of that saxophone! I'll never forget it. I had a bell full of money and a chicken dinner!"

But the battle was by no means over, as Barton knew. "I wasn't near ready, and she used to always refer to me as 'that little child.' It wasn't 'til years later. By then she lived in Washington, where she was a musicians' union delegate, and my group had a job in Annapolis, Maryland. She came down to the club—the big queen. Now, that time I was ready for her, and we settled *that* little score!"

In 1953 Barton and Myrtle Young, former Sweethearts tenor saxophonist, left Winburn to form their own unit, which they co-led until 1955. Barton then formed her own group called the Four Jewels. "That band was very successful," she recalls. "Bu Pleasant was on piano, and Gloria Coleman, who at that time was Gloria Bell, was on bass. I had met Bu in Cleveland, where she was playing with Arnette Cobb at the time. That was something—a young girl playing piano like that with an all-male band."

Barton's friendship with fellow tenor player Eddie "Lockjaw" Davis flourished during this period. "We're good friends. He used to be my agent one time, when he got disgusted with the music business for a while and decided he was gonna try to be an agent. So he booked me on a few jobs. I got to know him very well when he was with [organist] Shirley Scott. I was with the Four Jewels then, and we used to play the same circuit, the same clubs, so we'd always see each other. When Eddie would play, I used to go to the club with the intention of just sitting for one set and end up sitting all night. I like his sound."

Barton knew many of the great tenor saxophonists of jazz. "I got a chance to play with Ben Webster, Illinois Jacquet, Sonny Stitt and the man with the big sound, Gene Ammons. I would sit in with them, or they would sit in with my group. I met everybody except for Coleman Hawkins. One time in Chicago, both Sonny Stitt and Ben Webster were there. After the gig we all went up to Ben Webster's room and talked for a while. And I was surprised how shy he was, a very quiet kind of man. Later on he moved to Queens, and he came into a club I was working and used to sit in with us. One time a young horn player came in, to cut Ben, you know. And even though Ben was a little—under the weather, you might say—he proceeded to straighten that guy *out*. Later on, when we were packing up, I said to him, 'Ben, I sure hope you never do that to me.' He looked at me and said, 'I wouldn't do that to you, sugar.' "

A series of other New York–based groups, all of which worked steadily, followed the Four Jewels in the late fifties. "I formed another group of my own in 1956 and—this is the kick—they were all men. We played uptown at a little club called Connie's, right across the street from Small's Paradise. It was a real hole-in-the-wall kind of place, but all the musicians came in there. You see, there wasn't much going on downtown then, so all the musicians would drop in. With that group was George Tucker on bass and Gildo Mahones, who was a brilliant arranger, on piano.

"After that I hooked up with Dayton Selby, a fine organist, and we were together intermittently for about six years. Then I went with Melba Liston for a few months when she had an all-girl group [see Melba Liston profile], and she took that group to Bermuda. Finally, in 1959, I formed a group with a friend of mine named Elsie Smith, a tenor player. I met her when she was with Lionel Hampton's band. Then she got married and moved out here to Queens, so we decided to get ourselves a group. We used to rehearse all the time—it was the wildest group you ever heard!'' That group stayed together until the end of 1960.

But the sixties, when the always precarious business of jazz nearly toppled under the onslaught of rock and soul, forced Willene Barton to take a new direction in her career. "It got so bad in the sixties some kids didn't even know what the tenor saxophone was. They would ask me, 'Lady, what's that?' All they knew was the guitar." Barton's usually pleasant voice takes on a tired new tone. "I just dropped out. I got tired of leading a band, 'cause to afford a certain type of musician you have to be making a certain kind of money. So I couldn't afford the kind of musicians I needed, and there weren't too many of them around. Some of them had gotten out of the business." Barton herself took a day job, continuing to play her music only at occasional gigs in the New York area.

Barton has always been known and admired in the East Coast black musical network and among some white jazz fans, but like many black female musicians of her age group, she has seldom received adequate press coverage and professional management. "I always had managers who were more concerned with their little ten percent or whatever rather than with promotion," she says, but she is philosophical about her lack of "big breaks." Happily the eighties have witnessed a renewal in her career. "Recently, in 1980, Cobi Narita [director of the Universal Jazz Coalition, which sponsors many concerts featuring jazzwomen] came to me and said, 'Now, listen, you've stood behind somebody long enough. This time you're gonna do your own thing, you're gonna front your own band.' And she organized the people and we rehearsed, and when we played the response was overwhelming to me. I was surprised! We were playing for people who really came to hear jazz—the real jazz people, you can't fool 'em. So to get that kind of response from people like that is really overwhelming."

Willene Barton continues to find excitement in playing jazz, not only because of the thrill of building a dramatic musical statement, but because of the competition. "I keep telling these youngsters—some of them are kind of cocky, you know—'Listen, some of these older players may sound a little old-fashioned to you, but don't make a mistake and get up there on the bandstand with them, 'cause you don't have the experience they do.' I'll tell you, the main thing is not to have anybody make you get off the stage." She laughs a laugh deep with memory. "The Lord knows, with me it's been tried many times."

CARLA BLEY

Composer, Bandleader, Pianist

"I don't want any handicaps given to me. I've never been nurtured, and I wouldn't want to be."

A lean, stylishly slouched woman with a pale, planed Scandinavian face and frizzed caramel-colored hair prowls the stage in performance with her ten- to twelve-piece band. Like a mock-manic Groucho Marx imitating Frank Zappa, she throws her hands upward in seeming despair at the mess of music she hears, sings "Boo to you, too" at the audience and points a long, dramatic arm at the bandmembers as she directs their collective efforts. This is Carla Bley the entertainer, lover of the irreverent, the corny, the belly laugh. In this guise she'll pretend all sorts of outlandishness—that the band is a stuck record, perhaps, playing over and over in the same groove until the *pfft!* of the release. The jokes extend beyond the performances to the titles of her tunes, which often reflect her brand of humor ("Reactionary Tango," Latin American mock-romanticism on the album *Social Studies,* for example); visual chuckles include album covers like *Dinner Music,* which features Bley withdrawing a baked record from an oven.

But the humor, whether satirical or broad, is just one side of Bley's musical personality. Increasingly well-known and respected, Carla Bley is a largely self-taught bohemian who has managed to construct what comes close to being a musical kingdom. Not only is she an esteemed composer who steadily places high in the polls, she is Bley the bandleader, Bley the spare-playing pianist, wailing organist and occasional experimenter on diverse other instruments, Bley the co-producer of WATT Records, co-director of New Music Distribution Service, co-owner of a recording studio. Though some writers have dubbed her "empress of the new music" or "first lady of avant-garde jazz," she herself doesn't like to be called a jazz musician. Her works are culled from such varied musical sources as Kurt Weill, American minstrelsy, Duke Ellington, British music-hall numbers, Latin American music, the blues, and rock 'n' roll. Her band, stocked with fine soloists, is supple, precise, fresh-sounding. Carla Bley defies labels, cleverly confounding those who try to categorize her or her music. Her inventive powers also spill over into the area of her personal history; her past, as related in dozens of interviews and articles, is studded with ambiguities, inconsistencies, fabrications, and being "caught out" seems only to inspire her to greater storytelling efforts. As she told one interviewer, "I like to lie, it's so creative. I like to make mistakes, it makes me think up ways to correct them" (Howard Mandel, "Carla Bley: Independent Ringleader," *Down Beat,* June 1, 1978). Her skill in promoting freshly woven tales also makes for delightful music, full of contradictions. Slapstick entwines with lyric grace.

Having been entertained and impressed by Bley's music for some time, I looked forward to meeting the woman behind it. We scheduled an interview at her office in a large loft in Manhattan where New Music, the distribution service conceived by Bley and her husband, Vienna-born Michael Mantler, busily packages and ships all manner of music (including a record of whales in conversation). Carla Bley greets me with a long pipe clenched in her teeth and a tall glass of liquid refreshment. Interviews, she says right away, make her nervous; a bottle of gin stands by to soothe. Throughout the afternoon she resorts liberally to the pipe, drink and phone at her desk, using them like stage props.

Some interviewers and critics have called Bley an "enfant terrible," an epithet that seems to bother her not a bit; she often uses the word "outrageous" in describing herself and her band. She is an entertainer who loves the absurd but is dead serious about her music—not always an easy synthesis. She loves new-wave and punk bands—"I heard a band last Saturday night, a band of nobodies in Woodstock. They're all under nineteen. I like that," she told me—and she even did a brief stint as "Penny Cillin" with a punk-rock band called the Burning Sensation. But her taste for the outré and the camp is often at odds with her drive to compose according to her other voices—graceful, witty music alongside the more deliberately heavy-handed efforts—and with her desire to be given credence by the serious musical establishment. A good example of this ambivalence is her composition "Copyright Royalties," on *Social Studies:* it's both a takeoff on and a tribute to Duke Ellington's "Mood Indigo."

Though her projects and ideas enliven her and bring an easy flow of conversation, Bley balks at talking about herself. "I'm pretty tired of my childhood," she says. "I'd rather talk about my hundred-and-three-year-old grandmother. That's what interests me today. You know, she almost died a little while ago, and when she discovered she was still among the living, she got very excited about the whole experience." Long pause. "*Her* childhood," she continues in a low voice, "is much more interesting than mine. She was raised in a shoebox. That's the only bed she had. And she was sold as a slave when she was eight. There's all kinds of slaves. This was in Sweden: if you didn't have the money to raise your children, why, you sold them. In her case she was sold to a pastor. Later she worked in a gunnysack factory. She's got clarity. She's got a clarity—from being a freak."

I attempt to steer the conversation back to Carla Bley, but she responds, "What's interesting about a person without problems?" Indeed, Bley's life at present does seem miraculously unencumbered by the blemishes and struggles that are so often part and parcel of the jazz life. This free spirit appears to have things in remarkable order. Her marital and musical partnership with second husband Mantler seems serene, unlike her previous marriage, to pianist Paul Bley. "He helps me with my projects and I help him with his, so I devote almost half my time to his records and his bands. It's really unusual to find a person who can make it without another person." And there is her teenage daughter, Karen Mantler. "She takes care of herself all the time, her father and I take care of her alternately. She travels with me often and plays with my band. Glockenspiel. And I want her to play clarinet. She sings one of my songs, and now she's studying electric bass. So she's just a stage baby. She's been in on it from the very beginning. She's been on most of my records—she sang on *Escalator over the Hill* when she was four. We really didn't have time to let her have a lonely childhood." When Karen appears with the band at her mother's concerts, she is always at ease onstage, looking very much like a miniature Carla.

Bley's own childhood seems to have been a rather lonely one. Born Carla Borg in May 1938, she grew up in the San Francisco Bay area in a fervently religious atmosphere. Her mother died when she was about eight, and she was raised by her father, a piano teacher and choirmaster. Like her daughter's, Carla Borg's early years centered around music—"I played my first recital at the age of three"—but nothing like the loose, unfettered, heady music of an eclectic jazz band. Carla grew up amidst classical music and the hymns of Christian fundamentalism. In previous interviews she has alluded to those early years: "I spent the first fifteen years of my life playing music only for Jesus. Everything was Him: gospel songs, choir meetings, prayer meetings, Sunday morning services, Sunday school, Sunday evening services, and occasional piano solos for the revivals like Billy Graham" (Bret Primack, "Carla Bley: First Lady of the Avant-Garde," *Keyboard*, February 1979); "I'd play twelve variations of 'Onward Christian Soldiers,' one as a waltz, one as a march, one as a polka, one with big flourishes and lots of diminished chords" (Mandel); "I taught my own Sunday school class at eleven. It was a very good class, I thought. I used flour, sugar and baking powder to represent Jesus, the Holy Ghost, and God. I would demonstrate that when you added the Holy Ghost, it would rise" (Sy Johnson, "And Now, the Emerging Wacko Countess...Carla Bley!," *Jazz*, Spring 1978).

Sometime in her early teens, upon discovering the outside world, Bley abandoned religion, and music along with it. "During that time I had a lot of neuroses: I wasn't able to leave the house and I slept with my shoes on and ate cellophane and was almost totally crazy" (Mandel). She dropped out of high school at fifteen, as soon as she could, and turned up in New York a few years later, around 1955, working as a cigarette girl at the Birdland club. Her various accounts of the intervening period are somewhat vague as to detail. "Actually that's all that happened," she tells me, confirming what she has said elsewhere: "I only consider the stuff that happened to me after I went to New York interesting. . . . I'd rather talk about after I changed my life the way I wanted it" (Johnson).

In any event, music soon began to reclaim her. But now it was black music, jazz—emotional and intellectual experimentation, personal expression and freedom from enforced personas. Ignoring the advice of a string of psychiatrists who, she says, counseled her to give up her "obsession" with music, she glued herself to the Birdland bandstand, where great musicians like John Coltrane, Thelonious Monk and Dizzy Gillespie held forth. The music was a revelation to her; night after night she stood and listened, even as she had visions of becoming an aging cigarette girl or a hotel chambermaid, a sad-sack jazz groupie.

She was not yet writing music. Then, in true "starlet discovered at the soda fountain" fashion, a rescuer appeared in the form of a talented Canadian jazz pianist. Paul Bley fell for the shy, music-struck kid, bought some cigarettes from her even though he didn't smoke, and pursued her to the point of marriage. The couple soon settled in California, and Paul became involved with the musicians then forming the nucleus of the avant-garde jazz movement of the sixties, men like Ornette Coleman, Charlie Haden, Don Cherry. Meanwhile, "I didn't know I was in on anything when I was there in Los Angeles," Carla said. "I was just looking out through a crack in the wall, . . . just completely listening. Like one huge ear, with nothing attached to it. Maybe feet on the bottom and a little hair coming out on top. But I listened like I'm sure no musician could who played. I heard every note everybody played, every wart on every note everybody played. I'm sure that as a listener, I was unique. But I had so little self-esteem that I assumed that I would never be anything *but* a listener" (Johnson).

Carla credits Paul with launching her on her career as a composer, if not exactly inspiring her. In interviews she seldom misses an opportunity to suggest that his urging her to write was more a question of "keeping the royalties in the family" than of fostering her talent. "He'd come in and say, 'Well, I got a record date tomorrow and I need six hot ones.' I'd sit down and write six of them. I just functioned like that. Instead of cooking the dinner, that would be my job" (Primack). Interestingly, Paul Bley's second wife also became a composer after marrying him—a fact that prompted Carla to remark to an interviewer who mentioned that his own wife couldn't write a note of music, "Why don't you lend her to Paul Bley for a month?" (Johnson).

Whatever Paul's motivation, there is no doubt as to the results of Carla's efforts. By 1959 she was writing what she has called "miniature" or "haiku-like" pieces (Maureen Paton, "Bley Time," *Melody Maker*, September 10, 1977), and her compositions won almost immediate attention. "I was lucky," she says modestly. "People started playing my music as soon as I began to write it. It's always been that way. I don't know why. It just happened." And even though she insists she was "terrible," she was also getting jobs as a player (she often expresses reservations about her playing and is much more confident about her composing). Her anonymity was at an end.

The Bleys inhabited a California that was far removed from Billy Graham and the church. When they became part of the free jazz scene of the sixties, Carla found that her lack of formal musical skills was inconsequential. What mattered was her fresh and challenging approach to writing music, at a time when many artists were reaching beyond chord changes, exploring the music of other continents and otherwise departing from established conventions. Eventually she and other avant-gardists settled in New York. Her circle of acceptance widened there as important innovators like Jimmy Giuffre and George Russell began playing her works. Her major source of income is still the royalties she receives for the frequent use of her material by others.

The Jazz Composers Orchestra, begun in 1965, marked an important advance in Bley's career. The brainchild of a number of artists, including Michael Mantler, the orchestra existed to showcase the work of living experimental composers. Carla divorced Paul, married Mantler and became his partner in the new venture. As Bley describes it, "The Jazz Composers Orchestra was everybody's band, the community's band. All the composers who wanted to write for a large orchestra got to write for one." Gradually Bley and Mantler shifted their attention from the composers' showcase orchestra to a more central problem: how to get the music to the public. They began to think they could succeed with a do-it-yourself company aimed at the small, specialized markets scorned by the corporate recording industry. The two subsequently developed New Music Distribution Service, which acts as an umbrella for more than two hundred independent record companies and confers important status in the music community.

The success of New Music also gives Bley an opportunity to thumb her nose at the slick, commercially oriented musical world that demands hits just as adamantly as she demands autonomy. "New Music is a quite unglamorous end of the music business that I believe in very much," she says with animation. "It's the distribution of records, getting an order in the mail, picking a record off the shelf, putting it in a package and sending it to the person or the store. That's what we've been doing for over eight years, and the thing that distinguishes us from other distributors is that we don't pick the things that we think will make money. We pick everything. We let everything in the category of new music in the door." Or, as she put it elsewhere, "We're kind of like the Wildlife Preserve protecting all this possibly extinct music" (Primack). Bley's own WATT Records, produced at her and Mantler's Woodstock studio, are collector's items for the cognoscenti. For nearly a decade astute observers of contemporary jazz have been touting her tunes.

But it was a monumental work that really established Bley as a composer of international stature, a writer capable of much more than the mostly short pieces she was known for. This landmark achievement was *Escalator over the Hill*, an opera covering six record sides and taking five years (1967–72) and a great deal of money to produce. Bley shouldered much of the load herself, with loans, help from an angel or two and murmurs of interest from the record industry, which eventually backed off. She says that she could never afford to do such a long work again.

Escalator, which Bley has described as a "chronotransduction," uses music and musicians from all over the map. Its lengthy list of participants includes rock bassist Jack Bruce, singer Linda Ronstadt, sometime Warhol star Viva, guitarist John McLaughlin and saxophonist Gato Barbieri. It is multilingual and multicultural in its borrowings from musical sources around the world, including, of course, jazz. An ironic, engaging and poetic reading of the sixties, *Escalator* resists musical classification and is as stoned as the times it reflects. The surrealistic plot, drawn from poetry mailed in from India by a friend, Paul Haines, concerns the spiritual changes of a rock band wandering through a desert and a decaying grand hotel in the Orient. Considered by many a *tour de force*, the work won Bley rave reviews both abroad and at home.

It was also important as a personal artistic summation. Inspired by the music-hall and folk influences of the Beatles, then in their exciting *Sergeant Pepper* period, Bley used *Escalator* to explore her personal history and air her feelings as a white musician within the mostly Afro-American jazz community. "I started hearing the possibilities of not borrowing from black culture. Actually finding substance in white culture. The Beatles' best stuff was taken from Anglo-Saxon roots. I was amazed because up to then I thought only black music was important. I felt like an outsider" (Johnson). With its very large scale, *Escalator* also achieved something else. Women are often accused of not being able to do two things: architecture and composition. Here was a mammoth musical construction indeed, and one that seemed to free Bley to dip more liberally into the musical smorgasbord, embarking on a fertile, far-reaching period of composition that continues to date.

Like her contemporary, composer-pianist Toshiko Akiyoshi, Carla Bley maintains a band to play her music exclusively. And though she has publicly dissociated herself from jazz on numerous occasions, she is pleased by the increasing recognition of her music and her band in jazz circles. "I like the fact that my field of endeavor has finally accepted me," she says. "Like the International Jazz Critics poll—my band was voted the best new band. I'm usually in the other slots, but the fact that my band is accepted is really amazing to me. My band is doing so many outrageous things. I thought that the community wouldn't like it because it wasn't pure jazz or historically this or that. The fact that they accepted it made me very happy. And it's also good when people in the business who can help you, all of a sudden do. Now I have a very good lawyer, a very good publisher, a very good accountant—I have help. I don't need the help now, but instead of saying, 'You didn't help me when I needed you, fuck you,' I just decided to accept it and forget."

Bley strenuously denies having personally experienced any setbacks or problems as a woman in a predominantly male field. "I never had any problem, and that's the truth," she says firmly. "Until like a year ago, and all of a sudden it became a big thing. Someone's pointing out a problem I never knew existed, and all of a sudden I have a problem I never knew I had before. But I've never considered it a problem. I mean, it would be awfully boring if all of a sudden women were given a better chance than they deserve. I don't think of myself as a woman. I hate to be in a book about women, but I don't want to be, on the other hand, a snob in any way. A lot of women think—they look at themselves, they look at men, they say, 'You're a woman. You write music. Therefore, I'm a woman, *I* can write music.' The one doesn't follow the other at all, any more than that all redheads are astronauts."

What about the women who never got a chance? "Maybe not many of them were very good," Bley replies. "I don't believe in opening the gates to a group of people simply because they're a minority. If you give extra chances to redheads this year, think of all the brunettes that didn't get a chance. I'm not a liberal—I guess I'm a conservative." She laughs. "I believe that the same rules should be used for everyone, without any special consideration at all. I don't want any handicaps given to me. I've never been nurtured, and I wouldn't want to be. But maybe it's wrong not to be," she adds, lost in thought for a moment. Then she resumes. "In this world you have to fight all you can, no matter how dirty it is. So if the women want to fight to get what they want, I say, it's dirty fighting, but let them do it. I don't want to help it, but I won't hinder it."

With her generous gift, hard work and some breaks along the way, Bley has either circumvented or transcended a number of difficulties common to most women in jazz. Her self-confidence has grown through years of toughing it out and finally achieving success. She has simply not allowed being white or being female or being formally unschooled, unconventional and uncategorizable to deter or break her. Or perhaps it's a matter of selective perception, as she once suggested in an interview: "I don't suffer from being a woman.... Of course, someone could point it out—like Gary [tenor saxophonist Gary Windo, a member of Bley's band] just pointed out to me that one time in France, somebody shouted 'Go home and wash the dishes' but I didn't hear it" (Mandel).

Bley has persevered and succeeded largely by creating her own musical avenues. Her attitude toward music as a profession is totally unsentimental. "Music," she says, "is an exchange with society for food and clothing and a roof over your head. And if society doesn't particularly want your brand of music, they don't have to give you these things. You have to do something useful for society in order to get it back. So if your music is not useful to society, then you should do something else for society and pay for your music. Do it in your spare time. If you have any other possibilities open to you besides music, I think you should do them. Everybody. I don't think you choose music, I think music chooses you. If you have recourse to other professions, take them."

At the same time, Bley acknowledges that her free-market picture of musical enterprise is not without flaws. "People with money, they do create demand. It isn't a natural thing at all, and that's what I object to. I object to the bureaucracy in the foundations and in the government that creates things that aren't necessary or desirable. I think if you satisfy desire it's as wonderful and as important a part of life as if you satisfy necessity." This, indeed, is the goal that seems to animate Bley's own musical activities. She has profitably traded off among her various roles as bandleader, composer, performer and administrator, borrowing from Peter to pay Paul. Her performing doesn't buy the goods: her composing and business ventures do. Part of her energy appears to be devoted to shoring up the walls of her domain, keeping control. In her world, there are no middlemen to tamper with the idea; from inception to finished product, it is hers.

"My life is full of joy," Bley says earnestly. "I've got everything I ever wanted or needed. I appreciate it. I think about it all the time. I tend to think that if I don't constantly keep it in mind, I'll lose it somehow. I don't want to be unlucky, but I expect it when I walk out the door, 'cause everything is so great for me, it's about time something ridiculous happened. I just believe in chance. If you have heads twenty times in a row, every time there's more possibility it's going to turn tails. But I try not to look at it that way."

Whatever Bley's misgivings, they don't extend to her composing. "I'm terribly optimistic about writing," she says, "and I really do think that given a month I can write a piece of music, even if the first week is lost and I pace the floor. But I can't write every day now, because there are only certain days I have available. And lately I find I no longer need that week to prepare, that week of frustration—I just go right to it. But I have to know I've got a free month, or I don't even bother starting. I love to compose. That's my favorite thing in life, and I could do it every day, eight hours a day, even fourteen hours a day. But I do so many other things. I'm preparing material for a book, my forty-eight greatest hits, and I'm preparing for the Berlin Jazz Festival, and I'm working on one of my husband's records, which I'm producing and playing piano on, and I'm doing a short tour of the West Coast in September. And I have to replace the piano chair in my band, which means I have to rewrite the whole book, changing all the piano parts, 'cause I only like about three piano players and I can't get any of them, so I have to change the instrument itself.''

Bley relaxes down into her chair. The telephone rings and she begins a long, exuberant conversation about hiring a director for New Music. ''This space here is much too big,'' she says, hanging up. ''We've got to fill it up with records and orders and people. We're trying to make this organization permanent, trying to make it work by hiring somebody way above our heads in salary, someone we really can't afford, just to make it work.'' Another call comes in, this time about auditioning guitar players for the band.

''Well, you see what my life is like,'' Bley says. ''I've gotten into at least five things in the last ten years, and I feel obligated to all of them. I'm trying to keep them all going. One is New Music Distribution Service, which I believe in totally. I don't work here as much as I should—when I'm in town, I just really try to generate some energy about it. And I'm involved in having my own band, getting better gigs, working more and making records—all the stuff that entails. Then I'm involved in writing music on a pure level, and I'm involved in my husband's projects. It's almost too much. It's like having children, really. You can't cut back on a child. I used to want to be busy every moment, and now I am, so I guess it's my own fault. I like the feeling of having too much to do. I like the feeling of having things overlap, having to race from one thing to another—I *love* it. It makes me feel useful and wanted and important. That's a lot.'' She draws on her pipe, and gray-white smoke lazily uncurls and disperses as it rises into the air. ''It's a shame that we have to let people tell us what needs to be done to fill a demand that exists. Good things have a way of inserting themselves, of asserting themselves, into history.''

CLORA BRYANT

Trumpeter

"I started playing because I wanted to get out [of the house] at night."

When Dizzy Gillespie was asked at the 1981 Kool Jazz Festival to name women trumpeters worthy of mention as jazz players, he answered without hesitation, "Clora Bryant." Bryant, who also plays flugelhorn and drums, sings and composes, became active in California jazz in the forties and spent her formative years playing in the clubs along Central Avenue in Los Angeles. At the time that strip was the equivalent, in terms of black entertainment, of what was going on in New York in Harlem clubs and on Fifty-second Street. Bryant has been a working musician ever since, one of the few women horn players among the mostly male innovators of the bop era to remain active throughout ensuing decades and styles of the music. But although Dizzy and other confreres may remember her and laud her talents, Clora Bryant has been accorded relatively little attention by jazz writers.

We meet to talk at the College of Music on the UCLA campus, where Bryant, in her fifties, is completing a program she began in 1946 when she first came to California. She is acquiring now the formal musical training she had to put aside thirty-five years ago in order to get a job. She's an attractive woman, casually dressed, with her hair tied back in a kerchief, soft-spoken, but direct and candid in what she says. Why the lack of press on that uncommon phenomenon, a black woman who was a bebop trumpeter?

Bryant has obviously considered the question before, and her answer comes readily, not bitterly, but out of a seeming sense of genuine bewilderment. "Here in California, I was doing things jazz-wise—whether good, bad or indifferent. I was in with the 'in' people. But I really don't know why it is that I haven't got the credit; the documentation is not there. And it's been such a long time since anyone really wrote anything about me. Frankly, I'll be glad when it's just a fact instead of such a novelty that we do have women players. Because it *is* just a fact, you know. Ever since I started playing, it was treated as a novelty—it's always been that way. I think we do need to really get inside the women's playing, because I am sick of hearing that I 'play good for a woman,' " she says with conviction. Then she smiles. "Well, at least now they don't say *that* anymore." Recently Bryant has been both startled and pleased to find a new interest in her playing; suddenly not only jazz lovers of all ages but younger women trying to rediscover and learn from their own cultural role models want to hear the music of Clora Bryant, jazz trumpeter. Her stint as co-leader, with bassist Carol Kaye, of a bop-oriented combo brought recognition and good notices in the seventies.

Clora Bryant was born in Denison, Texas ("seventy-eight miles north of Dallas"), and raised by a strict but loving father, Charles Bryant; her mother died when she was only two. "When I was in high school," she remembers, "I wanted to play in the marching band so I could go to the football games, or otherwise my father wouldn't let me out of the house." She laughs. "So I started playing because I wanted to get out at night. My oldest brother played trumpet, and since my father couldn't buy another instrument, the only way I could join the band was to play his trumpet. And once I started I was hooked. Now, before that I could pick out anything on the piano. I always had a good ear, and the music was around—I was in the choir and I heard it in church, and my dad took me to hear the dance bands that came to town and such. But I wanted to *play*. So that was the only instrument available to me, and I found out it wasn't as hard as I thought. It was *hard*, but being determined and motivated, I did it."

Growing up in the harsh economic environment of the South during the Depression, Bryant was encouraged to pursue a career as a trumpet player when she showed aptitude. As she points out, entertainment was viewed by Southern blacks as an excellent vehicle to "be your own person. My dad wouldn't let me pick cotton and all of that." And she was encouraged by her instructor. "My high school teacher, Conrad Johnson, took an interest in me and had me buy an Arban trumpet book. He would take me over the scales and things that are in the book. He was a very good teacher. He originated the Cashmere High School band, a marching band which traveled all over the world—Japan, Germany—and won many awards.

"Once I got started, I played with the jazz band my last year in school. We played for the proms in Oklahoma and all around at various local places. In high school," Bryant observes, "you find girls playing instruments all the time. It's *after* you get out of high school, when you get that union card and you start competing one to one with guys, that it's hard. They don't like competing with each other, let alone a female!

"After high school I got scholarships to go to a couple of schools, but I went to Prairie View College in Texas because they had an all-girl orchestra. We had sixteen or seventeen pieces in that band. That was in 1943, '44 and '45, and I remember Bert Etta Davis—or 'Birdie,' they called her—she was there, and others came out of the Prairie View band." Indeed, several Prairie View alumnae joined trumpeter Tiny Davis' group in Chicago, and others, Bryant among them, later played with all-woman "jump" bands, notably the Sweethearts of Rhythm, then at the peak of their fame. Prairie View's Co-ed Orchestra made an East Coast tour in 1943–44, and Bryant appeared with it at Harlem's Apollo Theatre.

In 1945 Bryant left the school and settled in California, where she intended to further her studies at UCLA. "And there were very few blacks there at that time," she notes. But almost immediately she became active on the music scene, and when she had to drop out of school for lack of funds, she soon found a job with the Sweethearts. "I liked the band and thought [leader] Anna Mae Winburn was such a kick! But a problem for me was that, well, the all-girl bands have had a certain—connotation for many people for a long time . . . " Her voice trails off. Pressed, she admits that a common attitude had it that women playing in all-female groupings must be, ipso facto, homosexual. Bryant was one of the few women I interviewed who alluded to the problem of women being considered not only unfeminine but even "butch" for playing "male" instruments and stepping outside traditional roles.

"After a stint with the Sweethearts, I started playing with small women's groups, people like Anne Glasco [bass] and Willie Lee Terrell [guitar]. We had a group called the Four Bees. I started working with them, but they had to let me go because they found out I was underage and so I couldn't legally work in the clubs. Later there was another girl group with Matty Watson, the drummer, and Anne Glasco and myself. Willie Terrell, incidentally, died in the early fifties. In 1947 I played Vegas with one of these girl groups. They had just opened the Flamingo, before it became the huge place it is today. I remember in Vegas there was Doris Lura on bass and Minnie Hightower on sax. Then I went with a group after that led by Frances Grey, the drummer. We stayed up in the Seattle and San Francisco area for a long time."

Bryant's enthusiasm for playing with all-woman groups waned, though not because of the possible homosexual "stigma." "There was always this bickering—that's what got me through with women. Those little petty jealousies!" She shakes her head ruefully. But Bryant remembers individual women players fondly and with respect. "When I came out to California in the forties, there were only a few women trumpet players here. There was Valaida Snow. She was playin' at a theater in town when I saw her—they put on real good stage shows there—and she was *good*. And Billie Rogers was with Woody Herman. Then there was a girl from Beaumont, Texas, named Bessie Como. I never heard her, but I heard about her. She played with all-male orchestras. Melba Liston [trombone] was playing at the Million Dollar Theatre with Bardu Ali and the orchestra when I first got here. I used to go backstage—I didn't yet have a union card—and I would sit and listen. Then Melba went back East and joined Dizzy's group."

In her late teens and twenties Bryant made the rounds of the clubs and after-hours spots in Los Angeles, sitting in and jamming—the usual route for players trying to develop their strength, technique and jazz "chops," except that it wasn't so usual for women in those days. "There wasn't any other woman sittin' in—even Vi [Vi Redd, the alto sax player] wasn't going to clubs sittin' in then. I felt like if you played with somebody better, you'd learn; that was one reason why I'd go. I'd sit in, and when they'd start playing something hard the other guys would sit down. I'd stay and try it anyway"— she chuckles—"whether I succeeded or not. But you couldn't do it unless you tried it. And so many people were around then—Dexter Gordon, Sonny Criss, Teddy Edwards [tenor sax players]. So many I can't even remember!

"Around 1951, '52, something like that, because my daughter was a baby—she was born in '51, and I used to take her to rehearsals to nurse her—I also worked with a group at the Club Alabam. There were three clubs around then on Central Avenue, the Last Word, the Downbeat and the Alabam, right there on the block. Then you had the after-hours places, Brothers and a place called Dynamite's—there were about six clubs within a two-block radius. It was a good group we had at the Alabam, with Wardell Gray and Don Riverton; sometimes we added a couple other fellas, like 'Sweets' Edison and Britt Woodman. We played behind Josephine Baker, behind Billie Holiday, behind Foxx and White—Redd Foxx and Slappy White—behind Al Hibbler. Everybody came to the Alabam! And there were sessions at the breakfast clubs, like Jack's Basket Room. I used to play there, and one time it got written up, when Al Killian [lead trumpeter], who was with Duke Ellington, came by one morning. This was just before he got killed. He came by and he started hittin' those high notes. I'd play something, and he'd play something higher—it was a real fun night.

"Right after I started doing the Alabam, they had these all-girl orchestras doing local TV shows. And so they put out a call at the union to get trumpet players, and they gave me a call. I think I did one show or so with Ada Leonard.* There were so many complaint calls they had to take me off. They didn't want a black with the band. Now, this was '52 or '53. I didn't even think about *that*—I just thought, 'Well, your loss is my gain,' and I just shined it on.

"In the fifties I played quite awhile in an area called the Beach; I played the Lighthouse with Sonny Criss and Hampton Hawes. Then we played at a place called the High Seas, which is right next door to the Lighthouse. And

*Bryant has a number of other TV credits, including some 1951 appearances with a band led by Benny Carter on a local California TV show featuring black talent (the show was dropped for lack of sponsorship). Also in 1951 Bryant appeared with an all-female jazz combo on California TV, with Jackie Glenn on piano, Anne Glasco on bass, Ginger Smock on violin, Matty Watson on drums, Willie Lee Terrell on guitar and Vivian Dandridge doing vocals. In 1962 Bryant was part of an eight-piece band that appeared on the *Ed Sullivan Show* in a revue led by Billy Williams, and in 1967 she was on the *Tonight Show* in an eight-piece band promoted by Bill Cosby.

we had jam sessions on Sunday afternoons that started at two and went 'til two in the morning. On my break I'd hit the Lighthouse, 'cause at that time they had Shorty Rogers, Jim Giuffre, Bob Cooper, Marty Paich, Mel Lewis occasionally. Then they sent for Max Roach to come play, and *he* sent for Clifford Brown. And right before Charlie Parker was going back to New York, he came down to see Max. They tried all afternoon to get him to sit in, but he left and came over and spent the afternoon playing with *us*. The guy I was working with, Sid Calloway, his horn was so bad, but Charlie played it—he played the you-know-*what* out of it! It was a tenor, and Charlie blew it. Everybody emptied out of the Lighthouse to hear that."

But Las Vegas was Bryant's bread and butter, as it was and still is to innumerable other California-based jazz musicians. It began to really jump with entertainment and music in the fifties. "The second time I went to Vegas I went with [singer] Damita Jo. It was her show, and she was fronting the band. And we played opposite Harry James, who I idolized. One night I got ready to go to work and I couldn't find my horn. Someone had stolen my trumpet, so I went to work and I played Harry's horn, and I played everybody's in the trumpet section. Harry and I became very good friends; in fact, through Harry and Sammy Davis, Jr., I got a spot playing in an all-male orchestra in the movie *Pepe*. They were filming *Pepe* and *Oceans 11* at the same time, and I want to tell you, it was like New Year's Eve every night, because they had the 'Clan' there—Frank Sinatra and company. Boy, did we have fun! And I had a crush on Cantinflas [the star of *Pepe*]. He was like a little doll, and I just loved him.

"Out in Vegas [big-band trumpeter] Billy Williams heard me; when I closed with Damita Jo, I went right down the street to the Riviera with him, and I stayed with him for two and a half years. I was the only girl in that group; it was a seven-piece band, Horace Henderson's band, and then we had dancers and a vocal group. And I did an impression of Louis Armstrong. I even got a chance to play with Louis. We were in the lounge, and Louis was in the big room at the Riviera, so one night he marched his band into the room, got onto the stage, and we did 'Basin Street' together.

"With Billy Williams, we'd stay in Vegas for six months, then we'd do the Latin Quarter in New York. We played the Catskills, we played all the beaches, the Lido Beach—all the fabulous places. You'd be in the mountains in this beautiful club, and all these Rolls-Royces and Mercedes and Jags, the women with diamonds and gowns straight out of Paris. And we played Miami, Canada, Denver—all the beautiful supper clubs.

"And New Orleans. We stayed down in New Orleans six weeks. Now, *that* was a trip. That was just before integration, in 1961 and 1962, and they had just started sit-ins in New Orleans. We played on Bourbon Street at the Dream Room, down the street from where the trumpet player Al Hirt had just opened his club. We had to stay out of town, in Jefferson County, because there were no nice accommodations in town for us. So we stayed across the river at a motel, and we rented a station wagon to come and get us because the cab drivers wouldn't come and get us. So we'd be coming down the street, and on Bourbon Street there were a lot of strip joints. They'd have hawkers outside, and they'd see our station wagon coming, and the doors would start slammin'. They didn't want the guys in the group to be watchin' the [white] girls strippin'. Al Hirt had to come and pick us up to take us to his club, too, and bring us back. That's the way it was.

"And the governor, Long [Earl Kemp Long, brother of Huey], he had a crush on me. He would never approach me, but he followed us to New York to the Latin Quarter and would send money back to me—and write notes." Bryant laughs at the irony, and other wry memories seem to bubble up. Pulling a mock-serious long face, she says, "There were others, too. I don't want to *name* them, but I would never let it develop into anything. Well, if I wasn't in love, you know, I just couldn't see it. I missed a lot of opportunities. See, the agents—well, sometimes there would be a couch-like thing, see? I said, 'Well, if you can't hire me for my trumpet playing, forget it.' And the club owners. They'd want you to sit there and drink, like a B-girl. During the late forties, early fifties, B-drinking was still in. They still had a lot of soldiers around, and they were rippin' 'em off for their money. *You* drink Coca-Cola and the customer gets charged for a drink, see? In one place in Chicago—it was owned by gangsters—I finally had to do that there, because they threatened me. In order to keep a job I did it, and I stayed there about six months. But I wasn't raised that way, so I probably missed a lot of chances. A lot of the women in music playing horns and instruments, they were in it for the glamour and the hoopla—that made it easier to get connections. But from the jump, mine was strictly for music, and it still is."

As a jazz player, Bryant has been influenced by a number of different performers. She attributes her sound largely to her "coming up" and "hanging out" years. Great swing artists like Roy Eldridge and Charlie Shavers had an early effect on her, but it was Dizzy Gillespie, with his daring, exuberant, lightning-fast style, and the brilliant young trumpeter Clifford Brown, dead before he reached the age of thirty, who most impressed her.

Clora first heard Gillespie on the radio, and in the late forties she started buying up all his 78s. "Between the broadcasts and the records, I became a Dizzy freak," she allows. "I met him finally when he had his State Department band [1956], the one that had Melba Liston and Quincy Jones and Billy Williams, Charlie Persip and Lee Morgan on trumpet. They used to come over to my house. I'd fix breakfast, and we'd listen to Clifford Brown records. Now, when Clifford Brown first heard me play, it was at a place where we used to have jam sessions, a place called the California Club. Max Roach had sent for Clifford and organized a group at the Lighthouse. On this night at the California Club, my ex-husband, who is dead now—he played bass—was sitting in a booth with Clifford, and I was up there playing. They were talking, not looking up and paying attention, and all of a sudden Clifford looks up and sees that it's a woman playing. He turns to my husband and says, 'Why, who is that bitch up there blowin' trumpet?' My husband says, 'Well, that's my wife.' So Clifford said, 'Man, I'm sorry, but that bitch can *blow!*' That was one of my idols, so I wrote a song for him. Anybody I like I write songs for."

As she nears forty years in the music business, Clora Bryant is now more active than ever. She is studying composition at UCLA, where she also vigorously promotes jazz activities. Currently she is hard at work completing an ambitious five-part piece entitled "Suite for Dizzy," for which she received a jazz composer and performance grant from the National Endowment for the Arts. And this trumpet player who often doubles on drums is now concentrating on singing as well as playing. "I found out I had to sing—they want to get two for one. They don't want you to just stand and play, they don't appreciate you. That's one reason I started singing, but I also found out I like it, so I'm doing it more. Billy Williams advised me, 'Just sing like you play—*phrase* like you play.' And I found out that works."

Bryant has worked in the past in the trumpet sections of the bands of Duke Ellington, Lionel Hampton, Count Basie and Stan Kenton, as well as in numerous show bands. She is now an active player and often leader with small groups in the Los Angeles area, especially with Bill Berry's L.A. Big Band. "I took trumpeter Blue Mitchell's place in fourth chair in that band, and I don't know how Bill Berry swung it, but I've been accepted. I like section trumpet work. We do all Duke Ellington, his book. And I'm the only woman in the band." She pauses, eyes narrowing in thought. "You do see *one* woman in a band, never two or three," she observes. "Earl Hines, for example, had a violin section of all women in his orchestra—but not horns. This has been a hindrance right along the line for women players.

"Being a woman, and being a black woman, and playing a trumpet—that's three things I consider against me. Now, if I played piano, I don't think sex or race would enter into it. With the wind instruments, though, there's competition, period. No matter what color or what sex, there's a lot of competition in the trumpet section!" But Bryant is also quick to point to the positive influence of the men who guided her: her father, her high school band teacher, Harry James and especially Dizzy Gillespie. "We [Clora and Dizzy] became tight. He's supportive of anybody that acts like they're interested in music. He said, 'Learn to play the piano,' and that's what I'm doing. And *that's* when I really started writing. I have had a chance to get up on the stage with him. He mentioned on a TV show how I came up there and took his horn and blew the rim off of it. Well, he'll just stand there while you're playing, and his chest'll just puff out.

"The *real* musicians, they are *proud* of what you can do."

DOTTIE DODGION

Drummer

"Everything is your wrist and your placement of the beat. It isn't how much power you have."

The year is 1973, midwinter, the place an old-fashioned, friendly tavern in New Jersey where jazz is served up with the beer and hamburgers. I have come to the club to hear a friend, saxophonist Richie Cole, play his Bird-like alto. "I've got a new rhythm section," he advises me casually. "I think you'll dig my drummer." And he laughs, slightly mysterioso. He gets busy unpacking his horn and I settle in at the bar, prepared to enjoy the music.

A woman walks into the club, takes off her coat and seats herself behind the house traps as I do a rapid double-take: a woman drummer. I realized that I had never seen a woman on the traps—or almost any instrument, besides the piano. And I began right there to really wonder about that. Why was that so?

Several years later, when I got together with Dottie—Dorothy Giaimo Dodgion, the lady at the drums—I told her about my reactions that night in the New Jersey club. How I had simply not imagined a woman taking charge of the rhythm, and I had certainly never *seen* it happen. It fascinated me to watch Dodgion play. Her physical approach to the drums is lithe, graceful, easeful. Playing brings a constant, curving smile to her face as, like a painter, she wields her brushes over her palette of drums and cymbals or punctuates, light-wristed, with the sticks. Head tilted, she *listens*, and her rhythm swings.

Dottie Giaimo was born in Brea, California, in 1929. "They always ask me how I got into this," she says. "Well, my father was a drummer—still is, in San Francisco. And my mother was a dancer. So I come by it quite honestly. But I sang before I played drums." Dodgion still sings; she has a high, lovely voice and, like many players, phrases beautifully. As a teenager she worked with Charles Mingus and other jazz groups in the Bay area, intent on vocalizing. "I used to play on magazines with some brushes, to fill in for the drummer who was always late to the gig," she muses. "That's really how it started with the drums. And I thought that really it wasn't so hard. If I'd known it was going to be as hard as it is, I don't know whether I would have continued or not!" she jokes.

"Once on a gig when I was singing, I got stranded in Omaha, Nebraska, and I went to work playing cocktail drums just to get out of town and get back home. And then I just quit. I didn't even think about the drums for many years. I'd play a little brushes maybe, on a magazine or something, to keep time. If I'd go to a session and there wasn't a drummer there but a snare or some drums were set up, I'd sit in and play a little bit. But I didn't really start thinking about drums until later on, with Jerry."

Her marriage at age twenty-three to alto sax player Jerry Dodgion was the catalyst she needed to become a drummer. She had previously been married to bassist Monty Budwig, who thought her drumming "unladylike" (Hollie I. West, "A Different Drummer," *Washington Post*, May 8, 1979), but Jerry Dodgion was extremely supportive. "I know several lady players who were really very, very good, but they didn't get support from their husbands and they gave it up. That would be competition: 'Who do you love? Me or your instrument?' Isn't that a shame? If they only realized that the happier a woman is with herself, the happier she could be with him." She pauses. "You see, Jerry Dodgion was very much in love with me when I first started out, and he encouraged me to be a drummer. He helped carry my drums a lot. As I always say, that was true love, 'cause we lived in a place a hundred and fifty-six stairs up, and Jerry used to help carry my drums up all those stairs.

"Jerry, and later Gene Wright—a bass player who was with [tenor saxophonist] Gene Ammons later on—both of them really encouraged me. Eugene used to come to town, and the three of us would play in a trio and we'd get any piano player we could. And I would cook a whole lot of food, and we'd just play—for days!"

Her apprenticeship in the fifties, gigging in San Francisco and practicing in a congenial atmosphere, prepared Dodgion for a tougher playing environment when she and Jerry moved across the country to New York in 1961. "In the old days, when I first came to New York, it was like this: there'd be five male drummers after me, and all five of them would get to play first at a session. I would stay there 'til last, and they'd let me come up and play a tune. You had to prove yourself all the time, everyplace. A woman drummer—you think they were going to differentiate? But I really listened, tried not to get an attitude, tried not to be bitter because of that. Bitterness wouldn't have helped me at all to improve myself. So I really tried to take it and learn and listen."

Dodgion was serious, she was prepared, and when the breaks came she was ready. Like the job she landed with Benny Goodman's band. "It was an accident in a way," she demurs. "We had just come to New York. Benny had been trying out drummers, and he wasn't happy with them. Jerry had been with Benny's band in Las Vegas, and we had played in a session there where Benny Goodman sat in. He had a lot of fun with us that time, and that was all there was to it. Then, the first day we're in New York, I went out to buy myself a coat, I remember, and then I came back and looked up the band, which was at Basin Street East. And Benny told me, 'Hop up and take a set.' I thought we were just going to play a little, like we did at that session. And he looked at me and he closed the book! Now, you have to remember that I was *weaned* on Benny Goodman due to my father, since I was nine years old! A lot of Benny's charts hadn't been changed since then either. So I started playing, and he said, 'Fine. You start tonight.' And Zoot Sims [the tenor player] took me around the corner and we had a couple of fast belts.

"The show was an hour and a half, and it was *mean*, just to step in like that. He would wind up with 'Sing, Sing, Sing,' and I would wind up with mops for hands! It was a hard show. That lasted for some days, until Benny was going to cut an album in a different context. It was fun. And I used to rehearse once in a while with Duke Pearson's big band if Mickey Roker [the drummer] couldn't make it. At some of the rehearsals they had me sit in 'cause I knew the charts. Then I played a couple of times with Thad's band [then the Thad Jones–Mel Lewis Big Band] if Mel couldn't make it. And I knew the charts better than some other drummers."

Dodgion kept busy throughout the sixties, working with such musicians as Al Cohn and Zoot Sims, Carl Fontana, Wild Bill Davison, the Billy Mitchell–Al Grey Quintet, Marian McPartland and Ruby Braff. Still, she recalls, with an equanimity that speaks well for her self-esteem, instances where she was clearly denied work because she was a woman. "You have to be better than better," she says. "All the instruments are male-dominated. The way it's looked at, the drums are—pardon the expression—the balls of the band. When a guy turns around and sees a lady sitting there, it threatens his manhood some way. I'll say that this is how it *used* to happen," she amends. An example? "One time a friend of mine was trying to get me on Billy Butterfield's band, and the manager says, 'A chick on drums? Are you kidding? Forget it!' 'But she plays good. You haven't even heard her!' 'For*get* it!' Now, that," Dodgion pronounces distinctly, "is very typical. Not so much anymore. I think the guys are comin' around. They've been learning a whole lot—haven't we all?

"It used to be piano players and singers—that's the only thing the ladies were fit for. Guitar once in a while—although Mary Osborne is the only lady jazz guitar player that I know of. The women who are really professional, who have the experience, are in a minority. There were a few piano players, such as Terry Pollard. I knew her in Las Vegas. Jerry was working at the Moulin Rouge, the first black and white [integrated] club there. We called it the 'dust bowl.' And Terry was working with [vibraphonist] Terry Gibbs. She would get off early, and we would go out jammin' together. Two ladies in the dust bowl of Las Vegas, man! It was really funny. They would look at us and say, 'Sure, baby, you guys wanna play? Sure!'—and laugh their ass off. They weren't laughin' too hard when we finished! Terry was a real *cookin'* musician. I loved playing with her. Talk about people fitting—we fit beautifully rhythmically. Never had to work at it with her.

"Now, I wouldn't put anybody down for not hiring more women," she continues, "unless there's a choice where both a male and a female are qualified and they take the male because he's a male. You don't know how many times I've sat with other ladies and listened to them let off steam—the rancor because guys were picked over them. But you see, the bottom line is you can't let it get to you. You can protest, make a little bit of noise and put 'em on as much as you can, but you can't let it get out of hand, or else they'll *never* hire you 'cause they think that you're gonna be one of these—bitches that are always bitchin'. You don't knuckle under, but you don't go out and try to club 'em over the head either." She laughs softly.

In the seventies Dodgion moved to Los Angeles for a time, gigging locally. With the breakup of her marriage, she found herself in a position increasingly common for women in their mid-forties or early fifties: single again, with a daughter (Debra, now in her mid-twenties), and suddenly dependent on herself alone. Deciding to return to the East Coast, she quickly reestablished herself there. "In 1976 I moved to Washington because I wanted to be close to New York, where everything happens. Richie Cole introduced me to the lady who was managing a club called the Rogue and Jar, and I began hiring the musicians there, myself and a local trio. Pretty soon I was hiring musicians all the time. I had Flanagan come down [Tommy Flanagan, the pianist], and I'd get to work with him. And I hired groups like Roy Haynes, the Brecker Brothers. That went on for two years. We did so well they sold the club! Then I decided Washington was great if you're in politics. If I was a lawyer, I wouldn't move. But a musician, no."

At the time, arranger-trombonist Melba Liston was forming a new group in New York (see Melba Liston profile). Initially lukewarm to the idea of an all-female unit, Liston was persuaded to give it a whirl by Cobi Narita of the Universal Jazz Coalition, long a staunch Liston fan and supporter. "They talked to Carline [Carline Ray, electric bassist], and they sounded me," says Dodgion. "It was the people that Melba wanted at the time, and she felt very good about it. So then we all got together and she thought, 'Try it, anyway,' because she didn't want to be prejudiced either, just because they were women—not hire them, you know.

"Women are still in the minority in the music business. I think you'll find there are a lot of lady musicians who never wanted to work with other women because you just didn't feel they were serious enough about it. They were sold like they were a bag of meat and potatoes, strictly because they were women. And who wanted to be associated with that? Not any woman who's serious about music. Work yourself to death, knock yourself out, and then somebody says, 'Sure! A woman's band!'" Dodgion's tone is scoffing, dismissive; she has been around long enough to be wary of the periodic hype surrounding the "all-girl" gimmick. However, her tenure with Melba Liston's group was something else again. Relying as it did on Liston's arranging talent, the music demanded expertise, sensitivity and precision—in other words, musicianship. "This is a very good band, not just a fly-by-night band. It's not a gimmick band. Melba *writes*—she writes like Duke [Ellington]. Her music is so much fun to play, even the same tunes over and over. There's always a different flavor that you can add. She allows for that in her writing. Very unusual. I really love playing her music.

"This group is really Melba Liston and Company—not the 'All-Female Orchestra,' the 'All-Ladies.' They *always* do that, you know. They can't resist. It's just a natural selling point. Of course, we women never made any money off it, only the promoters. And nobody likes to be sold because of their gender. It's an understandable tendency and you can't help it, but you don't have to go along with it. In Melba's group two chairs now belong to men: Britt Woodman, who was trombonist with the Duke—a beautiful player; and Charles Williams on alto." (Personnel was to change several times.)

Rehearsals began in March 1980 with some of the cream of female jazz talent. Dodgion enumerates some of the women who worked with Liston's group at various times: "Sharon Freeman on piano, doubling on French horn; Erica Lindsay, a *fine* tenor player; Jean Fineberg was alto player, and Lollie Bienenfeld on trombone. And Melba, Carline and myself. We did a tour in June 1980, and European festivals in July." In the fall of 1980 Liston and her group did an Asian tour that Dodgion remembers with something like rapture. "Taiwan, Malaysia and Fiji. The people were just beautiful everyplace. That was where Melba added two fellas, because Jean and Lollie had something else going on musically. We were in Fiji and out-of-the-way places where they hadn't heard any jazz in I don't know how long. The audience was from every age group. We had the old beboppers, the young people, we played universities. And they were delighted—they were in awe! They don't see very much jazz, let alone *ladies*. I was big in Fiji!"

In 1981 Liston's combo regrouped, and Dodgion again sought free-lance work. "And I'm hoping maybe to get into singing again, a duo or something." Full circle from the teenager in San Francisco to the mature woman in New York. "I would like both to sing and play. I think I should use everything I've got." Dodgion also has tentative plans to do some teaching. Her ideas are definite and succinct, the fruit of nearly thirty years in the profession. "When I was out there listening, I found that a lot of things that drummers did really just turned me off. For instance, those who insist on covering up everybody else in the whole band. That's very undesirable to do. The sound shouldn't be sticking out; it should always be a blend. If any one person is sticking out too much, they're overblowing. Now, if you're gonna do a drum solo—well, do it, that's your *spot*. But all the rest of the time you're playing *with* each other, unless you're the lead trumpet player in a big band and you're supposed to have an edge.

"A lot of the drummers are so loud that the piano players and the bass players don't feel they're listening. So I can't blame them for not listening to the drummer. But the real pros, they know that you have to listen. There are very few musicians in the rhythm section who know that. God love the good bass player! They're very difficult to find. To me that's the hardest instrument to find a fit with. That's your soul, your ride cymbal, your division. It doesn't mean that I'm saying there aren't any good bass players— I'm just talking about that fit. Just *where* everyone is supposed to play during the time is not an easy thing to define. Whoever kicks it off is the time." She demonstrates by snapping her fingers, one-two three-four.

"But everybody hears *that* in a different way; no two people are going to hear it like a metronome. And it moves around. But you're not supposed to rush or drag. You move around *within* the time, within the breath that was kicked off—that's what's important. A lot of musicians take liberties with going outside that, and that's fine, *if* you can come back to it. And very few drummers can do that. They *think* they can, maybe, but they lean all over the piano player and the bass player. If the piano player and the bass player don't play 'one,' then the drummer can really mess 'em up." She sighs. "It's really difficult to describe what it's like inside a rhythm section, but I have certain beliefs, and I'd like to do some clinics on rhythm sections.

"Of course, there are some very good drummers around. Billy Higgins is one of my very favorite drummers. And Al Foster is very good. Kenny Clarke was probably the first drummer who really impressed upon me how versatile a drummer had to be, and how wonderful that is. He could take a small group—the Modern Jazz Quartet at the time—and then he'd turn around and play with a big band and *swing!* It didn't take away from either one. And at the time drummers specialized in one or the other, small group or big band. But he could do both. Jo Jones is probably another one. Pola Roberts is one of the women drummers I've heard who really swings. I heard her play at a session; she was filling in for Art Blakey. And Slide Hampton's niece,

Paula Hampton, is another." Dodgion also mentions Terri Lyne Carring-ton, already being talked about in her teens as one of *the* drummers of the future.

Dodgion, who has worked long and hard in all the playing situations she could find to get the experience so necessary to becoming a good jazz player, scoffs at some common assumptions. "For instance, that you have to be big and strong to play drums. First is your desire, your heart to play. Then you've got to be able to put it to your head, and then to your hands through your fingers. But everything is your wrist and your placement of the beat. It isn't how much power you have. Davie Tough [big-band drummer] was the littlest guy in the world, and Roy Haynes isn't exactly huge! You have to be doing it all the time to develop a certain amount of chops or stamina. To be able to produce it all the time in any situation."

Dottie Dodgion's skill and experience are well known to her fellow musicians, though she has been woefully underrecorded. Leonard Feather calls her a "sensitive drummer who fits into every modern jazz context" *(Encyclopedia of Jazz in the Sixties)*. Tap-dancing along with her radiant smile, she never pounds, doesn't crash or overwhelm but feeds into the music like a current into a river.

"When I go to work, which for me is when I set up my drums, I really go to do *that*, not to imagine what somebody else is thinking of what I'm doing. Your ego gets in your way if you're not very careful. Turn all of that crap loose when you're playing, it's going to filter in and hang you up. You're a musician first—you're going there to set up your drums because you're a drummer. And you're going to play because you're a musician. These other little assumptions that people have out there about you because you're a woman—if you start letting *that* get to you, boy, you're in trouble. You'll never play."

Playing jazz is just what Dottie Dodgion has been doing for the last several decades, her professionalism enriching the scene, her presence proof that a woman can be as effective behind the traps as behind the microphone. As she says, "There isn't any gender to music! I've always said that. It's a terrible misconception. Why, you can go back to Africa, where the women used to play those big kettledrums! You have to keep your mind open to every possibility to be able to *live*, not just exist."

As a card-carrying pioneer drummer among women jazz players, Dottie Dodgion has opened up a lot of minds—and probably blown a few.

HELEN HUMES

Vocalist

"I've been called a blues singer and a jazz singer and a ballad singer—
well, I'm all three, which means I'm just a singer."

Along with such fine singers as Mildred "Rockin' Chair Mama" Bailey, the
teenage Ella Fitzgerald with the Chick Webb orchestra and Billie Holiday
with the Count Basie band, Helen Humes helped to shape and define the
vocal sound of the swing era. Humes died on September 13, 1981, in a
California hospital; her passing brought outpourings of affection, eulogies,
tribute concerts and reminiscences from fellow musicians and fans. In the
fall of 1980 I met and talked with Helen Humes about her life and career.
Though ill even then, she was gracious, funny and generous with her time.

Helen Humes was a small, round, dimply person. Just five feet tall, she
looked up at the world through luminous brown eyes that suggested her
Indian ancestry on her mother's side of the family. She retained the gracious
Southern manner of her Louisville upbringing, and one felt no edge or bite
to her natural good nature. Bits of the girlishness that added to her vocal
charm seemed to peep through the dumpling figure of this lady in her
sixties, as when she folded her dainty hands in a quick prayer before eating a
snack during a break in our talk. Yet decidedly *not* a bland person: the
thoroughgoing niceness of Helen Humes was spiced throughout her
recollections of her long career with conviction, strength and an occasional
flash of stubbornness.

Her back stiffened, for instance, at attempted comparisons between her
singing style and anyone else's. An individualist in her approach, she
shrugged off labels. "I just sing the song in my own way, that's all," she
declared. Critics who attempted to "place" her exuberant style usually ended
by describing her simply as one of the outstanding vocalists on the
continuum of Afro-American technique. "I don't know of anybody that
influenced me musically. I never had singing lessons or anything like that. I
never listen to records; I've got a million tapes, but I never listen to them. And
people used to say, 'Who influenced you?' Nobody influenced me—I didn't
hear nobody," she said.

Humes was born in Louisville, Kentucky, in 1913, the only child of
Emma Johnson and John Henry Humes. Her father was a lawyer, and her

mother was musically inclined. Helen gravitated to the family piano when very young, began picking out tunes and was soon absorbing the music of her local church. "And when I was about eleven or twelve, my mother started in giving me piano lessons. I was playing before, but I didn't read. But now I had a German teacher, Professor Hermanspocher, and he used to have me play Bach and all that. But I would play what *I* wanted to play after practice, and I would sing with it. Then we used to go to church, and I'd sing in the choir and play for the Sunday school. But really I just learned how to sing at home. You know, everybody then could play the blues on the piano—we used to call them the 'struts.' " She illustrated by humming a boogie-woogie bass line and darted her eyes sidewise at me, breaking into laughter. "See! That's the struts!"

Then there was the instruction given by Miss Bessie Allen. One of so many energetic and community-minded black women who in myriad ways have encouraged and fostered the talents of black children, Bessie Allen operated an orphans' home and taught music. "She used to rent this big place where they had the Sunday school, every Sunday evening. She would teach you the instruments—she would do everything for the children. I tried a couple of them, trumpet and clarinet, but I didn't really like 'em, so I just stayed with the piano."

Many other musicians who later became well known got their start in Miss Allen's classes, notably trumpeter Jonah Jones and trombonist Dickie Wells. "Bessie Allen was a wonderful woman," Jones recalled. "She turned out a lot of good musicians. . . . When girls came in the band, Helen Humes played trumpet and sang, and then got on the piano. I met my wife in that band, when she was fourteen or fifteen, and played trumpet and clarinet" (Stanley Dance, *The World of Swing*, p. 162). Jones remembered their little band playing popular tunes like "Blue Skies" and "Sweet Georgia Brown."

"Now, Miss Bessie Allen had this marching band that she would take us out on," Humes continued, "and then at night, when it was time for the little theater band to play wherever, I would play in that. I would sing *and* play with the group. And I was about, oh, fifteen, sixteen, at this time." She was also a recording artist already. After the huge success of Mamie Smith's "Crazy Blues" (1920), which sold by the hundreds of thousands, record companies like Columbia and Paramount rushed to cash in on the blues craze. Dispatching talent scouts to the South, these companies "discovered" a wealth of black artists whose works they waxed and marketed to the black community on the "race records" of the period. Helen Humes was going on thirteen when she was first recognized as a potential talent. "It was about 1926, I think, and Spencer Williams, a blues singer, heard me. He had come down where our little group was playing a theater. I wouldn't get up and sing because I was sitting at the piano. But I would sing once in a while, just whatever was popular. Then Mr. Williams arranged for an audition by Mr. Rockwell [a producer for Okeh Records], and he brought him out to my house. He asked Mama would she bring me to St. Louis for a recording. So she did."

Humes breezed through the 1927 St. Louis session, recording the risqué, double-entendre blues then in vogue. Barely in her teens, she sang the country-style "Do What You Did" and "Papa Has Outside Lovin' " (a disc long out of print). "After I got there to the studio, they told me what tunes I was going to sing. They just said, 'You know, blues.' And then they gave me these songs. James C. Johnson was on piano."

This expectation of instant mastery of a tune was not confined to record producers of the twenties. "When I got with Basie, that's the way they did it in the Basie band. They'd come up and hand everybody the music, and if I hadn't known a little something about it, I don't know what would have happened to me. You know, they didn't *teach* me nothin'. They just handed you your piece like they handed the trumpets their piece. Basie or whoever wrote the arrangements did it. And in the studio they'd just hand me the words. If you didn't know the song—well, I'd just say, 'Well, I don't know nothin' about this tune.' Then *maybe* they'd come and hand me a piece of music. Then they just stood there and played it and I just sang it. They'd say, 'It goes like this.' " Humes' experience bears out the observation of jazz writer George Simon: "On recordings, singers often appeared to disadvantage because tunes were tossed at them at the last minute and they didn't have time to familiarize themselves with them" (*The Big Bands*, p. 35). Fortunately Humes was an instinctive vocal musician who usually managed to grasp a song's essence at a glance.

Humes looked back on her teenage record debut with the wry detachment that sustained her through the ups and downs of her long career. "After my first recording session we came back to Louisville, and when my record came out I didn't have a record player, so I'd go over to bug some of my friends. And I'd sit there and I'd listen." Humes' voice took on a scolding tone as she mimicked her friends. "They'd say, 'Oh, Helen, you don't never act like you like *nothin'*.' I said, 'I don't know—I always feel like I could have done better.' " Did making that record change her life? "Change my life?" She considered for a moment. "Well, I wasn't thinking about making singing a career. I wasn't into music, and I didn't know nothin' about the styles. I would just play and be happy. We'd have a little party and I'd sing. Like that."

But two years later, in 1929, Okeh Records called Humes and her mother to New York City for another recording session. This was a smoother, more commercial blues date, with the great Harlem stride pianist James P. Johnson accompanying (the resulting 78, "Race Track Blues" and "Black

Cat Moan," is also long out of print). Back in Louisville again, Helen continued along her undazzled way, completing her high school education. She then took on a series of jobs suitable for a proper young lady, assisting her lawyer father in his business, working as a bank clerk and as a waitress. "And I didn't really make any money off those early records, not really," she added, "nor off these late ones neither! 'Cause every time you look up, here's another record out, and you don't know how it got out and why they don't give you something, you know, for putting it out. But I don't let it worry me, then or now. I don't let *nothing* bother me."

A year or so later, visiting friends in Buffalo, New York, Helen was urged to get up and sing at a local club. In short order the Buffalo club hired her as vocalist, and she went on from there to land a job with the Midwestern territory band of tenor saxophonist Al Sears. After a stretch with Sears, Helen returned to Louisville and continued to sing locally until an attractive offer from Sears took her to Cincinnati's Cotton Club in 1937. There she made an impression not only on the local audience but on the great bandleader Count Basie. Pictures of Helen Humes dating from this period show a pretty, plump young woman with large brown eyes and a dazzling smile. Her attractive presence and light, clear, rhythmically sure voice prompted Basie, whose singer, Billie Holiday, had just left the band, to offer the spot to Humes. "But he wasn't offering but thirty-five dollars a week, and I was getting that already. So I turned him down." But the following year, 1938, during a New York engagement, she yielded to the persuasive arguments of record producer John Hammond and went with Count Basie's orchestra. It was undoubtedly the best move she could have made, for Basie's band had by then broken through to national fame, its sections stocked with great jazz players such as tenor saxophonist Lester Young.

Helen Humes stayed with Count Basie for four years, until 1942, sharing vocal chores with blues singer Jimmy Rushing. It was a time she remembered fondly. "I enjoyed it so much. It was the first time I ever really traveled around—me and the fellas. And they used to treat me like I was their little sister. When we would go somewhere and play, when I'd get on the bus after, I'd go to my seat and I'd sit there and play like I was sleepin'. And they would say, 'Is Humes asleep?' Or they used to call me Fanny, so they used to say, 'Is Fanny asleep?' You know, Fat Fanny," she pronounced, directing a deadpan look at me, then grinning broadly. "Then they'd start talking about *all* the happenin's. Now, I've had people tell me, 'Helen, I know you could write a book! Why don't you write a book about bein' in the Basie band and everything that happened?' And I say, 'Honey, I'll never write a book about it, 'cause I love those boys—and I don't want to see them killed!'" Rocking with glee, she hugged those untold tales to herself.

"You ask, is the road life hard? Well, it is a hard life if you make it a hard life. But when we finished the show, whatever we were doin', then sometimes I'd go out or go to a restaurant, or I'd get a sandwich and take it home. But whenever the boys would say, 'Come on, Humes, we're going to such-and-such a place,' I'd say, 'Well, you-all go on, just drop me off at home. I'll see you later.' Because, you know, I was *in* show business but I wasn't *of* show business. Every now and then you'd catch me out goin' to clubs, but I never did frequent the places too much. I guess I'm just a homebody, that's all I know. I just would feel comfortable at home, doin' something there or just sittin' up, listenin' to the radio or lookin' at TV. I never put on the record player—that's what I should be doin'!

"Oh, I heard some great music, 'cause all the greats were around then. You had Charlie Parker, Ben Webster, Coleman Hawkins, Hershel Evans. Now, Hershel was one of the greatest—he could play the prettiest tenor sax! And, of course, Fred Green [guitarist with the Basie band]—and he's still there! Before me, of course, Billie used to sing with the band. I took Billie's place. I was never palsy-walsy with her, but we'd speak when we'd see each other, we were just friends like that. But I hated to see her destroy herself, 'cause she was just a *nice* woman, as a singer and a person. Whatever she wanted, though, why, that's what she did.

"I went by to see Billie Holiday when she was working out in San Francisco one night—this was in the fifties. When I got there, there was a couple of fellas at the door, her husband and a plainclothesman. But her husband knew me and he says, 'Well, come on, Helen, I'll get you back.' He says, 'You know, we don't let nobody see her.' But he told the woman who was in front of Billie's door, 'This lady's all right,' and I got to go in and see her. I come to find out they wouldn't let nobody see her 'cause they thought they was bringin' her some—stuff. I sat there talkin' with Billie. She had her little dog. And she was just so mad she didn't know what to do! But Billie never did anything to anybody; everything she did she did to herself."

To successfully replace the great Lady Day in the hippest swing band in the country was no mean accomplishment; indeed, the two women's vocal styles—Humes' sunny, bouncing and infectious; Holiday's deep and shadowed, nearly always, with pain—were as unlike as their lifestyles. Humes recalled one incident that illustrates this difference and reveals her commonsense approach to life and work.

"This one night stands out clear. I remember we were in Chicago, and these friends of Basie's came by, and one of them wanted to take me out. 'We're going to take Helen out, we're going to a party tonight!' he says. And Basie said, 'Yeah, well, if she wants to go, take her. But don't think you're gonna get her drunk and then take advantage of her, 'cause she's gonna drink and *you* gonna get drunk, and she's gonna see that you get home safely!' And that's just what happened!" Helen noted, laughing slyly. "If I would drink all these drinks they gave me, then I would be the biggest drunk in town! They used to try to get me to smoke cigarettes. They said, 'When you go in these clubs and things, you gotta have a cigarette!' But I'm not a smoker, I'm not a drinker. I drink my rock 'n' rye, a few little drinks, or sometimes I don't have any."

A rather proper young lady, fond of home and family, alone in a sea of men. "Oh, I had a boyfriend in the band. Oh, yeah! My childhood beau, he was a trumpet player—he started out playing with Bessie Allen too. He was so nice, but I just didn't feel that I wanted to be cooped up with him for life! Why that is, I don't know, 'cause I just loved him. He was the sweetest thing and would always treat me nice." She shook her head as if to unravel this eternal mystery. "I should have married a musician, baby," she concluded after a pause. "But, well, this *other* young fella who was in the Navy—we did get married. And he was gone all the time. He would write to me every day. And I got *tired* of writin'. I mean, he'd be gone and then I'd be gone, and maybe we wouldn't get a chance to see each other for about three or four weeks. So I finally said, 'Oh, that was the biggest mistake I ever made.'" Another pause, brows knit in thought. "These women with their husbands that are musicians that have got to make a living and are always on the road—it takes a good woman to stand up to things like that. Takes a *very* good woman."

As for the women musicians she knew, such as her classmates in Miss Allen's Louisville band, "Oh, well, they got boyfriends, or they got married. Their boyfriends and their husbands were musicians. In those days, in my era, there weren't any women in the bands. I don't know why they didn't go on, unless they just didn't—develop. You know, there weren't too many places for them to play then unless it was a band."

But if women players were scarce, the twenties and thirties was the era of the great black women singers, and Humes heard many of the legends. "My mother took me to hear Ethel Waters when I was little. Josephine Baker was with her on the same bill. And then when I was in school, we had the opportunity to hear Ma Rainey and also Bessie Smith. And I caught the Calloway girl—Blanche Calloway and her band. She was singing and leading the band. Then there was Ida Cox and Edith Wilson—she was from Louisville."

Humes served with Basie's band primarily as an interpreter of pop songs and ballads but also gained a reputation as a superlative blues singer. Her audience always debated whether she was really a blues artist or a popular, jazz-influenced singer (rather, her *critical* audience debated it; to Helen Humes and her fans, such categorizing was hairsplitting). Humes loved to do ballads, which gave her an opportunity to sing at a measured pace from her lower register, where her voice took on an altogether different quality than it had in middle or top range. In her ballads, especially during her later years, the almost girlish wonder and the bright, sometimes strained effusion in higher keys yielded to a darker, richer sound in which one could sense that she was singing not just out of her lower reaches but out of the deeper emotional place where the private woman lived. (Hear, for example, her versions of "Stardust" and "Exactly Like You" on the album *Midnight at Minton's*, recorded at an after-hours session in 1945, for a splendidly relaxed, reflective set of choruses.)

"Jimmy Rushing used to be the blues singer with Basie, and I was really the pop singer," she said of her work during the Basie years. "That's how that worked out—two different types of singers. We were two different stylists, you see. That's why they had the women singers in those days, for ballads and pop songs." In an interview with Whitney Balliett, she explained it this way: "I've been called a blues singer and a jazz singer and a ballad singer—well, I'm all three, which means I'm just a singer" (*American Singers*, p. 46). But regardless of how she has been labeled, Helen Humes' ease of delivery and handling of dynamics, plus the fact that she was always in tune, enabled the listener to relax right into her music.

After she left Basie in 1942, Humes worked frequently at the prestigious Cafe Society club in New York. She then settled on the West Coast and began working in new contexts, among them recording soundtracks for such films as *Panic in the Streets* (1944) and *My Blue Heaven* (1950). In the latter part of the forties she showed her ability to deliver exuberant rhythm-and-blues material, which brought her some fortune and fame along with cries of distress from jazz purists. She had a hit in 1945 with "Ee Baba Leba" (also known as "Be Baba Leba" and "Oo Baba Leba"), backed by her favorite song, "If I Could Be with You." A Humes original, "Million Dollar Secret" (or "Helen's Advice"), was also very popular, but it was recorded off a live broadcast, and she received no royalties, only a flat fee. "And that was it then," she remembered. "I thought they were supposed to send it to have it copyrighted for me. Which they did—but I come to find out they had *their* names on it, the record company people." It was years before this injustice, all too common in the music business, was redressed.

Meanwhile Humes' career waned, though she recalled a number of artistic successes. "In the fifties I had some of my best records. That's when I went with [vibraphonist] Red Norvo. Then, in the early sixties and late fifties, I had some fine Contemporary Records sessions." Many of those older recordings have been or are now being reissued, including some that feature Helen Humes backed by strings. She also made a number of 78s for such labels as Decca and Discovery, rock 'n' roll and beautiful ballads, including songs like "Rock Me to Sleep," "He May Be Your Man," "Sad Feeling." And there were the concerts, including a triumphant tour of Australia.

In general, though, the late fifties and the sixties were lean years for jazz and for artists like Helen Humes, who felt she was hampered throughout her career by a lack of the personal management attention that proved so invaluable to singers like her contemporary Ella Fitzgerald. "I never had personal management since I began singing. I just had some agents. If I could see how it was doin' something for me—get me on the TV shows and things that I don't do for myself—then I could see it. But just to get a gig for me every now and then? I get as many gigs for myself as they do," she maintained. "To Helen, a singing career never seemed something that she had to have," one jazz writer has observed. "She lacked the single-minded commitment that drove Ella, Mildred and most of the others who made the top. Helen certainly never had the strong consistent booking management she deserved. . . . Not being a particularly aggressive person, she, more than most, needed that guidance" (John McDonough, "Still the Talk of the Town," *Down Beat*, May 20, 1975).

If things were slow professionally, Humes continued to enjoy herself all the same. Bingo later became her favorite mode of relaxation, but in the slow years of the late fifties, "all we did was play cards when I came out to Los Angeles. Honey, we used to play cards around the clock! When you wasn't workin', why then you had your little game, and that pays your rent and helps you out. And it was fun—you *know* I like to enjoy myself. We used to play blackjack, poker and pinochle, and maybe I shouldn't tell this, but we got raided too!" She laughed into her hand. "There was this girl out there in California. She was a singer, and her name was Helen too. But nobody never did come to her game. And she said, 'Helen, come on, have a game with me.' I said, 'Okay, I don't mind.' 'Cause she had her apartment and all the arrangements. Honey, we had a *crowd* then—about five tables, all full. So we used to cut the game. One night there we were, just playin', and somebody knocked on the door, and here come these two fellas. One of them is the mayor of Los Angeles now! He was the police chief or captain then. He comes in and says, 'Sit where you are sitting.'

"Now, there was a couple of fellas sittin' there who didn't have no money; they'd gotten broke. So I said, 'Get up and give these fellas a seat.' Well, *I* didn't know they was the police, 'cause I hadn't been around the police! So they took us down, and we went and paid our little ten-dollar fine and came back and played all night long! So I said, 'Well, well, well. Old Humes in a raid!' Then I went to sing it that way [in her rollicking blues, "They Raided the Joint"], and instead of singing, 'They raided the joint, took everybody down *but* me,' I sang, 'They took everybody down *and* me!' Oh, we had fun."

By 1967, in spite of intermittent recordings and concerts, Helen Humes' career had seemingly reached a nadir. That and the ill health of her mother convinced her to move back to Louisville, where she concentrated on caring for her parents, then in their eighties, and took a day job at a local munitions plant. As she explained it, she was sure that her career in music was behind her. So she sold her record player and her records and stopped singing. "I don't know whether I missed singing in those years or not," she considered. "I just didn't think about it anymore. And if it hadn't been for Stanley Dance [who coaxed her into coming to New York to perform at the 1973 Newport Jazz Festival], I guess I'd just be sittin' there not thinking about it still!"

Her Newport appearance launched Humes on a whole new career. She delighted not only those who remembered the Humes of the Basie years and the solo star of the forties and fifties, but a new crop of young people receptive to the rich jazz and blues heritage that had gone underground during the rock- and soul-dominated sixties. The veteran performer was thrilled at their enthusiastic reception, though a little unsure of herself after years away from the limelight. "Now I was scared. I had not been singing in so many years! And I was stopped up and everything. Nellie Lutcher [the jazz pianist and singer, popular especially during the forties and early fifties] was working down at the Cookery, and she got me all these lozenges and things and said, 'Now, you just take these, and I'm gonna stay right here with you until you come on.' And she did. And once I was singin', it felt good, and the people seemed to enjoy me. That's what makes you feel good. And they kept wanting me to sing more, though I was just supposed to sing one or two numbers.

"Five days later, that's when I went to France." Humes had been urged to go to Europe in the fifties by Mary Lou Williams, then based in France, but had declined. Her 1973 debut European tour was a smash success, and she recorded the award-winning album released in France as *Helen Comes Back,* for the Black and Blue label, with Milt Buckner, Jay McShann and other top-ranked musicians. "Then in '74 they sent for me to come back and do my own tour, so I took [pianist] Gerald Wiggins. And the album that came out of that [issued in America as *Sneaking Around*] came up for a Grammy award later." Thereafter Humes signed a contract with Columbia Records, and recordings appeared steadily. A final album, *Helen*, was made in 1980 and released in 1981 on Muse Records, with such artists as Joe Wilder, Buddy Tate and Norman Simmons.

"You know, I've had people tell me, 'Helen, you ought to get into something—scandalous!'" she said at the close of a long afternoon of talk that autumn day in 1980. "'Then they'd give you big headlines. Then you'll be a star!' Well, I don't want it. I'm not trying to be a star! I want to work and be happy and just go along and have my friends—and *that's* my career." To her many admiring fans, of course, this lady *was* a star. Her sunny, sure-pitched voice and her deft, swinging treatment of blues, ballads and pop remain to keep the memory of her fresh, alive and ever green.

SHEILA JORDAN

Vocalist

"What do I need to work for if I can't sing the way I feel?"

Reading a sheaf of record and concert reviews of Sheila Jordan's work is a little like thumbing through a thesaurus: she is called variously a "melody instrument," a "trumpet," "flugelhorn," "saxophone," a "master of ornament"; her voice strikes some as "broad-ranged," "supple," "pure," others as "throaty," "chesty," "acidy," "indistinguished in and of itself"; her technique ranges in critics' minds from "childlike naiveté" to "highly sophisticated," her effect from "cathartic" to "irritating"; some listeners adore the way she handles a lyric through the "slides, swoops, glides, shifts in tone and rhythm," others wish she would "stick closer to the words."

Confusing? Contradictory? If, as one writer, has it, she is "a paradox—a difficult singer who demands much but is never less than absorbing" (Richard M. Sudhalter, "Jordan Legend Rolls On," *New York Post*, January 18, 1980), the reason lies in her approach to singing. She always demands spontaneity and always takes risks, continuing to fine-tune her art. For her, more than for many other singers, this means exploring and sharing her interior emotional landscape. The result isn't always smooth. There is no safe resting place technically or emotionally for this singer, no neatly wrapped package of song. As she says, "Jazz singers sing out of the need to sing. I always try to approach songs as the first time I've ever felt them. Music is a religion to me, and it's also a love affair. It's the only thing that's kept me alive. I don't even know if I'd be alive today if it hadn't been for the music— that's how strongly I feel about it and how much I love it."

Sheila Jordan in conversation is warm, candid, spontaneous and humble about her high level of musicianship. Small in build and stature, with a pixieish face framed by bobbed hair, she moves with the easy, assured stride of a person who grew up in the country. In performance her body arches and bends as she pulls the music up and out, like a sax player. Her speaking voice retains the sharpish accents of her rural Pennsylvania childhood. At ease in an armchair in her apartment, which is filled with paintings, books, records and food, she unfurls her past—in both its brighter and dimmer aspects, a truly American story, full of grit, anger, stick-to-itiveness and, above all, triumph. A copper-bright thread of energy radiates through this up-and-down tale of the self-made artist, the odyssey of a poor white girl from the hills who journeys to a truly far country called jazz.

Sheila Jordan (née Dawson) was born in 1928. "My mother was married to my father the night she had me," she begins. "Mom was about sixteen at the time. She was working as a waitress in Detroit." (Billie Holiday, with whom Jordan is sometimes compared for the depth of emotional communion she achieves with her audience, began her story, and her life, in a similar fashion. "Mom and Pop were just a couple of kids when I was born—she was thirteen and he was sixteen," says Lady Day in the first line of her autobiography.) "My father married my mother to give me a name—you know, in those days they didn't like the idea that you were a marked woman, a scarlet woman, a tramp. This was in 1928. Of course they never had any life together. Within months he divorced her and married this other woman who was pregnant, to give her kid a name. I never knew my father, just that he was from Canada. He was a French Canadian, and he couldn't read or write.

"So I was born in a furnished room on a Murphy bed—the beds that come out of the wall. The doctor came in, and my father had to jump on the bed because it started going up when I was born. Probably my mother was having a lot of trouble giving birth to me, because she was very tiny and of course very young. It sounds like a comedy to me, it really does! My mother said when I was born my cry sounded like a musical note—she really felt that I sang when the doctor cracked me. I was just born singing! I always sang, I always felt that it was like breathing, another part of my body. But my mother couldn't take care of me, so she sent me back to my grandmother and grandfather in Pennsylvania."

Sheila's grandparents lived in Summerhill, which was fringed by coal mines. She spent the first fifteen years of her life in those tough, grimy Pennsylvania hills. "My grandfather was part American Indian, and my grandmother's family was Welsh. He was a house painter, and all my uncles worked in the mines. My grandmother had eleven children in all, and two of them died. With me there, there were nine of us kids. It was the Depression— very, very bad times. We and another family were the poorest in town. We didn't have any electricity at all, 'cause we couldn't afford it. We didn't have any water or heat in our house. We had two coal stoves to heat this huge old rundown house with eight rooms. We didn't have any indoor plumbing at all. We used to eat what my grandfather caught hunting—squirrel, rabbit, porcupine, pheasant—whatever you *could* eat. They made soup out of it. Greens and black-eyed peas, what they call gourmet soul food—all the stuff that poor folks, white and black, used. They charge a fortune for that food today! In those days it didn't matter what color you were—if you were poor, you ate poor food."

But for the little girl, being poor wasn't the worst of it. "I loved my grandmother dearly, and it was hard to see the way this woman worked. Heating huge aluminum tubs on the stove to wash clothes—can you imagine doing that once a week? She chopped wood, she did everything. The fact that we were that poor, and then my grandfather being part Indian, made it rougher. I didn't say anything about my background for years because of the harassment. It's like being born black but being able to pass for white—and I can understand doing that in those years. But the thing I feel bad about sometimes today is that in a family that size we weren't closer. There wasn't a lot of love in that house. It was being so poor, and it was rough. Everybody sang and drank in the beer gardens on Saturday night. That was the miners' only night, our form of recreation. We didn't have movies in the town." Elsewhere Jordan has said, "They drank back home—they didn't read or have cultural happenings like dance or plays. I used to spend lots of time in the beer gardens trying to get my grandfather to come home. And by Saturday night, after they'd paid off their bills at the company store, there wasn't much money left" (Joel L. Siegel, "Sheila Jordan and Jazz Singing," *Radio Free Jazz*, July 1979).

Instinctively she turned to singing. "I was constantly singing when I was a child. I used to have to go a long ways to the store for my grandmother and have to pass a graveyard, and I did a *lot* of singing passin' that graveyard! It was very natural for me to sing in this environment, because we lived right underneath a huge hill like a mountain. There was just something about singing in the mountains, in nature, that went together. So I would sing from the time I left the house. I can sit here now and see myself and remember the wonderful feeling of the freedom of voice and soul.

"The people loved my singing. Not the young people, my classmates— they would make fun of me, and they thought I was trying to show off because I'd get invited to radio stations to sing on the amateur contests. Out there we had just the old kinds of country and mountain tunes, made-up tunes, tunes of the days. Some people had radios. I knew that I was a singer and that I was accepted as a singer, because I was always asked to sing on all of the programs. But for a while, especially when I was in my first year of high school—the last year I lived in the mountains—I didn't sing, because my classmates were very cruel. By now I was approaching womanhood, where I was really self-conscious. I was very skinny and not very attractive. I just had no confidence in myself. But this need to sing was much stronger than the harassment I was going to take afterwards. My teacher kept on and on at me to sing in a duet situation at a school assembly, and that got me back into singing in front of kids. But I kept singing to the mountains and to nature."

Suddenly, during that first year of high school, Jordan's mother whisked her away from the isolated poverty of the mining hills and took her to Detroit. "I knew that I had a calling, and I just had to find it. I had to put this music I felt into a direction, and I didn't know my direction. In Pennsylvania I had heard a little jazz on the radio. You couldn't get any jazz stations there, but they were playing the standard tunes and the songs of the day, some great standard ballads, and they had these song sheets out at the time, where they put the words to tunes. Of course, the only way I got to hear any standards was by bein' at a friend's house who had a radio. I learned very quickly—I had to! My ears would be open when there was a radio program on.''

But in Detroit there was music all around, and Jordan found it fast. "I went to a high school in downtown Detroit, and they had a fantastic jukebox at a place nearby. It had Charlie Parker and His Reboppers. This was in about 1942, and I said, 'That's what I want to do. I want to sing this kind of music.' And this music was very new. Well, from then on I tried to find out where that music was. Unfortunately it was in black neighborhoods, and there was terrible prejudice—race riots.''

And not only prejudice. Betty Carter, a black singer who is Jordan's contemporary ("I'm two years older than Betty"), encountered another kind of resistance from her churchgoing family when she sought out the exciting new sounds of bop in the Detroit of the forties. She has described the situation vividly: "If you wanted to get into jazz, you had to go downtown where the pimps, prostitutes, hustlers, gangsters and gamblers supported the music. If it wasn't for them there wouldn't be no jazz! They supported the club-owners who bought the music. It wasn't the middle-class church people who said, 'Let's go hear Charlie Parker tonight'" (Barbara van Rooyen and Pawel Brodowski, "Betty Carter," *Jazz Forum*, January 1979).

Sheila Jordan didn't have a background of middle-class respectability to contend with, but her race made it difficult for her to gain entrée to the invaluable musical laboratory of the black clubs. Being white made the teenage singer highly visible in the black jazz community; for a while she was a minority of one, and an easy target of abuse—not, however, from blacks: "I was constantly harassed by the cops. It was a bore and it was terrible. I was always being taken down to the police station and questioned. The car was always being stopped if I was in the company of young black women and men. We had to show our age and our birth certificates. You had to carry your birth certificates on you! 'Cause they did not want white and black people associating—that's how sick it was. It was taboo. And I even got called in to the principal's office at school and asked why I hung around with black people.''

But the persecution merely quickened Jordan's resolve to continue with what soon amounted to total absorption in black music. "As soon as I started listening, it's the first time in my life I became very strong. And I have had only encouragement from all the black musicians. Generally speaking, when I was on the scene in Detroit, there were not many white musicians. I remember we had one nondrinking club called the Club Sudan where all the Detroit musicians hung out—Tommy Flanagan, Barry Harris, Kenny Burrell, all of us. We all grew up together, and I don't remember any white musicians at that particular time. Don't forget that I'm talking about the forties, and especially about '47, '48. After that more and more white musicians, such as Pepper Adams, came on the scene."

Though she completed high school ("I'm the only one in my family to do that") and toyed with the idea of becoming a sociologist, Jordan soon settled upon a method of coping with the chronic financial insecurity of being a jazz musician. She studied typing and bookkeeping and kept herself going by taking office jobs. But of course, her real life began in the evenings. It was a period of intensive musical apprenticeship. "We were all learning together, we were all enjoying the same thing. Jazz! Bebop! Like a family. In high school, with the few little pennies I got, I was down there buyin' Bird [Charlie Parker] and Dizzy and Monk records. I couldn't get enough of this music. And I couldn't absorb too much at once. I knew that I was going to learn from these guys, especially Bird."

Like most distinctive jazz singers, Jordan learned and developed her sound by listening to instruments rather than to other singers. "I'm ashamed to say that it wasn't the singers who affected me. Maybe that makes me sound like no singers were great enough, but I really have to be very honest. We're going back to a time where Billie and Ella were out there, and Sarah was comin' up. And that was it, except, of course, for the great blues singers. And Helen Humes was around then, and Mildred Bailey. Now, the first time I heard Sarah Vaughan, I was completely bowled over. I think she came naturally into what she was doing. But it didn't make me want to do that, 'cause I knew I couldn't. I could never have a voice like that. And with Billie, it was her feeling and emotion. Who the hell's going to want to sing like Billie Holiday, or even dare to pick her emotions and try to put them into your own? 'Cause she's singing her heart and what she's been feeling—that's why her sound is so unique."

In the late forties Jordan became part of a vocal trio that prefigured Lambert, Hendricks and Ross, who became famous a decade later for their minutely faithful vocal reproductions of jazz solos and instrumentation. "These two young black cats were singing in a club, and they were doing bebop tunes, Charlie Parker tunes and scat singing. I just went up to them and I said, 'I really would like to sing with you.' Of course they looked at me; but they didn't say, 'Aw, this white chick,' they said, 'Well, come on, let's get together.' And we did. We became Skeeter, Mitch and Jean—Skeeter Spight, LeRoy Mitchell and me. I used my middle name, from Jeanette, 'cause when I was a kid I got teased so much about my name—'Sheila, Sheeba, the jungle queen, Sheena'—that I didn't want to be called that anymore.

"So we scatted, and we did words too, to Charlie Parker's heads. Mostly they wrote the words, but I wrote some words too, to 'Round About Midnight.' " (She has, in fact, set lyrics to several Bird tunes that are still in her repertoire, including "Confirmation" and "Little Willie Leaps.") "We never did any recordings or appeared on any of the radio shows. We just sat in with Dizzy and Bird. When they came to town, the Detroit musicians used to tell them, 'Hey, let these kids sing. You gotta hear these kids sing!' They were kids themselves! And Bird used to ask us to get up and sing with 'em. And when I came to New York, years later, Bird remembered me, too."

Jordan's involvement with the music bred, perhaps inevitably, a deep identification with black culture. "Oh, I thought I was black for years, 'cause I never really felt white anyway. I always felt in the middle. Our family was always a minority group as far as the culture, and I had been harassed and knew the feeling of prejudice—of course, not with a black skin, but the prejudice of being poor and going through a lot of torment and unhappiness as a child because of people making fun of my background and the way we lived. So I always felt very comfortable in a minority group. I always felt I could say what I felt, I could sing the way I felt like singing, I could really relax and be myself. I didn't have to be ashamed of my background. I didn't have to bullshit anybody, say I was something I wasn't and had an education that I didn't have, or certain conveniences. So I felt very comfortable with black people. I just didn't want to be white. Of course, since then times have changed, and my feelings are different. But something saved me from having this race hatred and this prejudice. What was it, with my background and the way I was raised, that made *me* not be prejudiced?"

Jordan's roots, then, are emphatically in Afro-American music, and specifically in the great harmonic revolution of the forties and early fifties that we know as bebop. "I wouldn't be singing the kind of music I'm singing today if it hadn't been for black people and learning from them and their beliefs. And especially someone like Charlie Parker, who gave me all the inspiration in the world. There are people that say how terrible he was, how he ripped them off, but I can't say anything bad about Bird. He never did anything bad to me! He was always very encouraging, always treated me very nicely and with respect. Of course, I wasn't his girlfriend or his wife," she adds, her voice taking on a wry edge that indicates another, less serious side to the musically intense Sheila Jordan. In performance her sense of humor often pops up like a playful imp.

By 1950 she had had it with Detroit. "I couldn't stand the pressure of the prejudice anymore, and I wanted to basically be around Bird and his music. I wanted to be where I could be a little more free about going to these clubs without all of this hassle and the embarrassment to my black friends. I didn't feel that New York was going to be that much better, but I knew it was a little better. The last time I was taken down to the police station, I told the cop I was going to New York anyway. He said, 'Oh, yeah, that's where they let you-all live together.' I said, 'Yes, you mean it's very cos-mo-pol-itan.' I was cool, but I was burning inside."

In New York she became involved in the rich jazz underground, fast gaining a reputation among musicians as a fine singer. She married Duke Jordan, Parker's former pianist, and had a child. "In the early fifties, even my body changed. I wasn't like eighty, ninety pounds anymore—I had been very skinny. I started to get a little figure, and I had my daughter." The marriage was brief, and the financial and domestic responsibilities of raising the child became hers alone. Like single working mothers in any profession, Jordan found her mobility severely curtailed. This in itself was enough to cramp the development of her career as a singer, but there was another problem, about which she is typically straightforward: she began to drink, and the drinking magnified the pain in her life and tended to erode the good and glorious feelings that came from singing the music she loved.

Today, with years of sobriety behind her and a career moving rapidly toward a new level of success, Sheila Jordan reflects on this difficult period: "A lot of it came from the pain. Oh, it wasn't every *day*, but it got pretty bad." The requirements of caring for her daughter and, as she frequently stresses, the *need* to sing, combined to help her achieve a perspective about her drinking, what might be called a spiritual awakening. "The way I stopped drinking was I got a sort of shaking up, and I don't know whether I dreamed it or whether it actually happened. It was almost like a spirit that came to me and said, 'If you don't stop what you're doing to yourself, this is going to be taken away from you.' And to me, that would be like losing part of my soul, not being able to do music anymore. If you have a certain art and a special gift, you have got to nourish and respect it and take care of it. That means that you don't go out there and do anything to destroy this art."

The same credo has given Jordan the strength to stand fast in her choice of material and career decisions. "For me to go and sing something that I don't believe in is in essence taking away from my art. I would rather do anything except music I don't believe in." She pauses, and a puckish smile lights her face. "There are people who do that *other* music, like pop and disco, much better than I do anyway. And I think that the record people are the ones that make them change. They tell them how to approach a song: 'Do this tune, it's good for your career.' Then too, I feel a need to express myself in front of an audience, but not to the point where I'm gonna sing anything to do that. And I'm not going to hold back for a couple of dollars. What do I need to work for if I can't sing the way I feel?"

In New York, even during the troubled times, Jordan worked to broaden her knowledge and refine her skills. But though she studied music with various musicians, she eschewed formal voice training. "I was after the feeling, never technique. I didn't know what technique was. I never even thought about the voice as far as taking care of it, how to sing properly. I was just going by feeling and being knocked out by this music that all the great players wrote." Through practice she learned where the strengths and the limits of her instrument lay, experimenting with a fresh approach every time she sang. Thoroughly grounded in Charlie Parker's music, she branched out in new directions. Elsewhere she has described her musical evolution during those first New York years. "Through Duke [her husband] I met Charlie Mingus, who gave me the idea of studying with [pianist] Lennie Tristano. Lennie taught me harmony and theory, ear training and sight reading for nearly two years [1951-52]. When my daughter Tracy was born, I stopped studying with Lennie and concentrated on raising her. But emotionally I still needed to sing. . . . Thanks to a very special woman called Jacquie Howe, I got a job singing at the Page 3 in the Village. . . . One night in the early sixties, George Russell [the composer] heard me at the Page 3. George is the daddy of underground musicians; he sort of discovers people and puts them on record" (Siegel).

Russell's support led to Jordan's debut album, *Portrait of Sheila*. Released in 1963, it won her accolades and more work; prescient reviewers and listeners began to predict a brilliant future for her. Shortly afterwards, Jordan and Russell collaborated again, memorably reviving a dusty old piece of Americana. Jordan's beautiful twelve-minute rendition of "You Are My Sunshine" on Russell's album *Outer Thoughts* was a keening miners' blues that showed her country roots grafted onto black music. "I learned the *channels* that I must take to get across the feeling that I want to display through black music," she reflected in an interview. "Now, 'Sunshine' was for the coal miners. 'Sunshine' and 'Blue Skies' were their favorites. They liked songs that talked about light; their lives were so filled with darkness" (Burt Korall, "First Take," *Jazz*, Spring 1980).

But the sixties, which had begun with such promise, proved to be a dry period for jazz and for singers like Sheila Jordan and Betty Carter. Jordan continued to sing when she could, and many who didn't know she had the "chops" and the soul of a bopster labeled her an avant-garde singer—the kiss of death as far as record producers and most club owners were concerned. "I think many writers call me an 'out' singer because they can't compare me to other singers. They really feel that they have to be able to do that, and if they can't, they are at a loss for words. Of course I have been associated with avant-garde groups, and I have been involved with church liturgies written by jazz composers—because there were no other places for me to sing! Now, I would never be doing 'free' music if I didn't have my bebop roots. But I feel that I can certainly put my emotions and my musical feeling into any kind of creative music, as long as I know what the direction is. I always find a place to express the music that I need to express, whether it's the subway station, the church or my home."

Jordan's "avant-garde" explorations led to several recordings and a growing number of fans, but security within the established music business continued to elude her. Characteristically, she takes her lack of commercial success in stride. "Well, I'm shy. I cannot call up a record company and say, 'Would you like to record me?' I would feel like I'm tooting my own horn. Then too, I just never have really been out there looking for a manager, for starters. And most of the companies still think I sing too far-out. That's what they've been told." She laughs. "I've been fired from more jobs in my life by singing the way I sing than I could possibly tell you. I went all the way up to Newfoundland, stayed there for a week and got fired. I got fired from the Playboy Club, which was supposed to be a jazz room. I was too far-out. Also, it's not easy being white and singing jazz, or it didn't used to be. But mostly I've gotten fired because they didn't understand me.

"When you're a singer, oh, you're this chick that gets up and sings some songs and you look good—especially with the club owners. They could care less what you sing like; they're more concerned about what you look like. Not so much in the jazz clubs, but if you're out there trying to do your music, you're not always going to be invited to sing in a strictly jazz club. You're gonna try to take your jazz music into nonjazz or semijazz clubs. And of course, the owners don't know anything about music—they want to know what you look like." Critics have their weaknesses too: "I had two separate reviews from the same concert—top reviewers. One said I looked great but I didn't fulfill my capacity; in other words, I didn't sing that good, but I sure looked good. The other one said I didn't look too hot but, boy, could I sing."

In the late seventies Sheila Jordan's career finally began building steam as she linked up with pianist-composer Steve Kuhn and his group, touring Europe often and gigging more in the States. A 1980 Jordan-Kuhn recording excited the interest of fans old and new and elicited feelers from several record companies. Jordan's repertoire, always packed with standards—"If You Could See Me Now," "I'm a Fool to Want You," "Please Don't Talk About Me When I'm Gone," "A Sleeping Bee," "Falling in Love with Love," the jazz standards "Confirmation," "Dat Dere," "Lush Life," "St. Thomas," "My Favorite Things," "God Bless the Child"—became studded with Kuhn's songs as well. "They are very unique, special and very personal, so it took a long time before I could do his compositions. That's why I'd like to have time to just devote to music. I don't mean specifically learning new tunes all the time, getting new arrangements together. I mean really living with the music, learning things like what a composer like Steve Kuhn might have for me, or Steve Swallow." Jordan collaborated with Swallow on creating readings of

Robert Creeley's poems, a year long project that culminated in another 1980 recording.

Over the last decade Jordan has steadily chalked up awards and placed high in the jazz polls. Having weathered decades of virtual obscurity and scarce recording opportunities, she has emerged as a consummate craftswoman, a distinguished member of that small group of true jazz improvisers. Along with Betty Carter, she is one of the finest scat singers working today, and a searingly honest interpreter of ballads and blues. Jordan has been likened to a Venetian glass-blower, creating spun-glass sounds; one writer says that "she doesn't so much sing songs as melt them like candles" (Madora McKenzie, *Christian Science Monitor*, January 24, 1978). She is a singer who can emote like a seasoned actress, calling on all her experiences, telling stories and making up blues. Certain songs are indelibly hers—like "Lush Life." Above all, she is a singer who doesn't make compromises with her art.

"I'll keep working until I'm accepted. Until people that are in a position to record me or book me take me seriously and know that I've been out here for thirty-five years. Thirty-five years of believing in this music, working on it when I can, living it every day and protecting it from being false. Until they know that this is my sound and that there are people out there who would enjoy and get some pleasure from hearing it. I want to do as much music as I can while I'm around. To do nothing but music! That to me would be a dream come true."

HELEN KEANE

Manager and Producer

"The big companies still relegate women ... to where they don't have clout. There aren't many women in the record business in the kinds of positions to say, 'That's good and that's bad, and that's the final word.'"

Helen Keane has built a solid reputation and racked up impressive achievements as a manager and producer over her twenty-some years in the music business, a business in which women have been all but absent until recently. Keane managed the career of the great jazz pianist Bill Evans for eighteen years, until his death in 1980, producing all his recordings from 1967 on. She has also produced albums for guitarist Kenny Burrell, singers Morgana King, Mark Murphy, João Gilberto and Tony Bennett (with Bill

Evans), trumpeter Clark Terry, composer Steve Kuhn, guitarists Chuck Wayne and Joe Puma, and the all-woman group Alive! Her close attention to detail, executive ability and astuteness in handling what she terms the "career moves" of her artists reflect her deep concern for the musicians and the music they make.

We meet to talk in Keane's Manhattan office, a record-lined room complete with large, fluffy cat, constantly ringing phone, curios from her world travels and photographs of musician friends and her two sons. There are various ways to wave a visitor into your busy office. Helen Keane does it warmly, deals with her telephone efficiently and urges coffee on me. Her manner reveals what must be one of the keys to her success: the ability to make someone feel at home, at ease. Seated at a desk piled high with papers, she fixes me with an easy smile and focuses her considerable energy on her past, starting from the top with obvious relish.

"My career began in the fifties as a seventeen-year-old secretary in a company called MCA, which was the largest talent booking agency in the world. And I had a boss who said one day, literally, 'Kid, you have talent. You should be more than a secretary, and I'm gonna train you. You should be an agent.' And he trained me, very quietly. He was an executive in the television department and took me to the shows he booked and introduced me to the artists he was responsible for. A bit later I was working for him and for another agent as well, and the other agent was even more excited about me. By then I was actually functioning as an agent without officially doing it, because they had no female agents at MCA—there was a definite rule against it. There were no women executives, period, and there was no such thing as a female agent."

Earlier Keane had played with the idea of becoming an actress. "My aunt, who was in the theater, said, 'You have talent, there's no question about it, but are you ready for what you're gonna have to go through to make it?' After we talked a few times, I saw that I had no great desire to be onstage. If I *had* had the commitment, there was nothing she could have said that would have discouraged me. And she wasn't trying to discourage me, she was trying to find out how I really felt.

"So I knew very quickly that I did not want to pound the pavement and sit in casting offices. I had learned to type and take shorthand, so I got a job with MCA. And you know, when you're that age, every day is another adventure. And I was lucky. The men I worked for saw something in me, saw that I had a feeling for performers. So they—Bobby Sanford and Johnny Green—trained me, all very quiet. Then, after I'd been at MCA for about two years, they decided it was time to take a stand. They told me to go into the head man's office: 'We'll protect you.' But he—Sonny Werblin—said to me,

'That's ridiculous. We don't do that here.' So I put the word out, and William Morris, another agency that was a little less rigid, sent me a feeler. When MCA heard about that, they immediately promoted me, and I became the first female agent."

Keane made good on her potential. "My first winner was Harry Belafonte. Nobody else would talk to him at MCA, so he used to sit in my office. When he got the idea of singing folk songs, I presented him to the whole office. Everybody thought we were going together. They'd pat me on the head and say, 'Ah, kid, he's your boyfriend, right? What are you gonna do with a folk singer with a big production like that?' Well, I got rid of all the backup singers he had and put him in the Blue Angel and the Village Vanguard and got him a manager, and he was off and running. After that, of course, my career just moved like crazy."

Keane married in her twenties. "And got pregnant immediately," she adds. After she had her baby she went back to her MCA job. "But then I realized I could no longer do that job the way I had been. I was on the town every night looking for talent—that's how I found it, that's how I was so successful. So I left MCA and went to CBS. Now I was buying talent instead of selling, which is a lot easier. There were a lot of variety shows, and everybody came to me; I auditioned about fifty people a week. I found Jonathan Winters that way, and Carol Burnett, Artie Johnson, Dom DeLuise."

And now jazz reasserted itself in her life. "One of the shows I worked at the time was Garry Moore's. That was a very big show, and he was a closet jazz drummer. So my love of jazz came back through Garry Moore. I had loved jazz as a kid, because my older brother had collected the records and would take me to big-band things at the Paramount and so on. But I never said, 'This is going to be my career.' My desire was to be in show business. So I had tabled the jazz scene, but for Garry's show I started auditioning jazz talent. I auditioned Chris Connor and put her on the show, and Toshiko Akiyoshi and Marian McPartland. But you could only put jazz on the show if there was a gimmick. Toshiko was a Japanese lady who played piano; Marian was an English lady; Chris was a singer, and Garry loved singers. But jazz on television had to have a hook.

"I had a very successful six years at CBS. Then I got married again and got pregnant immediately again. And I did not want to work that way any longer. For one thing, I missed the children. So I left CBS and opened my own little management office, right in my apartment. Right in this same apartment, all these years later! My first client of my very own was [actor-choreographer] Geoffrey Holder, who was then getting a lot of recognition [in the Broadway show *House of Flowers*]. So I was able to start my business with somebody with a recognizable name. I had a lot of success with him—he had a big dance company. Then he married [dancer] Carmen DeLavallade, and I'm still exclusively her manager."

It was a simple, if momentous, step for Keane from the dance world to jazz. "Along the way I met a man named Gene Lees. He had just left his editorship at *Down Beat* magazine. After he came to New York we met, fell in love and were together for years. Right away he said, 'I want you to hear Bill Evans, the pianist. You should be his manager.' Now, I knew Bill Evans' work, because I never stopped loving jazz and listening to jazz. I just was not professionally involved with it. Gene took me to the Village Vanguard, where Bill and I met and liked each other immediately. So for eighteen years we were together.

"From there, I built my management company. Bill was struggling, and I was able to struggle with him because fortunately my income from Geoffrey and Carmen was considerable. And then I took on [dancer-choreographer] Alvin Ailey. So I was very active in dance, and I was able to give the dedication and commitment to Bill and build him without starving to death." The rapport between Evans and Keane was such that she went into a period of professional withdrawal after his sudden death. She still finds it difficult to discuss that lengthy association.

Managing the career of another pianist, whom Bill Evans much admired, has helped to ease Keane back into a full and busy schedule again in the eighties. "It was an unspoken thing with Bill that I would never really have an interest in another pianist. But in about 1978 Bill called me one day and said, 'Listen, I heard somebody the other night that you should manage named Joanne Brackeen. Do you know who she is?' It was just accidental that he had heard her, because musicians on his level don't really have the time to listen to other people—they're always traveling or recording or whatever. But she was playing in the Village Vanguard with [saxophonist] Joe Henderson, and Bill happened to hear her there.

"I became Joanne's manager right away. It was what *she* had wanted to happen, which is interesting. She came down to the Vanguard again later, when Bill was playing, and the three of us sat and talked at a table. And that was it. So it was meant to be. With Joanne, it's been hard work on both our parts, because it takes an awful lot of work to build an artist. And it's harder all the time. The record business is not good, and they are not signing artists the way they were a few years ago. And in the beginning every review of Joanne said, 'She sounds like a man.' But the fact that she's a woman quickly self-destructed, thank God, and it *was* beneficial in that she got so much press. Now she's being respected as just a great player, so the female thing is not a gimmick to the press anymore. Now it's her *performance*, and of course she's up to that. Her commitment is total. She knows where she's going and what she wants. And we know together how it has to be done. There's great understanding on her part and great strength."

Keane deliberately restricts her activities as a manager to a select group of artists, feeling that she can be more effective that way. She also wants to direct more and more attention to another aspect of the music business. "What I want to do is more producing. I'm very anxious to be an active record producer. I love that. I love that maybe best of anything. The ideal way to function as a manager is to be the producer. They are two separate functions, but the manager really knows more about the artist than anyone else—his or her creativity, life, habits, how disciplined or undisciplined they are when they work, what music they like best, how they choose their material, how they like to record. Therefore the manager can obviously be the best producer—that is, in personal management, where the artist trusts and will feel more comfortable with that person in the control room than almost anybody else. I'm just sorry more managers don't realize this.

"Actually, the word 'producer' is a misnomer. We're called producers, but that word is thought of as referring to the person who gets the money, who oversees the whole operation, who doesn't necessarily get involved in the actual creative aspects of the project. If we were called directors, what we do would be obvious—we direct the whole operation. Somewhere along the line with Bill Evans I first became a record producer. Creed Taylor was his producer with Verve Records, and he began asking me, 'What do you think of that tune?' and 'Why don't you talk to Bill about such and such?' After a while he said, 'You know, Helen, you are producing these dates.' So he opened the door for me, and eventually I got a contract at MGM-Verve as Bill's producer. It was certainly the ideal way to become a producer."

Keane's executive abilities have aided her in the recording studio. "A lot of producers feel it's very necessary to know the technical language, to know how to operate the engineer's board. I don't. I share the responsibility for what ends up on tape and put the engineers totally in charge of what they're doing. If I don't like what I hear, I ask them for something different. But I don't put it in technical language, because I feel the engineer knows what to do. I love delegating authority! I like to have people around me that I can say, 'This is yours—do it,' as long as I know they're able to. And an engineer is the boss of that section. *My* ears know when it's right or wrong, but when you give the engineer responsibility, *his* ears are going to be working if yours get a little tired. It's teamwork, it's much easier on the producer. I study the textures. If I was worried about the technical aspects, there's a lot that I probably wouldn't be as open to or as concentrated on. So that's how I try to listen.

"And I don't work on those giant speakers, those monsters in the control rooms that make everything sound like a hit. It's *not* what anybody hears when they buy the record. So I always work on small speakers, like JBLs, reasonable speakers so you really hear what's going to be on the record. In the world of rock 'n' roll nobody is realistic, and the speakers get bigger and bigger and bigger. Well, I don't do pop dates because I don't believe I could do them well. I think I would find myself getting real crazy."

Of the variety of jazz artists for whom Helen Keane has produced albums, the all-woman group Alive! represents a departure on two fronts. Musically Alive! is more eclectic than most of her other productions. And working with an all-female group was a new experience. "I began realizing that this Alive! date [done in the summer of 1981] was the very first time I had ever worked with women," Keane states, surprise in her voice. "A project totally organized by women—the producer, the manager, the entire band. And it was wonderful to be with and work with women, to just be a woman and sit and have coffee together. What it did was to create such a warm atmosphere between us that it was a joy. As hard as we were working, we were always happy, and that was kind of a revelation to me. I'm not saying that I now feel that I must work with women all the time. The women of Alive! are very unusual women, not only highly intelligent, but very mature in their approach and their commitment. Their friendship and their mutual respect is a very wonderful thing to see. There might be a difference of opinion, but they can talk it out, communicate, because of this respect. Now, in my career of working with and producing albums for men, in every situation there has always been a leader running the show as far as the musicians were concerned, one musician who was really the boss. But Alive! is a cooperative group, so they all have an equal voice. There is no leader."

Keane's achievements as agent, manager and producer are among the "firsts" for women in the entertainment and music industries, and her discussion of this other "first," an all-woman jazz record production, leads her into a summation of her own and women's achievements generally in the field since the fifties. "Being an agent at MCA back in the fifties had nothing to do with the record business, but certainly I opened the door there. I was the first woman with that company, and there are an awful lot of women agents now. I'm not saying I was responsible, but it did open it up. That was long before the word 'feminism' was being used. There was no women's lib, there was no women's movement. And I just got very lucky. I didn't make the salary I should have been making"—she chuckles ruefully—"but I had a lot of acclaim and a very successful career when I was very young. And that, I always say, is due to men. It's the truth, though it sometimes comes as a shock when I speak these days at symposiums and seminars. I like to qualify this statement by saying that though there has to be a certain radical aspect to everything, such as 'women in jazz' now being the big cause in the music, I'll be very happy when there isn't this prejudice and the consequent segregation. And this will come when women can make the full commitment to the music. The reason they haven't in most cases is due to their conditioning. Someday there will just be people playing music.

"As far as the record companies are concerned, the big companies still relegate women too often to the publicity department, to promotion, to artists' relations, to art—to where they don't have *clout*. There aren't many women in the record business in the kinds of positions to say, 'That's good and that's bad, and that's the final word.' There just aren't. And it doesn't seem to be changing, or there'd be more women like me producing albums. And even so, I'm working as an independent producer coming in. An outsider. I don't think I could get a position on staff in any of these companies—and I've worked for a lot of the biggies, Columbia, Warner Brothers, Fantasy—and be able to do what I've done.

"I do know women working in the business, sure, but it's usually a token thing. They don't let them do very much. And I don't know what's going to have to happen for that to change. They have women in the A-and-R departments of the big record companies, but they never walk through the door of a studio, of a control room. I've never understood that. But it's always tough for jazz anyway. Jazz has always been the stepchild of the record business and the concert and college concert fields. You don't get these gigs until you're a giant name in jazz, until you are a household jazz name. And until you're big, you can't get the record deal, you can't get the good jobs. So I don't think the state of the economy and the state of the record business today has really hurt jazz that much, or women in jazz. In jazz, the artist and the manager have to work so much harder to make the music succeed, to get the money out of it and the recognition."

Keane's telephone, which has been jangling on and off throughout the afternoon, is blessedly silent as she leans toward me over her desk, peering intently through big tortoiseshell glasses, to drive her final point home. "You can succeed in jazz. It can be done. But it's hard, hard work on everybody's part. I think that the proliferation of the independent record labels, the honest ones, is a good thing for jazz. That's where jazz will go. And that's where more and more women will then be heard."

MELBA LISTON

Trombonist and Arranger

"I had to prove myself, just like Jackie Robinson."

In 1974 Melba Doretta Liston, veteran jazz trombonist and arranger, left jazz and America for a new career as director of the Afro-American Department of the Institute of Music in Jamaica, there to immerse herself in cross-cultural educational activities. But in 1979 she came back to America, encouraged by fresh interest in her music. By then the women's movement was focusing attention on female contributors in music, and the Kansas City Women's Jazz Festival had become an important focus of activity. Its co-producers, Carol Comer and Dianne Gregg, persuaded Liston to return to the States, and to her hometown, to headline the 1979 festival. A critical and highly emotional success, she played to a sellout crowd of women and men; that show of support was instrumental in her decision to leave her teaching position in Jamaica and return to active involvement in the American jazz community. Comer and Gregg regard their successful long-distance per-suasion as one of their most important achievements. "We brought Melba out of retirement," Comer says proudly (interview with author, June 30, 1979). And Liston agrees. "Kansas City changed my life," she told me.

Few women instrumentalists (and not many men) have jazz credentials as impressive as Melba Liston's. She was for years the only woman in America to play jazz trombone seriously, and on a par with male musicians. And she played with the best from the beginning. In California her junior high bandmates included a future giant of tenor saxophone, Dexter Gordon, as well as alto saxophonist Vi Redd. Fresh out of high school, she joined the pit band at the Lincoln Theatre in Los Angeles, led by Bardu Ali, and began arranging almost immediately. Soon she was chosen as a member of an exciting new big band led by Gerald Wilson. Later she played with Count Basie, Dizzy Gillespie and Quincy Jones, and co-led a group with Clark Terry. She arranged and orchestrated for Gillespie, Duke Ellington, Count Basie, Dinah Washington and Diana Ross. In 1950 she helped form a group that backed Billie Holiday. In 1960 she orchestrated an entire album *(Lonely and Sentimental)* for singer Gloria Lynn in one week. Clark Terry commissioned her to write jazz figures for the Buffalo Symphony Orchestra, and she did important arrangements for pianist Randy Weston's recorded treatment of his *African Suite.* By 1980, reestablished in New York, she was arranging for, playing with and directing Melba Liston and Company, her own group. Speaking of Liston, singer Roberta Flack has observed, "Playing a trombone is considered anti-feminine—but here's a woman who hears the sound of a horn! If a woman picks up a horn, she's considered less than she is. There's that little area where you're allowed in. You can be *that* and be all right" (radio interview on WRVF, former New York jazz station, June 1979). The prejudices Liston encountered throughout her career were perhaps partly responsible for her retirement from performing throughout most of the sixties (she continued to do free-lance arranging) and for her move to Jamaica in 1974. It is heartening, however, that by 1979, when she returned to the States, conditions had begun to change. Since then she has generally been regarded simply as an experienced player who happens to be a woman.

Onstage Liston has that hard-to-define magnetism or charisma that draws empathy from the audience; it is there in her presence, in her physical bearing as she approaches the bandstand. She is lithe and tall, dresses in long, flowing, colorful dresses. A classic African beauty with hair cropped close to a finely shaped head, she has warm brown skin and Chinese eyes. When she turns to her audience ready to play, her face lights up; energy seems to surge up from within, and she is rendered ageless. She picks up her trombone and steadies it: the lowdown shiny brass instrument becomes an extension of herself, a delicate thing fitted to her graceful arms and long, tapering fingers. She begins to play, and her tone is warm, yet light and delicate; she brings forth a soufflé of sound. No pyrotechnics, no dazzle—but she swings. Better, she *sings* with her trombone (and on rare occasions with her voice, in a manner evocative, I think, of Billie Holiday—as if something were being broken, then put together in a new way).

Offstage, after a performance, there is the same sense of charisma, now at rest, and a kind of fragility. Her hands often fly upwards in a gesture artless as a child's, as if to ward off effusive praise from friends and fans. When an admirer compliments her singing she demurs immediately, showing a wry, earthy side: "Oh, that was just to surprise Ma. I don't know what possessed me to do that; I won't do it again." Her voice clips words strictly, rather like an old-time schoolmarm, and her accent is a curious admixture of black jazz musician and Jamaican lilt. She leans over as someone lights her cigarette for her, crushing a bunch of red roses in the lap of her ice-blue gown. She smiles and a glow comes over her, but in her eyes there is a certain saddened hauteur. She is not an easy person to describe.

I arrange for an interview and ride uptown on the appointed date to the Harlem apartment where Liston is staying. The welcome is almost formal, ritualistic. A Miles Davis record plays low on the stereo. Liston sits talking with friends. Drinks are brought round and introductions performed. The trombonist stands up, tall and long in a tie-dyed gown. "We'll go into the bedroom so we can talk privately," she says, then peeks into the room and bars the way. "Oh, my, no. You can't come in here like this. Let me clean this mess up." She scoops clothes into suitcases on the floor; she is leaving the next morning for Jamaica, "to settle things up" before returning to New York. "All right, now." She sits on one end of the white bedspread and begins. There is a mock-stern tone to her voice. "I've had interviews before"—she shakes her head ruefully—"like on TV, when I say, 'You will not ask me about this and you will *not* ask me about that. Agreed?' We shake hands. Soon as the camera's red light comes on, they'll ask, 'Have you ever been married?' Then I look right into them, and I pick up my trombone and I just start working the slide." She imitates the playing of a trombone and looks across the bed at me.

Liston starts from the beginning. She has the storyteller's gift, fresh wonder at the facts of her life: a poor black child born in 1926, growing up in the ghetto during the Depression, in Kansas City, where the South meets the Midwest. A lonely and wondering child. "Music was just something that seems like it was always there," she begins softly. "There was a piano in the house, and then we were pretty famous out there where we lived because we had a Majestic radio. And some of the people hadn't even received their electricity yet." She lived in Kansas City for her first ten years; in 1936 she moved with her mother across the country to Los Angeles. It was just the two of them. "I don't think my mama was making but thirteen dollars a week. And I never asked her for anything because that would mean I wouldn't see her for a long time, 'til she earned all this money. I really wanted to see my ma rather than have things. And so I was really a cool child.

"The only thing I ever really demanded was when I saw this trombone. It was just—oh! It did a thing to me, and I just had to have it. Just beautiful, standing up in the shop window like a mannequin, and I was just mesmerized by it. I was six or seven. My mom didn't question it, she just got on to business, tried to get herself together to get it for me."

But though the mother indulged the child, some of her other relatives were not so supportive. "Well, now, my grandfather was my cohort with the trombone. He encouraged me. But my grandma and my aunties were very much against it. They said it was going to make too cruel a life for me, and my mother should not do this thing to me. My grandmother said, 'You're exposing that child to this and that—dope and pimps and things.'" Liston chuckles. "As far as I know, my grandmother had never been no place but church. And how she knew about all these things that I didn't find out about until about forty years later, it still amazes me! Every now and then I run across something and I say, 'Boy, Grandmama said I was going to run into this.' "

From childhood on, the trombone was Liston's link to the world. The musical connection was there even before the instrument: "Oh, even before I started school, three, four years old. I didn't have any sisters or brothers. And there weren't any girls my age in the neighborhood. So I was a tomboy, right? But sometimes the boys didn't want to be bothered with me, so I'd be alone. And when I was little I found out I could do this [she sings the notes in the octave, numbering them one to eight, in a childlike, innocent voice]. Now, there was a song I really liked at that time, I think it was by Fats Waller. It used to come on the radio, but I would always forget it. But then after I remembered this one-two-three business, then when the song came on again I said, 'Oh! Two-six-five-two!' So before I even went to school I had a little system, except for there were some things that would come in between that I didn't figure out. But I would make some kind of mark or arrow." She spreads her hands in a broad gesture of explanation. "See, now, later when I saw music, the teachers and the church people said, 'Oh she's a genius' [this in a voice grown up, pompous, solemn and a little ominous]. But I wasn't a genius. It's—I can't stand not to figure things out, because there's supposed to be a reasonable answer to whatever it is. And being a lonely child, I would always puzzle it out."

For Liston, school meant mostly music too, though she loved math—"puzzling it out." Glee club, band class and church music filled her days. "I was a loner," she repeats. "I didn't pay attention to anybody that didn't love music. And so it was just me and the fellas all the time. I never was"—she hesitates, makes a face of wry disdain—"with the girls. You know, in the frillies and wearin' nice clothes. They never had nothin' to do with me, black or white. It wasn't about race or nothin', it had no color. I just was an outsider to everybody that didn't love music. But I was good friends with anybody that loved music, and it was only there that I had any friends."

Already naturally drawn to music, at age ten Liston became involved in an extraordinary educational project, a program of musical instruction run by Mrs. Alma Hightower. During the twenties, a new pride in black culture had been sparked by the Harlem Renaissance and other flowerings of black talent. Writers like James Weldon Johnson, Countee Cullen, Langston Hughes and Zora Neale Hurston emerged to give voice to black experience, and black accomplishments began to be recognized. In the thirties the Work Projects Administration (WPA), a Depression relief agency that supported various cultural undertakings, gave assistance to certain projects aimed at fostering these developments. One of them was the program Liston enrolled in.

Mrs. Hightower had made passing on black culture her life's work. She had taught generations that remembered slavery, and their children who "escaped sharecroppin' in the South," according to Liston. "Old Mrs. Alma Hightower: that was [alto saxophonist] Vi Redd's great-auntie. Even after the WPA phased out, she stayed at the playground and was in charge of handin' out bats and balls. But there was a piano there, and all the music kids, she'd just grab us up and make us go in there and play. And we were the best group she had. There was Alice Moore, Hobson now—that's a most talented girl. She played piano. There was Vi Redd. And Minnie Moore, she was playin' sax, very good too. And Mrs. Hightower had a very special thing for me. She'd say, 'This one is goin' places.' She made us do everything. We played at the Y, we represented the Department of Parks and Recreation at the Fair in Sacramento for two summers, in 1939 and 1940. Miss Hightower's band. Miss Hightower and the Melodic Dots." She laughs at the memory. "I had forgotten the name of that band."

With that foundation, Liston left Mrs. Hightower as soon as she turned sixteen and could get her union card and start working professionally. "Yes, we left her. Rather rudely, I suspect." She shakes her head in disapproval. "These days, when I watch my students, I remember Mrs. Hightower. I watch their feet to see them pat in time. What I say is, in my older days when I settle down, wherever I settle down, I'm gonna be Aunt Alma all over again, gonna go out and grab up *all* the pickaninnies in the neighborhood that got any talent and make 'em sing and pat in place. That's my retirement work."

For Liston, those early professional years in Los Angeles were exciting ones. "I was meetin' all the musicians. They see this girl with a trombone, and so those persons that really loved music, you know, they watched me out and finally invited me to come and play with them here and there. I was serious about music. I listened hard, and they didn't have to tell me nothin' twice about things involving the music." But Liston was shy about her playing; even today she is self-deprecating about her skills. Repeatedly her fellow musicians urged her to get up and play when she felt like holding back. "Everybody had more confidence. I didn't know what was goin' on. They knew I could do a thing that I didn't know I could do. Well, I had the love. The guys carried me all the way."

Soon after leaving Alma Hightower, Liston and other Melodic Dots alumni were hired to work in the pit band of L.A.'s Lincoln Theatre, under Bardu Ali. It was wartime, and jobs were more plentiful for young (and female) musicians because so many men were in the service. "The big black acts would come and work downtown for a week," she recalls. "Then they would come over and work our theater before they left town. So we were getting some of the best people. Sometimes they wouldn't have their music for our size orchestra, and one time the pianist who did our emergency arrangements took sick. Now, I think Bardu thought I was out of college rather than high school. He said, 'Can you write?' I said, 'Oh, yes.' Then I had to run back to my schoolteachers and make them show me how to set up a score and things. They'd been trying to get me to do it all the time.''

This was Liston's introduction to—and a great deal of her instruction in—the arranging and writing of music, at which she excelled. "Ah, well, the rest was follow-through,'' she adds modestly. "Of course, as a trombone player sittin' in the band, I learned. A trombone player—you sit in the middle of the band and know the blends in another way. And trombone players have more patience. They're not as flighty as a reed player.'' What Liston presents as so casually and easily acquired—the ability to arrange music in complex, exciting combinations—is a talent given to precious few in music: she is indeed specially gifted this way.

With her job at the Lincoln, the teenager of the 1940s entered an exciting world: the jazz world of the big stars. "Gerald Wilson [the bandleader] comes along and snaps many of us out of that pit band. And we started workin' in nightclubs and stuff. We're grown now!'' Melba was introduced to Duke Ellington, Count Basie. "Everybody that came out to California wanted to see this girl trombone player, friend of Gerald's. And I was copying for Gerald, who was an excellent arranger.''

In 1945 she cut her first record. "That's the first time I was in a record studio in my life. Dexter Gordon dragged me in there. I was the dumbest thing in the world. See, this was through my association with the guys in the school. They loved me. Whenever they heard of something they'd say, 'Come on, Melba.' I'd say, 'I can't do it.' They'd say, 'Come on, bitch,' and I'd say, 'Well, okay,' because I don't know what they're gonna do if I don't go. So I would go and do it.'' Her reputation as player and arranger grew. "Whenever they would come to town and there was any little slot where they could fit me in, they would. Benny Carter and all of them—[bandleaders] Les Hite, Fletcher Henderson, Lucky Millinder.''

Liston played with Gerald Wilson's outfit in 1947-48, and when it disbanded she went with Count Basie. A big break came along in 1949. Dizzy Gillespie had put together a band that featured top musicians (at the time including saxophonists John Coltrane and Jimmy Heath) and played one of the most advanced books of modern jazz arrangements. To play in that band was an honor for any up-and-coming musician, and Dizzy called for Liston to come to New York to join him. For a top-ranked bandleader to sign a woman instrumentalist—much less bring one all the way across the country—was just about unprecedented. Woody Herman hired women to play in one or another of his Herds—trumpeter Billie Rogers, vibist Margie Hyams. Mary Lou Williams was pianist, composer and arranger for Andy Kirk's Clouds of Joy for years. But Duke Ellington had never hired a woman player, nor had Basie, except for Liston's brief stint. Gillespie's choice was not a popular one with the players in his band.

"Gerald Wilson brings me to New York and drops me in Dizzy's lap, with all these giants. This was at the end [of the band's engagement], the last six months or so. I was so in awe of all these persons, and I didn't have any idea of what I was doin' there, although I could read the music. But Dizzy had great faith in me. He had called me in California and said, 'Well, you know, the brothers, they got their friends that they want to be in the band.' But he laid this all out, and he told me to bring at least two arrangements with me when I came.

"The first thing, all the guys in the band said, 'Goddamn, Birks, you sent all the way to California for a *bitch?*' Dizzy said, 'That's right.' He said, 'Did you bring the music that I told you to write?' I said, 'Yes, sir.' He said, 'Pass it out to these muthafuckas and let me see what a bitch you are.' He said, 'Play the music, and I don't want to hear no fuckups.' And of course they got about two measures and fell out and got all confused and stuff. And Dizzy said, 'Now who's the bitch!' Dizzy was really something. So after that I was everybody's sister, mama, auntie. I was sewin' buttons, cuttin' hair and all the rest. Then I was a woman again."

A few years later Liston rejoined a newly formed Gillespie band that traveled the world on State Department–sponsored tours. During a Middle East tour in 1956 she was responsible for writing a musical summation of the styles and sounds of jazz, a history of the music, as it were. "I take off some Benny Goodman, I take off some Lunceford and this and that, and I orchestrate these things," she explains in her nothing-to-it way. Her arranging talents continued to be much in demand.

But in 1957 there came a lean period. Dizzy's band was out of work again, and Liston began looking around for other possibilities. A booking agent called and tempted. "You don't have to lay off 'cause the guys are off. I got a job—if you'll take some girls." Melba grumbled; the agent cajoled. "It's only for four weeks—in Bermuda! Have you ever been to Bermuda? It's a beautiful place." Liston succumbed and set about putting together a group: Bu Pleasant on piano, Gloria Coleman on upright bass, Pola Roberts on drums, Willene Barton on tenor sax.

"Well, we have a few rehearsals before we go, and I find out they don't read so well. I get it together, though, and we go down there—and we up*set* Bermuda! We have 'em jammed up against the walls. Old folks came to the club that had never been in a nightclub in their lives, and all the children. This was a spot. And they held us over an extra time, and the people were invitin' us all out to dinners and stuff. They'd never seen women play. We were cookin'. Yes, we were *cookin'*. And we managed that out, we got through Bermuda, held over and everything."

But the trip wasn't all roses. There were some problems with various bandmembers, some unpleasant scenes—"I had boo-hooin' on the goddamn bandstand"—and Liston's patience was wearing thin. "Now we come back and I am informed that we got to go to the Bluebird in Detroit, to something in Pittsburgh—that agent done booked me all over the East Coast. I didn't have nobody and didn't know if he was allowed to do this, but I didn't have no job anyway. Well, Bu discovered she was pregnant, so that let her out. They sent me somebody else who was ridiculous, so I got my first man. I had Melba Liston and her All-Girl Band with a male piano player." She grins.

"As we moved around, somebody else left. Anyway, when we got back to New York at Small's Paradise, we had Charlie Rouse on tenor, and the only girls left were Gloria and me. She toughed it on out. And the dude that manages Small's, he said, 'Melba, next time you come, you don't have to have no women at all.' And the guys said, 'You put any sign you want out there. If it's Melba it doesn't matter—we'll come anyway.' And I ended up with cats, with the boss's approval." Her grin broadens, and then she suddenly becomes serious and deliberate as she expresses grave reservations about the "all-girl" format. "I don't think I'll ever have a girls' band again. But I will deal with women, and I love them," she adds. "And I've been very happy to remeet up with some of these people, like Willene Barton, who was at the gig the other night."

When asked to name some women musicians she feels are important, Liston is generous in her praise. "In the past is Mary Lou Williams, pianist and composer. She is like my mentor as far as women musicians, and she won't even tell *me*, but I know some of the stuff that *she* went through in her day. But the guys are much kinder to me than they were to those persons.

"And Valaida. Valaida Snow"—the trumpeter who sang sweet and played hot all over the world. Liston, just beginning her career, met Snow toward the end of hers, in 1945, when her days of glory were past. "I worked on a show with Valaida Snow," she remembers. "Now, there was something about her, the way she acted, that saddened me and that I never forgot. This was right there at the Lincoln Theatre. I said, 'Boy, when I get her age I'm not going to let that happen to me'—whatever it was. She was so talented, so beautiful and so sweet. But she was so unhappy. She was like hurt all the time. In my youth I didn't understand. But I felt the pain from her all the time. I figure she must have been forty-something, and she didn't last much longer. [Actually Snow lived for another decade, until 1956.] I loved that lady! There was that confusion there that I couldn't understand in my youth, but I promised myself—when I get old, I'm not gonna be onstage with my trombone and let nobody do that to me."

Liston's seven-piece group, Melba Liston and Company, has undergone several changes in personnel since its inception in 1979 as an all-female unit.

By 1981 it was a truly mixed company that included tenor saxophonist Erica Lindsay and pianist Chessie Tanksley among its female players. Among former women members are drummer Dottie Dodgion, bassist Carline Ray, reed player Fostina Dixon, Sharon Freeman on French horn and piano, and Janice Robinson on trombone—the first female player to seriously challenge Liston's title to uniqueness.

"Women's lib," says Liston. "I had no business with that. But it did bring a lot of attention to the trials that are going on. The male-female thing is really something else." She purses her lips as if tasting something sour. "And that has not changed too much. You don't see it quite so clearly, and you don't hear it quite so clearly, but it's nothin' changed. Like, well, they're doin' it to Janice Robinson. I worry about Janice, who is a most talented girl. And she is not accepted just for that by the musicians. And they don't even *know* it. It's not what they intend to do—the brothers would not hurt for nothin'. But this attitude is just a deeply imbedded thing. It's just a *habit*.

"No, they are not treating her properly," she concludes, her syllables distinct as her voice thickens with intensity. "They used to call her 'Little Melba.' I told them that's wrong. I told them two, three years ago. When she was down in Jamaica with Thad Jones [trumpeter, writer and arranger], all the cats was standin' there, and they said, 'Hey, little mama!' I said, 'She ain't no little mama.' I said, 'That's *Janice Robinson*. Hopefully, she is not goin' to follow in *my* footsteps and let you do the same thing to her that you did to me. And you just quit it.' 'Cause she is so smart, she's smarter than anybody in the band, and she has to take low still, right now!

"Oh, yeah! They knew they had me. I mean after I got over the hump, after proving myself. I had to prove myself, just like Jackie Robinson. Now I belong to all the guys, and they will take care of me. I don't have to worry. I'm free all over the world. Musicians will take care of Melba. Not to worry. But another young woman musician comes along, they're not going to get that. They're not giving it to Janice. 'We can't let no woman come here and do this here thing,' " she mimics, pausing. Then, with a faraway look, she adds, "They would give me money, they would take care of me or anything. But they couldn't let me have the job."

As afternoon deepens to dusk, Liston shares her thoughts about the role black women have played in jazz history. Looking away at a view of rain-drenched trees in the gray-green New York twilight, she speaks softly. "Do you know, in Bessie Smith's time and all that, you don't hear too much about the men. They were piano players. But onstage it was the black *woman*. But now, to get an instrument? No, sir, a woman couldn't bring an instrument in no house, especially with a husband that was a musician. And not today either.

"But if it wasn't for the women there wouldn't be no culture a-tall, a-tall.

There were women—why, it was plant the garden, work the fields, raise the children and pacify the men. All the men did was do their labor and take their straps, and then the women had to take care of him as well as take care of all that other business. She still had to keep his ego up. And we still have to do it, just like back in slavery times."

Her hands fly upward, like birds. "Oh, Lord! Oh, Lord! Oh, Lord! Oh, Lord! The exact terminology that we're using today—say, 'Come off the plantation, mother!'"

MARY OSBORNE

Guitarist

"Everything I accomplished was because this was the business I was in and this was what I was—a musician."

Mary Osborne was one of the first electric jazz guitarists on the scene. A Charlie Christian–inspired player, she built a highly successful career on the East Coast in the forties and fifties before moving to California in 1968 with her husband, trumpeter Ralph Scaffidi. Based in Bakersfield, the couple has since operated the Osborne Guitar Company, which makes quality guitars and amplifiers. Osborne also teaches music and continues to play locally and in Los Angeles. In 1981 she traveled to New York for one of her rare appearances outside California, playing at the Kool Jazz Festival's Women Blow Their Own Horns concert and fulfilling a two-week club date in Manhattan. She also recorded an album for Stash. An excellent technician and articulate soloist, Osborne is often described as the only woman worthy of mention as a jazz guitarist. However, she herself is quick to praise other women guitarists whose playing impressed her, including some rare figures indeed. Osborne happened upon one of them, Sidney Bell, in a music store working and teaching in almost total obscurity. "She was a really fine player, with a really professional instrument, an Epaphone guitar," she remembers. "And don't forget Mary Kay"—the professional name of a Hawaiian guitarist especially active in Las Vegas in the fifties and sixties.

As she sits for our interview in the living room of her Bakersfield home, there is little about Osborne or her surroundings to suggest the world of jazz—except for her hand-crafted Bill Baker-model guitar, made in Toledo, Spain, in 1963, which holds the place of honor reserved for the TV in most middle-class households. No suburban matron, she. "Never once in my life did I say, 'I'm not going to play. I'll just become a housewife,' " she assures me, chuckling at the thought. "Maybe I can't go skippin' off on the road, but never in my life did I think I had dropped out of the scene." Indeed, as afternoon wears into evening on that warm California day, she prepares for her regular Sunday night gig as featured soloist with an excellent local big band that plays to a packed and appreciative neighborhood audience, using charts that span the spectrum from Benny Goodman and Jimmy Dorsey to latter-day Thad Jones. Trumpeter Scaffidi takes the high notes in the band, and Osborne's daughter and son, both in their twenties and musically inclined, come along for the ride. (Another son is in the Navy and is, she avers, a fine musician too.)

Mary Osborne was born in North Dakota in 1921. Both her parents were musically inclined; her mother played guitar, and her father's occupation provided an eclectic musical education. "My dad moved the family to Minot, North Dakota, which was considered a pretty big city there. And he opened a barbershop for business, but he continued with music—he was a musician since he was five years old, played the violin and any instrument. His barbershop became a meeting place for musicians. My dad used to make violins in a workshop he had, and he would bring home every kind of instrument he could get his hands on. Well, I would end up playing them all. Before I had a chance to form any kind of opinions, it was just the most natural thing in the world to play."

The tenth of eleven children, little Mary shone with particular musical promise. "I learned to read music in the first grade, and by the second grade I was playing violin with an orchestra," she says. "I had a mandolin, a ukelele and a mandolia—a guitarlike instrument shaped like a lute, cut down from twelve to six strings." At age nine Osborne acquired her first guitar, and in the mysterious way that instruments and players "meet," it was love at first sight. "When I picked up that first guitar, that was it," she says. "I knew that's what I wanted to play the rest of my life."

Aside from playing with school groups, Osborne was featured on her own radio show at age ten (it lasted until she was fifteen). Soon she began working local jobs. "The first group I worked with professionally was a girls' trio that formed one summer. By this time I was twelve years old. Actually, I really was singing and using the guitar as an accompanying instrument. I had gotten hold of a book which I think was written by [guitarist] Eddie Lang—a very fine book on bar chords. I just learned those chords. I don't think I ever played first-position chords, just in kidding around, in country music. Only we didn't call it country then—we called it hillbilly. Anyway, I worked with this girls' trio in Bismark. We played dinner music, light classics, with two violins. I doubled on violin, and all three of us sang."

Already Osborne's ears were reaching beyond to the big challenge of improvising. "You didn't hear the word 'jazz,' " she remembers. "There was just music, good music. The pop music of the day really was so different than today. I'm not saying it was better, but concert people studied it." The radio served as primary ear-opener: "When I was a little girl at home, I used to hear Red Norvo and Mildred Bailey live from the Blackhawk Restaurant in Chicago. I used to listen to them every night—the first jazz musicians I ever listened to, incidentally. My mother used to say, 'Honey, go to sleep, it's eleven o'clock.' I'd say, 'Okay Mom,' but I'd listen to the whole program. This was before I knew the word 'jazz' at all. I just thought, 'What are they doing?' " These many years later, Osborne remains loath to label, alive to the limitations of categorizing. "If you were in a jazz field, you just did jazz," she says of the marketing mentality. "If you were in commercial big-band music, why, then that's what you did. There was a market for what you did, and they were all categorized. All the record companies did that. A lot of people wouldn't accept jazz per se or anything like that, so everything I did had to be with *vocals* and guitar."

Whether she knew the word or not, by 1939, at seventeen, Mary Osborne had become a stone jazz freak. "I think I must have listened to every 78 record. One time when I was going to school I stayed at a YWCA, and they had them all in their recreation room. The first octave guitar thing I ever heard used in jazz was by Django Reinhardt, and everybody called him an original. The first time I heard Charlie Christian [the great black electric jazz innovator, then with Al Trent's territory band], when my friends took me out to listen to him that year at a local dance, I knew those choruses of Django's by heart. I had played them over so many times, I knew every note in every song that he did! So the first thing that Charlie played at the floor show was 'St. Louis Blues' by Django Reinhardt. But Charlie didn't say that, he just played it, only it was on electric guitar. Later, when they introduced me to him, I said, 'I heard you play Django's chorus on "St. Louis Blues," ' and he said, all excited, 'You know that chorus?' It was the idea that who knew Django Reinhardt? So Charlie and I became friends, and he let me sit in and he showed me things.

"I was trying to play jazz violin at the time, but I was playing chord choruses and so on," Osborne continues. "That's all I thought I could do. So when Charlie Christian came out with guitar *jazz solos,* so great with that sound and everything—phrased like a horn—I knew I wanted to do *that*. And I thought I might be able to." The teenage Charlie Christian's concept of hornlike phrasing on guitar elevated that instrument from a rhythm accompaniment to the front line as another solo instrument, and the teenage Mary Osborne jumped to the possibilities. "That's like 1939, and until 1952 or '53 that's all you heard. That's all there was"—Christian's approach to guitar in jazz. "In fact," she adds, "if you did anything else, nobody would listen to it."

Soon—with a newly acquired Gibson electric guitar just like Christian's—Osborne was on the road with a trio of women musicians led by Winifred McDonald. The group gained considerable attention in the music business: "I think that if we had continued, we would have probably been one of the biggest groups in the country." Playing some jazz and popular material, the trio joined Buddy Rogers' band as part of his show after he heard them play in St. Louis. "Then we left Buddy Rogers and had a lot of good dates. But the band broke up because we all met guys at the same time and got married at the same time. We were in New York, and we hadn't been there more than a month when I met my husband."

Based in New York in the early forties, Osborne quickly caught on as a performer and recording artist. "I had met a lot of the musicians before I ever got to New York, so I already had a lot of connections and had sat in with many bands. Musicians get the word around more than any announcer. What really makes an impression is your musicianship, not just that you can play jazz on guitar." Osborne jumped right into the active playing scene. "The first year I was in New York they used to have jam sessions on the off-nights on Fifty-second Street and at the Village Vanguard. They would pay certain musicians and pick a leader. What this did was encourage everybody in town to come and sit in at the club. Like the first time I ever played at Kelly's Stables was at a jam session. And one night they had maybe four or five trumpet players up there—Roy Eldridge, Dizzy Gillespie, you name 'em and they would be there sittin' in. There'd be twenty-five guys up there playing! And there I am, sitting in, playing! That's why I'm so glad I was around then. That kind of thing could never happen again. And I felt completely at home in that environment, because that's what I'd been doing all my life."

In the forties Osborne played and/or recorded with numerous top-ranked musicians. She went out on the road with leader Russ Morgan and with jazz violinist Joe Venuti around 1941, replacing his longtime partner, guitarist Eddie Lang (Venuti offered her Lang's old guitar as an inducement to stay on). She later worked and recorded with Mary Lou Williams, Ethel Waters, Coleman Hawkins and others. Until 1949 she led her own trio that played at many of the important clubs on Fifty-second Street. "We were at Kelly's Stables for a year, and we had every musician, every act or bandleader that came to New York ending up coming to Fifty-second Street; we must have performed for everyone. Then I played a lot at the Hickory House, across the street, and that was first-rate. Every jazz musician played at the Hickory House."

Both in performance and on recordings, Mary Osborne carefully explains, her trio (whose personnel included Sanford Gold and Frenchy Cauette around 1946, and later Jack Pleis on piano) was not strictly a jazz trio. "I love the way [guitarist] Bucky Pizzarelli describes the kind of thing we were doing—he calls it disguising jazz as hotel music. And that's just about what it was. We really included everything; as one instance, a song called 'Cement Mixer' was very big, and we had a good arrangement of that. We recorded first for Signature Records, then Decca and their subsidiary, Coral. On Decca it was strictly commercial. They had vocals and small groups like Nat Cole's. My group was in that same vein—no drums, just bass, piano and guitar. I knew that if we ended up as just a jazz trio, we'd disappear. I wanted people to like us—and to sell."

Commercial considerations notwithstanding, Mary Osborne cut some fine guitar instrumentals and good solos with her trio, especially for Signature. And her guitar was often heard at jazz concerts. One of the first was a 1944 concert in Philadelphia at the Academy of Music. "Everybody was on that one—Coleman Hawkins and Art Tatum, Denzil Best and Al McKibbon—and oh, my God, [producer-writer] Leonard Feather just urged me to go onstage. So I ended up sittin' in, and I got this fantastic write-up in the Philadelphia papers the next day, when I wasn't even supposed to be there! Then I did a jazz concert in New Orleans, the first one I ever did in my life where I was like one of the stars. That was with Louis Armstrong, Leon Prima and Irving Fazola. They must have taped that; it was recorded for overseas, those V-discs [records made for servicemen during the war years]. So the guy who produced Stash Records must have got hold of that air check—isn't that crazy? My first jazz concert, and it's true, lots of people who never heard me otherwise have heard that one.

"Around this time different things began happening. I started doing a lot of personal appearances on television shows in New York—Arthur Godfrey's show, and *We the People* with an all-girl program. The show was a documentary about women musicians. We had just done a series of recordings—Leonard Feather set up these recordings with all women, including an album called *Cats vs. Chicks*, which a lot of people tell me they have—and so they had us appear on the show, not as an oddity, but we *were* different and it was interesting."

Perhaps the job that most brought Osborne's name and sound to public attention was a local New York radio show hosted by Jack Sterling, on which she performed regularly from 1952 to 1963. "They decided to put on live musicians, and we had a nice little quartet with Elliot Lawrence as bandleader. It was only supposed to be for a short time, but the show got very big and so we were there eleven years. We had some great arrangers—people like Al Cohn and Tiny Kahn, and Johnny Mandel wrote some things for us. We had a chance to play everything, and I was also singing, and we had to read scripts. It happened that I was good at what I did, and being a girl didn't hurt."

With some few exceptions, Osborne feels that she encountered little prejudice or resistance from her mostly male peers during her years as an active New York free-lancer. In part, no doubt, this was due to her even disposition and professionalism—qualities always welcome in the music business, which has more than its share of temperament and unreliability. Thinking hard, she dredges up one unpleasant incident when a male guitarist and colleague insinuated that her success had to do with her sex— that is, the "girl gimmick." "All I could say was 'I'm disappointed in you as a person' and walk away," she remembers. In general, though, Osborne was much more likely to hear praise from her fellow musicians. In fact, by the sixties, it was the very polish and ease of her playing that began to concern her.

"I got very bored with my playing and with music in general. I was living a very full life, so it didn't have to do with being stagnant. But I'd listen to the playbacks from the show, and we'd do all these nice, tough little things, and I'd hear myself playing just nice, perfect. In fact, somebody said to me, 'Don't you ever play a wrong note?' I said, 'Well, I *should*.' Not to be afraid to try a new thing, that's what it was. And I thought, 'I know exactly what's going to happen there. But I'm *better* than that. I can do more than that.' " So in 1962 she tried a new musical avenue—Spanish classical guitar. "It was a thrill to study classical techniques. I thought, 'Look at this, there's so much more!' And my teacher, Alberto Valdez-Blaine, was wonderful. He just sat down and gave me what I had to do. So now I was practicing two hours every day! And of course it was playing with no pick, and I'd never done that. I knew my real strength lies in what I do—jazz—and that classical could never be my forte. But it's beautiful music and made me hear so much more. And when I started to learn that right-hand finger technique, I started to play pop and jazz things with my fingers, so it really aided my development as a musician and a guitar player."

Leaning back in her chair, Mary Osborne reflects on her career. "It's the preparation that a person has to do for anything like music, dancing, acting. The time spent is not always financially rewarding for a long time, and maybe never. If you've got a wife or husband that's doing the same thing, they understand it. You know, it's hard to say, 'Look, I'm not going to pay any attention to my children today' or 'The house needs cleaning but I have to practice now.' . . . I used to think, 'What's the big deal about a woman musician?' I know so many women who are musicians. When that attitude came along later—'Gee, you don't *look* like a musician'—well, what are musicians supposed to look like? It took me a long time to know that anybody would think this way, because I never did. But I never got jobs because I was a girl, I never kept them because I was a girl. Everything I accomplished was because this was the business I was in and this was what I was—a musician."

ANN PATTERSON

Bandleader and Alto Saxophonist

"I believe that if I'm thoroughly prepared to do the job and I have a way to let it be known that I can do it, then I'm going to get work."

When Maiden Voyage met the International Sweethearts of Rhythm during a tribute to the Sweethearts at the 1980 Women's Jazz Festival, the encounter had more than nostalgic significance. Technically Maiden Voyage players may be better schooled than their swing-era predecessors and may appear much more assertive about pursuing careers in jazz as composers, arrangers, studio musicians and soloists; after all, they have thirty years of jazz and social development on their side. But today's jazzwomen too share the problem of exclusion from most of the existing bands; they too find themselves still on the outskirts of the music. Like their sisters of the thirties and forties, these big-band players of the seventies and eighties have found it necessary to band together to play the music.

Maiden Voyage began in 1979 as a rehearsal band for women musicians in the Los Angeles area and quickly evolved into a seventeen-piece performance unit with an attractive, eclectic band book that includes arrangements by such top writers as Bobby Shew, Don Menza, Tommy Newsom, Bob Enevoldsen and Brad Dechter. The group, which also actively solicits the work of women arrangers, has seen a constant upgrading of personnel since its inception. In 1981 Voyage boasted a number of fine soloists: Ann Patterson, leader and reeds (primarily alto sax); trumpeters Louise Berk and Stacy Rowles; flugelhornist Ann Petereit; trombonist Betty O'Hara (who also plays trumpet and double-belled euphonium, sings with the band and writes); and saxophonists Carol Chaiken and Leslie Dechter. Maiden Voyage was originally co-led by drummer Bonnie Janofsky and veteran alto saxophonist Roz Cron, who was one of the first white women to join the Sweethearts in the forties. Both Janofsky and Cron eventually left the group; Janofsky now leads her own all-male big band and free-lances in other large ensembles, and Cron continues as an active free-lance musician.

Headed since 1980 by Ann Patterson, Maiden Voyage has made an impressive start in its short history: the band has played a number of jazz festivals, including the Playboy and Concord festivals in 1981 and the Women's Jazz Festival in 1980; it has been seen on the *Tonight Show* and regularly gigs at various California clubs, notably Donte's in Los Angeles. As of this writing, a debut album is in the works, and Voyage aggressively seeks bread-and-butter jobs on the concert, college concert and women's concert circuits. And favorable press continues to build interest in the group.

Leader Ann Patterson's story might well serve as an example of what the current generation of emerging women jazz musicians both aims for and is up against. Born in Snyder, Texas, in 1947, Patterson was classically trained as an oboist before coming to jazz. As she explains, "I always wanted to play jazz, but I felt, especially at the time [the sixties], that it was not something I could do. Because I never saw any women playing jazz—especially horn players. I went to North Texas State [a college especially active in big-band ensemble music], and I used to go listen to the lab bands there and sort of wish that I could do that."

But during the seventies she began rethinking her options. "By about 1975 I was a thoroughly schooled classical musician with a master's degree in oboe. I had done professional work in symphonies and taught school at the college level. I was becoming a freer person at that point in my life, and this desire to play freer music, where I could express my own individuality, was a part of that desire to play jazz. And I was not very happy at the time, because I wasn't playing very much. I just decided to do what would make me happy— so since then I've been really studying and working hard to become a good jazz player."

As an altoist Patterson has an attractive urgency about her playing, an "edge" to her full, rich tone that, together with her solid technical background, makes her an interesting improviser. "The only reason we haven't seen very many women play saxophone well," she observes thoughtfully, in a voice characteristically soft but intense, "is that the saxophone is a very free-blowing horn—you have to be very aggressive to play it. I think that just sociologically women are not aggressive, so it's more difficult to overcome whatever passive way they're used to being and be aggressive when they play."

After several years' tenure as lead altoist with the musically challenging band led by the late Don Ellis, Patterson was approached by Bonnie Janofsky about working with the still-unnamed women's rehearsal band. "Bonnie started the big band with another woman in 1979; that band split in two a few months later, when they had some differences. And Bonnie asked me to come and play. I thought the band needed to be rehearsed more, and I had some teaching experience, so I asked if I could rehearse the band. And we got together and started working on that band to see if we could make it just as good as it could be with the existing women players." When Janofsky left to form and lead her own band, Patterson became leader and chief spokeswoman for the newly christened Maiden Voyage.

Patterson and her fellow bandmembers concentrate a large part of their energy on Maiden Voyage, but they also work with other groups, in show and theater bands, and as teachers. Above all they try for lucrative Los Angeles studio work. "The band rehearses once a week, so it's not a full-time job for any of us. It's more a labor of love," Patterson says. "We started out with just a rehearsal band book—everybody else's tunes. But now we've been changing the book so that we can have our own charts written for our own unique sound and style." Voyage has been praised for its tight, precise ensemble playing. "And the band plays very sensitively on ballads," Patterson points out. "Also our percussionist, Judy Chilnick, is a very fine vibes player, and in adding a vibes double in some of our trumpet and saxophone lines, I think we have the beginning of the development of our own sound. And we are very interested in women writers—in fact, we have a couple of people in the band who can write, too."

Despite the inevitable problems in keeping such a large organization functioning, Patterson sees the Maiden Voyage experience as positive in a number of respects. "First, it gives women who are potentially top-flight musicians the experience they've had difficulty getting elsewhere," she says. "Second, it showcases women musicians and exposes their abilities so they might get other work and get better known. The third thing is to give women some work" (A. James Liska, "Maiden Voyage," *Down Beat*, November 1981). Comparing Maiden Voyage with other big bands, Patterson feels that "there's less fighting and difference than in the men's bands I've played in. We have a sort of camaraderie. There's more caring about each other than I've seen in other bands. We're not feminists, but we have a sisterhood feeling within the band. When I played with Don Ellis' band, there was never that good feeling that our band has. Oh, we cared about Don and his music, but it wasn't there as far as individuals in the band.

"The only problem we *do* have sometimes is that some of the women have not learned to be tough, that it doesn't matter if you didn't sleep last night or you have a hundred-and-two-degree fever—you gotta play the gig! But they're learning to be tough now, learning that the music is the important thing." During the Maiden Voyage tribute concert to the Sweethearts at the 1980 Women's Jazz Festival in Kansas City, I witnessed an unfortunate freak accident that underscored Patterson's point about the growing professionalism and supportiveness of these women players. Midway through the concert, a bandmember who was perched on the edge of a raised platform fell, trumpet, chair and all, to the floor a good distance below. With a broken arm and white with pain and shock, she was taken from the hushed concert hall, but managed to restore everybody's spirits when she raised her good arm in a salute and exhorted the band to "keep on playing!" The sixteen remaining musicians stood to applaud her, as did the audience. Amid a standing ovation, the show went on.

Maiden Voyage and its sister groups across the country—indeed, the world—usually strive to mix sisterly camaraderie and solidarity with their musicianship. Patterson is optimistic about the future for such a band, and for jazzwomen in general. She reiterates what many of her contemporaries and many veteran players from the Sweethearts era have said: "We're trying to change attitudes about women musicians. It's funny, but a male musician is just assumed good until proven otherwise. For women it's the other way around. . . . It's really difficult to get work as a musician in this town if you're a woman. But where it helps to be a woman is that other musicians remember you if you're good" (Liska). Speaking of that important studio recording work that makes the difference between scuffling and living comfortably, Patterson observes, "I know that the *very few* women horn players I see in the studios are better than good, but I think there are going to be more women in the studios in the next five years or so. Because I believe that if I'm thoroughly prepared to do the job and I have a way to let it be known that I can do it, then I'm going to get work."

The example of Maiden Voyage proves that women can succeed in the highly competitive, male-dominated field of big-band jazz. They and their sister artists everywhere—as leaders, players, vocalists, composers, producers and managers in all styles of the music, all over the world—are writing a new, hopeful chapter in the ongoing story of women in jazz.

Notes

CHAPTER 1: THE ONES THAT GOT AWAY

1. Quoted in David Ewen, *The Life and Death of Tin Pan Alley*, p. 21.
2. Eugene D. Genovese, *Roll, Jordan, Roll: The World the Slaves Made* (New York: Pantheon, 1974), p. 490.
3. Quoted in Victoria Ortiz, *Sojourner Truth: A Self-Made Woman* (New York: J. B. Lippincott Co., 1974), p. 131.
4. Orrick Johns, quoted in Ewen, *Tin Pan Alley*, p. 82.
5. Ewen, *Tin Pan Alley*, pp. 82–84.
6. Quoted in Genovese, *Roll, Jordan, Roll*, p. 249.
7. Quoted in Nat Shapiro and Nat Hentoff, *Hear Me Talkin' to Ya*, p. 243.
8. Susan Cavin, "Missing Women: On the Voodoo Trail to Jazz," *Journal of Jazz Studies* 3, no. 1 (Fall 1975): 4–27. Cavin cited Robert Tallant's *Voodoo in New Orleans* (New York: Collier Books, 1974), and Tallant derived the lyrics from a New Orleans newspaper of 1924.
9. Quoted in ibid., p. 10.
10. Ewen, *Tin Pan Alley*, p. 31.
11. Quoted in Robert C. Toll, *Blacking Up*, p. 162.
12. D. Antoinette Handy, *Black Women in American Bands and Orchestras*, pp. 157–58.
13. Frank Driggs, "Women in Jazz," p. 5.
14. Tom Dardis, *Keaton: The Man Who Wouldn't Lie Down* (New York: Charles Scribner's Sons, 1979), p. 5. Mrs. Myra Keaton also played piano, bass, fiddle and cornet.
15. See, for example, Chris Albertson, *Bessie*. This biography of the great blues singer provides a detailed look at the rough-and-tumble life of black traveling shows. See also Sandra Lieb, *Mother of the Blues: A Study of Ma Rainey*.

16. Quoted in Ann Charters, comp. and ed., *Ragtime Songbook*.

17. Al Rose, *Eubie Blake*, pp. 24–26.

CHAPTER 2: FIRST LADIES OF EARLY JAZZ

1. Bunk Johnson and Jelly Roll Morton quoted in Alan Lomax, *Mister Jelly Roll*, pp. 20–21; Spencer Williams quoted in Nat Shapiro and Nat Hentoff, *Hear Me Talkin' to Ya*, p. 7.

2. Quoted in Shapiro and Hentoff, *Hear Me Talkin'*, p. 6.

3. Quoted in Martin Williams, *Jazz Masters of New Orleans*, p. 168.

4. Quoted in Shapiro and Hentoff, *Hear Me Talkin'*, p. 30.

5. Quoted in Danny Barker, *Bourbon Street Black*, p. 69.

6. Quoted in Williams, *Jazz Masters*, pp. 89–90.

7. Richard Hadlock, *Jazz Masters of the Twenties*, p. 10.

8. Quoted in Alan C. Weber, liner notes to *Sweet Emma Barrett and Her New Orleans Music*, Southland LP 241, 1963. I have drawn heavily on Weber's notes for information on Sweet Emma Barrett.

9. For information on Jeanette Salvant Kimball I have relied on interviews with Kimball conducted by William Russell on February 10, 1962, and by Barry Martyn, Lars Edegran and Richard B. Allen on June 16, 1969. The interview transcripts are in the William Ransom Hogan Jazz Archive of Tulane University, New Orleans, Louisiana.

10. Ione Anderson, quoted in D. Antoinette Handy, *Black Women in American Bands and Orchestras*, p. 173.

11. For information on Billie Pierce, I have relied on interviews with Billie and De De Pierce conducted by Ralph Collins and William Russell on April 2, 1959; by Ernest Trepagnier, Ralph Collins and Richard B. Allen on October 7, 1959; and by Richard B. Allen on November 20, 1963 (digest of interview). The transcripts are all in the Hogan Archive at Tulane.

12. Interview of April 2, 1959, p. 13.

13. Interview of October 7, 1959, p. 7.

14. For information on Dolly Adams, I have relied on Handy, *Black Women*, pp. 170–71; and on an interview with Dolly Adams, Mr. Adams and Justin Adams conducted by William Russell on April 18, 1962. The interview transcript is in the Hogan Archive at Tulane.

15. See, for example, Frank Driggs, "Women in Jazz," p. 7.

16. Barker, *Bourbon Street Black*, p. 35.

17. Handy, *Black Women*, pp. 121–24.

18. In a phone conversation with the author, June 26, 1981.

19. Hadlock, *Jazz Masters*, p. 106.

20. Brian Rust, *The Dance Bands*, p. 21.

21. My account of Lil Hardin Armstrong's career is a composite based on material in

Shapiro and Hentoff, *Hear Me Talkin'*, passim; in the files of the Rutgers University Institute of Jazz Studies in Newark, New Jersey, and the Lincoln Center Library for the Performing Arts in New York City; and in the transcript of an interview with Hardin Armstrong conducted by William Russell on July 1, 1959, in the Hogan Archive at Tulane.

22. Quoted in Shapiro and Hentoff, *Hear Me Talkin'*, p. 92.
23. Quoted in ibid., p. 93.
24. In ibid., p. 102.
25. Williams, *Jazz Masters*, p. 175.
26. Quoted in Shapiro and Hentoff, *Hear Me Talkin'*, p. 102.
27. George Avakian, liner notes to *The Louis Armstrong Story*, Columbia LP CL-583.
28. Interview of July 1, 1959, p. 5.
29. Quoted in Shapiro and Hentoff, *Hear Me Talkin'*, p. 94.
30. Quoted in ibid., p. 93.
31. For information on Lovie Austin I have drawn on Norman Stevens and Ray Webb, liner notes to *Lovie Austin and Her Blues Serenaders*, Fountain Records FJ-105 (Vintage Jazz Series); and on correspondence between Austin and George Hoefer in the files of the Rutgers University Institute of Jazz Studies, Newark, New Jersey.
32. Mary Lou Williams, liner notes to *Jazz Women: A Feminist Retrospective*, Stash Records ST-109, 1977.
33. Quoted in Shapiro and Hentoff, *Hear Me Talkin'*, pp. 247–48.
34. Stevens and Webb, liner notes to Fountain FJ-105.
35. Stanley Dance, *The World of Earl Hines*, p. 179.
36. Quoted in Dance, *Earl Hines*, p. 181.
37. Quoted in Tony Heilbut, *The Gospel Sound*, p. 177.
38. Frank Driggs, liner notes to *Women in Jazz: Pianists*, Stash Records ST-112.
39. Heilbut, *Gospel Sound*, p. 219.
40. Driggs, "Women in Jazz," p. 6.
41. Quoted in Stanley Dance, *The World of Swing*, p. 32.
42. Quoted in ibid., p. 48.
43. Maurice Waller and Anthony Calabrese, *Fats Waller*, p. 18.
44. Quoted in Ira Gitler, *Jazz Masters of the Forties*, p. 154.
45. Quoted in ibid.
46. Slide Hampton, in a telephone interview with the author, June 1981.
47. Ross Russell, *Jazz Style in Kansas City and the Southwest*, pp. 58–59.

PART TWO INTRODUCTION: "MY SAX IS A SEX SYMBOL"

1. Susan Yank Porter and Harold F. Abeles, "The Sex Stereotyping of Instruments," *Journal of Research in Music Education* 26, no. 2 (Summer 1978).

2. G. E. Britton, "Sex Stereotyping and Career Roles," cited in Susan Yank Porter and Harold F. Abeles, "So Your Daughter Wants to Be a Drummer?," *Music Educators Journal* 65, no. 5 (January 1979): 47–49.

3. Porter and Abeles, "So Your Daughter Wants to Be a Drummer?," p. 50.

4. American Music Conference, "The Women of Music," *Music Journal* 30, no. 1 (January 1972): 22.

5. *Boston Post*, October 14, 1929.

6. "The Women of Music," p. 20.

7. Francis Bebey, *African Music*, p. 115.

8. "The Women of Music," p. 20.

9. Joachim Berendt, *The Jazz Book*, pp. 277–78.

10. Harold C. Schonberg, "The Distaff Side: Many Women Are Fine Artists but Find It Hard to Get Public Acceptance," *New York Times*, March 25, 1962. He further states, "Many women play much more beautifully than men, but men can provide more of the physical excitement that any audience, no matter how sophisticated, comes to share."

11. Harold C. Schonberg, "How Sex Plays a Role at the Piano," *New York Times*, May 27, 1979.

12. Quoted in "Are Women Musicians People?," *Musical Courier*, February 1937. See also "Women Bristle at Iturbi's View They're Inferior," *New York Herald Tribune*, February 5, 1937.

13. *Down Beat*, March 1938.

14. Baldassare Castiglione, *The Book of the Courtier*, trans. Sir Thomas Hoby (London: J. M. Dent & Son, 1928), p. 194.

15. Whitney Balliett, *New Yorker*, May 2, 1964.

16. In examining historical precedents, we are hampered by a lack of in-depth studies concerning the attitudes of societies—ancient and modern, preliterate and industrialized—toward women in music (and in many other areas). However, some pioneering research has been done. For my historical discussion, I am particularly indebted to "The Women of Music," the American Music Conference paper cited above.

17. John Rublowsky, *Black Music in America*, pp. 23–32.

18. Ibid., pp. 30–31.

19. J. H. Kwabena Nketia, *The Music of Africa*, pp. 58, 61.

20. "Some Women of Marrakech," a production aired on the *Odyssey* series on PBS, New York, December 22, 1981.

21. Quoted in Irene V. Jackson, "Black Women and Afro-American Song Tradition," *Sing Out!* 25, no. 2 (July-August 1976): 12.

22. See Eugene Genovese, *Roll, Jordan, Roll: The World the Slaves Made* (New York: Pantheon, 1974), pp. 209–32 passim.

23. Quoted in Marshall Stearns, *The Story of Jazz*, p. 59.

24. Leroy Ostransky, *Understanding Jazz*, p. 281.

25. *Down Beat*, July 15, 1942.

CHAPTER 3: THE LADIES IN THE BAND

1. D. Antoinette Handy, *Black Women in American Bands and Orchestras*, p. 23.
2. Duncan Schiedt, *The Jazz State of Indiana*, pp. 204–6.
3. David Ewen, *The Life and Death of Tin Pan Alley*, p. 35. Ewen says the Atlantic Gardens "featured the country's first woman orchestra."
4. Cecil Smith, *Musical Comedy in America*, pp. 222, 255.
5. Stanley Dance, *The World of Earl Hines*, p. 180.
6. Maurice Zolotow, "Phil Spitalny and His All-Girl Orchestra," *Swing*, August 1938.
7. "A Critical Briton Has a Gentle 'Go' at Us," *New York Times Magazine*, July 14, 1946. A rebuttal by conductor Hans Kindler of Washington, D.C., included the following statement: "The women in the orchestras I have . . . conducted, not only in my own National Symphony Orchestra, but recently in Mexico City, Guatemala, Panama, Chile, Peru and Canada as well, proved themselves to be not only fully equal to the men, but to be sometimes more imaginative and always especially cooperative" (*New York Times*, October 20, 1946).
8. Quoted in *Newsweek*, March 8, 1976. The feminist Women Musicians Collective subsequently picketed concerts of the Los Angeles Philharmonic.
9. Letter to the Editor, *London Times*, June 22, 1975. Solti had a distinguished predecessor in Leopold Stokowski, who said in 1916, "An incomprehensible blunder is being made in our exclusion of women from symphony orchestras. . . . When I think of women as I see them in the musical world, what they are capable of doing, their fine spirit, excellent technic, I realize what a splendid power we are letting go to waste in this country and in other countries, too" (quoted in Frederique Petrides, "Women in Orchestras," *The Etude*, July 1938).
10. On the *Tonight* show in 1979, per Women's Jazz Festival.
11. Frank Driggs, "Women in Jazz," p. 18.
12. Quoted in Stanley Dance, *The World of Swing*, p. 186.
13. For information on the Melodears I have drawn on the clipping files of the Lincoln Center Library for the Performing Arts in New York City; Driggs, "Women in Jazz"; George Simon, *The Big Bands*, pp. 260–61.
14. Film information from jazz film archivist David Chertok, in a June 1981 conversation with the author, who promised not to disclose the identity of the skeptical male critic.
15. Richard Lamparski, *Whatever Became of . . . ?*, 4th series (New York: Crown, 1973), p. 123.
16. Quoted in "Ina Ray Hutton Comes Up the Hard Way from Queen of Burlesque to Sophisticate," *New York World-Telegram*, September 16, 1940.
17. *Down Beat*, April 1937.
18. "Why Women Musicians Are Inferior: Should Be Able to Get More Out of a Horn Than a Mere Cry for Help" and Rita Rio rebuttal, *Down Beat*, February 1938.
19. "The Hormel Girls' Caravan," *International Musician*, November 1951.
20. *Swing*, August 1938. After retiring, the Spitalnys settled in Miami and became music critics. Phil Spitalny died in 1970.

21. D. Antoinette Handy, "Conversation with Lucille Dixon, Manager of a Symphony Orchestra," *Black Perspective in Music*, Fall 1975.
22. All quotes from former Sweethearts personnel are taken from my transcript of a March 1980 interview conducted by Leonard Feather during a live tribute to that band at the Women's Jazz Festival in Kansas City, Missouri.
23. Marian McPartland, "The Untold Story of the International Sweethearts of Rhythm," p. 5.
24. Quoted in ibid., p. 3.
25. S. Frederick Starr, *Red & Hot: The Fate of Jazz in the Soviet Union* (New York: Oxford University Press, 1983).
26. Driggs, "Women in Jazz," p. 23.
27. Unidentified, undated interview in clipping files, Lincoln Center Library for the Performing Arts, New York City.
28. *Independent Woman*, February 1936.
29. Florence Haxton Bullock, "Women Musicians Make Good in the Big-Time Orchs," *New York Times*, February 13, 1944. Bullock's article carried the subheadline "War Has Given Them New Impetus and Opportunities but Progress Had Been Made Before That, Despite Opposition of Conductors."

CHAPTER 4: THE LADIES AT THE KEYBOARD

1. Alan Lomax, *Mister Jelly Roll*, pp. 6-8.
2. Barry Ulanov, *Metronome*, July 1949.
3. Dan Morgenstern, liner notes to *Jazz Pioneers*, Prestige Records 7647.
4. Mary Lou Williams, liner notes to *Jazz Women: A Feminist Retrospective*, Stash Records ST-109, 1977.
5. John S. Wilson, interview with Mary Lou Williams, June 1973, Jazz Oral History Project of the National Endowment for the Arts at the Rutgers University Institute of Jazz Studies, Newark, New Jersey. I have relied heavily on this interview for my account of Mary Lou Williams' career.
6. Ibid.
7. Ibid.
8. Quoted in John S. Wilson, "Mary Lou Williams: A Jazz Great Dies," *New York Times*, May 30, 1981.
9. Oral History Project interview.
10. *Melody Maker* interview with Mary Lou Williams, published in eleven weekly installments from April 3, 1954, to June 12, 1954.
11. Ibid.
12. Ibid.
13. Ibid.
14. Morgenstern, liner notes to Prestige 7647.
15. *Melody Maker* interview.
16. Quoted in Regina Weinreich, "Play It, Momma," *Village Voice*, July 3, 1978.

17. *Melody Maker* interview.
18. Quoted in *Time*, September 16, 1957.
19. Quoted in *Down Beat*, October 17, 1957.
20. Oral History Project interview.
21. Ibid.
22. Ross Russell, *Jazz Style in Kansas City and the Southwest*, p. 218.
23. Quoted in Whitney Balliett, "Something Better Out There," *New Yorker*, April 7, 1980.
24. Frank Driggs, liner notes to *Women in Jazz: Pianists*, Stash Records ST-112.
25. Maurice Waller and Anthony Calabrese, *Fats Waller*, p. 108.
26. Driggs, liner notes to Stash ST-112.
27. Patricia Willard, interview with Nellie Lutcher, January–February 1979, Jazz Oral History Project of the National Endowment for the Arts at the Rutgers University Institute of Jazz Studies, Newark, New Jersey.
28. D. Antoinette Handy, *Black Women in American Bands and Orchestras*, p. 179.
29. Driggs, liner notes to Stash ST-112.
30. As recalled by Lutcher in the Oral History Project interview.
31. Ibid.
32. Ibid.
33. Ibid.
34. Gary Giddins, *Village Voice*, November 6, 1978.
35. Quoted in *Melody Maker*, July 7, 1951.
36. Quoted by Whitney Balliett, *New Yorker*, January 20, 1973.
37. Quoted in *Melody Maker*, July 7, 1951.
38. Quoted by Balliett, *New Yorker*, January 20, 1973.
39. Quoted by Ralph Gleason, *New York Journal American*, December 19, 1959.
40. *Down Beat*, August 27, 1947.
41. Quoted in "Barbara Carroll Trio Plays Jazz in Broadway Show," *Down Beat*, July 1, 1953. The show was Rodgers and Hammerstein's *Me and Juliet*.
42. Ira Gitler, liner notes to *Soft Winds*, Jazzland LP-61, 1961.
43. Tony Outhwaite, "Organ Trios Still Roar," *Jazz* 3, no. 1 (Fall 1978): 52–55.
44. Richard Sudhalter, *New York Post*, September 8, 1980.
45. Quoted in the *New Orleans Times-Picayune*, September 11, 1973.

CHAPTER 5: BREAKING THE TABOOS

1. From a Hyams interview with Chris Albertson in *Stereo Review*, quoted in Art Napoleon, liner notes to *Women in Jazz: All-Women Groups*, Stash Records ST-111, 1978.
2. Walter C. Allen, *Hendersoniana*, pp. 270, 274, 308, 507.
3. D. Antoinette Handy, *Black Women in American Bands and Orchestras*, p. 42.
4. Quoted in Stanley Dance, *The World of Earl Hines*, p. 180.
5. Jazz film archivist David Chertok, in conversation with the author, June 1981. Chertok has this short in his collection.

6. Mary Lou Williams, liner notes to *Jazz Women: A Feminist Retrospective*, Stash Records ST-109, 1977.

7. Bobby Short, *Black and White Baby*, p. 99.

8. *Down Beat*, May 1938.

9. Frank Driggs, liner notes to *Women in Jazz: Swingtime to Modern*, Stash Records ST-113.

10. Quoted in Napoleon, liner notes to Stash ST-111.

11. Quoted in Leonard Feather, "Girls in Jazz: This Chick Plays Like Navarro," *Down Beat*, April 6, 1951.

12. Leonard Feather, "Focus On: Vi Redd," *Down Beat*, September 13, 1962.

13. Quoted by Hal Holly, *Down Beat*, June 15, 1951.

14. Driggs, liner notes to Stash ST-113.

15. All Carline Ray quotes from conversation with the author, June 10, 1980.

16. See, for example, Giles Oakley, *A Devil's Music;* Samuel B. Charters, *Sweet As the Showers of Rain;* Sheldon Harris, *Blues Who's Who;* and Steve LaVere and Paul Gordon, "Memphis Minnie," *Living Blues*, Autumn 1973.

17. William Broonzy, *Big Bill Blues*, p. 104. Most other sources agree that Memphis Minnie's recording debut was in 1929.

18. Woody Mann, "A Blues Guitar Teach-In," *Sing Out!* 25, no. 2 (1976): 28.

19. Broonzy, *Big Bill Blues*, pp. 104–6.

PART THREE INTRODUCTION: VOICE AS INSTRUMENT

1. Francis Bebey, *African Music*, p. 115.

2. Linda Prince, "Betty Carter: Bebopper Breathes Fire," *Down Beat*, March 13, 1979.

3. Henry Pleasants, *The Great American Popular Singers*, p. 26.

4. Humphrey Lyttleton, *The Best of Jazz*, pp. 79, 83.

5. Richard Hadlock, *Jazz Masters of the Twenties*, p. 224.

6. Pleasants, *American Popular Singers*, p. 46.

CHAPTER 6: THE BLUESWOMEN

1. John Godrich, "Ma Rainey," *Storyville*, June 1971. For a detailed study of Ma Rainey see Sandra Lieb, *Mother of the Blues*.

2. Giles Oakley, *The Devil's Music: A History of the Blues*, p. 99. Other contemporaries called Ma just plain "ugly"; see Derrick Stewart-Baxter, *Ma Rainey and the Classic Blues Singers*, p. 42.

3. Quoted in Oakley, *The Devil's Music*, p. 103.

4. Quoted in Stewart-Baxter, *Ma Rainey*, p. 42.

5. Stewart-Baxter, *Ma Rainey*, p. 18. I have relied heavily on Stewart-Baxter's book for background information on Hegamin and other "classic blues" singers.

6. Quoted in ibid., p. 21.

7. Stewart-Baxter, *Ma Rainey*, p. 81.
8. D. Antoinette Handy, *Black Women in American Bands and Orchestras*, p. 64.
9. "Lizzie's Return, " *Time*, October 3, 1955.
10. Stewart-Baxter, *Ma Rainey*, p. 27.
11. Ibid., p. 62.
12. In performance at the Cookery, New York City, April 29, 1982.
13. Chris Albertson, "The Roots of Jazz," *Stereo Review*, December 1977. Albertson is currently working with Alberta Hunter on her autobiography, to be published by G. P. Putnam's Sons.
14. Quoted in Nat Shapiro and Nat Hentoff, *Hear Me Talkin' to Ya*, p. 86.
15. Quoted in Leslie Bennetts, "Fame Comes Again, to Alberta Hunter," *New York Times*, November 25, 1978. I have drawn on Bennetts' article for many of the details of Hunter's career.
16. Quoted in ibid.
17. Conversation with the author, April 29, 1982.
18. Quoted in Oakley, *The Devil's Music*, p. 115.
19. Performance of April 29, 1982.
20. Hettie Jones, *Big Star, Fallin' Mama*, p. 48. Jones asserts that Thomas Edison, father of the phonograph and owner of one of the earliest recording companies, considered Bessie's voice "no good."
21. Oakley, *The Devil's Music*, p. 108.
22. See especially Chris Albertson, *Bessie*, for a discussion of this point.
23. Stewart-Baxter, *Ma Rainey*, p. 48. For other glowing assessments of Bessie Smith's contributions to jazz singing, see especially Richard Hadlock, *Jazz Masters of the Twenties;* and *John Hammond on Record*, the autobiography of the Columbia Records impresario.
24. Leonard Feather, *The Book of Jazz*, p. 152.
25. Quoted in Shapiro and Hentoff, *Hear Me Talkin'*, p. 149.
26. Barry Ulanov, *A History of Jazz in America*, p. 32.
27. Pearl Bailey, *The Raw Pearl*, pp. 24, 26.
28. Quoted in Shapiro and Hentoff, *Hear Me Talkin'*, p. 88.
29. Oakley, *The Devil's Music*, pp. 99–100.
30. Quoted in Stewart-Baxter, *Ma Rainey*, p. 56.

CHAPTER 7: THE "CANARIES"

1. John Hammond, *John Hammond on Record*, p. 195.
2. George Simon, *The Big Bands*, p. 33.
3. Ibid., p. 36.
4. *The Baton*, October 1, 1941.
5. *Down Beat*, September 9, 1946.
6. Ted Toll, "The Gal Yippers Have No Place in Our Jazz Bands," *Down Beat*, October 15, 1939.
7. *Swing*, October 1938.

8. Bucklin Moon, quoted in booklet accompanying *Mildred Bailey's Greatest Performances 1929–1946*, Columbia Records C31-22, 1960.
9. Ibid.
10. *Down Beat*, June 1938.
11. Stanley Dance, *The World of Swing*, p. 391.
12. Quoted in Chris Albertson, liner notes to *Ella Fitzgerald, The Cole Porter Songbook*, Verve Records VE-2-2511.
13. Taft Jordan, quoted in Dance, *The World of Swing*, p. 87. The details of Fitzgerald's debut vary from eyewitness to eyewitness, but the theme of initial resistance and subsequent triumph runs through all the accounts.
14. "The Rise of a Crippled Genius," *Down Beat*, February 1938.
15. Quoted in *Down Beat*, June 1, 1955.
16. Quoted in Simon, *The Big Bands*, p. 270.
17. Ibid., p. 307.
18. Quoted in ibid., p. 33.
19. Quoted in Dance, *World of Swing*, p. 275.
20. Conversation with the author, February 20, 1983.
21. Quoted in Barbara van Rooyen and Pawel Brodowski, "Betty's Groove," *Jazz Forum*, January 1979.
22. Simon, *The Big Bands*, p. 184.

CHAPTER 8: THE JAZZ SINGERS

1. Alice Adams, *Listening to Billie* (New York: Alfred A. Knopf, 1978), p. 1.
2. Maya Angelou, *The Heart of a Woman* (New York: Random House, 1981), p. 17.
3. Quoted in Hettie Jones, *Big Star, Fallin' Mama*, p. 96.
4. Billie Holiday, *Lady Sings the Blues*, pp. 16–17.
5. John Hammond, *John Hammond on Record*, p. 92.
6. Quoted in John Chilton, *Billie's Blues*, p. 26.
7. See Lena Horne, *In Person: Lena Horne*; and *Lena*.
8. Quoted in Chilton, *Billie's Blues*, p. 86.
9. Quoted in Barbara Gardner, interview with Sarah Vaughan, *Down Beat*, March 2, 1961.
10. Quoted in Don Gold, interview with Sarah Vaughan, *Down Beat*, May 30, 1957.
11. John S. Wilson, *New York Times*, July 4, 1974.
12. Quoted in Harvey Siders, "Perfectionist Carmen McRae," *Jazz*, Fall 1978.
13. Quoted in Sammy Mitchell, "The Magic of Carmen McRae," *Down Beat*, December 12, 1968.
14. See Anita O'Day, *High Times, Hard Times*, for the singer's own account of her struggles.
15. Nat Hentoff, *Books and Art*, September 14, 1979.
16. Quoted in ibid.
17. Quoted in Linda Prince, "Betty Carter: Bebopper Breathes Fire," *Down Beat*, March 13, 1979.

18. Quoted in "The Jazz Singer," *Newsweek*, July 10, 1978.
19. Quoted in Barbara van Rooyen and Pawel Brodowski, "Betty's Groove," *Jazz Forum*, January 1979.
20. Quoted in Prince, "Betty Carter."
21. Quoted in John S. Wilson, "Betty Carter Sings Jazz on Broadway," *New York Times*, November 24, 1978.
22. Quoted in Prince, "Betty Carter."
23. Guregian, record review of Carter's *Social Call*, *Down Beat*, October 1979.
24. Quoted in van Rooyen and Brodowski, "Betty's Groove."
25. Ibid.
26. Leonard Feather, *The Encyclopedia of Jazz*, 1960 ed.
27. Conversation with the author, January 1981.
28. Dan Morgenstern, *Down Beat*, November 12, 1970.
29. Irene V. Jackson, "Black Women and Afro-American Song Tradition," *Sing Out!* 25, no. 2 (1976): 22.
30. Tony Heilbut, *The Gospel Sound*, pp. 136, 302.
31. Jones, *Big Star*, p. 131.
32. Heilbut, *The Gospel Sound*, pp. 302-3.
33. Quoted by John Tynan, *Down Beat*, January 2, 1964.
34. Quoted in Siders, "Perfectionist Carmen McRae."
35. Quoted in van Rooyen and Brodowski, "Betty's Groove."
36. Conversation with the author, March 1981.

CHAPTER 9: THE CONTEMPORARY SCENE

1. Quoted in Takashi Oka, "Japanese Jazz Artist Perfects Skills in U.S.," *Christian Science Monitor*, October 12, 1956.
2. Quoted in Nick Dean, "Toshiko Akiyoshi," *Metronome*, April 1956.
3. Quoted in Leonard Feather, "Toshiko Akiyoshi: The Leader of the Band," *Ms.*, November 1978.
4. Peter Rothbart, "Toshiko Akiyoshi," *Down Beat*, August 1980.
5. Quoted in Charles Gans, "T.A.L.T. Conference: A Conversation with Toshiko Akiyoshi and Lew Tabackin," *Jazz Forum*, February 1980.
6. Conversation with the author, March 1981.
7. Quoted in Rothbart, "Toshiko Akiyoshi."
8. Conversation with the author, March 1981.
9. Quoted in Gans, "T.A.L.T. Conference."
10. Conversation with the author, March 1981.
11. Quoted in Gans, "T.A.L.T. Conference."
12. Ibid.
13. Conversation with the author, March 1981.
14. Rothbart, "Toshiko Akiyoshi."
15. Quoted in Joachim Berendt, *The Jazz Book*, p. 115.
16. Quoted by John S. Wilson, *New York Times*, December 17, 1978.

17. Ibid.
18. Quoted in J. N. Thomas, "Profile: Jessica Williams," *Down Beat,* June 1981.
19. Quoted in George Nelson, "Joanne Brackeen, Pianist for a New Era," *Down Beat,* July 1980.
20. Quoted by Amy Duncan, *Baltimore Sun,* May 25, 1980.
21. Interview with the author, June 1981.
22. Quoted by Don Nelson, *Jazz Times,* April–May 1981.
23. Ibid.
24. Ibid.
25. Quoted in Fred Bouchard, "Profile: Jane Ira Bloom," *Down Beat,* December 1981.
26. Ibid.
27. Conversation with the author, July 1979.
28. Conversation with the author, May 1981.
29. Ibid.
30. Leonard Feather, *Encyclopedia of Jazz in the Seventies.*
31. Quoted in Yusef A. Salaam, "Profile: Janice Robinson," *Down Beat,* April 1981.
32. Quoted in Richard Brown, "Profile: Terri Lyne Carrington," *Down Beat,* March 22, 1978.
33. Feather, *Encyclopedia of Jazz in the Seventies.*
34. Quoted in Lee Underwood, "Blindfold Test," *Down Beat,* November 18, 1976.
35. Videotaped interview by Burrill Crohn of Stop-Time Productions, aired on ABC-TV cable affiliates in 1981–82.
36. Quoted in Regina Weinreich, "Play it Momma," *Village Voice,* July 3, 1978.
37. Crohn interview.
38. Quoted in Weinreich, "Play it Momma."
39. Quoted in Stephen Holden, "Brazilian Pianist on Expatriate Road to Stardom," *New York Times,* August 19, 1983.
40. Quoted in Jim Dulzo, "Alive! and Well," *Detroit News,* October 5, 1979.

CHAPTER 10: BUILDING A SUPPORT SYSTEM

1. Quoted in John S. Wilson, "A Salute to Women in Jazz Will Open," *New York Times,* June 25, 1978.
2. "Studio Red Top: A Loft Performance Space and Resource Center for Jazz Women and Men," 1981 press release distributed by Cathy Lee.
3. Interview with the author, June 1979.
4. Ibid.
5. Ibid.
6. Quoted in Amy Duncan, "Women's Jazz Festival: A Swinging Minority," *Christian Science Monitor,* March 31, 1980.
7. Interview with the author, June 1979.

More Women in Jazz

This appendix covers women who were omitted from the text (or mentioned only in passing) either because information about them is scarce or because their involvement with jazz was brief or peripheral. It also includes many contemporary jazzwomen. It is divided into five parts: Instrumentalists and Bandleaders; Vocalists; All-Woman Bands; Women Songwriters and Lyricists; and Organizations That Promote Women in Jazz.

Instrumentalists and Bandleaders

CAROL ANDERSON, *piano:* Contemporary Los Angeles–based performer.

WILHELMINA "WILLA" BART, *piano:* Deceased. Born about 1900, she played with many New Orleans–based groups, including Willie Pajeaud at the Alamo Dance Hall in the 1920s, the New Orleans Creole Jazz Band, and groups led by Jimmy Noone, Joe Oliver and Amos White.

ROSEMARY BEARSE, *tenor sax:* Led the Girls' Swing Band based in Tucson, Arizona, in the 1930s.

WINI BEATTY, *piano, vocals:* California-based musician active in the 1940s; performed with a group led by bassist Vivien Garry.

PEGGY BECHEERS, *tenor sax:* Played both lead and second (solo) sax with the International Sweethearts of Rhythm during the swing era, then settled in California.

FLORIDA BECK, *piano:* Early player from Florida. Her contemporary, pianist Billie Pierce, said of Beck and her fellow Floridian Willie Woods, "They could really play

piano. They played with bands, usually at private parties rather than in clubs"
(transcript of interview conducted by Ralph Collins and William Russell on April 2,
1959, p. 5, in the William Ransom Hogan Jazz Archive of Tulane University).

RENEE BERGER, *trombone:* Contemporary New York–based performer.

LOLLIE BIENENFELD, *bass trombone:* Contemporary New York–based performer,
formerly with Melba Liston and Company, a member of the Mel Lewis Orchestra as
of 1982.

KAY BLANCHARD, *tenor sax, clarinet, symphonic oboe:* West Coast–based veteran;
appeared with the all–woman combo Quintess at the 1980 Women's Jazz Festival.

ESTHER BLUE, *piano:* Emerging contemporary player, originally from Boston, now
based in New York.

BESS BONNIER, *piano:* Veteran Detroit–based player, active as a performer and teacher.

KAREN BORCA, *bassoon:* Associated with "free" or avant-garde jazz, she studied with
pianist Cecil Taylor and has played with Taylor, saxophonist Sam Rivers and
drummer Andrew Cyrille, and the Jimmy Lyons Quartet. She has also led her own
groups, including an 11–piece unit at the 1979 Salute to Jazzwomen in New York.

ANDREA BRACHFELD, *flute:* Contemporary New York–based player who has worked
with the CETA Orchestra and with the Latin-jazz orchestras led by Tito Puente and
Machito.

PAULINE BRADDY, *drums:* Played with the International Sweethearts of Rhythm from
1939 to 1948, and with various groups under former Sweethearts leader Anna Mae
Winburn until 1955. She then played with Vi Burnside's Orchestra and the Edna
Smith Trio before forming her own group, Two Plus One.

LILLIAN BRIGGS, *trombone:* Worked in various ensembles during the formative years
of jazz.

HADDA BROOKS, *piano, vocals:* Began performing as a jazz-influenced pianist and was
a popular performer on the West Coast during the late 1940s and early 1950s. In the
early 1950s she had her own local TV program, *The Hadda Brooks Show.*

JEANE BROWN, *bandleader:* Led a studio band in Fort Wayne, Indiana, with a coast-to-
coast radio show in 1940.

LISE BROWN, *sax:* Contemporary New York–based performer who studied with Karl
Berger at the Creative Music School in Woodstock.

JUANITA BURNS, *piano:* Active during the formative years of jazz. Her married name
was Mrs. Abe Bolar.

ANITA BYRNES, *bandleader:* Commercially successful dance-band leader and pianist
of the swing era. Historian Frank Driggs says that she rose from dancing-school
accompanist to "one of the highest-paid and most sought–after bandleaders,
rivalling Meyer Davis...and others in a highly competitive and lucrative industry....She retired to Atlantic City, a wealthy woman" ("Women in Jazz," p. 5).

ALICE CALLOWAY, *drums:* Veteran of vaudeville; worked with Walter Barnes' band in the 1920s.

BABY CALLOWAY, *bandleader:* Led the Rockin' Rhythm Orchestra based in Tulsa, Oklahoma, in the 1940s.

HARRIET CALLOWAY, *bandleader:* Headed a revue with Red Perkins' Dixie Ramblers and briefly fronted King Oliver's band.

JEAN CALLOWAY, *bandleader:* Led the Fess Whatley Orchestra and the Alabama-based Yellowjackets in the 1930s.

DONA CARTER, *piano:* Contemporary New York–based performer who worked with Ornette Coleman; formed her own group, the Peacemakers, in 1977; and currently leads a combo.

CAROL CHAKIAN, *reeds:* Contemporary Boston–based player, currently in a trio with pianist Lee Ann Ledgerwood and drummer Terri Lyne Carrington.

OLIVIA "LADY CHARLOTTE" CHARLOT, *piano:* New Orleans–based performer active beginning in the 1930s as teacher, player and leader of her own group, Lady Charlotte and Her Men of Rhythm.

KIM CLARKE, *electric bass:* Contemporary New York–based performer.

GLORIA COLEMAN, *bass, organ, vocals:* Played bass with organist Sarah McLawler in the 1950s, then switched to organ and led several trios in the 1960s.

JOYCE COLLINS, *piano, vocals:* Played with bassist Oscar Pettiford in the mid-1950s before resuming formal musical studies.

MARY COLSTON, *piano:* Played with the George Morrison Orchestra in Denver in the early 1930s, then married bandleader Andy Kirk and gave up playing professionally.

ESTHER COOK, *trombone, trumpet:* Worked with the International Sweethearts of Rhythm in 1947–48; later became a music teacher and scholar.

OLIVIA COOK. See OLIVIA CHARLOT.

ELISABETH COTTEN, *guitar:* Veteran performer, self-taught in the folk-blues idiom, based in Washington, D.C., for many years; wrote "Freight Train."

MARGE CREATH, *piano:* Active in St. Louis in the early 1920s. The sister of legendary riverboat performer Charlie Creath, she was very popular in her own right. She stopped playing professionally upon her marriage to drummer Zutty Singleton.

MARILYN CRISPELL, *piano:* Contemporary New York–based player who has worked with saxophonist Anthony Braxton.

CONNIE CROTHERS, *piano:* Contemporary New York–based player, student of late pianist Lennie Tristano.

BEVERLY DAHLKEY, *baritone sax, reeds:* Contemporary West Coast–based player; worked with the Akiyoshi-Tabackin Big Band, then joined Harry James' big band in the late 1970s.

DESDEMONA DAVIS, *piano:* Worked with the George Morrison Orchestra out of Denver in the 1930s.

JEAN DAVIS, *trumpet:* Veteran player active professionally since the 1950s. She studied with trumpeter Doc Cheatham and has worked with numerous groups, including Oliver Nelson's band, Al Madison's band and several Dixieland bands. Played with the Jazz Sisters, an all-woman combo led by pianist Jill McManus, in the 1970s, and currently freelances out of New York.

MARTHA DAVIS, *piano:* Popular in the 1940s as a swing and boogie-woogie player; made several film shorts.

LYNN DELMONICO, *cornet, trumpet:* Active freelancer; appeared with an all-woman combo at the now-defunct Jazz Museum in New York in 1973.

DIANE DEROSA, *baritone sax:* Contemporary player who has worked with Clark Terry's Big Bad Band.

CLARA DE VRIES, *trumpet:* Dutch player, probably part of the European big band Jac and Louis De Vries' Internationals during the 1930s. *Down Beat* praised her highly as a soloist and bandleader in 1937.

GARVINIA DICKERSON, *piano:* Player and leader in Chicago during the 1920s.

MARILYN DONADT, *drums, percussion:* Contemporary Los Angeles–based player; appeared with the all-woman quintet Quintess at the 1980 Women's Jazz Festival, where she was featured producing special sound effects on "found" objects, including various kitchen utensils and giant gongs.

ANN DUPONT, *clarinet, reeds:* Active freelancer during the late 1930s and 1940s, when she was compared in the trade papers to Artie Shaw; led her own all-male group, the Masters of Swing.

GLADYS EASTER, *piano, vocals:* Veteran performer still active in the later 1970s.

RUTH ELLINGTON, *bandleader:* Headed King Kolax's big band in 1936.

PAMELA EPPLE, *oboe:* Contemporary New York–based player.

SUSAN EVANS, *percussion:* Contemporary New York–based freelancer and active studio musician; played with Gil Evans (no relation) and orchestra in the late 1960s and 1970s, and with pianist Steve Kuhn in the 1970s.

JANE FAIR, *sax, reeds:* Emerging contemporary performer based in Toronto, Canada; played with the Jim Galloway Big Band, composed music for the film *Passages,* leads and records with her own combo.

STEPHANIE FAUBER, *French horn:* Contemporary New York-based player, with the Mel Lewis Orchestra as of 1982.

MERCEDES GORMAN FIELDS. See MERCEDES GORMAN.

EDNA MITCHELL FRANCIS. See EDNA MITCHELL.

NADINE FRIEDMAN, *reeds:* Played with Ina Ray Hutton and the Melodears in the 1930s; *Down Beat* praised her solo work in 1937.

LAURIE FRINK, *trumpet:* Contemporary New York-based performer and active freelancer. She often appears with East Coast big bands and has played lead with Gerry Mulligan's ensemble.

MARIAN GANGE, *guitar:* Rhythm player with Ina Ray Hutton and the Melodears in the late 1930s and early 1940s; also active as a freelancer.

JULIE GARDNER, *accordion, blues vocals:* Veteran performer who came to attention with the Earl Hines Orchestra in 1943. She has since worked with various ensembles and as a soloist.

JANE GETZ, *piano:* West Coast-based performer. During the 1960s she played in the McCoy Tyner style in groups led by saxophonist Pharoah Sanders, bassist Charles Mingus and others.

GOODSON SISTERS (Edna, Ida, Mabel, Dalla), *piano:* Sisters of the better-known Billie and Sadie Goodson. All were active, separately, in the teens and twenties in various parts of the South, including New Orleans, where Edna served a stint with sister Billie's husband, trumpeter De De Pierce.

MERCEDES GORMAN, *piano:* New Orleans-based performer active during the formative years of jazz; played with Manuel Perez's band in 1926, and intermittently with Papa Celestin's Orchestra into the 1930s and 1940s.

LIZ GORRILL, *piano:* Emerging contemporary player based in New York. A student of late modernist pianist Lennie Tristano, she is active in jazz circles he influenced.

JUNE GRANT, *bandleader:* Led an all-woman band in the 1940s.

JOANN GRAUER, *piano:* Veteran West Coast-based player, active in the 1980s as a soloist and accompanist in the Los Angeles area.

IDA GUILLORY, *accordion:* Veteran San Francisco-based performer, active in the 1980s with Queen Ida's Bon Ton Zydeco Band, a washboard group.

ANNIE HARRIS, *bandleader:* Leader and pianist of an all-woman orchestra in Chicago in the 1930s.

LOTTIE HIGHTOWER, *piano, bandleader:* Had a popular all-male band in Chicago in the 1920s.

JANE HIMINGWAY, *piano:* St. Louis-based player who worked with riverboat leader Charlie Creath in the 1920s.

JEAN HOFFMAN, *piano:* Active California-based freelancer in the 1950s.

JULIE HOMI, *piano:* Contemporary player, based during the 1970s in California, where she worked with the all-woman group Alive!; moved to New York in the late 1970s.

BERTHA HOPE, *piano:* East Coast performer, widow of pianist Elmo Hope, with whom she cut an album.

OZZIE "BUMPS" HUFF, *bandleader:* Fronted the all-woman Darlings of Rhythm in the 1930s; later married bandleader Clarence Love.

REVELLA HUGHES, *organ:* Veteran East Coast–based player, still performing occasionally in the 1980s.

BOBBI HUMPHREY, *flute, piccolo, alto sax:* Studied with flutist Hubert Laws and performed with flutist Herbie Mann, then went on to success as a pop player in the 1970s.

NADINE JANSEN, *trumpet:* Veteran player who worked with guitarist Mary Kaye after World War II on the West Coast and in Las Vegas. She still freelances.

LOUISE JOHNSON, *piano:* Active in New Orleans during the formative years of jazz.

MARY JOHNSON, *piano:* Performed with husband Willie Austin's band in the Midwest in the 1930s.

DEBBIE KATZ, *drums:* Emerging contemporary performer based in Chicago, playing with the all-woman big band Maiden Voyage as of 1982.

MARGARET KIMBALL, *piano:* Played with cornetist husband Andrew Kimball and in pit bands at the Lynn and Lyric theaters in New Orleans in the early 1920s. She later moved to the Gulf Coast.

ROSA KING, *sax:* American-born player based in the Netherlands for many years; performs in r&b style and makes occasional visits to the States.

MARY COLSTON KIRK. See MARY COLSTON.

RUTH KISSANE, *trumpet, flugelhorn, arranger:* Veteran Los Angeles–based player, formerly leader of the all-woman combo Quintess, and a member of the all-woman big band Maiden Voyage as of 1982.

MARCELLA KYLE, *piano:* St. Louis–based player who worked with riverboat performer Charlie Creath in the 1920s.

JOAN LEE, *bandleader:* Led an all-woman band in the 1940s.

GERTRUDE LONG, *bandleader:* Led the Rambling Night Hawks in Pittsburgh in the 1930s; Duke Ellington reportedly praised the band as "ready for the big time" (D. Antoinette Handy, *Black Women in American Bands and Orchestras*, p. 43).

PAMELA LUCIA, *bandleader:* In the early 1940s led all-woman bands and combos on society dates in St. Louis.

ANN LUNCEFORD, *bandleader, vocals:* Probably also performed under the names Joan Lunceford and Baby Briscoe. She recorded with the Jules Robichaux Big Band on Vocalion in the 1930s. Touted as "the next Ella," she was killed in a club brawl.

KIT MCCLURE, *tenor sax, reeds:* Contemporary New York–based freelancer. She leads an all-woman big band formed in 1982.

SARAH MCLAWLER, *organ, piano:* Played piano with an all-woman combo, the Syncoettes, in the 1940s, worked with bassist Gloria Coleman in the 1950s and currently freelances as organist and vocalist.

IDA MAE MAPLES, *piano:* Led her own band in Chicago in the 1920s.

GERTRUDE ELOISE MARTIN, *bandleader:* Conducted the 25-piece show band for the *Blackbirds* revue in 1939–40.

NYDIA "LIBERTY" MATA, *percussion:* Contemporary New York–based performer. A member of the combo Deuce, she appeared at a concert of women performers at the 1981 Kool Jazz Festival in New York.

LYNN MILANO, *bass:* Contemporary performer who has gigged with pianist Duke Jordan, trumpeter Charlie Shavers and pianist Marian McPartland; played with the Jazz Sisters, an all-woman group led by pianist Jill McManus, in 1977–78.

ETHEL MINOR, *piano:* Early performer who played with Estella Harris' Ladies Jass Band in Chicago in 1916.

EDNA MITCHELL, *piano:* New Orleans–based performer during the formative years of jazz; married drummer Albert Francis.

ANNA RAY MOORE, *bandleader:* Led the Milt Larkins Orchestra during the swing era.

PAT MORAN, *piano:* Emerged in New York in the 1950s as leader of her own trio, which played at the Hickory House in 1959. She worked with vibraphonist Terry Gibbs in the early 1960s, before moving to California.

KATHRYN MOSES, *flute:* Based in Toronto, Canada, since the early 1970s, she freelances and has produced her own album.

PATTY PADDEN, *drums:* Emerging contemporary freelancer based in Los Angeles; student of drummer Bill Douglas.

GLADYS PALMER, *piano, vocals:* Jamaican-born performer who moved to the U.S. and appeared at jazz rooms such as Chicago's Three Deuces in the 1930s. She served as Billie Holiday's accompanist for two years and continued to perform into the late 1960s.

MARY FETTIG PARK, *alto sax, reeds:* Emerging contemporary player based on the West Coast.

BU PLEASANT, *organ, piano:* East Coast–based freelancer who got her start in the 1950s and worked with an all-woman group led by Melba Liston in the late 1950s.

NANCY HILDEGARDE PRATT, *trumpet:* Worked with Anna Mae Winburn's International Sweethearts of Rhythm in the early 1950s. She married and left professional music, returning after the death of her husband. Since the 1970s she has freelanced in the New York area.

PATTI PRIESS, *bass:* Emerging contemporary performer; toured with the Carla Bley Band in Europe in 1978.

DARALYN RAMEY, *drums:* Contemporary East Coast–based performer.

YVONNE RICHARDSON, *sax, oboe, piano:* Emerging contemporary performer based in Houston.

JUDY ROBERTS, *piano, vocals:* Contemporary jazz-influenced performer based in Chicago.

LULA ROBERTS, *tenor sax:* Florida-born player who worked with Sarah McLawler in the Syncoettes, an all-woman combo, during the 1950s.

MICHELLE ROSEWOMAN, *piano:* Contemporary New York–based freestyle player.

JUNE ROTENBERG, *bass:* Played and recorded with a number of women jazz musicians during the 1940s, including Mary Lou Williams and Marjorie Hyams, then became a classical musician and symphony player.

STACY ROWLES, *trumpet, flugelhorn:* Contemporary West Coast–based performer; appeared with a big band at the Monterey Jazz Festival in 1973 and with an all-woman big band led by Clark Terry at the Wichita Jazz Festival in 1976. She is a member of the all-woman big band Maiden Voyage as of 1981.

KATHY RUBBICO, *piano:* Contemporary West Coast–based performer.

"QUEENIE" ADA RUBIN, *piano:* New York–based performer active in the Fifty-second Street jazz clubs during the swing era.

LAURA RUCHER, *piano:* New York–based performer during the formative years of jazz.

PATRICE RUSHEN, *piano:* Contemporary performer who showed considerable invention as a teenage jazz musician in the 1970s and was often compared to the young Herbie Hancock. She subsequently began playing in a more commercial vein.

HILARY SCHMIDT, *soprano sax, flute:* Contemporary New York–based performer.

DOROTHY "DOT" SCOTT, *piano:* Player-leader in Chicago in the 1920s and early 1930s; backed Victoria Spivey on recordings.

RHODA SCOTT, *organ:* Veteran performer.

DELOIS SEARCY, *piano:* Began her career in the Midwest in the 1920s, then moved to the East Coast and continued to perform for many years.

DARYL SHERMAN, *piano, vocals:* Emerging contemporary New York–based performer and songwriter.

AUZIE CRAWFORD SHOFFNER, *piano:* Originally based in St. Louis, she began playing professionally in the 1920s and continued to play in the Midwest into the 1940s.

MATTIE SIMPSON, *cornet:* A true pioneer, she played with the Mahara Minstrels in the 1890s.

MARGE CREATH SINGLETON. See MARGE CREATH.

KATHRYN SKEFFINGTON, *bandleader:* Led Grandma's Ragtime Band in Chicago in the late 1940s: "The one requirement for membership . . . was that you had to be at least a grandmother" (D. Antoinette Handy, *Black Women in American Bands and Orchestras*, p. 24).

EDNA SMITH, *acoustic bass, trombone, guitar:* Played with the International Sweethearts of Rhythm, with groups under Anna Mae Winburn in the 1940s and 1950s, and with the Vi Burnside Orchestra, then formed her own trio.

JERI SMITH, *bandleader:* Active in New Jersey in the 1930s as a dance-band leader and pianist.

LEONA MAY SMITH, *cornet:* Garnered excellent reviews in the 1930s, probably as a "straight" (nonsoloing) player. *Down Beat* called her "Queen of the Cornet" and the "greatest lady cornetist of our time" after concerts in 1937 at the Roxy Theatre and Radio City Music Hall in New York.

MARY SOUCHON, *piano:* Active in New Orleans from the teens to the 1940s in groups led by her husband, Edmond Souchon.

PEGGY STERN, *piano:* Contemporary New York–based performer.

JEAN STRICKLAND, *flute:* Contemporary freelancer based in Los Angeles.

CAROL SUDHALTER, *baritone sax, reeds:* Contemporary East Coast–based performer.

DONA SUMMERS. See DONA CARTER.

CHESSIE TANKSLEY, *piano:* Emerging contemporary performer based in New York; member of Melba Liston and Company since 1980.

BLANCHE THOMAS, *piano:* New Orleans–based performer active during the formative years of jazz.

BARBARA THOMPSON, *sax, reeds:* Contemporary performer based in England; member of the jazz fusion group Paraphernalia.

CAMILLE TODD, *piano:* Born in 1888 and active in New Orleans jazz for many years; pianist with the Maple Leaf Orchestra (1919-20) and other concert groups. She became a popular music teacher and church organist in her later years.

RUBY MAY TOWNSEND, *piano:* Mentioned by fellow New Orleans pianist Jeanette Salvant Kimball as a good player during the early years of jazz.

JEAN WALD, *bandleader:* Led an all-woman band in the 1940s.

BERNARDINE WARREN, *drums:* New York–based performer who has frequently worked with organist Sarah McLawler and tenor saxophonist Willene Barton since the 1970s.

MARY WATKINS, *piano:* Contemporary San Francisco–based musician/composer in the jazz fusion style. She was awarded a 1981 grant by the National Endowment for the Arts to perform and record four original jazz compositions with a 36-piece orchestra.

THELMA WHITE, *bandleader:* In the early 1940s led a white all-woman band, reportedly very good, and made at least one film short.

EDITH WILLIAMS, *piano:* Based in Kansas City in the 1920s; performed in barrelhouse and boogie styles.

PAULINE BRADDY WILLIAMS. See PAULINE BRADDY.

SHERRY WINSTON, *flute:* Contemporary East Coast-based performer.

WILLIE WOODS, *piano:* Florida-based player of the teens and twenties, praised by her contemporary, pianist Billie Pierce (see FLORIDA BECK, above).

EVELYN YOUNG, *alto sax, tenor sax:* Veteran Memphis-based player; toured with a group backing bluesman B.B. King in the 1940s and has since worked in blues, jazz and r&b backup bands.

VICKIE ZIMMER, *piano:* Active as a performer in the 1940s.

Vocalists

CARMEN BARNES: Contemporary East Coast-based performer; in the late 1970s sang with the female vocal trio Joyspring, which also included Nancie Manzuk and Lionelle Hamanaka.

ANN BURTON: Contemporary singer based in the Netherlands.

LODI CARR: Active into the 1950s.

SAVANNAH CHURCHILL: Born in New Orleans in 1919, died in 1974. She began her professional career at Small's Paradise in Harlem, then performed with Benny Carter's orchestra (1942–44). She went on to become a solo attraction, singing blues and r&b material with some jazz stylings.

CARLOTTA DALE: Sang with the Jan Savitt Big Band and with Will Bradley's Big Band.

SASHA DALTON: Contemporary Chicago-based singer; performed a Tribute to Dinah Washington in Chicago in 1981.

DOLLY DAWN: Born in 1919, she became popular in the 1930s with the George Hall Band, which she led in 1941–42. She recorded as Dolly Dawn and Her Dawn Patrol and continued to perform into the 1980s.

DORIS DAY: Vocalist with the Les Brown Orchestra at age 17, in 1940–41, and again from 1943 to 1946, prior to becoming a solo star in movies and TV.

LU ELLIOT: Sang with various bands in the 1950s, including a stint with Duke Ellington; continues to perform as a solo attraction in the 1980s.

ANITA ELLIS: Born Anita Kert in Montreal, Canada, in 1920. A noted ballad stylist, she began as a child actress in Hollywood, performed on radio shows in the 1940s, was the movie voice for many stars, and reemerged as a performer in the 1970s.

ETHEL ENNIS: Jazz-influenced stylist; won an amateur singing contest in her hometown of Baltimore in 1950 and toured with Benny Goodman in 1958; continues to perform in the 1980s.

DALE EVANS: Big-band singer with the Anson Weeks and Herman Waldman bands in the 1930s; later became famous as wife and partner of Roy Rogers.

PAM GARNER: Active in the 1950s.

MABEL GODWIN: Veteran cabaret performer, a fixture at Greenwich Village boites in the 1960s and 1970s.

CONNIE HAINES: Big-band singer, best known for stints with Harry James (1939) and Tommy Dorsey (1940–42), with whom she recorded a hit, "Will You Still Be Mine?" She then went out as a soloist, performing in movies and on records.

JANE HARVEY: Began professionally during the swing era after a successful audition at Cafe Society Downtown. She worked with the Benny Goodman band and had a long musical association with pianist Ellis Larkins. She then settled on the West Coast, performing on the club circuit and recording again in the 1970s, and finally relocating in New York.

HARRIET HILLIARD: Born Peggy Lee Snyder, she got her start as a dancer in vaudeville. She sang with Ozzie Nelson's band in the mid-1930s, later married him and starred with him in the popular 1950s TV series *Ozzie and Harriet*.

LURLEAN HUNTER: Born in Mississippi in 1928; settled in Chicago and in the 1950s became a popular vocalist with some jazz influence.

DAMITA JO: Born in Austin, Texas, in 1930; in the 1950s worked with Steve Gibson and the Recaps, an r&b-style band, then became a versatile solo artist.

ETTA JONES: Veteran pop-soul singer, born in South Carolina in 1928, notable for her timing and phrasing. She worked in jazz contexts in the 1940s and was with the Earl Hines Sextet from 1949 to 1952. She stopped working professionally in the 1950s, made a comeback, and since the late 1960s has performed with saxophonist Houston Person on the black club circuit in what one reviewer called a "classic Harlem lounge jazz act."

JEZRA KAYE: Emerging contemporary vocalist based on the East Coast.

EARTHA KITT: Born in South Carolina in 1928, she joined Katherine Dunham's dance troupe at age 16 and soon became the troupe's vocalist. She went out as a solo act, worked in movies and still performs in the 1980s in her highly mannered, idiosyncratic style, marked by a curt delivery and punctuated by growls.

JOAN LA BARBERA: Contemporary opera-trained vocalist who works in an experimental, free-form style, often utilizing electronic media.

BARBARA LEA: Born Barbara LeCocq, she apprenticed as a singer in Boston and New York, where she settled in 1954 and made her first record for Riverside. She has since done mainly theater work.

KITTY LESTER: Born in Arkansas in 1934, she has been based since the 1950s in Los Angeles, where she has performed and recorded.

CARMEN LUNDY: Emerging contemporary vocalist based on the East Coast.

GLORIA LYNNE: Born in New York in 1931, she began singing in church and later received concert training. She made her professional debut in 1951 after winning an amateur contest at the Apollo Theatre. She became increasingly influenced by and oriented to jazz in the late 1950s.

MARY ANN MCCALL: Band singer of the late swing era, born in Philadelphia in 1919; with Tommy Dorsey (1938), Woody Herman (late 1930s, 1946–49), Charlie Ventura (1954–55). Based on the West Coast in the 1960s and 1970s, in 1976 she cut her first recording in 15 years.

SUSANNAH MCCORKLE: Contemporary New York–based cabaret performer, notable for her tasteful handling of material and selection of obscure but excellent songs.

MARILYN MAYE: Veteran ballad stylist.

MARY MAYO: Studied classical singing at Juilliard and has been a popular ballad stylist since 1946, with the Glenn Miller Orchestra and other groups; did a series of New York club dates in the 1970s. She also sang with Duke Ellington in his spiritual concerts and recorded for Columbia.

VELMA MIDDLETON: Born in 1917; best known for her long tenure with Louis Armstrong, from 1942 until her death in 1961.

ANNE MARIE MOSS: Veteran singer born in Toronto, Canada, and based in New York; noted for her taste and musicality. She got her first important professional job with Maynard Ferguson's orchestra in 1960 and was teamed with then-husband Jackie Paris in the 1960s and early 1970s. A solo artist since, she made her debut recording as a leader in 1981.

MAGGIE NICHOLS: Contemporary British singer who often works with the Feminist Improvising Group in Europe.

JUDY NIEMACK: Emerging contemporary vocalist based on the East Coast.

ODETTA: Jazz-influenced folk singer. Born in Birmingham, Alabama, in 1930, she began singing professionally in San Francisco in the early 1950s, then settled on the East Coast later that decade.

DELORES O'NEILL: Sang with Bob Chester's Big Band and with Artie Shaw and Gene Krupa for a short time in the late 1930s to mid-1940s and made some recordings.

PATTI PAGE. Began her professional career as a band singer; with the Jimmy Joy Band in 1947 on radio in Chicago, and the Benny Goodman Septet in 1948. In the 1950s she became a big pop star with hits like "Tennessee Waltz." She continued to perform in the 1980s.

JANN PARKER: Emerging contemporary vocalist based on the East Coast.

DENISE DE LA PENHA: Contemporary singer who bases her style on Afro-Brazilian vocal improvisation.

ESTHER PHILLIPS: Veteran blues and r&b-style performer, born Esther Mae Jones in Galveston, Texas, in 1925; billed as "Little Esther" during a stint with the Johnny Otis Band from 1949 to 1952. She dropped out of professional music in the 1950s, made a comeback in the mid-1960s and currently performs in a sophisticated jazz-influenced style somewhat reminiscent of Dinah Washington.

MARTHA RAYE: Born Margaret Yvonne Reed in 1916, she began performing at age three. Before succeeding as an actress and comedienne, she sang with the Paul Ash Orchestra, with Louis Prima and in swing-era clubs in New York.

LUCY REED: Popular Chicago-based singer of the 1950s, born in Wisconsin in 1921; was with the Woody Herman Sextet in 1950 and the Charlie Ventura Big Band in 1951.

DELLA REESE. Born in Detroit in 1932, she sang in church choirs as a child, was part of the Mahalia Jackson Troupe from 1945 to 1949 and had her own gospel group while attending Wayne State University. She later joined Erskine Hawkins and band in New York, becoming a prominent solo performer in 1957.

IRENE REID: Born in Georgia in 1930, she won an amateur talent contest at New York's Apollo Theatre in 1948 and became a solo artist in the 1950s. She toured with Count Basie and Orchestra in 1962, then resumed solo work.

BEVERLY ROHLEHR: Emerging contemporary vocalist based on the East Coast.

SHARON RUSSELL: Contemporary vocalist formerly based in Paris, now active on the West Coast.

KEISHA ST. JOAN: Emerging contemporary vocalist based on the East Coast.

DINAH SHORE: Born in 1917, she became a very popular radio singer in the late 1930s, recorded with Xavier Cugat in 1939–40, then went on to star as a film and TV personality.

MARY STALLINGS: Self-taught San Francisco–based singer, born in 1939; began her professional career in the late 1950s with the encouragement of Dizzy Gillespie.

ALLISON STEWART: Emerging contemporary vocalist based on the East Coast.

LEE TORCHIA: Emerging contemporary vocalist based on the East Coast.

ROSEANNE VITRO: Emerging contemporary vocalist based on the East Coast.

FRAN WARREN: Born in 1926, she sang with Claude Thornhill's Big Band in the 1940s and with Charlie Barnet's Big Band; she has been active in the musical theater since 1949 and still concertizes.

PATTY WATERS: Free-form stylist of the 1960s and 1970s.

FRANCIS WAYNE: Born in 1924, she sang with Woody Herman's Herd in the mid-1940s. In 1952 she co-led a big band with her husband, arranger Neal Hefti, and recorded with him. She died in the late 1970s.

MIDGE WILLIAMS: Born in 1908, she toured the Orient extensively as a vocalist in the 1930s, toured with pianist Fats Waller, sang with Louis Armstrong's band (1938–41) and then went out as a solo performer.

NANCY WILSON: Born in 1937 into a musical family, she sang in her church choir as a teenager and performed in local clubs. Cannonball Adderly brought her to the attention of the music industry in 1958, and she became a commercial success in the 1960s with her cool, vibrant tone and sleek delivery. Her later work retains traces of jazz influences, but her early style was closer to jazz phrasing, reminiscent of Dinah Washington.

GAIL WYNTERS: Contemporary vocalist based in New York, versatile and at home with jazz, country and r&b styles.

All–Woman Bands

In addition to famous groups like the International Sweethearts of Rhythm and Ina Ray Hutton and Her Melodears, the swing era spawned all sorts of all-woman big bands and combos. Like the all-male bands of the period, some were lightweight novelty groups, some good swing units; but all helped to disprove the myth that women didn't participate in jazz. Among the all-female groups active in the 1930s and 1940s, in addition to those mentioned in the text and elsewhere in this appendix in connection with women bandleaders, were the following: Sara Battles' Band, Joy Caylor (trumpet) and Her Band, Helen Compton and Her Band, the Coon Creek Girls (mainly country music), the Coquettes, the Diplomettes, Dody's Swingtet (Las Vegas-based), the Girls of the Golden West (all-brass ensemble), the Golden Gate Girls, the Hollywood Debs, Alex Hyde's Musical Darlings (vaudeville material), Vincent Lopez' Debutantes, Ruth Noller and Her Band, Sally Sharon and the Dixie Debs, Mitzie Shelton and Her Band, the Southland Rhythm Girls, Glenna Thompson and Her Band, Anna Wallace and Her Band, Peggy White's Texas Rockets (Western swing), Velma Wuench and Her Band.

Women Songwriters and Lyricists

There have always been women songwriters—for that matter, women composers of all types of music—though they have always been in a minority. The more curious among music critics (also in a minority) have from time to time attempted to analyze the array of social restrictions and prejudices that have shackled potential women composers over the centuries, but most writers tend to frame the issue in terms of the dearth of female Bachs, Beethovens and Irving Berlins, and many claim that composing requires certain mental powers lacking in the female sex (see "Why Haven't Women Become Great Composers?," *HiFi/Musical America*, February 1973, for a typical example of such a discussion).

However, the question of genius—the "Shakespeare's sister" syndrome analyzed so tellingly by Virginia Woolf in *A Room of One's Own*—more often than not serves as a convenient excuse for ignoring the historical record and overlooking the real achievements of women on a more human scale. The contributions of women popular composers have yet to be examined as a body. Their work has been wispily compiled and infrequently mentioned (for example, David Ewen's *Popular American Composers*, a voluminous index, lists only one woman composer, Carrie Jacobs Bond). Only recently have there been attempts to give a more accurate and thorough survey. In 1977 the National Academy of Popular Music produced a Tribute to Women Songwriters that called attention to the contributions of a number of long-neglected women and sparked a musical revue called *Womansong*. At the 1982 Kool Jazz Festival, singer Sylvia Sims organized a concert that showcased music and lyrics by women. Serious research into the subject has only begun, but as the preliminary results come in, it turns out that quite a respectable number of popular composers and lyricists of the last century have been women.

For example, several pioneer women songwriters broke into Tin Pan Alley or had ragtime hits around the turn of the century. Many of the blueswomen wrote their own material, of course, and later performers like Abbey Lincoln, Nina Simone and Betty Carter have made notable contributions as songwriters or lyricists. Carla Bley and Toshiko Akiyoshi are among the leading contemporary jazz composers. The songwriting achievements of these and other women discussed in the text have already been noted. This section surveys the contributions of women composers of the better type of American popular song, which has always been a sturdy branch of the eclectic jazz tree.

Women worked in the vital field of American popular music from its beginning in vaudeville and Tin Pan Alley song-peddling through the eras of theater, radio and film. A surprising number of the standards of Americana were penned by women, including "Rock-a-Bye-Baby" (Effie Channing), "America the Beautiful" (Katherine Lee Bates), "Happy Birthday to You" (Patty and Mildred Hill), "Swing Low, Sweet Chariot" (Sarah Hannah Sheppard), "The Battle Hymn of the Republic" (Julia Ward Howe), "When It's Springtime in the Rockies" (Mary Hale Woolsey), "Shine On, Harvest Moon" (Nora Bayes, with husband Jack Norworth) and "Sweet Rosie O'Gradie" (probably written by Maude Nugent). Early in this century, when popular music was still at the toddler stage, women composers of songs in the European tradition of opera and operetta ("art" songs) were prolific, but their work often went unpublished or was self-published and not widely distributed.

Vaudeville spawned a number of female songwriters, many of whose achievements have undoubtedly been lost or appropriated by others. Among the names that survive are the sister team Rosetta and Vivian Duncan, who worked in vaudeville and the theater in the twenties and thirties. They wrote the music and lyrics to *Topsy and Eva* (1925), a musical version of *Uncle Tom's Cabin*. Later they became music publishers, produced a number of tunes and recorded, "I Never Had a Mammy," "Do Re Mi" and "The Moon Am Shinin', Someday Soon." Another vaudeville performer who turned to songwriting in the thirties was Bernice Petkere ("Close Your Eyes," "Lullabye of Leaves," "The Lady I Love," "By a Rippling Stream," "Stay Out of My Dreams," "It's All So New to Me"). Twins Sue and Kay Werner wrote mostly novelty tunes in the vaudeville tradition; Ella Fitzgerald sang their "I Want the Waiter (with the Water)," "Rock It to Me" and "I've Got the Spring Fever Blues."

Popular song in America was immeasurably enriched by the developing American musical theater, which attracted and supported the best songwriting talents. By the 1920s, American musicals as we have come to know them were growing up: the elements of entertainment and song began to adhere to plot, and the music and words of the songs reflected the American experience (unlike light opera and operetta, which, though popular, were imported from Europe and less closely attuned to American realities). And the great pop music from the shows lived on after the shows themselves closed or folded. This pre-Depression Jazz Age atmosphere was a heady mix of youth, energy, insouciance and talent, a new field of opportunity: the young Kern, the Gershwins, scores of abundantly talented composers writing beautiful popular music. Among them were a number of women.

Kay Swift was born in 1905. After studying at Juilliard and the New England Conservatory of Music, she was attracted to popular music, partly through her friendship with George Gershwin. He took an interest in her and suggested that she get to know the musical theater business by working as a rehearsal pianist, as he had done. Swift followed his advice and was hired for *A Connecticut Yankee* in 1927. Her apprenticeship paid off in a hit song, "Can't We Be Friends?," written for a sophisticated 1929 revue called *The Little Show* (the song has since been recorded by many singers, including a recent version by jazz singer Betty Carter). A year later Swift followed with two more hits, "Fine and Dandy," from the show of the same name, and "Can This Be Love?" for the *Garrick Gaieties* revue. Other popular Swift songs, many written with lyricist husband Paul James, include her own favorite, a wistful, bluesy ballad called "Up Among the Chimney Pots," "Forever and a Day," "Calliope," "A Moonlight Memory" and "I Gotta Take Off My Hat to You."

Petite and blonde, Kay Swift may have looked "like a French boudoir doll" to a thirties reporter, but she was tough and determined when it came to her career. During the Depression, for example, she managed to land a job as staff composer at Radio City Music Hall—an ideal position for plugging her own songs. In 1940, after divorcing Paul James, she married the top ranch hand at the World's Fair Rodeo and temporarily abandoned New York for the West, where she raised three daughters. In the late forties she began working in films, adapting Gershwin's music for *The Shocking Miss Pilgrim* (1947) and writing the music for *Never a Dull Moment* (1950), which starred Irene Dunne as a New York songwriter who marries a rancher and tries to be at home on the range. Back in New York in 1952, Swift wrote music and words for a charming Cornelia Otis Skinner play called *Paris '90*. In 1958 she contributed music to Marc Connelley's play *Hunter's Moon,* and in 1962 she composed music for the Seattle World's Fair. George Balanchine commissioned her to write a ballet, *Alma Mater,* and she was still actively writing instrumental and piano pieces into the 1980s.

Composer Ann Ronell, born around 1910, is best remembered for writing the music and words to "Willow Weep for Me." Among her other popular compositions are "Baby's Birthday Party" (a hit in 1930), "Rain on the Roof" (1932) and the lyric to "Who's Afraid of the Big Bad Wolf?" (1933), as well as songs and scores to several musicals. Ronell is the first woman credited with having written both music and lyrics to a Broadway show: *Count Me In* (1942) was praised by critics for the taste and wit of its score, though it was not a commercial success.

Ronell was also guided by George Gershwin when she began popular writing. She met Gershwin when she interviewed him for Radcliffe's college magazine, of which she was music editor, and he inspired her to study harmony and theory seriously. After finishing college, she followed his advice and Kay Swift's example by taking a job as a theater rehearsal pianist. This experience, plus persistence, paid off. Seeking help from established songwriters, she haunted Irving Berlin. "I got to his office at 8:30 one morning and was met by the scrub woman," she recalled. "I didn't know then that he usually got in about 10:30. But I waited. And when he came in, he just couldn't escape me—I told him I'd been waiting a long time" (quoted in Jessie Ash Arndt, "Song Writer as Plucky as Three Little Pigs," *Christian Science Monitor,* January 3, 1955).

The first female songwriter-lyricist on Broadway, Ronell also became the first woman to compose and conduct movie soundtrack music in Hollywood in the thirties. She scored the background music for many movies and wrote songs and/or scores for others, including *Champagne Waltz* (1937), *Algiers* (1938), *Commandos Strike at Dawn* (1942), *Tomorrow the World* (1944), *The Story of GI Joe* (1945), *Love Happy* (1949) and *Main Street to Broadway* (1953). Her "Linda, My Love" was an Academy Award nominee for Best Song in 1945, and her "Ernie Pyle Infantry March" from *The Story of GI Joe* was a popular hit.

Like George Gershwin and Scott Joplin, Ronell had an enduring interest in writing opera in an American manner. Presumably *Porgy and Bess* inspired her own opera, *O Susanna,* based on the life of Stephen Foster. In 1938 her adaptation of the opera *Martha* by Flotow was acclaimed as outstanding; she later adapted the work further for presentation by the Metropolitan Opera in 1961. Ronell continued to adapt classical works, including Strauss' *The Gypsy Baron,* and to write commissioned works, such as the score for the State Department–sponsored feature film *Meeting at a Far Meridian* (1964), which she also conducted.

A third woman who became active in popular songwriting during the twenties and thirties was Louisiana-born child prodigy Dana Suesse. Born in 1911, Suesse began to win prizes and scholarships at age nine. She was a serious composer who turned to popular music for her bread and butter. Working chiefly with lyricist Ed Heyman, she worte tunes that became part of the popular repertoire: "You Oughta Be in Pictures," "Whistling in the Dark," "The Night Is Young and You're So Beautiful," "Yours for a Song," "My Silent Love" and others. But more extended works of composition ultimately claimed Suesse's attention. As early as 1932, when she was twenty-one, her "Jazz Concerto in Three Rhythms" debuted at Carnegie Hall, played by Paul Whiteman and orchestra; he also performed her "Symphonic Waltzes" and a suite called "Young Man with a Harp." Other orchestras, including the prestigious Philadelphia, Boston and New York Philharmonics, played her compositions.

Prestige was one thing; it was Suesse's writing for the theater, movies and musical revues that continued to pay the rent. From roughly 1939 to 1949, she actively worked in pop music, writing scores for a nightclub revue *(The Casa Mañana Show)*, for Billy Rose's World's Fair Aquacade and for the film *Young Man with a Horn.* She then moved to Paris to write for films and to study composition with, among others, the world-famous Nadia Boulanger. From then on, she devoted herself to formal composition. Little is known of her later life.

Another popular songwriter who studied classical composition (with Claude Debussy, among others) was Maria Grever. This Mexican-born composer penned more than eight hundred published songs, including at least one musical score, a number of film scores and what she termed "song dramas" and "concert cameos." And, of course, pop songs: Her "Besame (Mucho)" attained worldwide fame, and "What a Difference a Day Makes" was immortalized by singer Dinah Washington. Married at age fourteen, mother of eight children, blinded by a freak accident in the thirties (she later recovered her sight), Grever compiled an impressive record of achievements; the songs seem to have simply poured from her. Opera star Enrico Caruso praised her work lavishly. "It is a pleasure to sing your songs," he told her. "They are so unique and immense in their drama[tic quality]."

Musical child prodigies often seem to be the rule rather than the exception—and Mable Wayne was no exception. Wayne was born in 1904. As a youngster she studied classical composition at the New York School of Music and in Switzerland, and began performing as a concert singer and pianist. But like other composers, she was drawn to popular music and became a vaudeville pianist-performer, which in turn led her to writing pop songs. Several have become standards. Her string of hits includes "In a Little Spanish Town" (1926), "Ramona" (1927), "Chiquita" (1928), "Little Man, You've Had a Busy Day" (1934), "It Happened in Monterey" (1940), "I Understand," "A Dreamer's Holiday" and "Why Don't You Fall in Love with Me?"

Another songwriter with a classical background was Doris Fisher, daughter of songwriter Fred Fisher, with whom she collaborated in "Whispering Blues" in 1930. This Juilliard-trained songwriter formed her own group, Penny Wise and Her Wise Guys, for which she played the piano and sang. Eventually, with Allen Robert, she began to write film scores and a series of songs that are still in the pop repertoire, among them "Angelina," "You Always Hurt the One You Love," "Invitation to the Blues," "Tampico," "Into Each Life a Little Rain Must Fall" and "Tutti Frutti" (with Slim Gaillard).

Kay Thompson, born in 1902, was a child piano prodigy who debuted with the St. Louis Orchestra in 1918, at age sixteen. Thompson was a talented singer, pianist, vocal coach (her most famous pupil was Judy Garland), arranger and lyricist. She began in show business with the Mills Brothers, before they were famous, and went on to work as arranger and vocalist with Fred Waring's orchestra. During the forties she performed numerous vocal chores for films and composed for the movies *Ziegfeld Follies* and *No Leave, No Love,* among others. She made a notable appearance in the 1956 movie musical *Funny Face.* As lyricist and/or composer, Thompson wrote the songs, "Eloise" (she also wrote the book of the same title), "Promise Me Love," "This Is the Time," "You Gotta Love Everybody," "Just a Moment Ago," "Vive l'Amour," "Love on a Greyhound Bus," "What More Can I Give You?" and "Isn't It Wonderful?"

New Yorker Doris Tauber, who began her career as a secretary to Irving Berlin, made good with a number of enduring songs: "Them There Eyes" (definitively sung by Billie Holiday), "I Was Made to Love You," "Why Remind Me?," "Let's Begin Again" and "Drinking Again" (a torrid mixture of defiance and sadness sung memorably by Dinah Washington).

Alberta Nichols was a versatile composer who wrote for vaudeville, radio, commercials and Broadway (including the revues *Blackbirds of 1933* and *Rhapsody in Black).* Nichols scored over one hundred published songs in collaboration with her husband. Among them are "Why Shouldn't It Happen to Us?," "A Love Like Ours" and "Until the Real Thing Comes Along."

Irene Higginbotham, sister of jazz trombonist J.C. Higginbotham, played trombone and piano when young and was a concert pianist in her teens. Her small repertoire of compositions includes "Good Morning Heartache" (a song associated with Billie Holiday), "Harlem Stomp" and "Blue Violets."

Another musician who turned to songwriting was Ruth Lowe. In the thirties, as pianist for Ina Ray Hutton and the Melodears, Lowe wrote many tunes, then promptly filed them away. A tragedy made one of those songs famous. Lowe's husband died suddenly, and in her grief she remembered a melody she had written years before that seemed to express her sadness perfectly. She showed it to bandleader Tommy Dorsey, who liked it so much that he recorded it soon after. Thus did "I'll Never Smile Again" become one of the big, big hits of 1939. Lowe followed up with others, including "My First Love" and "Put Your Dreams Away," which Frank Sinatra used as a radio theme song.

There are many other women songwriters of the thirties, forties and fifties about whom information is sketchy or who are primarily remembered for one or two notable songs. Barbara Belle collaborated with Anita Leonard on "A Sunday Kind of Love" for singer Fran Warren. Belle also supplied material to Louis Prima ("Little Boy Blew His Top"), Louis Armstrong and Lucky Millinder. Anita Leonard worked on summer stock productions and scored ballets. The popular "Scarlet Ribbons" (1949), a song associated with Harry Belafonte, was written by Evelyn Danzig, and Rosemary Clooney popularized Dee Libbey's song "Mangos." Composer/lyricist Inez James wrote "Vaya con Dios," "Come Baby, Do," the score for the TV show *Mr. Big,* and other music for films and TV. Singer Joan Whitney, who had her own radio show for a while, wrote and published (with husband Alex Kramer) "High on a Windy Hill," "It All Comes Back to Me Now," "Candy," "My Sister and I" and others. Also worthy of mention is Anna Sosenko, theatrical archivist, historian, producer of star-studded tributes. In the fifties Sosenko managed singer Hildegarde to fabulous success and wrote Hildegarde's theme song, "Darling, Je Vous Aime," as well as "J'Attendrai," "Let's Try Again," "I'll Be Yours" and "Ask Your Heart."

That special breed of person who puts lyrics to music—a craft where, as lyricist Carolyn Leigh has observed, "a good combination of music and lyrics will seem almost inevitable"—is often underrated. Lyricists are not poets and not exactly songwriters, though there is much of both arts in their specialized skill. Not surprisingly, the theater has been the birthplace for a large body of the lyricists' work, though it has often brought more fame to the composers than to the people who wrote the words to their hit songs (and often the book or libretto of the show as well).

Three women lyricists were of particular importance during the era of European-style light comic opera, before the development of a native American theater. Of them, Rida Johnson Young (1869-1929) is perhaps best known. Young performed in the theater before becoming a lyricist and librettist. In 1910 she scored a great success with *Naughty Marietta*, for which she wrote the book and lyrics to Victor Herbert's music. Some of her most popular songs from that score include "Ah! Sweet Mystery of Life," "I'm Falling in Love with Someone" and "My Dream Girl." Other successes were her book and lyrics to Sigmund Romberg's music for *Maytime* (1917) and *Sometime* (1918), which included the hit song "Will You Remember?" She also wrote numerous straight plays and collaborated as lyricist and/or librettist on many musicals with composers Rudolf Friml and Emmerich Kalman. Young contributed the lyrics to "When Love Is Young in Springtime," "I Can't Take My Eyes Off of You," "The Road to Paradise" and "Italian Street Song," among many others.

Anna Caldwell O'Dea (1867-1936), two years older than Young, was another versatile, prolific lyricist. O'Dea came from a theatrical family and married a songwriter. She wrote some twenty-five librettos and/or show lyrics from 1907 to 1928, including *I Know That You Know* (with Vincent Youmans), *A Night in Spain* (with Jean Schwartz) and several collaborations with Jerome Kern, including *The Night Boat* and *Hitchy Koo* (both 1920) and *Good Morning, Dearie* (1921). Like many of the compositions of the later lyricist team of Betty Comden and Adolph Green, most of O'Dea's songs work well within the context of the show but do not succeed on their own. In the thirties O'Dea wrote film scenarios for Hollywood musicals, including *Babes in Toyland* and *Flying Down to Rio*.

The third important woman lyricist of this period was Dorothy Donnelly, born in 1880 into a musical family; her father ran an opera house. Donnelly started as an actress and then began writing for the theater. In 1921 her lyrics and libretto to *Blossom Time* were very successful; the showstopper was her "Song of Love." Her most famous and enduring effort was the book and lyrics to Victor Herbert's *The Student Prince*, which opened in 1924 and is still revived today. Donelly's hits from that show include "Drinking Song" and "Deep in My Heart, Dear." She also wrote the popular songs "Silver Moon" and "Your Land and My Land," and the shows *Fancy Free* (1918), *Poppy* (1923), *My Princess* and *My Maryland* (both 1927).

Lyricist Elsie Janis (1889-1959) was a versatile talent who performed in vaudeville and on Broadway, starring in *The Vanderbilt Cup* in 1906. After appearing in many other shows, she began writing librettos and lyrics; in 1916 her show *The Century*

Girl was mounted. During World War I she entertained troops and continued to write shows; afterwards she wrote the book and some of the music and lyrics to *Puzzles of 1925*, in which she also starred. By 1929 she had become a movie producer and had penned the scenario to an early talkie called *Close Harmony*. She followed with many movie scripts, books and song lyrics.

Among other early female lyricists was Beth Slater Whitson, who collaborated with songwriter Leo Friedman. The team scored big with "Meet Me Tonight in Dreamland" (1909) and "Let Me Call You Sweetheart" (1910), which sold about five million copies of sheet music. Theodora Terris is best known for her lyric to "Three O'Clock in the Morning." She frequently worked with her husband, songwriter Theodore F. Morse. The first woman to join the American Society of Composers, Authors and Publishers (ASCAP), Terris often had to use a pseudonym (Alfred Scott) at her publisher's insistence. Ruth Etting, a hugely popular singer of the twenties and thirties, wrote lyrics and/or music to several songs, including "Wistful and Blue" (1927), "When You're with Somebody Else" (1928) and "Maybe—Who Knows?" (1929).

In the Roaring Twenties and the thirties, the predictable formats and stylized language of the light operas and operettas were supplanted by a native musical theater inspired by jazz and American speech and humor. The wit and style of lyricist Lorenz Hart, of songwriter-lyricist Cole Porter, of prose writers like Robert Benchley, Damon Runyan and Dorothy Parker, made their mark on revues, skits and Broadway shows. (Parker, surprisingly, did not try her hand at songwriting until 1956, when she contributed lyrics to "I Wished on the Moon," "Gavotte" and "How Am I to Know" for Leonard Bernstein's ambitious musical *Candide*.) Among the crowd of talented young people writing for the theater were a number of women.

Sparkle and metal-hard wit gleamed in the songs and stories of Nancy Hamilton, an author, lyricist and frustrated actress who explained her songwriting efforts with the remark: "The only way to get a show is to write a show." The revues she wrote, chock-full of talented unknowns who later became stars, pulled in chic New York audiences. A gifted satirist, Hamilton wrote *One for the Money* (1939), *Two for the Show* (1940) and *Three to Get Ready* (1942). She also worked on film scripts, documentaries and an adaptation of Cole Porter's *Du Barry Was a Lady*. Her best-known lyric was to Morgan Lewis' music for "How High the Moon," a song that attracted little attention when it appeared in *Two for the Show* but went on to become the national anthem of forties jazz modernists, who liked to improvise on its changes.

Nancy Hamilton's personal style was as fashionably cheeky as her work. Reviewers called her "impudent," "acidic," "a writer with point and bite," and found her good copy. A news photo from the forties shows her seated at a piano in a business suit, sporting a short, severe haircut, puffing on a cigarette and quaffing a glass of beer. An interviewer once asked this "gay and chatty bachelor girl who authored Broadway revues" (as he called her) about her marriage plans. Hamilton coolly responded, "I have always preferred my own freedom. I am the individual versus the state of matrimony." (Wambly Bald, "Bachelor Girl Makes Good on Broadway," *New York Post*, April 10, 1946).

The first lady of lyricists is undoubtedly Dorothy Fields (1905–1974), who once summed up her philosophy in typically succinct fashion: "Write songs that become popular—not popular songs." Depending on whom you consult, there are between 450 and 800 published Fields songs. Many are both pop and jazz standards today, long outliving the shows in which they admirably served. In half a century of professional lyric writing, Fields worked with just about every important songwriter, won every kind of award, and remained current with changes in manners, morals and language.

Fields' father, the vaudeville comedian Lew Fields, was a gentleman of the old school who did not want his daughter involved in show business. (The same objections didn't hold for his two sons. Both became well known in show business as writers and producers, and Dorothy later collaborated with brother Herbert on a number of shows.) So Dorothy dabbled; she played piano at a dancing school and worked for a while as a receptionist and as a lab technician. But the lure of songwriting soon became too strong to resist, and Fields determined to try peddling her song lyrics on Tin Pan Alley. Eventually she teamed up with songwriter Fred Cootes at fifty dollars a song. After toiling briefly on hack pop ditties, she left what she called her "rude beginnings" for a partnership that clicked.

With songwriter Jimmy McHugh, Fields soon became a famous lyricist, and a wealthy one. The team got their big break when they were commissioned to write the score for the *Blackbirds of 1928* revue. For this show, inspired by the sight of a young couple staring longingly into the window of Tiffany's, they produced the smash hit "I Can't Give You Anything But Love," which aptly anticipated the fast-approaching Depression. It was the first of a dazzling string of Fields-McHugh collaborations, including "On the Sunny Side of the Street," "I'm in the Mood for Love" and "Exactly Like You."

Fields went on to write the lyrics and/or libretto for more than twenty Broadway shows, as well as numerous movie songs. Among her many top-notch collaborators, she cited Jerome Kern as one of the greatest. Fields was assigned to Kern by the Hollywood studio she was working for in the thirties, and her first effort for the exacting composer was the marvelous "Lovely to Look At." Although many lyricists bemoaned Kern's martinet manner, Fields adored him. They became good friends and collaborated on several scores, including *I Dream Too Much*, *The Joy of Living* and the Astaire-Rogers movie *Swingtime* (songs from which include "A Fine Romance," "Pick Yourself Up" and "Bojangles of Harlem"). They were in the midst of working on the score for *Annie Get Your Gun* when the great composer died in 1945. Fields' last show, decades later, was *Seesaw* (1973) with Cy Coleman.

Fields' scope and writing range were vast. She wrote charming turn-of-the-century lyrics to Sigmund Romberg's period-piece musical *Up in Central Park*, and rather raunchy, exuberant words for *Sweet Charity*. She was tender and romantic in her lyrics to "The Way You Look Tonight," which won an Academy Award. She was wry and witty in "Don't Blame Me," and she excelled in satire, as in "A Lady Needs a Change" and "A Fine Romance." Fields was a cultured woman with an elegant and disciplined mind. Her substantial contribution to American popular music is reinforced by the countless performers who keep her songs green in our memory. She had style and—magic words for jazz—her lyrics swung.

Another important lyricist and veteran of the musical theater is Betty Comden, who has been teamed with lyricist Adolph Green since the forties. Both began as performers and went on to great success using Nancy Hamilton's "write your own show" formula. They had a smash hit with their lyrics for *On the Town*, written to the music of their then-unknown friend Leonard Bernstein; the show opened on Broadway in 1944. Comden and Green (each married to someone else) have been a close and prolific lyricist team ever since. Their credits are so long that we can but skim the cream: their movie work includes *Singin' in the Rain* (1952) and *The Band Wagon* (1953); in 1953 they collaborated again with Bernstein, on a show entitled *Wonderful Town*; and they did several shows with composer Jules Styne, including *Subways Are for Sleeping, Hallelujah Baby* and the outstanding *Bells Are Ringing*. Their old friend Judy Holliday sang two of the memorable songs from *Bells*, "The Party's Over" and "Just in Time," both now standards. Among other enduring Comden-Green songs are "New York, New York" and "Make Someone Happy." Their lyrics, often studded with literate allusions, reflect the inimitable attitude of the New Yorker, to whom wit means survival and style often crowds out substance.

Marilyn Bergman is the female half of another established lyricist duo, this one married personally as well as professionally. Marilyn and Alan Bergman have been active since the fifties, working mainly on films and television shows and doing special material for stars like Frank Sinatra. They wrote the lyrics to several Michel Legrand songs that became hits, notably "What Are You Doing the Rest of Your Life?," "The Windmills of Your Mind" and "The Way We Were." Marilyn Bergman describes their approach to writing lyrics as follows: "It's not a question of fitting words to the melody. It's more freeing words that are implicit in the music" (*New York Daily News*, April 27, 1976).

Carolyn Leigh is another outstanding lyricist who emerged during the fifties. Born in New York, she began her career writing radio and advertising copy. In 1951 a song publisher gave her a contract on the basis of her evident promise. Leigh made good that promise a short two years later—but only after writing hundreds of song lyrics that remained unpublished (even today, she says, about nine lyrics are discarded for every one used). The song that did the trick was "Young at Heart," with Leigh's lyrics to Moose Charlap's music. Actress Mary Martin recalls in her autobiography (*My Heart Belongs*, William Morrow, 1976) that when she happened to hear "Young at Heart" on the radio, she decided to use "whoever had written those lovely lyrics, that haunting melody," on her forthcoming project, *Peter Pan*. With Charlap, Leigh then wrote, "I've Gotta Crow" and "I'm Flying" for *Pan*, and her career took off. She went on to work on many Broadway shows and TV musicals, including *The Chocolate Soldier, The Merry Widow, Heidi* and *The Great Waltz*. Among her well-known songs are "Real Live Girl," "The Best Is Yet to Come," "Pass Me By," "Witchcraft," "Hey, Look Me Over," "You Fascinate Me So," "I Walk a Little Faster," "I've Got Your Number," "When in Rome" and "Firefly." Leigh performs her own songs in concert from time to time, as at a well-received club date in 1980 at Michael's Pub in New York.

A woman writer whose lyrics lend themselves especially well to a jazz context is Fran Landesman. She was an art student before marrying writer Jay Landesman and moving with him to St. Louis in the fifties. There she began collaborating with pianist-composer Tommy Wolfe, and in 1959 they did a musical adaptation of Jay Landesman's hipster book, *The Nervous Set*. Using a jazz combo instead of a show orchestra, the successful musical swung through tunes that were both topical and amusing: "How Do You Like Your Love?," a cleverly spun query from a sexually frustrated hipster; "New York," as satirical and wickedly realistic view of "glamorous Gotham"; and "Ballad of the Sad Young Men," a melancholy sketch of urban isolation and loneliness. Other Landesman lyrics include "Season in the Sun," "Laugh, I Thought I'd Die," "Night People," the cleverly hypochondriac "Lovesick" and, best known, "Spring Can Really Hang You Up the Most."

A number of other women made noteworthy if less sustained contributions as lyricists during the forties and fifties. Gladys Shelley penned the lyrics to "How Did He Look?" "Paper Roses" and "Jelly Roll," as well as writing for the theater, films and children's operettas. Stella Unger was a multitalented woman. A pop lyricist who wrote extensively for theatrical productions, she was also an actress, a newspaper columnist, a radio personality, and a writer of plays and scripts, including *Cabbages and Kings*. Phyllis McGinley scored in the theatrical world in 1948 with her lyrics to Billing Brown's music for *Small Wonder*. And Jean Kerr, the author and playwright, worked with her husband, Walter Kerr, and Joan Ford on the lyrics, score and libretto to *Goldilocks* (1958).

Since the fifties, popular songwriting has become much less important as a source of inspiration for jazz musicians. With the rise of rock 'n' roll, and then folk, folk-rock, hard rock, disco and new wave, the melodically and harmonically sophisticated popular music that served as a basis for jazz interpretation became the exception rather than the rule. Most jazz musicians have found the pop music of recent decades too simplistic or alien to their tastes to provide a springboard for jazz improvisation.

Nevertheless, the early rock 'n' roll sound, though unrelated to jazz and aimed mainly at a teenage audience, was characterized by a lot of good songs with fresh, lively melodies and clever, insightful or heartfelt lyrics. Among the most prolific and successful of the women working within this music were Cynthia Weill, Toni Stern, Ruthann Friedman, Ellie Greenwich, Toni Wine, Carole King and lyricist Carole Bayer Sager, who went on to work on many theatrical shows. They (especially King and Sager) can be found on the credits for many of the "oldies but goodies."

The rock 'n' roll era also gave rise to the pop singer-songwriter phenomenon, where the singer tended to become identified with the song, if not to surpass it in importance in the listener's mind. The cult of the star performer was already well established, of course, but it became more widespread in the sixties, when the personalities of pop performers appeared to dwarf the music. Carole King abandoned her bubblegum hits for new success as a singer-songwriter working in the "poetic," confessional style. She developed a substantial audience, as did Laura Nyro, Janis Ian, Dory Previn and Joni Mitchell.

Of these women, Mitchell is the most relevant to a discussion of jazz, because after the late sixties and seventies she consciously turned to the music, and the musical backing, of jazz musicians. The early Joni Mitchell established herself as a writer of songs that stood on their own as popular hits: "The Circle Game, "Both Sides Now," "Free Man in Paris," "Chelsea Morning" and many more. She dealt with rock-drugs-alienation themes, adding a generous dose of the old "my man done left me" refrain, hippie-style. Her lyrics were a translation of her private emotional world, tunneled through her unusual vocal instrument. By the eighties, however, her restless spirit had taken her far from her folk-rock roots to a looser, more swinging style of music showing greater maturity and self-irony. This is evident on the album *Mingus*, a posthumous tribute to the late jazz bassist Charles Mingus, featuring four of his compositions, with jazz accompaniment by the band Weather Report.

Since the late fifties, women composers and lyricists have turned to the musical theater in increasing numbers. Gwen Davis wrote the lyrics to Phil Springer's music for *Cock o' the Walk* (1962). Joan Davis wrote the words to the music for *Young Abe Lincoln* (1961) and *Hotel Passionato* (1965). Screenwriter Helen Deutsch authored *Lili* (1961), a musical play based on her book to the show *Carnival*, and featuring the hit song "Hi-Lili, Hi-Lo." Composer-lyricist Micki Grant scored the award-winning "soul-jazz-gospel" show *Don't Bother Me, I Can't Cope* (1970) and many other musicals *(Bury the Dead; Step Lively, Boys; I'm Laughin', but I Ain't Tickled; The Prodigal Sister)*. Novelist Maya Angelou wrote the lyrics to Lalo Schifrin's music for *And I Still Rise* (1976) and has also written song lyrics ("I Know Why the Caged Bird Sings," sung by Abbey Lincoln).

Lyricist Eve Merriam wrote the words to Helen Miller's music for the "street cantata" *Inner City*, among other shows, and has also contributed lyrics to singer Nina Simone and composer Michel Legrand. Mary Rodgers, daughter of famed composer Richard Rodgers, did the music for the Broadway shows *Hot Spot* and *Once Upon a Mattress*, and has written for TV, nightclubs and concerts. Dorothea Freitag contributed the music or was musical director for several shows, including *Oh, Kay!* (1960), *Zorba* (1968) and the revue *Mask and Gown*, for which she also wrote the lyrics. In 1970 Freitag served as musical conductor of *Mod Donna*, billed as the "first women's liberation musical." The music of Gretchen Cryer and Nancy Ford has also been linked to the theme of women's liberation. Cryer is the lyricist of the team, and Ford the composer. Together they wrote *The Last Days of Isaac* and *Shelter* before scoring a hit in 1977 with *I'm Getting My Act Together and Taking It on the Road*. Composer-lyricist Carol Hall made it big on Broadway with her show *The Best Little Whorehouse in Texas*, a country-western musical. Hall, who sometimes records her own material, also served as composer for the TV special and album *Free to Be You and Me*. Contemporary composer Elizabeth Swados has many musical credits, including her dramatization of Euripides' *Medea* and *The Trojan Women*, the musical play *Runaways* and the 1977 *Nightclub Cantata*, with Andrei Serban.

Jazz performers, always hungry for new material, glean whatever they can from the music around them. The pop music of the day is constantly culled by jazz musicians, and often improved beyond recognition. As this survey has shown, American popular music is studded with memorable works by women. In addition, since the days of Mammy Lou in turn-of-the-century New Orleans, jazzwomen have written and performed their own material. And today's up-and-coming jazzwomen, better-schooled technically than their foremothers, are even more likely to put pen to paper and compose their own classics.

Organizations That Promote Women in Jazz

ROSETTA RECORDS, 115 West 16th St., New York, NY 10011. Director, Rosetta Reitz.

STUDIO RED TOP, P.O. Box 6004, Boston, MA 02209. Director, Cathy Lee

UNIVERSAL JAZZ COALITION, 156 Fifth Ave., Rm. 817, New York, NY 10010. Director, Cobi Narita; publishes a directory of women jazz artists in the New York area.

THE WOMEN'S JAZZ FESTIVAL, P.O. Box 22321, Kansas City, MO 64113. Co-producers, Carol Comer and Dianne Gregg; publishes an annually updated *National Directory of Female Jazz Performers*.

Discography

This discography is a selective listing of the recordings of women instrumentalists, vocalists and bandleaders in jazz. It might better be called "Toward a Discography of Women in Jazz," because it is far from complete; much patient digging awaits future researchers. Even the most extensive compilation of recordings in the jazz field, Walter Bruyninckx's *Sixty Years of Recorded Jazz, 1917–1977*, omits much of the material included here. My purpose was not to compile a definitive discography. Rather, I hope that the following pages will give those interested in jazz and in women's participation in jazz a fairly detailed roadmap.

The discography is arranged alphabetically by artist. The listing for each artist is divided, where appropriate, into 78s, 10″ records and LPs; 78s and 10″ records are grouped together, with citations arranged alphabetically by label and separated by semicolons; LPs follow alphabetically by label, with each label beginning a new paragraph and individual album citations separated by commas. Each citation includes the record number and/or title, with additional information, if any, following parenthetically. Where the artist's name appears in record titles or in the parenthetical information, it is represented by her initials. A key to abbreviations used in the discography follows.

ABBREVIATIONS

GENERAL

acc	accompanies, accompanying	*rec*	recording
arr	arranged, arrangements	*vol*	volume
incl	included, including	*w*	with
orch	orchestra		

INSTRUMENTS

arr	arranger	*har*	harmonica
as	alto saxophone	*keybd*	keyboards
b	bass	*misc*	miscellaneous instruments
bb	big band	*o*	organ
bl	bandleader	*p*	piano
bs	baritone saxophone	*per*	percussion
cl	clarinet	*prod*	producer
com	composer	*s*	saxophone
cor	cornet	*ss*	soprano saxophone
d	drums	*synth*	synthesizer
el	electric	*tr*	trumpet
fl	flute	*trom*	trombone
flg	flugelhorn	*ts*	tenor saxophone
fr horn	French horn	*vi*	vibraphone
g	guitar	*vo*	vocalist

RECORD LABELS

Atl	Atlantic	*Mls*	Milestone
Beth	Bethlehem	*Mon-Ever*	Monument-Everest
Bio	Biograph	*Para*	Paramount
Br	Brunswick	*Pres*	Prestige
Cap	Capitol	*Riv*	Riverside
Chi	Chiaroscuro	*Rou*	Roulette
CJ	Concord Jazz	*Sav*	Savoy
Col	Columbia	*ST*	Stash
Dec	Decca	*Sto*	Storyville
Dis	Discovery	*Stp*	Steeplechase
Fk	Folkways	*UA*	United Artists
IC	Inner City	*Van*	Vanguard
Imp	Impulse	*Ver*	Verve
Main	Mainstream	*Vic*	Victor
Mer	Mercury	*Voc*	Vocalion

Anthologies and Collections

RAGTIME:

   Van VSD-79402 *The Ragtime Women*
   World Records *Those Ragtime Years, 1899–1914* (rags played by Elsie Janis)

BLUES:

   Arhoolie/Blues Classics BC-26 *When Women Sang the Blues* (incl Lillian Glinn,
Bertha "Chippie" Hill, Bernice Edwards, Bessie Jackson, Memphis Minnie)
      CBS 52798, 66232 *Story of the Blues, Vol. II*, 63288, 64218
      Col CG-30008 *The Story of the Blues* (incl Bessie Smith, Bertha "Chippie" Hill,

Memphis Minnie, Lillian Glinn)

  MCA 2-4064 *Singin' the Blues*

  Pres/Bluesville BR-1052 *Songs We Taught Your Mother*

  Riv 12-121 *Great Blues Singers*

  Rosetta RR-1300 *Independent Women's Blues, Vol I*, RR-1301 *Women's Railroad Blues*, RR-1302 *Red White & Blues*, RR-1303 *Piano Singers' Blues*

  Sav SJL-2233 *Ladies Sing the Blues, Vol I* (reissues from the '40s by Viola "Miss Rhapsody" Wells, Esther "Little Esther" Phillips, Albinia Jones, Linda Hopkins & Big Maybelle), *Ladies Sing the Blues, Vol II* (reissues, 1944–57)

  ST 106 *AC-DC Blues*, 117 *Streetwalking Blues*, 118 *Straight & Gay*

  Vic/RCA LPV-534 *Women of the Blues* (incl Alberta Hunter, Margaret Johnson, Lizzie Miles, Monette Moore, Mamie Smith, Victoria Spivey, Sippie Wallace)

GOSPEL:

  Sav (wide selection available on this label)

  ST 114 *All of My Appointed Time: 40 Years of A Capella Gospel*

JAZZ:

  Col DC-36811 *Billie, Ella, Lena, Sarah* (incl reissues of recs by Billie Holiday, Ella Fitzgerald, Lena Horne, Sarah Vaughan)

  Fk 403 (incl Ella Fitzgerald, Billie Holiday, others)

  New World NW-295 *When Malindy Sings: Jazz Vocalists 1938–1961*

  ST 109 *Jazzwomen: A Feminist Retrospective* 2 vol, 111 *Women in Jazz: All-Women Groups*, 112 *Women in Jazz: Pianists*, 113 *Women in Jazz: Swingtime to Modern* (a unique source of documentation on jazzwomen as players; wide selection of instrumentalists from the '20s up to the '60s)

  Sto STLP-916 *The Women in Jazz* (incl Lee Wiley, Mary Lou Williams, Teddi King, Toshiko Akiyoshi, Jackie Cain & Milli Vernon)

Performers and Groups

MADAME ADAMI *p/ragtime*

  78s: Zonophone 1060 "The College Rag" (London 1913)

TOSHIKO AKIYOSHI *p, bl, com*

  Asaki Sonorama E-23 (Japan 1961)

  Ascent ASC-1000 *Farewell to Mingus* (Akiyoshi-Tabackin Big Band)

  Candid CM-8012 (w Charlie Mariano *as*)

  Chi CR-2026 *Together* (w Steve Kuhn *p*)

  CJ 69 *Finesse*

  Col PS-1185 (Japan 1965), XM-510008CT *Top of the Gate* (Japan)

  Dan VC-6001 (Japan 1971)

  Dauntless DM-4308 (1963)

  IC S-6046 *Dedications*, S-6066 *Notorious Tourist from the East*

  Jam 5003 *A Tribute to Billy Strayhorn* (1978), 5006 *Tanuki's Night Out* (Akiyoshi-

Tabackin Big Band; 1981)
  Jazzman 8000 *Toshiko-Mariano Quartet* (reissue of 1960 rec)
  King SKC3 (Japan 1961)
  Liberty LPC-8049 (Japan 1970)
  Metrojazz E-100 (1958)
  Nippon NS-1001 (Japan 1963)
  ST 112 *Women in Jazz: Pianists*
  Sto STLP-912 *The Toshiko Trio,* STLP-918 *TA* (1954–55)
  Vee Jay VJ-2505 (Japan 1964)
  Ver MGN-22 (Japan 1954), MGV-0236, MGV 8273 (1957), MV 2570 IMS
  Vic JV-5084 (Japan 1963), CD4B-5007 (Japan 1971)
  Vic/RCA (all by Akiyoshi-Tabackin Big Band) AFL1-1350 *Long Yellow Road*
(1974–75), AFL1-3019 *Kogun* (1975), AFL1-0723 *Tales of a Courtesan* (1975), CPL2-
2242 *Road Time* (1976), AFL1-2678 *Insights* (1976), *March of the Tad Poles* (1977),
Live at the Newport Jazz Festival (1977), RCV (RCA/Japan) *Salted Ginko Nuts*
(1978), RCV *Sumie* (1979), RCV *Live at Newport II* (1980)

LOREZ ALEXANDRIA   *vo*
  Argo 663, *Early in the Morning* (1960), 682 *Sing No Sad Songs for Me* (1960), 694
Deep Roots (1962), 720 (1963)
  Dis DS-782 *How Will I Remember You?* (1978), DS-800 *A Woman Knows* (1978),
DS-826 *LA Sings the Songs of Johnny Mercer* (1981)
  Imp A-62 *Alexandria the Great* (1964), A-76 (1964)
  King LD-542 (1957), LD-565, LD-657 (1959), LD-676

ALIVE!   *combo*
  Redwood *Alive! Live*
  Urana/Wise Women Enterprises WWE-84 *Alive! Call It Jazz*

LAURIE ALTMAN   *p*
  Progressive *For Now at Least* (1981)

ERNESTINE ANDERSON   *vo*
  CJ 31 *Hello Like Before,* 54 *EA Live from Concord to London,* 102 *EA Live at the
Concord Jazz Festival,* 109 *Sunshine,* 147 *Never Make Your Move Too Soon*

IVIE ANDERSON   *vo*
  Col KG-32064 *Duke Ellington Presents IA* (2 vol; reissue of 1932–40 recs)
  Design 238 *Pearl Bailey, Rose Murphy, IA*

ANDREWS SISTERS   *vo*
  MCA 4024, 4093, AB-4003

DOLLY ARMENRA.   See DOLLY JONES.

IRENE ARMSTRONG (WILSON)
  78s: Col *Leave Me Mr. Strange Man* (w Eloise Bennet *vo*; 1929)

LIL HARDIN ARMSTRONG   *p, vo, com*
  10": Riv RLP-1029 (w Louis Armstrong & King Oliver's Creole Jazz Band; reissue)

Col CL-851/852 *The Louis Armstrong Story* 4 vol (LHA incl on 2 vol)

Epic LA-16003 *King Oliver & His Orchestra* (LHA incl on)

Gardenia 4005 *LHA & Her Swing Band, 1936–1940*

Heritage 112 *Gut Bucket Blues & Stomp* (LHA incl on; reissue of 1926–28 recs)

MCA 510123 *Swinging Small Bands, Vol 4* (LHA incl on; reissue)

Riv RLP 12-101 *Young Louis Armstrong* (LHA incl on; reissue), RLP 12-120 *Satchmo & Me* (LHA tells her own story), RLP 12-122 *Louis Armstrong: 1923* (LHA incl on; reissue), RLP-401 *LHA & Her Orchestra* (1961)

DOROTHY ASHBY   *harp*

Argo LP-690 (1961)

Atl 1447 *The Fantastic Harp of DA* (1965)

Cadet 690 (1963), S-809 *Afro-Harping* (1968), S-825 *Dorothy's Harp*, S-841 *Rubaiyat*

Fantasy F-9508 (w Stanley Turrentine *ts;* 1976)

Jazzland LP-61 *Soft Winds* (w Terry Pollard *p, vi;* 1961)

Pres 7638 *Best of DA* (1969), 7639 *DA Plays for the Beautiful People*, 7140

Regent MG-6039 *Jazz Harpist*

VERA AUER   *vi*

Br 10062 (Europe 1956)

Harmona 17081 (Europe 1950), HL-132 (Europe 1951)

Honey Dew 6621 *Positive Vibes*

LOVIE AUSTIN   *p, com, bl*

Bio 12032 *Queen of the Blues* (LA & Her Blues Serenaders incl acc Ma Rainey *vo;* reissue of 1923–24 recs)

Fountain FJ-105 *LA & Her Blues Serenaders* (reissue of 78s)

Riv RLP-147 (LA & Her Blues Serenaders incl acc Ida Cox *vo*), RLP-418 (LA acc Alberta Hunter *vo*), 154 *Tommy Ladnier Blues & Stomps* (LA incl on), 1016 (LA acc Ma Rainey *vo*), 1026 *Tommy Ladnier & the Blues Serenaders* (LA incl on), RLP 12-104 *Johnny Dodds* (LA incl on), RLP 12-135 *In the Alley* (LA & Her Blues Serenaders incl on), 8808 *LA & Her Blues Serenaders*

ALICE BABS   *vo*

Bellaphon BLST-6504 *Duke Ellington & Orchestra* (AB incl on)

Dec LK-4326 *Alice & Wonderland*

Pres P-24045 *Second Sacred Concert* (w Ellington & orch)

RCA APL2-0785 *Sacred Concert* (w Ellington & orch)

Reprise *Serenade to Sweden* (w Ellington & orch; Sweden 1963)

MILDRED BAILEY   *vo*

10": Dec DL-5387 *The Rockin' Chair Lady*

AFJ 269E *MB*

Col Special Products C31-22 *MB: Her Greatest Performances* 3 vol (also as JC 3L22)

Ever 269 *MB*

Hindsight 133 *Uncollected*

Mon-Ever 6814 *All of Me*
Regent 6032 *Me & the Blues* (reissue of Majestic 78s)
ST 108 (w Delta Rhythm Boys)
Sunbeam 209 *Radio Show, 1944–45* (w Woody Herman *cl;* reissue)
Vic CPL1-3370 *Legendary Performer—Hoagy Carmichael* (MB incl on)

PEARL BAILEY   *vo*
  Col CL-985 *The Definitive PB*, ML-4969 *House of Flowers* (Broadway cast album)
  Coral CRL-57037 *PB*
  Mer MG-20187 *The One & Only PB Sings*
  Rou R-25063 *PB Sings Porgy & Bess & Other Gershwin Melodies*, R-25144 *The Best of PB*, RE-101 *Echoes of an Era: The PB Years* 2 vol

ANDREA BAKER   *vo*
  Skyline *All the Things You Are* (1981)

JOSEPHINE BAKER   *vo*
  78s: Card 2053/Phantasie 17201; Col (France 1926); Federal 5163 (under pseudonym "Dorothy Dodd"; 1921)
  Mon-Ever 7023E *Songs from the 30s*

LA VERN BAKER   *vo*
  Atl-1281 *LVB Sings Bessie Smith*, 8002, 8036, 8050, 8071, 2-504 *Soul Years* 2 vol, 8078 *Best of LVB*
  Br 754160 *Let Me Belong to You*

SWEET EMMA BARRETT   *p*
  78s: Okeh 8215, 8198 (w Original Tuxedo Jazz Orch; 1925)
  GHB 141 *Sweet Emma*, 142 *At Disneyland*
  Nobility LP-711 *Sweet Emma the Bell Gal & Her New Orleans Jazz Band at Heritage Hall*
  Riv LP 356/357 *New Orleans, the Living Legends* 2 vol (SEB incl on; 1961), 364 *The Bell Gal's Careless Blues* (1961)
  Southland LP-241 *SEB & Her New Orleans Music* (1963), 242 *Sweet Emma at Disneyland* (1965)
  VPH/VPS-2 *New Orleans Sweet Emma & Her Preservation Hall Jazz Band* (1964)

WILLENE BARTON   *ts*
  Design DLP-37 *The Feminine Sax* (WB *bl*)

YOLANDE BAVAN   *vo*
  Vic LSP-2747 *At Newport '63* (w Lambert, Hendricks & Bavan *vo combo*) LSP-2635 *Lambert, Hendricks & Bavan at Basin Street East* (1963)

WINI BEATTY   *p*
  78s: Coast 8045, 8055; Keynote 506; Lamplighter 101 (w Red Callender *b*)

GLADYS BENTLEY   *vo*
  Raretone RTR-24010 (w Bertha "Chippie" Hill *vo;* reissue of 78s)

LOLLIE BIENENFELD   *trom*
 Telarc DC-10044 (D) *Naturally* (w Mel Lewis Orch; 1979)

BIG MAYBELLE.   See BIG MAYBELLE SMITH.

CARLA BLEY   *com, bl, keybd*
 Col FC-37307 *Fictitious Sports* (CB *com, keybd;* 1981)
 ECM 11 *Social Studies* (CB *com, p, o, bl;* 1981), ECM W12 *Live!* (1982)
 ESP 1108 *Barrage* (CB *com,* w Paul Bley Quintet; 1965)
 Imp S-O 9183 *Music Liberation Orchestra* (CB *arr, com, p;* 1969)
 Jazz Composers Orchestra Association *Escalator Over the Hill* 3 vol (CB *com, misc*)
 New Wave 881010 *Jazz Realities*
 Scholastic Records CC-0603 *Six Songs from a Wreath of Carols* (CB *arr, prod, bl;* 1968)
 Vic/RCA LSP-3900 *A Genuine Tong Funeral* (CB *com,* w Gary Burton Quartet; 1968)
 Watt 1 *Tropic Appetites* (CB *com;* 1973–74), 2 *No Answer* (CB *p, o, clavinet;* 1974), Watt Works *3/4* (CB *com, p;* 1975), 4 *The Hapless Child* (CB *p, clavinet, synth;* 1976), 5 *Silence* (CB *p, vo;* 1977), 6 *Dinner Music* (CB *com, p, o;* 1977), 8 *European Tour '77* (CB *com, bl*), 9 *Musique Mechanique* (CB *com, bl;* 1979)

JANE IRA BLOOM   *ss, as, reeds*
 Anima 1-J85 *All Out* (w Jay Clayton *vo*)
 Enja 3089 *Of the Wind's Eye* (w Dave Friedman *vi*), *Mighty Lights* (1982)
 Outline OTL-137 *We Are* (JIB *bl*), OTL-138 *Second Wind* (JIB *bl;* 1981)

LUCILLE BOGAN   *vo/blues*
 Yazoo L-1017 (w Walter Roland; reissue of 1927–35 recs)

BESS BONNIER   *p*
 Argo 632 *Theme for the Tall One* (BB *bl;* 1958)
 MGS LP *26th Floor*

BERYL BOOKER   *p*
 78s: SIW 527, 529, 539 (1948); Vic 0147/20-3088 (w Mary Osborne *g*, June Rotenberg *b;* 1946)
 10": Cadence LPC-1000 *BB Trio* (1954); EmArcy MG-26007 *Girl Met a Piano*
 Birdland LP (w Miles Davis *tr;* air check, New York, April 25–26, 1952)
 Dis DL-3021 (w Bonnie Wetzel *b*, Elaine Leighton *d;* 1954), D-3022 (w Don Byas *ts;* 1954)
 MEM E-255 *Cats v. Chicks: A Jazz Battle of the Sexes* (w Terry Pollard *bl*)
 Mer MG-8294 (w Jimmy Cobb Orch, Dinah Washington *vo;* 1952), MG-20247 (1952–53), MG-26077 (1953), MVL-300
 Session SR-106 (w Count Basie Orch, Dinah Washington *vo*)
 ST 109 *Jazzwomen: A Feminist Retrospective,* 111 *Women in Jazz: All-Women Groups,* 112 *Women in Jazz: Pianists,* 113 *Women in Jazz: Swingtime to Modern*

Vogue LD-203 (1954)
Wing MGW-12140 (w Dinah Washington *vo*)

KAREN BORCA   *bassoon*
Hat Hut Y/Z/Z *Push Pull* 3 vol (w Jimmy Lyons; 1978)

CONNEE BOSWELL   *vo, arr, com*
Ace of Hearts LP(E)AH-116 *Nothing Was Sweeter Than the Boswell Sisters* (English reissue of 78s)
Bio C-3 *Boswell Sisters* (reissue of 1932–35 recs)
Col 36523, 38298 (reissues)
Dec DL-8356 *Connee*
Design DLP-68 *CB Sings Irving Berlin*
Take Two TT-209 *CB: Early Solos* (reissue of 1931–35 recs)
Totem 1025 *On the Air* (reissue of radio broadcasts, 1935–41)
Vic LPM-1426 *CB & the Original Memphis Five in Hi-Fi*

PATTI BOWN   *p, arr*
Bellaphon BJS-4024 (w Illinois Jacquet *ts*), BJS-40100 (w Oliver Nelson & orch)
Cadet CA-50040 (New York 1974)
Col CL-1379 (PB *bl, com;* 1959)
Fontana 6430130 (w Quincy Jones & orch)
Imp AS-11, IA 9342/9343 (2 vol; PB *p, arr;* w Quincy Jones & orch)
Mer MG-20444 (1959), MG-20612 (1960), PPS-2014 (1961), MG-20653, 71940, MG-20799, 6336705 (PB *p, arr;* w Quincy Jones & orch)
Pres PRLP-208, PRLP-225 (w Oliver Nelson Big Band; 1961), 7275, 7445 (1961), P-24079 (w Gene Ammons Quartet), 7287 (w Gene Ammons *ts*)

JOANNE BRACKEEN   *p, com*
Antilles 1001 *Ancient Dynasty*
Catalyst CAT-7902 (w Art Blakey & Jazz Messengers '70; 1970)
Choice CRS-1007 *Captured Alive* (w Toots Thieleman *har*), CRS-1009 *Snooze* (1975), CRS-1016 *Tring-a-ling* (w Mike Brecker *ts*), CRS-1040 *Prism* (w Eddie Gomez *b*, Jack DeJohnette *d*)
Freedom 147303 *Invitation*
IC 1040 *Stan Getz Gold* (w Stan Getz *ts*)
MPS 68211
Pausa 7045 *Mythical Magic* (1978)
Stp SCS-1073/1074 (2 vol; w Stan Getz *ts*), SCS-1099 (w John McNeil), SCS-1154 *Clean Sweep*
Tappan Zee 36075 *Keyed In*, 36593 *Ancient Dynasty*
Timeless SJP-103 *New True Illusions*, 115, 123, 302 *Aft* (1977)

DARDANELLE BRECKENRIDGE   *p, vo*
Audiophone 145 *Echoes Singing Ladies*
MCA 510103-IMS, 510112-IMS, 510117-IMS (w Lionel Hampton & orch; 1945)
ST 202 *D Sings for New Lovers*, 204 *New York, New York: Sounds of the Apple* (DB incl on), 109 *Jazzwomen: A Feminist Retrospective*, *The Colors of My Life* (1982)

FANNY BRICE   *vo/vaudeville*
   Vic LPV-561 (w Helen Morgan *vo*)

THE BRICKTOPS   *bb*
   78s: Br "I'll Still Think of You" / "I Still Love You"

DEE DEE BRIDGEWATER   *vo*
   Atl 18137 *The Wiz*
   Elektra 6E-119 *Just Family*, 6E-188 *Bad For Me*, 6E-306 *DDB*
   Horizon SP-701 *Suite for Pops* (also listed as Horizon MLJ-701; DDB incl on one track w Thad Jones-Mel Lewis Orch; 1972)
   Labor LRS-7002 *Brains on Fire* (w Reggie Workman *b;* 1973), LRS-7003 (w Reggie Workman; 1973)
   Main MRL-349 (w the Loud Minority Big Band, Frank Foster *bl;* 1974)
   Pausa PR-7012
   Production Associates 6.22663-AS

HADDA BROOKS   *p*
   78s: Crown (1947); London (1950); Modern (1945–50); Okeh (1952, 1953)
   ST 112 *Women in Jazz: Pianists*

CLEO BROWN   *p, vo*
   78s: numerous on: Cap; Dec (incl Dec 477 "Pinetop's Boogie Woogie"; 1935)
   MCA 1329 *Kings & Queens of the Ivories*, 510090-1MS
   ST 112 *Women in Jazz: Pianists*

OLIVE BROWN   *vo/blues*
   JTP-103

RUTH BROWN   *vo*
   Atl 1308, 8001, 8004 *Rock & Roll*, 8010, 8021, 8026, 8080
   Blue Note LA-392 *Thad Jones/Mel Lewis* (RB incl on several tracks)
   Cobblestone 9007 *Real RB*
   Dobre 1041 *You Don't Know Me* (1976)
   Main M-56034, MRL-369 *Softly*
   Philips PHM-200-028, PHM-200-055, 652020-BL
   Skye SK-13 *Black Is Brown*

CLORA BRYANT   *tr, bl*
   Mode LP-106 (CB as *bl;* 1957)

VIOLA "VI" BURNSIDE   *ts*
   78s: Guild; RCA 40-0146, "Vi Vigor"/"Don't Get It Twisted"
   ST 111 *Jazzwomen: A Feminist Retrospective*, 113 *Women in Jazz: Swingtime to Modern*

ANN BURTON   *vo*
   IC 6026 *By Myself Alone*, 1094 *New York State of Mind*

SHIRLEY CAESAR   *vo/gospel*
Sav 14202
Vesper 1, 2, 4, 5, 8

JACKIE CAIN   *vo* (in vocal duo Jackie & Roy, w Roy Kral)
ABC-Para 120 *The Glory of Love*, 163, 207, 267
Br BL-54025 *Here's Charlie* (w Charlie Ventura *bl*), BL-54026, BL-58026
Cap ST-2936 *Grass*
CJ 115 *Star Sounds*, 149 *East of Suez*
Col CL-1469, CL-1701 *Double Talk*, CL 1931
CTI 6019 *Time & Love*, 6040 *A Wilder Alias*
Rou R-25278 *By Jupiter & Girl Crazy* (JC & RK *arr*)
Sto SLP-904, SLP-915
Studio 7-402 *By the Sea*
Ver MGV-8668 *Changes*, 8688 *Lovesick*

BLANCHE CALLOWAY   *bl, vo*
78s: Okeh 8279 (w Louis Armstrong *tr;* 1925); BC & Her Joy Boys: Perfect 16054 (1934); Vic 22640, 22641, 22661, 22717, 22733, 22866 (1931); Voc 3112 (1935), 3113 (1935)
Collector Classics CC-32 (reissue of 78s by BC & Her Joy Boys)
Raretone RTR-24005 (reissue of 78s by BC & Her Joy Boys)
ST 105 (BC & Her Joy Boys incl on)
Timely Tunes C-1578, C-1587 (BC & Her Joy Boys under pseudonym "Fred Armstrong & His Syncopators")
Vic/RCA (F)42392 ("Fred Armstrong & His Syncopators"; France)

VALERIE CAPERS   *p*
Atl S-3003 *Portrait in Soul*
KMArts *Affirmation*

UNA MAE CARLISLE   *p, vo*
78s: numerous on: Beacon; Bluebird (incl "Walkin' by the River"/ "I See a Million People," 1941); Col, Sav, Vic (1938)
ST 109 *Jazzwomen: A Feminist Retrospective*, 112 *Women in Jazz: Pianists*, 113 *Women in Jazz: Swingtime to Modern*
Vic/RCA (F)741117 *The Greatest of the Small Bands* Black & White Series Vol 106 (incl UMC reissues; France), (F)FXM1-7121, Vol 141 (UMC incl on; France), LPV-578 *Swing, Vol 1* (UMC incl on)

JUDY CARMICHAEL   *p*
Progressive 7065 *Two-Handed Stride* (1983)

JEAN CARN   *vo*
Ovation 1702 *Higher Ground* (w Doug Carn)
Philips International JZ-34394 *Happy to Be with You*, JZ-36196 *When I Find You, Love*

Pres P-10086 (w Azar Lawrence *as*)
Tops FZ-36775 *Sweet & Wonderful*

THELMA CARPENTER *vo*
Coral CRL-57433

TERRI LYNE CARRINGTON *d*
CEI Records *TLC & Friends* (w George Coleman *s;* 1982)

BARBARA CARROLL *p*
Blue Note 1977 *BC*
Dis 129, DS-847 *At the Piano* (1980)
Pres PRLP-7813 *Memorial Album* (w Oscar Pettiford *b*)
ST 112 *Women in Jazz: Pianists*
UA LA-778-H *From the Beginning*
Ver MGV-205 *Barbara*
Vic LJM-1001, LJM-1023 *Lullabies in Rhythm*, LPM-1296 *We Just Couldn't Say Goodbye*, LPM-1396 *It's a Wonderful World*

NORMA CARSON *tr*
MGM E-255 *Cats v. Chicks: A Jazz Battle of the Sexes* (w Terry Pollard *bl*)
ST 109 *Jazzwomen: A Feminist Retrospective*, 111 *Women in Jazz: All-Women Groups*

BETTY CARTER *vo*
ABC-Para ABC-363, ABC-385 (w Ray Charles *vo*)
Atco S-33-152 *Round Midnight* (w Oliver Nelson & orch; 1963)
Bet-Car MK-1001 *BC* (1971), MK-1002 *BC Album* (1972), MK-1003 *BC with the Audience, Whatever Happened to Love?* (1982)
Col JC-36425 *Social Call* (reissue of 1955–56 recs)
Epic LN-3202 *BC & Ray Bryant*
Imp ASD-9321 *What a Little Moonlight Can Do* 2 vol (incl arrangements by Melba Liston; reissue, incl ABC-Para ABC-363)
MCA Coral 82018-2 (2 vol; w Lionel Hampton & orch)
Pres PR-24017 *King Pleasure, The Source* (BC incl on one track; reissue)
Progressive Jazz PJL-P90 (1958)
Rou SR-5000 *Finally BC* (1969), 5001 *Round Midnight*, 5005 *Now It's My Turn* (also released as RA-20243 in 1976)
UA UAS-5639 *Inside BC*, UAL-3379

ANN CHARTERS *p/ragtime*
FK (F6)3563 *Essay in Ragtime*
Kicking Mule SW-101 *Scott Joplin & Friends*

JEAN CHEATHAM *p*
Jazz Chronicles 104 *Meet Grover Mitchell* (JC in *bb:* 1979), *Devil's Waltz* (w Grover Mitchell *bl*)

JUNE CHRISTY *vo*
Cap T-167 *Artistry in Rhythm*, T-656 *Duet*, T-725 *The Misty Miss Christy*, T-833 *Fair & Warmer*, T-1006 *This Is JC*, T-1114 *The Song Is June*, T-1202 *Those Kenton Days*, T-1398 *Cool School*, T-1498 *Off Beat*, TBO-1327 *Road Show* 2 vol, SM-516 *Something Cool*, SM-1196 *Best of JC*
SeaBreeze 2002 *Impromptu* (w Bob Cooper)

SAVANNAH CHURCHILL *vo*
78s: Arco: Cap (w Benny Carter & Orch); Col; Manor
Jazz Anthology JA-5224 (w Jimmie Lunceford Orch)
Vic/RCA/Hot 'n Sweet HOL-6426 (1943 recs)

JAY CLAYTON *vo*
Anima IJ-35 *JC All-Out* (JC *bl;* 1981)
Choice CRS-1015 (w Bob Mover Sextet)
Earplay *Scat Malisma* (w Kirk Nurock)
ECM 1129 *Steve Reich & Musicians*, 1-1168 *Octet-Music for a Large Ensemble* (Steve Reich *com*)
Ellipsoid *The Silver Apple* (w Peter Fish)
EPI *Blow Through Your Mind* (w Unity group)
New York Composer CC-722 *Interface*
Sweet Dragon *Songs, Dances and Prayers* (w Marc Levin)
Tomato *She's Asleep* (w John Cage)

ROSEMARY CLOONEY *vo*
Cap SM-11736 (w Bing Crosby *vo*)
CJ 47 *Everything's Coming Up Rosie*, 50 *A Tribute to Duke*, 60 *Rosie Sings Bing*, 81 *Here's to My Lady* (tribute to Billie Holiday), 112 *RC Sings Ira Gershwin Lyrics*, 144 *With Love*
Col CL-872 *Blue Rose* (w Duke Ellington Orch), CL-1006 *Ring Around Rosie* (w the Hi-Lo's *vo combo*)

DOROTHY LOVE COATES *vo/gospel*
Sav 14466, 14500
Specialty 2134-E, 2141-E

GLORIA COLEMAN *o, vo*
Imp AS-47 *Soul Sisters* (w Pola Roberts *d;* 1963)
Main MRL 872 (1965)

JOYCE COLLINS *p, vo*
Dis *Moment to Moment* (1981), *A Tribute to Johnny Mercer* (w Bill Henderson *vo;* 1982)
Jazzland JLP-24 (w Ray Brown *b;* 1961)

ALICE COLTRANE *p, o, harp, tamboura, misc*
Col PC-32900Q *Illuminations* (w Carlos Santana *g*)
Imp AS-9120 (w John Coltrane *reeds;* 1967), AS-9124, AS-9221, AS-9223, AS-9225,

YB-8508/8509/8510 (3 vol; Japan 1966), AS-9156 (1968), AS-9185 (1969), AS-9196 (w Pharaoh Sanders *ts, misc;* 1970), AS-9203 (w Pharaoh Sanders; 1970), AS-9210 (1971), AS-9218 (1971), AS-9224 (1972)

    Limelight LM-82005 (w Terry Gibbs *vi;* 1963)

    Mer MG-20812 (w Terry Gibbs *vi;* 1963)

    Pathe/EMI C064-95637 *The Elements* (w Joe Henderson *ts;* 1973; also released on Bell BLP-S19184, Germany)

    Time 52105 (w Terry Gibbs; 1963)

    Vogue JL-72 (w Terry Gibbs; 1963)

    Warner Bros BS-2916 (1975), BS-2986 (1976), BS-3077 (1977)

CHRIS CONNOR   *vo*

    ABC-Para 529 *CC Sings Gentle Bossa Nova*

    Atl 2-601 *Gershwin* 2 vol, 1228 *CC*, 1290 *Chris Craft/CC*, 1307 *Ballads of the Sad Cafe*, 8032 *Witchcraft*, 8046 *Portrait of Chris*, 8061 *Free Spirits*

    Beth BCP-20 *This Is Chris*, BCP-56 *Chris*, BCP-6004 *CC Sings Lullaby of Birdland*, BP-1001 *The Finest of CC* 2 vol (reissue)

    Clarion 611 *CC Sings George Gershwin*

    Progressive Jazz 7028 *Sweet & Swinging* (1978)

    Rou R-52068 *Two's Company* (w Maynard Ferguson *tr*)

    Stanyan 10029 *Sketches*

ELISABETH "LIBBA" COTTEN   *g, vo/folk-blues*

    Cap 81002/81003 (2 vol; Geneva, Switzerland, 1979)

    Fk FG-3526, FG-3537, FB-31003

IDA COX   *vo/blues*

    78s: numerous on Para

    10": Riv RLP-1019

    Fountain FB-301 *IC Vol 1* FB-304 *IC Vol 2*

    Mls 2015 *Blues Ain't Nothin' Else but...*

    Riv RLP-147 *The Moanin' & Groanin' Blues*, RLP-9374 *Blues for Rampart Street* (w Coleman Hawkins *ts;* 1961)

    Rosetta RR-1304 *Wild Women Don't Have the Blues* (Foremothers Series Vol. 1; reissues)

MARILYN CRISPELL   *p*

    Hat Hut 1984 *A B Composition 98* (w Anthony Braxton *reeds;* 1981)

CONNIE CROTHERS   *p*

    Jazz Records *Perception* 2 vol

    Stp SCS-1022 *CC Trio* (1974)

MEREDITH D'AMBROSIO   *vo*

    Palo Alto *Little Jazz Bird* (1983)

BARBARA DANE   *vo/blues*

    Cap T-1758 (1961)

Dot DLP-3177 (1959)
Fk FA-2468, FA-2471
Horizon WP-1602
Tradition 2072
Van VRS-9063 (1959)

DARDANELLE. See DARDANELLE BRECKENRIDGE.

BERT ETTA DAVIS. See ERNESTINE "TINY" DAVIS.

ERNESTINE "TINY" DAVIS   *tr, bl*
   78s: Dec 48122, 48220, 48246 (all ETD & Her Orch, w Bert Etta Davis *as,* Maurine Smith *p,* Helen Cole *d,* Margaret Backstrom *ts,* Eileen Chance *b*)
   ST 111 *Women in Jazz: All-Women Groups,* 113 *Women in Jazz: Swingtime to Modern*

MARTHA DAVIS   *p*
   78s: Coral 60890 (w Art Blakey *d;* 1951), 65048; Dec 24335, 24383, 48174 (1949); Jewell ON-2002 (1948), ON-2003 (1949); Urban 120, 121, 126, 127 (all 1946)

BLOSSOM DEARIE   *vo, p, com*
   Barclay (F)EP-74017 (France 1956)
   Cap T-2086 *May I Come In?* (1963)
   Daffodil BMD-101 *BD Sings, Vol 1* (1974), BMD-102 (1975), BMD-103 *My New Celebrity Is You* 2 vol (1976), BMD-104 *Winchester in Apple Blossom Time* 2 vol (1977), *Needlepoint Magic* (w Bob Dorough *vo, com*)
   DRG DAR-C2-1105 *Blossoms on Broadway* 2 vol (reissue)
   Felsted SDL-86034 (France 1955)
   Fontana TL-5399 (1966), TL-5454 (1967), (E)6309015 (England 1970)
   Pres PR-24017 *King Pleasure: The Source* (BD incl on one track), VIJ-5036 *Al Haig Sextet* (BD incl on)
   Ver MGV-2037 (1956), 2018/MV-2036 (1958), MGV-2109 (1959), MGV-2111/2317107 (1959), MGV-2125, MGV-2133

FOSTINA DIXON   *b, cl, reeds*
   Esoteric *Our Music Is Your Music* (FD *bs, cl;* w Leslie Drayton Orch; 1980), ER-1002 *Turning a Corner* (w Leslie Drayton Orch; 1981)

DOTTIE DODGION   *d*
   Chi CR-115 (w Ruby Braff *cor*)
   Halcyon HAL-115 *Now's the Time* (w Marian McPartland *bl;* 1977)

BARBARA DONALD   *tr*
   Arhoolie 8003 *Manhattan Egos* (w Sonny Simmons *s;* 1969), 8004/8005 *Smiley Etc.* 2 vol (BD incl w Smiley Winters *bl*)
   Contemporary 7623 *Ruma Suma* (BD incl on), 7625/7626 *Burning Spirits* 2 vol (BD incl on; 1970–71)

ESP 1043 *Music from the Spheres* (w Sonny Simmons *s;* 1966), S-1030 *Staying on the Watch* (w Sonny Simmons *bl;* 1967)

DOROTHY DONEGAN   *p*
  78s: numerous on: Continental 6033, 6034, 6051, 6056, 6057, 6058; Miltone 5269
  Cap T-1155 *DD Live!*, T-1226 *Donnybrook with Donegan* (1959)
  Dec 5486 *The Feminine Touch*
  Four Leaf Clover FLC-5006 *DD Trio & Quartet*
  Jubilee LP-11
  Mahogany 558101 *The Many Faces of DD* (1975)
  MGM E-278
  Regina 285 *Swingin' Jazz in Hi-Fi* (1963)
  Rou R-25010 *DD at the Embers*, R-25514
  ST 109 *Jazzwomen: A Feminist Retrospective,* 112 *Women in Jazz: Pianists*

LES DOUBLE SIX OF PARIS   *vo sextet*
  Col FPX-188 (DSP incl Monique Aldebert, Mimi Perrin, Christiane Legrand; Paris 1959), FPX-202 (DSP incl Mimi Perrin, Claudine Barge, Monique Guerin; Paris 1961)
  Philips PHS-600-026 *The Swingin' Singin' Double Six,* PHS-200-106 *Dizzy Gillespie & the DSP* (Paris 1963), PHS-600-141 *DSP Sing Ray Charles* (w Jerome Richardson Quartet), 652054BL

MEMPHIS MINNIE DOUGLAS   *g, vo*
  78s: numerous 1929–54 on: Bluebird (1935); Checker (1952); Col (w Kansas Joe McCoy *g;* New York 1929); Dec (1934, 1935); JOB (1954); Okeh (1933, 1940, 1941, 1944); Okch-Col (1946, 1947, 1949); Regal Bio (w Sunnyland Slim; 1949); Vic (w Memphis Jug Band; 1930); Voc (w Bumble Bee Slim, 1936; 1934–39)
  Arhoolie BC-1 *MM* (1934–42 recs), BC-13 *MM II* (w Kansas Joe McCoy)
  Bio 12035 *MM/Blind Willie McTell: Love Changin' Blues* (1949)
  Blues Classics 1 *MM* 2 vol, 13 *MM Vol 2* (w Kansas Joe McCoy)
  Col CG-33566 *Fifty Years of Jazz Guitar* 2 vol (MM incl on)
  Flyright LP-108/109 *MM 1934–1949* 2 vol
  Muse MR-5212 *Cryin' in the Morning: An Anthology of Post-War Blues* (MM incl on)
  Paltram PL-101 *Early Recordings of MM & Kansas Joe McCoy* (1929–36)
  ST 109 *Jazzwomen: A Feminist Retrospective*
  Yazoo L-1021 *Memphis Jamboree* (reissue of 1927–36 recs)

ARIZONA DRANES   *p, vo/gospel-blues*
  78s: Okeh (1926–28)
  Blues Classics CL-BC18 (reissue of 78s)
  Col 1445-D/Truth 1001 (w Texas Jubilee Singers; 1928)
  Herwin 210 (reissue of 78s)
  Parlophone PM-C1174 (reissue of 78s)
  ST 112 *Women in Jazz: Pianists*

URSZULA DUDZIAK   *vo, synth*
   Heritage/Pausa 7047 (w Michal Urbaniak, *violin*), 7114 *Daybreak*
   IC 1066 *Future Talk* (UD *bl*)
   Warner Bros 9058, 9065, 9081

ANITA ELLIS   *vo*
   Orlon ORS-79358 *A Legend Sings*

ETHEL ENNIS   *vo*
   Cap *Change of Scenery, Have You Forgotten*
   Jubilee 1021 *Lullabies for Losers*
   Pickwick S-3021 *EE*
   Vic LSP-2786 *This Is EE* 2 vol (1964), LSP-2862 *My Kind*, PSP-2862 *Once Again*
(1964)

RUTH ETTING   *vo/vaudeville*
   Bio C-11 *Hello, Baby* (reissue of 1926–31 recs)
   Col ML-5050 *Original Recordings of RE*

SUSAN EVANS   *per*
   Ampex A-10102 (w Gil Evans Orch; 1969)
   Atl 40528 (w Gil Evans Orch; 1974)
   Cobblestone CST-9020 *Steve Kuhn Live* (SE incl on; 1972), CST-9022 (w Bobby
Jones, 1972)
   ECM 1052-ST *Trance* (w Steve Kuhn *p;* 1974)
   Philips RJ-6043 (w Gil Evans Orch; 1974)
   Polyjazz SX-0636 (w Gil Evans Orch; 1976)
   Vic/RCA (all w Gil Evans Orch) CPL1-0667 (1974), AFL1-1057 (1975), (F)PL-
25209 (France 1978)

JANE FAIR   *s*
   RCI (JF *bl;* Canada 1975)

STEPHANIE FAUBER   *fr horn*
   Pausa 7115 *Mel Lewis & the Jazz Orchestra Play Music of Herbie Hancock* (SF incl
on; live at Montreux, Switzerland)

FRANCES FAYE   *vo*
   Beth BCP-23, BCP-62 *Relaxin' with FF* (1956), BCP-6006 (1956), BCP-6017 (1957),
BCP-6040 *Porgy & Bess* 3 vol (w Betty Roche & Mel Torme *vo;* also released as Beth
3PP-1)
   Cap T-512 (1953)
   GNP 41 *Caught in the Act, Vol 1*, 92 *Caught in the Act, Vol 2*
   Verve V6-8434 *Singin' All the Way with FF* (1961–62)

JEAN FINEBERG   *s, fl, cl*
   Atl SD-19209 *C'est Chic* (w Chic), SD-5209 *We Are Family* (w Sister Sledge)
   Buddha BDS-5626 *Ain't No Backin' Up Now* (w Isis), BDS-5605 *Isis* (JF incl on)
   Col PC-34786 *Season of Light* (w Laura Nyro *vo*)

Marlin 2204 *Short Trip to Space* (w John Tropea)
Olivia *Let It Be Known* (JF *horn arr;* w Teresa Trull)
Phantom BPL1-0995 *Deadly Nightshade* (JF incl on)
UA LA-706-G *Breaking Through* (w Isis)
Vic/RCA ADL1-0098 *Young Americans* (w David Bowie)

ELLA FITZGERALD   *vo*
Cap SM-11793 *Brighten the Corner*
Col PG-32557 *EF at the Newport Jazz Festival* (1973)
Dec DX5-7156 *Best of Ella* 2 vol, DL-8695 *First Lady of Song,* DL-9223 *King of the Savoy, Vol 2* (w Chick Webb Orch; reissue of 1937–39 recs)
MCA 215E/MGV 4024 *EF Sings Gershwin,* 4047E *Best of Ella II,* 4016E *Volume II*
Pablo 2310-702 *Take Love Easy,* 2310-711 *Ella in London,* 2310-751 *Montreux '75,* 2310-759 *Ella & Oscar* (w Oscar Peterson), 2310-772 *EF & Joe Pass...Again,* 2310-814 *Dream Dancing,* 2310-825 *Lady Time* (w J. Davis), 2310-829 *Fine and Mellow,* TD-0231-2110 *EF & Count Basie—A Perfect Match,* L-2308-206 *EF with Tommy Flanagan,* 2630-201 *EF Embraces Jobim* 2 vol, *Ella à Nice* (reissue), *Today* 2312-138 *The Best Is Yet to Come*
Pickwick 3259 *EF*
Sunbeam 205 *Ella & Her Orchestra* (w Chick Webb Orch; reissue)
Ver 2507/MGV-4011 *Porgy & Bess* 2 vol, 2511/MGV-4001-2 *EF Sings Cole Porter Songbook* 2 vol, 2519/MGV-4002-2, *EF Sings Rodgers & Hart* 2 vol, 2525 *EF Sings Gershwin Songbook* 2 vol, 2535 *EF Sings Ellington Songbook* 2 vol, MGV-4046-2 *EF Sings Harold Arlen* 2 vol, MGV-4054 *EF Swings Brightly with Nelson Riddle,* MGV-4056 *Rhythm Is My Business,* 2-8811 *Ella & Louis* 2 vol, 2-64072 *EF with Duke Ellington, Cote d'Azur* 2 vol, UMV 2636 *Ella in Hollywood* (reissue, 1961)
Voc 73797E *EF*

ROBERTA FLACK   *vo, p*
Atl 8230 *First Take,* 1569 *Chapter 2,* 18131 *Feel Like Makin' Love,* 19154 *Killing Me Softly,* 1594 *Quiet Fire,* 16013 (w Donny Hathaway *vo*), 2-7004 (2 vol; w Peabo Bryson *vo*)

HELEN FORREST   *vo*
10″: Dec DL-5243 (w Dick Haymes *vo*)
Camden CAL-515 *Artie Shaw Swings Show Tunes* (HF incl on), CAL 584 *One Night Stand* (w Artie Shaw)
Cap T-704 *Voice of the Name Bands*
Col CL-523/524 (2 vol; w Benny Goodman & Orch; reissue)
Harmony HL-7159 (w Harry James)
Vic LSP-2830 (w Tommy Dorsey Orch), LPM-1570 *Any Old Time* (w Artie Shaw Orch)

ARETHA FRANKLIN   *vo/soul*
Arista 9538 *Aretha,* 9552 *Love All the Hurt Away*
Atl SD-7292, SD-8207, SD-8265, SD-18176 *Sparkle,* SD-19102 *Sweet Passion,* 7205 *AF at Filmore West,* 7213 *Young, Gifted & Black,* 8139 *I Never Loved a Man,* 8295

Greatest Hits, 18204 *10 Years of Gold*, 19248 *La Diva*, 2-906 *Amazing Grace* 2 vol, QD-8305(Q) *Best of AF*, (F)40504, (F)50031, (F)50445

Checker 861/LP-10009 (w New Bethel Baptist Church of Detroit Choir; 1955–56)

Col CS-8879 *Laughing on the Outside*, CS-8963 *Unforgettable* (tribute to Dinah Washington), KC-31953 *First 12 Sides*, CG-31355 *Beginning* 2 vol, C2-37377 *Legendary Queen of Soul* 2 vol

LAURIE FRINK   *tr*

DRG SL-5194 *Walk on the Water* (w Gerry Mulligan Orch; 1980)

MARIAN GANGE   *g*

78s: (w Ina Ray Hutton & Her Melodears)

ST 111 *Women in Jazz: All-Women Groups*, 113 *Women in Jazz: Swingtime to Modern*

VIVIEN GARRY   *b, vo, bl*

78s: Exclusive 11; Guild 124; Sarco 101, 102, 103; Skylark 521; V-Disc 690; Vic 20-2352, 40-0144 (1946)

ST 111 *Women in Jazz: All-Women Groups*

LORRAINE GELLER   *p*

Dot DLP-3174 (*LG* bl; 1956)

EmArcy MG-36040 (w Herb Geller; 1954), MG-36044 (1955), MG-36045 (1955)

Imperial EP-121 (w Herb Geller Quartet; 1954)

Trip TLP-5539

JANE GETZ   *p*

Debut VIJ-5012 (w Charles Mingus *b*)

ESP-1003 (w Pharaoh Sanders *bl*)

ASTRUD GILBERTO   *vo*

CTI 6008 (w Stanley Turrentine *ts*)

Ver V-8643 *Look at the Rainbow* (Gil Evans *arr*), 2332072-IMS, MV-2099-IMS (w Stan Getz, João Gilberto), MV-9041/9042-IMS (w Stan Getz, João Gilberto), 2332050-IMS, 2352066-IMS (w Stan Getz), V08608 *The AG Album* (w Antonio Carlos Jobim)

ADELE GIRARD   *harp*

78s: Musicraft 328 (1945), 329 (1945)

Allegro 3104 *Joe Marsala's Sextet* (AG incl on)

Saga 6927 *AG* (w Joe Marsala *cl*)

ST 109 *Jazzwomen: A Feminist Retrospective*

Tops 1639 *Joe Marsala & Orchestra* (AG incl on)

LIZ GORRILL   *p*

Jazz Records, JR2 *I Feel Like I'm Home*

ROSE GOTTESMAN   *d*

ST 109 *Jazzwomen: A Feminist Retrospective*, 111 *Women in Jazz: All-Women Groups*, 113 *Women in Jazz: Swingtime to Modern*

JOANNE GRAUER *p*
   Mode LP-113 (JG *bl;* 1957)

LIL GREEN *vo*
   78s: numerous on: Aladdin; Bluebird (1940–42)
   Vic LP-V574 *LG, Romance in the Dark* (reissue of 78s)

VERA GUILAROFF *p*
   78s: numerous on: Compo (Canada); HMV (England 1937)
   Bio BLP-12047 (VG incl on 1926 rec of "Maple Leaf Rag")
   ST 112 *Women in Jazz: Pianists*
   Supertone 21178 (VG incl on 1926 rec of "Maple Leaf Rag")

CONNIE HAIMES *vo*
   Camden CAL-800 *Dedicated to You* (w Tommy Dorsey Orch; reissue)
   Tops L-1606 *A Tribute to Helen Morgan*

CORKY HALE *harp, misc*
   Atl SD-1642 (w Herbie Mann *bl;* 1973)
   GNP 17 *Modern Harp* (1955–56), 9035 *CH Plays Gershwin & Duke*
   Ver (both w Buddy Bregman Orch, Anita O'Day *vo*) MGV-2000, MGV-2036

LIL HARDIN. See LIL HARDIN ARMSTRONG.

JANE HARVEY *vo*
   Classic Jazz CJ-15 *You Fats, Me Jane* (w Zoot Sims *ts*)
   Vic/RCA LP-L15030 (1974)

JENNELL HAWKINS *o*
   Atco S-33157 *Lady Soul* (w Vi Redd *bl, as;* 1962)

LEORA MEOUX HENDERSON *tr*
   78s: Melotone M-12340/N "Casa Loma Stomp" (w Fletcher Henderson Orch;
   1932; later issued in U.S. on Perfect and Domino, and in 1932 in England on Br
   [E]1319-A and in France on Br [F]A-500191)
      Col CL-1685 *Study in Frustration: The Fletcher Henderson Story* 4 vol (anthology
   of 1923–38 recs; LMH incl on "Blue Moments," recorded in 1932 but not issued until
   this collection)

LIL HARDAWAY HENDERSON *p*
   78s: Dec 7193 (1936), 7241, 7247, 7276
   Herwin 112 (LHH incl on; reissue of 1928 recs)
   ST 109 *Jazzwomen: A Feminist Retrospective*

BERTHA "CHIPPIE" HILL *vo/blues*
   Raretone RTR-24010 (w Gladys Bentley *vo;* reissue)

HARRIET HILLIARD *vo*
   Imperial 9049 *Ozzie & Harriet Nelson*

THE HIP CHICKS *combo*

ST 113 *Women in Jazz: Swingtime to Modern* (incl Jean Starr *tr*, L'Ana Webster *ts*, Marjorie Hyams *vi*, Vicki Zimmer *p*, Cecilia Zirl *b*, Rose Gottesman *d*, Marian Gange *g*, Vivian Garry *vo*; 1945)

JUTTA HIPP *p*

Blue Note 1515, 1516, 1530 (w Zoot Sims *ts*), 5056
Dec *Das Ist Jass* (JH *bl*; Germany)
MGM *Cool Europe* (w Hans Koller; Germany)
ST 112 *Women in Jazz: Pianists*, 113 *Women in Jazz: Swingtime to Modern*

JEAN HOFFMAN *p*

Cap (S)T-2021 (1963)
Fantasy 3260 (JH *bl*; 1957)

BILLIE HOLIDAY *vo*

AFJ 265E *BH*, 310E *BH, Vol II*
American Recording Society G-409
Atl SD-1614 *Strange Fruit*
Col CSP P-14338 *Swing, Brother, Swing*, CL-637 *Lady Day* (w Teddy Wilson *p*), CL-2666 *BH's Greatest Hits*, C3I-21 *BH: The Golden Years* 3 vol, C3-40 *BH: The Golden Years, Vol 2* (3 vol), CL-1157, CL-1036 *The Jazz Makers* (BH on one track), CL-821 *The Vintage Goodman* (BH on one track w Benny Goodman *cl*), CL-1098 *The Sound of Jazz* (BH on one track), CG-30782 *God Bless the Child* 2 vol, C-32060 *BH: Original Recordings*, KC-32080 *Billie's Blues*, CS-8048 *Lady in Satin*, PG-32121 *BH Story, Vol I* (w Teddy Wilson, Lester Young), PG-32124 *BH Story, Vol II*, PG-32127 *BH Story, Vol III*
    Commodore XFL-14428 *Fine & Mellow*, 30008, 30011 (w Eddie Heywood *p*)
    Dec 8215, 8701, 8702, DXB-161 *The BH Story* 2 vol (also released as DXS-7161)
    Esp-Disk 3002 *Lady Lives Broadcasts* (1949–52)
    Hall 622E *I've Gotta Right to Sing*
    Main 6022 *Once Upon a Time*
    MCA 4006E (2 vol), 275E *Greatest Hits*
    MGM E-3764 *BH*
    Mon-Ever 7046E *Gallant Lady*
    Para PAS-6059 *BH, Songs & Conversations*
    Score 4014
    Time-Life STL-J03 *BH* 3 vol
    Trip 50243 *BH Live*
    UA LI-5635 *Lady Love*
Ver 2503 *First Verve* 2 vol, 2529 *All or Nothing at All* 2 vol, V-8026 *Songs for Torching*, 8027, 8074, 8096, 8098 *Jazz Recital*, 8099, 8197, 8234, 8239, 8257 *Songs for Distingué Lovers*, 8302, 8329, MGV-8338-2 *The Unforgettable Lady Day* 2 vol, Clef MGC-686 *Recital by BH*, MGC-721 *Lady Sings the Blues*, (E)2304-104 *BH: The Voice of Jazz* 10 vol (reissue series), 68074 *Solitude*

LIBBY HOLMAN   *vo/vaudeville*
  Dec DEA-7-2 *Those Wonderful Thirties* 2 vol
  Mon-Ever MRS-6501 *The Legendary LH*

BERTHA HOPE   *p*
  Riv VIJ-5050 *Elmo & BH* (w Elmo Hope *p*)

LINDA HOPKINS   *vo/blues-pop*
  Ampex 40101 *Purlie* (LH on original cast album)
  Col PC-34032 *Me & Bessie* (LH on original cast album; 1975)
  Vic/RCA LSO-1171 *Inner City* (LH on original cast album; 1972)

SHIRLEY HORN   *p, vo*
  ABC-Para ABC-538 (1965)
  Mer MG-20761 (1963), MG-20835
  Stp 1111 *A Lazy Afternoon* (1978-79), *Violets for Your Furs* (1982)

LENA HORNE   *vo*
  10": MGM E-545
  Buddha BOS-18-SK *Watch What Happens* (w Gabor Szabo *g*)
  Gryphon G-918 *Lena & Gabor* (w Gabor Szabo *g*)
  Lion L-70050 *I Feel So Smoochie*
  Qwest/Warner Brothers QW-3597 *LH: The Lady & Her Music* 2 vol (live on Broadway; 1981)
  Spotlite SPJ-100 (w Billy Eckstine & orch)
  Sunbeam 212 (w Fletcher Henderson & orch; reissue of 1944 recs)
  Tops L-1502 *LH,* L-910 (w Phil Moore Orch)
  20th Fox TFS-4415 *Here's Lena Now*
  Vic LPT-3061, LOC-1928 *LH at the Waldorf Astoria,* LPM-1148 *It's Love,* LPM-1879 *Give the Lady What She Wants,* LOP-1507 *Porgy & Bess* (w Harry Belafonte *vo*), RCA 26.28034-DP *Artie Shaw & His Orchestra* (LH incl on), RCA BXL-1-1799 *Lena: A New Album*

HELEN HUMES   *vo*
  Audiophone 107 (1974)
  Black & Blue 33050 *Helen Comes Back* (France)
  Black Lion BLP-30167 *On the Sunny Side of the Street* (England)
  Classic Jazz 110 *Sneakin' Around,* 120 *Let the Good Times Roll!*
  Col PC-33488 *Talk of the Town,* G-31224 *Count Basie Super Chief* 2 vol (HH incl on several tracks)
  Contemp 7571 *Tain't Nobody's Bizness If I Do* (1959; reissued 1981), 7582 *Songs I Like to Sing* (1960; reissued 1981), 7598 *Swingin' with HH* (reissued 1981)
  Jazzology 55 *Incomparable*
  MCA 2-4050 *The Best of Count Basie* 2 vol (HH incl on), 2-4064 *Singin' the Blues* 2 vol
  Muse MR-5217 *HH & the Muse All-Stars,* MR-5233 *Helen* (1980)

Onyx ORI-208 *Midnight at Minton's* (w Don Byas *ts;* reissue of 1945 after-hours session)

Sav 2215 *Black California* (HH incl on; reissue), 2242 *Black California, Vol 2* (HH incl on; reissue)

Van VSD-47/48 *From Spirituals to Swing* 2 vol (HH incl on)

Vic/RCA FPM-17018 *HH with Red Norvo & His Orch* (Black & White Series; reissue of Vic LPM-1711 *Red Norvo in Hi-Fi* and Vic LPM-1729 *Red Plays the Blues*)

BOBBI HUMPHREY *fl*
    CBS 88286 *Montreux Summit*
    Col JE-36368 *Best of BH*
    Epic JE-35338 *Freestyle*, JE-35607 *The Good Life*

ALBERTA HUNTER *vo/blues*
    Col JS-355 *Remember My Name* (film score; AH *com, vo*), 36430 *Amtrak Blues*, FC-37691 *The Glory of AH* (w Gerald Cook *p;* 1982)
    DRG SL-5195 *The Legendary AH: The London Sessions, 1934* (reissue of 78s w orch)
    Riv RLP-101 *Young Louis Armstrong* (AH incl on; reissue), RLP-418 *AH with Lovie Austin & Her Blues Serenaders* (1961)
    ST 115 *Classic AH* (reissue)
    Vic LPV-534 *Women of the Blues* (AH incl on; reissue)

LURLEAN HUNTER *vo*
    Vic LPM-1151 *Lonesome Gal*

DOLLY HUTCHINSON. See DOLLY JONES.

INA RAY HUTTON & THE MELODEARS *bb*
    78s: various on Elite; Okeh; Vic; Voc
    ST 109 *Jazzwomen: A Feminist Retrospective*

L'ANA HYAMS. See L'ANA WEBSTER.

MARJORIE HYAMS *vibes*
    78s: Dis 105, 106; MGM (w George Shearing *p*), Signature 28106, 28119 (w Flip Phillips *ts*)
    Col C3L-25 *The Thundering Herds* 3 vol (MH incl on; reissue of recs by Woody Herman & orch)
    Dis DL-3002/Sav MG-120 (w George Shearing Quintet; 1949)
    MGM E-3265 *Touch of Genius* (w George Shearing *p*)
    Onyx LP 20-2174 (w Mary Lou Williams *p;* reissue of Vic 78s)
    ST 111 *Women in Jazz: All-Women Groups*, 113 *Women in Jazz: Swingtime to Modern*

THE INTERNATIONAL SWEETHEARTS OF RHYTHM *bb*
    78s: Guild 141; Magic 715; RCA 40-0146 (1946)
    ST 109 *Jazzwomen: A Feminist Retrospective*, 111 *Women in Jazz: All-Women Groups*, 113 *Women in Jazz: Swingtime to Modern*

JACKIE & ROY. See JACKIE CAIN.

MAHALIA JACKSON   *vo/gospel*
  Apollo 482 *No Matter How You Pray*
  Col CS-9686 *MJ*, CS-9727 *Christmas with MJ*, CL-30744 *MJ Sings America's Favorite Hymns*, CG-31379 *The Great MJ*, CS-8804 *MJ: Greatest Hits, Bless This House, Best-Loved Hymns of Dr. King, Garden of Prayer, Great Gettin' Up, I Believe, MJ in Concert, Mighty Fortress, My Faith, Power & the Glory, MJ Recorded in Europe, Right Out of the Church, What the World Needs Now*
    Harmony HL-11279 *You'll Never Walk Alone*
    Kenwood *The Best of MJ*

BONNIE JEFFERSON   *g/blues-folk*
  Advent *San Diego Blues Jam*

DODIE JESHKE   *d*
  ST 111 *Women in Jazz: All-Women Groups*

DAMITA JO   *vo*
  Camden S-900 (1965)
  Epic BN-26131 *This Is DJ* (1965), BN-26164 *One More Time* (1965)
  Mer 60818 (1963)
  Vic 1137 *DJ Sings* (1965)

BESSIE JOHNSON. See LUCILLE BOGAN

MARGARET JOHNSON ("Countess" or "Queenie")   *p*
  Col C-3L-40 *Billie Holiday: The Golden Years* 3 vol (MJ incl on 4 tracks acc BH *vo*; reissue of 1938 rec)

DOLLY JONES   *cor, tr*
  78s: Okeh 8350 "That Creole Band" (w Al Wynn & His Gutbucket Five; 1926)
  ST 109 *Jazzwomen: A Feminist Retrospective*

ETTA JONES   *vo*
  Muse 5099 *Ms. Jones to You*, 5145 *Mother's Eyes*, 5175 *If You Could See Me Now*, 5178 *The Nearness of You* (1981), 5214 *Save Your Love For Me* (1981) (5175–5214 all w Houston Person *ts*)
  Pres S-7186 *Don't Go to Strangers*, S-7204 *So Warm*, S-7241 *Lonely & Blue*, S-7272 *Love Shout*, S-7284 *Hollar*, S-7443 *EJ: Greatest Hits*, S-7784 *Love Is the Thing*

SHEILA JORDAN   *vo*
  Arista AL-1006 *Flexible Flyer* (w Roswell Rudd *bl*)
  Black Saint BRS-0023 *Free to Dance* (w Marcello Melis *bl*, Jeanne Lee *vo*; Italy 1979)
  Blue Note 9002 *Portrait of Sheila* (SJ *bl*; reissue of 1963 rec; Japan 1980)
  East Wind *Confirmation* (Japan 1975)
  ECM 1-1159 *Playground* (w Steve Kuhn Band; 1980), 1-1160 *Home* (w Steve Swallow *b, com*, to poetry by Robert Creeley; 1981), *Last Year's Waltz* (w Steve Kuhn Band; 1981–82)

Jazz Composers Orchestra Association 2002 *Numatick Swing Band* (w Roswell Rudd *bl*), 3LP-EOTH *Escalator over the Hill* (SJ incl on; Carla Bley *com*)
Riv 440 *The Outer View* (SJ incl on, w George Russell; 1964; reissued on Mls as *Outer Thoughts*)
Steeplechase SCS-1081 *Sheila* (SJ *bl;* w Arild Andersen *b;* Norway 1978)
Vista-RCA TLPI-1082 *Perdas de Fogu* (w Mario Schiano *bl;* Italy)
Wave LP-1 *Looking Out* (w Peter Ind *b, prod*)

CAROL KAYE   *el b*
Col CS-9889 *The New Don Ellis Band Goes Underground* (CK incl on; 1969)
Mer MG-21063 (w Quincy Jones & orch; 1965)
Pres P-10080 *Brasswind* (w Gene Ammons *bl, ts*), P-10088 *Northern Windows* (w Hampton Hawes *bl, p*)

JOANN KELLY   *vo/blues*
Blue Goose 2009 (w John Fahey *g*)

EMME KEMP   *p, vo*
EBM *Eubie Blake & His Girls* (EK incl on)

BEVERLY KENNEY   *vo*
Dec DL-8743 *BK Sings for Playboys* (w Ellis Larkins *p*)

JEANETTE SALVANT KIMBALL   *p*
78s: Col (w Original Tuxedo Jazz Orch; 1926–27)
Dulai 800 *Traditional New Orleans Jazz* (JSK incl on)
Second Line 0112 (JSK incl on)
Southland SLP-206 *Oscar "Papa" Celestin's Golden Wedding* (JSK incl on; 1954), SLP-212 (w Paul Barbarin & His Jazz Band), SLP-218 *Crescent City Music* (JSK incl on), SLP-239 *Echoes of New Orleans* (JSK incl on)

MORGANA KING   *vo*
Muse MR-5166 *Stretching Out,* MR-5190 *Everything Must Change,* MR-5224 *Higher Ground,* MR-5257 *Looking Through the Eyes of Love* (1982)
Wing 60007 *Helen Morgan Songs*

NANCY KING   *vo*
IC 1049 *First Date* (w Steve Wolfe *s*)

TEDDI KING   *vo*
10": Sto 302
Audiophone 117 *Lovers & Losers,* 150 *Someone to Light Up Your Life*
IC 1044 *This Is New* (w Dave McKenna *p*)
Sto 314, 903 *Now in Vogue*
Vic LPM-1313 *To You from TK,* LPM-1147 *Bidin' My Time,* LPM-1454 *A Girl & Her Songs*

EARTHA KITT   *vo*
Caedmon 1267 *Folk Tales of the Tribes of Africa*
Camden ACL-7030 *Golden Hit Parade*

GNP 2008
Kapp 3046 *Fabulous EK* (1959), 3192 *EK Revisited* (1960)
MGM S-4009 *Bad But Beautiful*
Stanyan 10040
Vic LPM-1661 (1957), LPM-1183

IRENE KRAL   *vo*

Cap ST-2173 *My Fair Lady* (w Shelley Mann *bl, d;* 1964), *Guitar from Ipanema*
Catalyst 7625 *Kral Space*
Choice CRS-1020 *Gentle Rain,* CRS-1012 *Where Is Love?*
Main *Wonderful Life*

KARIN KROG   *vo*

Enja 2030 (KK-Arild Andersen Duo)
MPS 88040-2 (KK *bl*)
Polydor 2382051-IMS (w Steve Kuhn Trio), 2382044-IMS, 2382045-IMS

JOAN LA BARBERA   *vo, com*

Chi CR-195, CR-196 *Tapesongs*

CLEO LAINE   *vo*

Black Lion 162028 (w John Dankworth *s*)
Buddha 5607 *Day by Day*
GNP 9024E *Cleo's Choice*
London 6.30110EM (w Ray Charles *vo*)
Stanyan 10067 *Day by Day,* 10092 *Easy Livin',* 10122
Vic/RCA CLP2-1831 *Porgy & Bess* 2 vol (w Ray Charles; 1976), AFL1-1937 (w John Williams), AFL1-2926 *Gonna Get Through,* AFL1-3628 (CL & James Galway), AFL1-3751 *Carnegie Hall,* AFL1-2407 *Return to Carnegie Hall,* AFL1-3805 *Beautiful,* AFL1-5000 *I Am a Song,* AFL1-5015, AFL1-5059 *A Beautiful Thing,* AFL1-5113 *Born on a Friday*

LAMBERT, HENDRICKS AND ROSS. See ANNIE ROSS.

JANET LAWSON   *vo*

IC 1116 *JL Quintet* (1981)

BARBARA LEA   *vo*

Audiophone 86 *A Woman in Love,* 119 *Devil Is Afraid of Music,* 125 *Remembering Lee Wiley*

JEANNE LEE   *vo*

Affinity AFF7 *My Angel* (w Archie Shepp *ts;* 1969)
Birth (w Gunter Hempel et al) 001, 003, 005, 007, 008, 009, 0010, 0011, 0012, 0013, 0016, 0017, 0021, 0022, 0024, 0025, 0026
Black Saint BSR-0023 *Free to Dance* (w Marcello Melis *bl,* Sheila Jordan *vo;* Italy 1979)
Calig 30605 (w Marion Brown Sextet)
Earthform 1

ECM 1004-IMS *JL*
IPS ST-002 *Celebration* (w Andrew Cyrille *d*)
Trio 3008/3009 (2 vol; w Anthony Braxton *s*; Japan)
Vic/RCA LSP-2500 *JL & Ran Blake*

JULIA LEE   *p, vo*
  78s: numerous in '30s & '40s on: Cap; Dec "That's What I Like" (w Benny Carter *s*);
Premier "Lotus Blossom" (1945)
  10": Cap H-228 *Party Time*, H-240 (JL incl on 2 cuts w Jay McShann *p*)
  Cap T-1057 (JL incl on, reissue of recs by Kansas City pianists)

PEGGY LEE   *vo*
  10": Cap H-151 *Rendezvous*; Col CL-6033 (w Benny Goodman Orch; reissue)
  A&M SP-4547 *Mirrors*
  Atl *Let's Love*
  Cap SM-386 *Is That All There Is?*, SM-1290 *Latin à la Lee*, SM-1520 *PL at Basin St.
East*, SM-1857 *I'm a Woman*, SM-11833 *PL, Vol 1*, SN-16140 *PL Sings the Songs of
Cy Coleman*, T-1049 *Things Are Swingin'*, T-1219 *Beauty & the Beat* (w George
Shearing *p*), T-1401 *Pretty Eyes*, T-1743 *PL Sings Her Greatest Hits*, T-1776, STBB-
2979 *Christmas*, DKAO-377E *PL's Greatest*, ST-1671 *Blues Cross Country* (w Quincy
Jones & Orch), ST-1860 *Mink Jazz*, ST-2320 *Pass Me By*, ST-2732 *Extra Special*, ST-
2781 *Somethin' Groovy*, ST-2887 *PL Hits*, ST-11077 *Norma Delores Egstrom*
  Col LP PG-31547, *All-Time Greatest Hits* (w Benny Goodman Orch)
  Dec DL-5482 *Black Coffee*, DL-8166 *Pete Kelly's Blues* (w Ella Fitzgerald *vo*)
  DRG SL-5190 *Close Enough for Love*
  Harmony HL-7005 (reissue)
  Legend GL-6023 *You Can Depend on Me* (1981)
  MCA 2-4049 *Best of PL* 2 vol

CAROL LEIGH   *vo/blues*
  Circle/Audiophile *Blame It on the Blues* (1983)
  GHB 88 *Wild Women Don't Have the Blues*

ELAINE LEIGHTON   *d*
  10": Cadence LPC-1000 *Beryl Booker Trio* (1954)
  Atl 664, 668 (w Jackie & Roy *vo*; combo incl Marilyn Beaout *cello*)
  Dis DL-3021 (w Beryl Booker Trio; 1954)
  MGM E-255 *Cats v. Chicks: A Jazz Battle of the Sexes* (w Terry Pollard *bl*)
  Pres LP-179 (w Jimmy Raney *g*; Sweden 1954)
  ST 109 *Jazzwomen: A Feminist Retrospective*, 111 *Women in Jazz: All-Women
Groups*
  Sto SLP-302 (w Teddi King *vo*, Bonnie Wetzel *b*; 1953)

ABBEY LINCOLN   *vo*
  Candid SMJ-6169(9002) (w Max Roach *d*), SMJ-6187(9022) (w Jazz Artists Guild),
SMJ-6190(9015) (AL & Her Orch)
  Col JC-36581 *What It Is*
  IC 6040 *People in Me*, 1117 *Golden Lady*

Imp AS-8 *Percussion Bitter Sweet* (w Max Roach *d*), A-16 *Max Roach Chorus & Orchestra* (AL incl on)

Jazz Man *Straight Ahead* (reissue)

Muse MR-5244 *The Maestro* (AL incl w Cedar Walton *p*)

Riv 6088 *Abbey Is Blue*, RLP-12-251 *That's Him*, RLP-12-277 *It's Magic*

MELBA LISTON   *trom, arr*

78s: Aladdin 534 (w Gerald Wilson Orch; 1947) Mer 8010 (ML in orch acc Dinah Washington *vo;* 1946)

Atl LP-1312 (ML in orch acc Ray Charles *vo*)

Blue Note BN-LA-598-H2 *Little Niles* (ML *trom, arr,* in orch w Randy Weston *bl, p;* reissue of 1958 rec UN-UAL-4011)

EmArcy MG-36141 (ML in combo acc Dinah Washington *vo;* Newport Jazz Festival 1958)

Ever LPBR-5063 (ML *arr, trom,* in orch acc Gloria Lynn *vo;* 1959)

Imp A-11 (w Quincy Jones Orch; 1961)

Limelight LM-82002 (w Quincy Jones Orch; 1964)

Mer (all except last w Quincy Jones Orch) MG-20444 (1959), MG-20612 (1960), MG-20653 (1961), MG-20799 (1963), MGV-8444 (ML w *bb;* 1962)

Metrojazz SC-1013 *ML & Her Bones* (ML *bl, com;* 1958)

Pres LP-7225 (w Oliver Nelson Orch; 1961), LP-7206 (ML w *bb;* 1960)

SOS LP-121 (w Gerald Wilson Orch; reissue of 1946 recs)

ST 109 *Jazzwomen: A Feminist Retrospective*

UA UAL-4045 *Destry Rides Again* (1959)

Ver (all w Dizzy Gillespie Orch) MGV-1084 *Dizzy Gillespie & His Orchestra* (1956), MGV-8017, Clef 8174 (1956), MGV-8222 (1957), MGV-8242 (1957), MGV-8244, MGV-8444 (1962)

Xanadu 120 *Bebop Revisited* (w Dexter Gordon *ts;* reissue of 1946 recs)

BARBARA LONDON   *fl, vo*

Morning Sky Records *Sea of Dreams* (BL w Morning Sky; 1976)

JULIE LONDON   *vo*

Liberty 3006, 3060, 3100, 3119, 3171, 5501, 7434, 7493, 7514, 7546, 7609

Sunset 5161

NELLIE LUTCHER   *p, vo*

78s: numerous on: Cap "Hurry On Down"/"The Lady's in Love with You" (1947); Col; Dec; Imperial; Liberty

10": Cap H-232 *Real Gone*

Liberty 3014 *Our New Nellie*

ST 112 *Women in Jazz: Pianists*

Sunset 1124 *Delightfully Yours*

GLORIA LYNN   *vo*

Ev LPBR-5022 (1958), 5063 (1959), 5090 (1960), 5101 (1960), 5126, 5128 (1962), 5208, 5220

Imp 9311

MARYANN MCCALL   *vo*

   78s: Col; Roost

   10": Dis 3011 *MM Sings* (1948)

   CJ 22 *Kansas City Express* (MM incl on)

   Coral (E)FEP-2040, (E)FEP 2041, (E)FEP 2042

   Jubilee JLP-1078 *Detour to the Moon* (1958)

   Regent MG-6040 *Easy Living* (1956)

   Ver V-8143 (w Charlie Ventura)

SUSANNAH MCCORKLE   *vo*

   IC 1101 *The Songs of Johnny Mercer,* 1131 *The Songs of Yip Harburg, The Music of Harry Warren* (1982)

ELLEN MCIWAINE   *vo g*

   Blind Pig *Everybody Needs It* (1982)

SARAH MCLAWLER   *o, vo*

   78s: Br (1953); King (1951–52); Premium/Chess 857 (1950); Vee Jay (1956)

   MCA 4113 (2 vol; SM incl on)

   ST 109 *Jazzwomen: A Feminist Retrospective*

   Vee Jay LP-1003 (1957), 1006 (1958), 1030 (1960)

JILL MCMANUS   *p*

   Muse MR-5093 *As One* (w Richard Davis *b;* New York 1975)

MARIAN MCPARTLAND   *p*

   10": Sav MG-15027 *MM Moods,* MG-15032 *Jazz at the Hickory House*

   Argo 640 *MM at the London House*

   Bainbridge *MM* (reissue), *The Music of Leonard Bernstein* 2 vol (reissue, also on Time R)

   Cap T-574 *MM at the Hickory House,* T-699 *After Dark,* T-785 *MM Trio,* T-895 *With You in Mind*

   CJ 86 *From This Moment On,* 101 *Portrait of MM,* 118 *At the Festival* (MM *bl;* w Mary Fettig Park *as*), 171 *Alone Together* (w George Shearing *p;* 1981), CJ-202 *Personal Choice* (1982)

   Dot 25907 *MM Performs the Classic Hits of Sam Coslow*

   Halcyon 100 *Interplay,* 103 *Ambiance,* 105 *Delicate Balance,* 107 *Live at the Monticello* (w Jimmy McPartland *cor*), 109 *MM Plays Alec Wilder,* 111 *Solo Concert at Haverford* (1974), 113 *Concert in Argentina* 2 vol (MM incl on), 114 *Swingin'* (w Jimmy McPartland), 115 *Now's the Time* (MM *bl;* w Mary Osborne *g,* Vi Redd *as,* Lynn Milano *b,* Dottie Dodgion *d;* 1977), 117 *MM Live at the Carlyle* (1979), 118 *Marian Remembers Teddi* (tribute to Teddi King *vo*)

   Improv 7115 *Fine Romance*

   Jazztone J-1227 *The Middle Road* (w Jimmy McPartland), J-1241 *Dixieland Now & Then*

   MPS 68122 *Duo*

   Sav 12004 *MM at Storyville & Hickory House,* 12005 *Lullaby of Birdland,* 12016 *Great Britains,* SJL-2248 *MM at the Piano* (reissue)

ST 109 *Jazzwomen. A Feminist Retrospective*
Time 52013 *Music of Leonard Bernstein*

CARMEN MCRAE *vo*
America AM-015116
Atl SD-2-904 *The Great American Songbook* 2 vol (1970), 8165 *Portrait of CM* (1967), SD-8143 (London 1967), 8200 (1968), 1568 (1970)
Bainbridge *The Sound of Silence* (reissue, 1968)
Beth 6004 *So Easy to Love* (1954)
Black Lion 162025, 284980-4U (London 1970)
Blue Note 709-H2 *Great Music Hall* 2 vol, LA-462-G (1975), LA-635-G (1976), LA-709-H2 (1976)
Buddha 6501 *I'm Coming Home Again*
Catalyst 7904 *As Time Goes By*
CJ 128 *Two for the Road* (w George Shearing *p*), CJ-189 *Heat Wave* (w Cal Tjader *vi*; 1981)
Col CS-8530 *CM Sings "Lover Man" & Other Billie Holiday Classics* (also released as PC-37002), CL-1730 (1961), CL-1943 (1962), CL-2316 (1964)
CSP JCS-9116 *Take Five* (w Dave Brubeck *p*)
Dec DL-8173 (1955), DL-8583 (1957), DL-8662 *Mad About the Man* (1957)
Ember (E)NR5000 (England 1961)
Focus 334 *Bittersweet* (1964)
Groove Merchant 522 (1972), *Ms. Jazz* (w Zoot Sims *ts*; 1973)
Jazzman *November Girl*
Kapp KLP-1117 (1958), KLP-1135 (1959), KLP-1169 (1959)
MCA 4111 *Greatest of CM* 2 vol (reissue of 1954-59 recs)
Main MRL-309 *CM*, MRL-338 *Carmen's Gold*, MRL-352 *CM in Person*, MRL-387 *I Want You*, MRL-403 *Live & Doin' It*, MRL-800 (1965), 56044, 56065
Quintessence 25021 *Ms. Jazz*
Realm (E)RM-194 (England 1963)
Stanyan 10115 *Mad About the Man*

CHARLOTTE MANSFIELD *p*
Cap T-1057 (CM incl on one track; anthology of Kansas City pianists)

TANIA MARIA *p, vo*
Accord ACV-130005 *TM Live* (Copenhagen)
CJ Picante P-15 *Piquant* (1981), Picante P-175 *Taurus* (1981)

ROBERTA MARTIN *vo/gospel*
Jewel 1044
Sav (RM w Roberta Martin Singers) 7018, 14008, 14022, 14221

SARA MARTIN *vo/blues*
10": Riv 1007 *Plays the Blues* (SM incl on)
Parlophone PMC-1177 *Jazz Sounds of 20s, Vol 4* (SM incl on; reissue)
Riv 12-130 *Back o' Town* (w King Oliver *cor*)

THE MELODEARS. See INA RAY HUTTON & THE MELODEARS.

MABEL MERCER   *vo*
   10": Atl 402 *Songs by MM*, 403
   Atl 1213 *MM Sings Cole Porter*, 1244 *Midnight at MM's*, 1301 *Once in a Blue Moon*, 1322 *Merely Marvelous*, 2-602 *The Art of MM* 2 vol, S-604 *MM at Town Hall* 2 vol, MM4-100 *A Tribute to MM* 4 vol
   Audiophone 161/162 *Echoes of My Life* 2 vol
   Dec DL-4472 *MM Sings*
   Stanyan 10108

HELEN MERRILL   *vo*
   Atco LP SD33-112 (1959)
   Catalyst 7903 *HM Sings & Swings* (w Teddy Wilson *p*), 7912 *Autumn Love*
   IC 1060 *Something Special*, 1080 *Chasin' the Bird*, 1125 *Casa Forte* (1981)
   Main M-56014 (1964)
   Mer 1150 (w John Lewis *p*)
   Metrojazz E-1010 (England 1959)
   Miles MLP-1003 (1967), MSP-9019 (1968)
   Polygram *The Nearness of You* (reissue, 1957)
   Trip 5526 *HM Sings with Clifford Brown* (reissue), 5552 *HM with Strings* (reissue)
   Vic/RCA LPM-10094 (Italy), LPM-10105 (Italy 1960), SJET-8166 (Japan 1969)

VELMA MIDDLETON   *vo*
   78s: Dootone M-001, M-002 (1948), M-004, M-005 (1951)
   Col Special Products JCL-591 *Louis Armstrong Plays W.C. Handy* (VM incl on), JCL-708 *Satch Plays Fats* (VM incl on)
   Dec DL-8041 *Satchmo at Pasadena* (VM incl on)
   MCA 2-4057 *Satchmo at Symphony Hall* (VM incl on)

LYNN MILANO   *b*
   Halcyon 115 *Now's the Time* (w Marian McPartland *bl*)

LIZZIE MILES   *vo/blues*
   Cap T-792 *A Night in New Orleans* (w Sharkey Bonano)
   Cook 1182 *Moans & Blues*, 1183 *Hot Songs My Mother Taught Me*, 1184 *Torchy Lullabies My Mother Taught Me*
   Ver MGV-1009 *Bourbon Street* (w Bob Scobey)

MILLS CAVALCADE ORCHESTRA   *bb*
   ST 113 *Women in Jazz: Swingtime to Modern*

MEMPHIS MINNIE. See MEMPHIS MINNIE DOUGLAS.

MEREDITH MONK   *vo*
   ECM-1-1197 *Dolmen Music* (1981)

MONETTE MOORE   *vo*
   78s: numerous on: Ajax (1924); Col (1925); Dec (1936, 1947); Gilt-Edge (1945–46);

Para (1923, 1924); Vic (1927), Voc (1924)
   Vic/RCA 741-065/066 *Charlie Johnson, Lloyd Scott, Cecil Scott* (Black & White Series, Vols 70 to 71; MM incl. on), LPV-534 (incl reissues of MM 78s)

GAYLE MORAN   *vo, keyb*
   CBS 69076 (w Mahavishnu Orch)
   Warner Bros WB-56801 (w Chick Corea)

PAT MORAN   *p*
   Beth BCP-6018 *While at Birdland* (PM *bl;* 1957), BCP-6040 *Porgy & Bess* (PM incl as *bl* of quartet), FCP-4014 *Bethlehem's Finest, Vol 14* (PM incl on)
   Mer MG-20704 (reissued as SR-60704; 1962)
   Ver (all w Terry Gibbs *vi*) MGV-2151, MGV-8447 (1969), MGV(S6)-8496

HELEN MORGAN   *vo/vaudeville*
   Audio Rarities 2330 *HM Sings the Songs She Made Famous*
   Epic LN-3188 *Here Come the Girls*
   Vic LPV-561 (w Fanny Brice *vo*)

KATHRYN MOSES   *fl, vo*
   CBC Records LM-437 *KM* (Canada)
   PM Records/Holy Moses PMR-107 *Music in My Heart*

ANNE MARIE MOSS   *vo*
   ST 211 *Don't You Know Me* (1981)

ROSE MURPHY   *p, vo*
   Big A's Records MG-658, MG-659 (w Slam Stewart *b*)
   Black & Blue 33158 (France 1980)
   Design 238 *RM—Ivie Anderson—Pearl Bailey*
   ST 112 *Women in Jazz: Pianists*
   Ver MV-2613-IMS (RM *bl*)

AMINA CLAUDINE MYERS   *p, o*
   Delmark 900252-AO (w Maurice McIntyre Ensemble)
   Leo Records LR-100 *Song for Mother E* (ACM *bl;* 1979), LR-103 *ACM Salutes Bessie Smith* (ACM *bl;* 1980)
   Soul Note SN-1006 (w Martha Bass, Fontella Bass, David Peaston *vo*)
   Sweet Earth SER-1005 *Poems for Piano* (ACM *bl;* 1979)

JUDY NIEMACK   *vo*
   SeaBreeze SB-2001 *By Heart* (w Simon Wettenhall *tr;* 1978)

DOROTHY NORWOOD   *vo/gospel*
   Jewel 0134
   Sav 7042, 14083, 14140, 14217, 14259, 14515

HELEN O'CONNELL   *vo*
   Camden CAL-529 *Green Eyes*, CAL-706 *HO Today*
   Dec DL-4248 *Remember Jimmy* (w Jimmy Dorsey & orch; reissue), DL-4853

Jimmy Dorsey's Greatest Hits (HO incl on), DL-8153 *Latin American Favorites*
   Mark 56-710
   Vic LX-1093 *Green Eyes*, VPM-6076 *This Is HO* 2 vol
   Warner Bros WB-1403 (w Bob Everly *vo*)

ANITA O'DAY   *vo*
   Col C-2L-29 *Drummer Man* (w Gene Krupa; reissue of 1941–45 recs incl Col 10″
CL-6017)
   Creative World 1028 *Stan Kenton: Fabulous Alumni* (AO incl on), 1029 *Kenton:
Some Women I've Known* (AO incl on; reissue)
   Emily 9578, 9579 *AO Live in Tokyo*, 11279 *My Ship*, 11579 *AO Live at Mingo's*,
102479 *AO Live at the City, Angel Eyes* (Japan; 1975 & 1978), *The Second Set*
   Glendale 6000 *Once Upon a Summertime*, 6001 *AO*
   GNP/Crescendo 2126 *Mello'Day*
   Pausa 7092 *AO in Berlin* (Germany)
   Polygram *AO Sings the Winners*
   Ver 2534 *Big Band Sessions* 2 vol (reissue), MGV-2000 *Anita*, MGV-2008 *Drummer
Man* (w Gene Krupa), MGV-2043 *Pick Yourself Up with AO*, MGV-2050 *An Evening
with AO*, MGV-2113 *AO at Mister Kelly's*, MGV-2145 *Waiter, Make Mine Blues*,
MGV-2157 *Trav'lin' Light*, MGV-6059 *AO Swings Cole Porter*, MGV-8259 *AO Sings
the Most*, MGV-8442 *All the Sad Young Men*, MGV-8472 *Time for Two*, MGV-8485
AO Sings the Winners

BRIDGET O'FLYNN   *d*
   78s: Continental (w Mary Lou Williams *bl;* 1946); RCA (w Mary Lou Williams *bl*)
   Onyx ORI-210 *Café Society* (w Mary Lou Williams *bl;* reissue of 1946 Continental
78s)
   ST 111 *Women in Jazz: All-Women Groups*
   Vic/RCA (F)741106 *The Greatest of the Small Bands* (Black & White Series, Vol 96,
w Mary Lou Williams *bl;* reissue of RCA 78s; France)

ODETTA   *vo/blues-folk*
   RCA LSP-2573 *Sometimes I Feel Like Cryin'*
   Riv RLP-9417 *Odetta and the Blues*

MARY OSBORNE   *g, vo*
   78s: numerous on: Aladdin 530, 3010 (1947); Continental; Coral 60058 (1948); Dec
24308 (1947); Saga (E)6924 (England 1945); Signature 15077, 15087 (1946); Vic (w
Mary Lou Williams & Girl Stars, Stuff Smith *violin;* 1946; not released)
   10″: Remington 1025 (w Ethel Waters *vo;* reissue of 78s), Rou (w Gene Krupka *d*)
   Halcyon 115 *Now's the Time* (w Marian McPartland *bl;* 1977)
   MGM E-255 *Cats v. Chicks: A Jazz Battle of the Sexes* (w Terry Pollard *bl*)
   Onyx ORI-210 *Café Society* (w Mary Lou Williams *bl;* reissue of 1945 rec)
   ST 109 *Jazzwomen: A Feminist Retrospective*, 111 *Women in Jazz: All-Women
Groups*, 215 *Now & Then* (MO *bl;* incl 1981 recs w Charlie Persip *d;* reissue of 1959
recs)
   Vic LJM-1017 *The All-American Esquire Jazz Band* (w Coleman Hawkins *ts*)
   Warwick LP-W2004 *A Girl & Her Guitar* (MO *bl,* w Tommy Flanagan *p;* 1959)

JEWEL PAIGE *p*
   78s: Dec 7863, 7891 (1941)
   ST 109 *Jazzwomen: A Feminist Retrospective*

GLADYS PALMER *p*
   78s: Dec 7106, 7107 (1935); Federal 12006 (w Floyd Hunt Orch; 1947); Miracle (all 1947–48) M-104, M-123, M-129, M-149, M-507

PARISIAN REDHEADS. See THE BRICKTOPS.

MARY FETTIG PARK *as, reeds*
   CJ 118 *At the Festival* (w Marian McPartland *bl*)

ANN PATTERSON *as, reeds*
   Atl SD-18227 *Music from Other Galaxies & Planets* (w Don Ellis & orch; 1977), SD-19178 *Live at Montreux* (w Don Ellis & orch)

ANNETTE PEACOCK *vo*
   RCA *I'm the One* (w Paul Bley *p*)
   Tomato 7025 *X-Dreams*, 7044 *Perfect Release*

ESTHER PHILLIPS *vo*
   Atl 50521, S-1565
   CTI 63028, 63036
   Kudu 05 *From a Whisper to a Scream*, 09 *Alone Again (Naturally)*, 14 *Black-Eyed Blues*, 18, 23, 28 *For All We Know*, 31 *Capricorn Princess*
   Mer 3769 *Here's Esther*, SRM-1-4005 *Good Black Is Hard to Crack*, SRM-1-3733 *All About EP*, SRM-1-1187 *You've Come a Long Way, Baby*
   Original Sound 8859 *Oldies But Goodies, Vol 9* (EP incl on; reissue)
   Power 288

BILLIE PIERCE *p, vo*
   Atl SD-1409 *Jazz at Preservation Hall*, Vol 2 (BP incl on)
   Center CLP-15 (1953)
   Folk-Lyric LP-110 (w De De Pierce *tr;* 1959; also released as Arhoolie 2016)
   Fk FA-2463 (1954)
   Jazzology JCE-25 *Legends Live* (w De De Pierce; 1960)
   Music of New Orleans LP (1963)
   Preservation Hall VPS-3 (1966)
   Rarities 15 (w Preservation Hall Band; Copenhagen 1967)
   Riv LP-370 *Billie & De De Pierce* (1961), LP-394 (1961), RLP 356/357 (2 vol; BP incl on), RLP-9394 *Blues & Tonks from the Delta* (BP incl on; 1961)
   VPH/VPS-3 *Billie & De De & Their Preservation Hall Jazz Band* (1966)

BU PLEASANT *p, o*
   Muse MR-5033 *Ms. Bu* (1973)
   Sto STLP-916

TERRY POLLARD *p, vibes*
   Beth BCP-1, BCP-15 (w Terry Gibbs *v;* 1955)

Br (all w Terry Gibbs) BL-54009, 54027 (1953, 1954), 58055

EmArcy (all w Terry Gibbs) MG-36047, MG-36064, MG-36065, MG-36075, MG-36085, MG-36087, MG-36103

Jazzland JLP-61 *Soft Winds* (w Dorothy Ashby *bl*)

MGM E-255 *Cats v. Chicks: A Jazz Battle of the Sexes* (TP *bl*, w Elaine Leighton *d*, Bonnie Wetzel *b*, Norma Caron *tr*, Mary Osborne *g*, Beryl Booker *p*; "against" Kenny Clarke *d*, Horace Silver *p*, Percy Heath *b*, Tal Farlow *g*, Urbie Green *trom* Clark Terry *tr*, Lucky Thompson *ts*)

ST109 *Jazzwomen: A Feminist Retrospective*, 111 *Women in Jazz: All-Women Groups*, 113 *Women in Jazz: Swingtime to Modern*

FLORA PURIM   *vo*
   CTI 63044
   ECM 1022
   Fantasy F-9505 (w Nat Adderly *tr*)
   Miles, MSP-9052, 9058, 9065, 9070, 9077, 9081, 9095
   Warner Bros BSK-3163, 3344

MA RAINEY   *vo/blues*
   78s: numerous on Para
   10": Riv 1003 *MR, Vol I*, 1016 *MR, Vol II*
   Bio 12001 *Blues the World Forgot, Vol I* (reissue of 1924–29 MR recs), 12011 *Oh My Babe Blues, Vol II* (reissue of 1924–28 MR recs), 12032 *Queen of the Blues, Vol III* (reissue of 1923–24 MR recs; incl Lovie Austin & Her Blues Serenaders)
   Mls MLP-2001 *Immortal MR*, 2008 *Blame It on the Blues*, 2017 *Down in the Basement*, M-47021 *MR* 2 vol (reissue)

BONNIE RAITT   *g, vo/blues-rock*
   Asylum DP-90002 *Urban Cowboy*
   Warner Bros 1953 *BR*, 2643 *Give It Up*, 2729 *Takin' My Time*, B-2818 *Streetlights*, 2864 *Home Plate*, B-2990 *Sweet Forgiveness*, 3369 *The Glow*

CARLINE RAY   *el b, g*
   ST 111 *Women in Jazz: All-Women Groups*

MARTHA RAYE   *vo*
   78s: Br; Col; Dec
   10": Dis 3010 *MR Sings*
   Epic LN-3061 *Here's MR*

LUCY REED   *vo*
   Fantasy 212 *The Singing Reed*

VI REED   *as, vo*
   Atco S-33157 *Lady Soul* (VR *bl*; 1962)
   Bellaphon BLST-6509 (w Howard McGhee Quintet)
   Halcyon HAL-115 *Now's the Time* (w Marian McPartland *bl*; 1977)
   Pres P-10010 *Chase* (w Gene Ammons *ts*, Dexter Gordon *ts*)
   ST 113 *Women in Jazz: Swingtime to Modern*

Tangerine *Shades of Grey* (w Al Grey *trom*)
UA UAS-15016 *Bird Call* (VR *bl;* 1962)

DELLA REESE *vo*
ABC S-524 *C'Mon & Hear* (1965), S-598 *One More Time* (1967), S-612 *DR on Strings of Blue* (1967), S-636 *I Gotta Be Me* (1968)
Jazz à la Carte *One of a Kind, Vol 3*
Jubilee 1026 *Melancholy Baby*, S-1083 *Amen!* (also released as 6009), 1116 *And That Reminds Me*, S-1071 *DR at Mr. Kelly's* (1958), S-1095 *Story of the Blues* (1959), S-1109 *What Do You Know About Love*
Vic LSP-2157 *Della* (1960), LSP-2280 *Cha Cha Cha* (1960), LSP-2391 *Special Delivery* (1961), LSP-2419 *Classic Della* (1962), LSP-2568 *DR On Stage* (1962), LSP-2711 *Waltz with Me* (1963), LSP-2872 *Basin St. East* (1964)

DIANNE REEVES *vo*
Palo Alto *Welcome to My Love* (1982)

IRENE REID *vo*
Glades 7506 *Two of Us*
MGM S-4159 *It's Only the Beginning* (1963)
Polydor 244040 *World Needs What I Need* (1971)
Rou (all w Count Basie & Orch) (S)R-52086 (1961), (S)R-52106, (S)R-52113 (1962), REP-1049 (Sweden 1962)
Sav 1170
Ver MGV-68621 *Room for One More* (w orch directed by Oliver Nelson; 1965), MGV-5003 *It's Too Late* (1966)

EMILY REMLER *g*
CJ 138 *It's All in the Family* (w the Clayton Brothers), 162 *Firefly* (ER debut as *bl*, w Hank Jones *p;* 1981)

RITA REYS *vo*
CBS S-53026 (Europe 1971), S-65037 (Europe 1972), S-65620 (Europe 1973)
Philips B-08006L (1956), B-08010L (1957), 422444-BE, P0-8203L (1958), P0-8052L (1960), P0-8099L (1963), P12700L (1965), P12955L (1965), 844048PY (1967), 849013PY (1969)

MISS RHAPSODY. See VIOLA WELLS.

JUNE RICHMOND *vo*
78s: Dec
MCA 2-4105 *The Best of Andy Kirk* 2 vol (JR incl on)

RUTH RITCHIE *per*
Atl SD-18227 (w Don Ellis Orch; 1977), SD-19178 (w Don Ellis Orch; 1977)

JUDY ROBERTS *p, vo*
IC 1978 *The JR Band*, 1088 *The Other World*

POLA ROBERTS *d*
Imp AS-47 (w Gloria Coleman *bl, b;* 1963)

JANICE ROBINSON   *trom*

Col YQ-7522 (w Frank Foster *bb;* Japan 1975)

Denon XY-7521 *Manhattan Fever* (w Frank Foster *bb;* Japan 1977), XY-7545-ND *Shiny Stockings* (w Frank Foster *bb;* Japan 1978)

Horizon (w Thad Jones–Mel Lewis Orch; 1975) SP-701 *Suite for Pops,* SP-707

Van VSD-79355 *Clark Terry's Big B.A.D. Band* (JR incl on; 1974)

West 54-8001 *World of Trombones* (JR incl on; Slide Hampton *bl*)

BETTY ROCHÉ   *vo*

Beth BCP-64 *Take the "A" Train*

Pres 9198 *Lightly & Politely*

BILLIE ROGERS   *tr, vo*

78s: Dec 4176 (w Woody Herman *bb,* BR *vo, tr solos*); Majestic (all w Jerry Wald Orch; 1945) 7129, 7130, 7137, 7138 "Clarinet Boogie Blues"; Musicraft 15027 (1944), 15028

Joyce LP-1018 *One Night Stand with BR* (reissue of 1944 recs)

MCA 2-4077 (2 vol; w Woody Herman *bb;* reissue)

ST 109 *Jazzwomen: A Feminist Retrospective*

BOBBI ROGERS   *vo*

Focus Productions 337 *Tommy Wolf Can Really Hang You Up the Most,* 338 *Crystal & Velvet*

ANNIE ROSS   *vo*

78s: Dec (E)F-10514 (England), (F)10620 (France 1955); Esquire 10-354 (1954); Met B-647 (1953); Pres 794, 839 (1952)

Col (all AR w Dave Lambert *vo* & Jon Hendricks *vo,* as Lambert, Hendricks & Ross *vo combo*) OL-5850 *The Real Ambassadors* (w Dave Brubeck *p,* Carmen McRae *vo,* Louis Armstrong *vo*), CL-1510 *LH&R Sing Ellington,* CL-1675 *High Flying,* CS-8198 *The Hottest New Group in Jazz,* C-32911 *Best of LH&R,* PC-37020 *LH&R*

Dec (E)SKL-5099 *You & Me, Baby* (England 1964), DL-4922 *Fill My Heart with Song*

Ember (E)EMB-5182 *Handful of Songs* (also released as NR-5008; England 1963)

HMV (E)CLP-1082 (England 1956–57)

Imp A-83 *Sing a Song of Basie* (LH&R)

MCA 510135, 510132-IMS (w Fletcher Henderson Orch)

MPS (G)SBI-5082 *AR & Pony Poindexter with the Berlin All Stars* (Germany 1966)

Muza (P)XL-0285 (Warsaw 1965)

Odyssey 32160292 *Way-Out Voices* (LH&R)

Pres PRST-7828 *The Bebop Singers* (AR incl on)

Pye PEP-604 (also released as Nixa NJT-504 and NJE-1035; 1956)

Rou RE-102 (w Count Basie Orch)

Sav MG-12060 (AR incl w Blossom Dearie *p;* 1952)

Transatlantic (E)TRA-107 (England 1962)

World Pacific WP-1253 (w Gerry Mulligan Quartet; 1958), WP-1264 *The Swingers*

(LH&R), WP-(ST) 1276 (w Buddy Bregman Orch; 1958–59), WP-(ST)-1285 (w Zoot Sims *ts;* 1959)

JUNE ROTENBERG   *b*
   78s: Vic 0147 (w Beryl Booker *p;* 1946)
   ST 109 *Jazzwomen: A Feminist Retrospective*
   Vic/RCA (F)741106 *The Greatest of the Small Bands* (Black & White Series, Vol 96; JR incl on, w Mary Lou Williams; reissue of Vic 78s; France 1946)

PATRICE RUSHEN   *p*
   CJ 89 *The Clayton Brothers* (PR incl on)
   Fantasy F-9493 (w Stanley Turrentine *ts;* 1975)
   Pres PR-10089 *Prelusion* (1974), PR-10098 *Before the Dawn* (1975)

IRENE SCHWEIZER   *p*
   Ex-Libris GC-324 (Zurich 1962), GC-365 (Zurich 1964)
   Free Music Productions FMP-0010, 0190 (1974), 0290, 0330, 0500, 0550, 0590, 0630
   Hat Hut X *The Very Center of Middle Europe* (w Carl Rudiger; 1978)
   MPS 15142 (Cologne 1967)
   Ogun OG-500 (Zurich 1973)
   Philips P-14438L (Vienna 1965)

DOROTHY SCOTT "DOTT"   *p*
   MCA Coral 82040-4 *Sweet Pease Spivey & Her Dott Scott's Rhythm Dukes*

HAZEL SCOTT   *p*
   78s: Col (1947); Dec (1940, 1942, 1945, 1955); Signature (1946)
   10": Cap H-364; Dec DL-8474 *Round Midnight*
   Cap CRL-56057
   Col CL-6090 *Great Scott* (reissue)
   Debut DLP-16 *Relaxed Piano Moods* (w Charles Mingus *b;* 1955)
   Dec LP-5130 *Swingin' the Classics* (reissue of 78s)
   ST 112 *Women in Jazz: Pianists*

SHIRLEY SCOTT   *o, p*
   Atl SD-1515 (1968), SD-1532 (1969), SD-1561 (1970)
   Blue Note BLP-4081 (w Stanley Turrentine *ts;* 1961), BLP-4129 (1963), BLP-4150 (1963), BLP-4162 (1964), BST-84315 (1968)
   Cadet CA-50009 *Mystical Lady* (1971), CA-50025 (1972)
   Imp AS-51 (1963), AS-67, AS-73, AS-81, AS-93, AS-99 (1963), AS-9109, AS-9115 (1966), AS-9119, AS-9133, AS-9141, IA-9341 *Great Lives* 2 vol
   King LP-605, LP-606 (w Eddie Lockjaw Davis *ts;* 1956)
   Moodsville LP-4 (1960), LP-5 (1960), LP-19 (1960), LP-30 (1960)
   Pres PR-LP 7143, 7155, 7163, 7173, 7182, 7195, 7205, 7226 *Hip Twist,* ST-7240, LP-7262, 7267, ST-7283 *Satin Doll,* ST-7305 *Drag 'Em Out,* ST-7328 *Travelin' Light,* ST-7360 *Sweet Soul,* ST-7376 *Blue Seven,* ST-7392 *Soul Sister,* 7424, ST-7440, LP-7456, (following recs w Eddie "Lockjaw" Davis *tr)* LP-7141/P-24039 (1958), LP-7154

(1958), LP-7301 (1958), LP-7161 (1958), LP-7219 (1958), LP-7171 (1959), 7710 *Best of Eddie Davis with SS*, (following recs w Stanley Turrentine *ts*) ST-7312 *Soul Shoutin'*, ST-7338 *Blue Flames*, 7707 *Best of Stanley Turrentine with SS*, 7773 *Best for Beautiful People*, 7845 *Soul Is Willing*

Rou R-52007/30123 (w Eddie Davis *tr* & Count Basie *p*; 1957), R-52019 (w Eddie Davis; 1958), RLP-2227 (1958)

Strata-East SES-7470 *One for Me* (1974)

BLOSSOM SEELEY *vo/vaudeville*

VJM (E)14 *The Georgians* (reissue)

ELLEN SEELING *tr, flg*

Atl SD-19209 *C'est Chic* (w Chic), SD-5209 *We Are Family* (w Sister Sledge)

Buddha BDS-5626 *Ain't No Backin' Up Now* (w Isis)

Col PC-34786 *Season of Light* (w Laura Nyro *vo*)

Fania JM-00527 *Larry Harlow Presents Latin Fever* (ES in all-woman Latin salsa *bb*)

Marlin 2204 *Short Trip to Space* (w John Tropea)

UA LA-706-G *Breaking Through* (w Isis)

LINDA SHARROCK *vo*

Atco SD-36-121 *Paradise* (1975)

Byg 529337 (1970)

Muse MR-5114 *Angel Eyes* (LS incl on)

Vortex SD-2014 *Black Woman* (1969)

NINA SHELDON *p, vo*

PM (NS *bl*, w Dave Liebman *s*; 1982)

JOYA SHERRILL *vo*

Col CL-951 *A Drum Is a Woman* (w Duke Ellington & Orch), CS-8207 *Sugar & Spice*

Design DLP-22 *Jumps with Joya* (w Sammy Davis Jr. *vo*), DLP-1467 *Spotlight on Sammy Davis Jr.* (JS incl on)

20th Century TFM-3170 *JS Sings Duke Ellington* (1965)

Vic LPT-1004 *Duke Ellington's Greatest*

DINAH SHORE *vo*

Harmony HL-7010 *DS Sings Cole Porter & Richard Rodgers*

NINA SIMONE *vo, p*

Beth BCP-6028, 6041 (1957)

Colpix CP-407 (1959), 409 (1959), 142 (1960), 419 (1961), 421 (1961), 455 *NS at Carnegie Hall* (1963), 465 (1964), 495 (1964)

CTI 7084 *Baltimore*, 63041 *NS & Orchestra*

Festival (F)ALB-167 (France 1975), (F)ALB-189 (France)

Marble Arch (E)MAL-895 (England)

Philips PHM-200-135/PHS-600-135 *NS in Concert*, 200-148, 200-172 *I Put a Spell*

on You, 200-187, 200-202, 200-207, 200-219, PIIS-200-148 *Broadway, Blues & Ballads,*
PHS-600-298 *The Best of NS* (reissue)
PM 018 *A Very Rare Evening*
Quintessence 25421 *Silk & Soul*
Trip TLP-8020 *NS Live in Europe* 2 vol
Vic/RCA ASP/AFL1-4374 *Best of NS,* ASP/AFL1-4536 *Here Comes the Sun,*
AFL1-1788 *Poets,* LPM/LSP 3789 (1966–67), LPM/LSP 3837 (1967), LSP 4065
(1968), LSP-4102, LSP-4152, LSP-4248

SYLVIA SIMS   *vo*
Atl SD-18177 *Lovingly*
Movietone 71022/72022 *In a Sentimental Mood*
Pres S-7489 *For Once in My Life*

CAROL SLOANE   *vo*
Choice 1025 *Cottontail*
Col CL-1766 *Out of the Blue* (also released as CBS BPG-62074; 1961), CL-1923
(1962)
Honey Dew HD-6608 *Carol & Ben* (w Ben Webster *ts*)
Progressive Jazz 7047 *Carol Sings*

BESSIE SMITH   *vo/blues*
78s: numerous on Col (later reissued)
Col CG-33 *The World's Greatest Blues Singer,* CG-30126 *Any Woman's Blues,*
CG-30450 *Empty Bed Blues,* CG-30818 *The Empress,* CG-31093 *Nobody's Blues But
Mine,* CL-855 *BS Story, Vol 1,* CL-856 *BS Story, Vol 2,* CL-857 *BS Story, Vol 3*
Fk 2802 *Jazz, Vol 2* (BS incl on), 2804 *Jazz, Vol 4* (BS incl on)
Olympic 7104 *Blues Heritage* (BS incl on)
Sine Qua Non 124 *Best of the Blues* (BS incl on)

CARRIE SMITH   *vo/blues*
Classic Jazz 139 *Do Your Duty*
West 54 WLW-8002 *CS* (1978)

CLARA SMITH   *vo/blues*
78s: numerous on Col (1923–32)
Jazzum 2 (CS incl on; reissue)
Vintage Jazz Mart VLP-15, VLP-16, VLP-17

ELSIE SMITH   *ts, cl*
World Record Club TP-1952 (ES w Lionel Hampton Orch; 1958)

LAURA SMITH   *vo/blues*
78s: Okeh (1924–27); Pathé-Act (1927); Vic (1927)
VJM VLP-40 (LS incl on; reissue of 1927 rec)

MAMIE SMITH   *vo/blues*
78s: Ajax (1924), Okeh (1920–30, incl 4113 "That Thing Called Love"/"You Can't
Keep a Good Man Down," debut female blues rec, Feb. 14, 1920); Vic (1920)

Col KG-30788/CBS-67203 (MS incl on)
Vic LPV-534 *Women of the Blues* (MS incl on)

BIG MAYBELLE SMITH   *vo/blues*
Br 754107 *What More Can a Woman Do* (1962), 754142 *Gospel Soul* (1969)
Encore 22011 *Gabbin' Blues* (1968)
Savoy 14005 *Big Maybelle Sings*
Scepter 522 *Soul*

TRIXIE SMITH   *vo/blues*
Riv RLP-101 *Young Louis Armstrong* (TS incl on)

GINGER SMOCK   *violin*
78s: Vic (w Wini Beatty *p*, Dodie Jeshke *d*, Vivien Garry *b*, Edna Williams *tr*, 1946)
ST 111 *Women in Jazz: All-Women Groups* (credited as GS or "Emma Colbert")

VALAIDA SNOW   *tr, vo, bl*
78s: Bel-Tone; Chess 1558 (1953); Dec; PAR (w Billy Mason Orch; London 1935–37); Sonora; Tono (all w Lulle Ellboj Orch; Sweden 1939); Tono & Ekko (Copenhagen 1940)
Gold Star 5657 (w Buzz Adlam Orch; 1945; reissue)
Halo LP-50280 (w Jimmy Mundy Orch; 1950)
Jubilee Air Series H-11 (VS incl on Armed Forces Radio Series, program #145, #1)
Rosetta RR-1305 *Hot Snow: Queen of the Trumpet Sings & Swings* (Foremothers Series, Vol 2; reissue)
ST 109 *Jazzwomen: A Feminist Retrospective*, 113 *Women in Jazz: Swingtime to Modern*
Swingfan (Germany; reissues) 1008, 1012
World Records SH-309 *High Hat Trumpet & Rhythm* (reissue)

JERI SOUTHERN   *vo*
Dec DL-8055 *The Southern Style*, DL-8214 *You Better Go Now*, DL-8394 *When Your Heart's On Fire*, DL-8472 *Jeri Gently Swings*, DL-8761 *Southern Hospitality*

PHIL SPITALNY & HIS ALL-GIRL ORCHESTRA   *bb*
78s: Col C-72, C-108, C-114; Vic; Vogue 733
10": Col CL-6042 *Hymns*

SWEET PEASE SPIVEY   *vo/blues*
MCA Coral 82040-4 *SPS & Her Dott Scott's Rhythm Dukes*

VICTORIA SPIVEY   *vo/blues*
78s: numerous on: Br; Okeh (1926, 1927); Vic; Voc
Blue Horizon (England 1969)
Bluesville BVLP-1044 (VS incl w Lonnie Johnson *g;* 1961), BVLP-1054 (1961)
Fk 3541 *Blues Is My Life*, FS-3815 (1962)
GHB 17 (w Easy Riders Jazz Band; 1966)
Spivey 1001 *Victoria & Her Blues* (1962), 1002 (1962), 1004 *3 Kings & the Queen* (1962), 1006 *The Queen & Her Knights* (1965), 2001 *The VS Recorded Legacy of the*

Blues (reissue of 78s); *Queen Vee Souvenir 1* (1961)

Vic LPV-534 *Women of the Blues* (VS incl on)

JO STAFFORD *vo*

10": Col CL-2501 *Soft & Sentimental*

Cap 57-604 *Smiles/Bop* (w David Lambert *vo*)

Col CL-584 *JS Sings Broadway's Best*, CL-910 *Ski Trails*, CL-1124 *Swingin' Down Broadway*, CL-1332 *Ballad of the Blues*, CL-1561 *Jo Plus Jazz*, CL-6286 *Garden of Prayer*

Corinthian COR-105 *GI Jo*, COR-106 *JS's Greatest Hits*, COR-108 *Jo Plus Jazz*, COR-112 *Jo Plus Broadway*, COR-114 *Jo Plus Blues*

Reprise (S)R9-6090 *Getting Sentimental over Tommy Dorsey*

JEAN STARR *tr*

ST 111 *Women in Jazz: All-Women Groups*, 113 *Women in Jazz: Swingtime to Modern*

KAY STARR *vo*

Cap H/T-211 *Songs by KS*, T-125 *Movin'*, T-1303 *Losers Weepers*, T-1358 *One More Time*, T-1681 *I Cry by Night* (w Ben Webster *ts*; 1961)

Coronet CX-106 (reissue)

Liberty LRP-9001 *Swingin' with the Starr* (reissue)

Premier K-584 *KS Sings* (reissue)

DAKOTA STATON *vo*

Cap T-876 *The Late, Late Show* (1957), T-1170 (1954–55), T-1003 (w George Shearing *p*; 1957), T-1054 (1958), T-1241 (1959), T-1325 (1959), T-1387 (1959), T-1427 (1960), T-1490 (1960), T-1597 (1960), T-1649 (1961)

Groove Merchant GM-510 (1972), GM-521 (1973)

London 3495 (1967)

UN UAL-3262 (1963), UAL-3312 (1963), UAL-3355 (1964)

KATHLEEN STOBART *ts, reeds*

78s: Decibel P2, P3 (KS & Her Orch; London 1951)

Black Lion (KS w Humphrey Lyttleton Orch; England) BLP-147005, BLP-162004, BLP-162005, BLP-162009, 12134

Dis 2001

London (AM)LL-3132, PS-178 (England)

Parlophone (KS w Humphrey Lyttleton Orch; London 1957)

Spotlite SPJ-503 *KS–Joe Temperley Quintet* (England), SPJ-509 *KS Quintet (England)*

ST 109 *Jazzwomen: A Feminist Retrospective*, 113 *Women in Jazz: Swingtime to Modern*

MONNETTE SUDLER *g*

Philly Jazz PJ-1004

Stp SCS-1062 *Time for a Change* (MS *bl, g, vo*; 1976), SCS-1087 *Brighter Days for You* (1979), SCS-1102 *MS Live in Europe*

MAXINE SULLIVAN *vo*

78s: numerous on: Apollo; Col; Dec; International; MGM; Vic (1937–38); Voc/Okeh

AFJ 307 (w Jack Teagarden *trom;* 1955–56)

Audiophone 128 *We Just Couldn't Say Goodbye*

Beth BCP-67 *The Complete Charlie Shavers with MS*

Chi CR-107 *Earl Hines & MS at the Overseas Press Club* (1970)

Fat Cats Jazz 136 *Queen of Song*

Jazzology 17 *Manassas Jazz Festival*

Mon-Ever MES-6919 *Close as Pages in a Book* (w Bob Wilber *reeds;* 1969), MES-7038 *Shakespeare* (w Dick Hyman *p;* 1971)

Period SLP-1113 *Flow Gently Sweet Rhythm* (1956), SLP-1207 (1956), RL-1909 *MS, 1956* (also released as Met MEP-1084, 1085 & 1104)

Vic/RCA (F)430686 (w Benny Carter *reeds;* French reissue of 1941 recs, also released as 741073)

EVA TAYLOR *vo/blues*

Audubon AAN *ET & Her Anglo-American Boy Friends* (1967)

Rarities (E)RA-161 (ET incl on one side; English reissue)

KOKO TAYLOR *vo/blues*

Alligator AL-4706 *I Got What It Takes* (1975), 4711 *The Earthshaker*, 4724 *From the Heart of a Woman* (1981)

Black & Blue 33505 (France 1973)

Chess LPS-1532 *KT*, CH-50018 *Basic Soul* (1972)

Sonet SNT-775 (1977)

Spivey LP-1003 (KT incl on), 1009 (KT incl on; 1964)

NORMA TEAGARDEN *p*

Commodore XFL-14940 (1944)

Dec 53 (NT incl on 4 cuts)

Ember CJS-803 *Jack Teagarden & His Orchestra* (NT incl on)

London HMC-5007-AN (England), 6.24060-AG (Europe)

Pumpkin 106 *Big T & the Condon Gang* (w Jack Teagarden *bl*)

ST 109 *Jazzwomen: A Feminist Retrospective*

Sto SLP-704-AO

THELMA TERRY *b, bl*

78s: Col (1928)

Sunbeam MFC-5 *Hodge-Podge of the Off-Beat, Vol 2* (TT incl on one cut w her Playboys; reissue of 78)

SISTER ROSETTA THARPE *vo/gospel-soul*

10": Dec DL-5354 *Blessed Assurance*

Dec DL-5382, DL-8782 *Gospel Train*

Diplomat 2234 *Spirituals in Rhythm*

MCA 510129-IMS (w Marie Knight; 1951), 510148-IMS (1946–48), 510056-IMS (w the Gospel Singers & Trio), 150187-IMS *The Gospel Book* (RT incl on)

Mer MG 20412 *The Gospel Truth*
Sav SGL-7029 *The Best of SRT* 2 vol
Ver MGV-8439 *The Gospel Truth*

IRMA THOMAS   *vo/blues*
Imp LP-9266 (1963–64)
Minit MLL-40004 (1968)
Record Company of the South RCS A-1004 *Safe with Me*

BARBARA THOMPSON   *reeds*
Dec 6.23985 *Neil Ardley & His Harmony of the Spheres* (BT incl on)
MCA Coral 62117 *BT Quartet*
Spotlite SPJ-502 *The Don Rendell Five* (BT incl on)

"BIG MAMA" WILLIE MAE THORNTON   *vo/blues*
78s: Peacock (1951–57)
Arhoolie F-1028 *Big Mama in Europe* (1965), F-1032 *BMT & the Chicago Blues Band* (1966), LP-1039 (1968)
Atl 60036 (1972), 90003 (BMT incl on; 1973)
Back Beat BLP-68
MCA 68 *She's Back*
Mer 134234 MCY *Stronger Than Dirt* (1970)
Tomato 2-7006 *Blues Roots* 2 vol (BMT incl on)
Van VSD-79351 (1975), VSD-79354 *Sassy Mama* (1975)

TERI THORNTON   *vo*
Col CL-2094 (1963–64)
Dauntless DM-4306 (1963), 6306
Riv RLP-352 *Devil May Care* (w Clark Terry *tr*, 1960–61), RM-3525 *Lullaby of the Leaves*

MARTHA TILTON   *vo*
Tops L-1577 *We Sing the Old Songs* (w Curt Massey), L-1607 *Pal Joey*
Vic LPT-6703 *The Golden Age of Swing* 5 vol (MT incl w Benny Goodman Orch)

SOPHIE TUCKER   *vo/vaudeville*
Edison cylinders: from 1910 into the teens
Dec DL-8355 *The Great ST*
Mer MG-20035 *Her Latest & Greatest Spicy Songs*, MGW-20126 *The Spice of Life*, 12176 *Bigger & Better Than Ever*, 12213 *Cabaret Days*

SARAH VAUGHAN   *vo*
AFJ- FS-250-E, 271-E, 325
Atl 16037 *Songs of the Beatles*
Col (J)CL-660 *After Hours with SV*, CL-745 *SV in Hi-Fi* (also released as CSP P-13084)
Coronet CX-277 *SV Belts the Hits*
EmArcy MG-36089 *Sassy*, MG-36109 *Swingin' Easy*, 2-412 *SV Live* 2 vol
Main MRL-340 *A Time in My Life*, MRL-361 (w Michel Legrand), MRL-379

Feelin' Good, MRL-404 *SV & the Jimmy Rowles Quintet,* MRL-412 *Send in the Clowns,* MRL-2401 *Live in Japan,* MRL-419 *More from Japan Live*

Masterseal MS-55 *SV Sings*

Mer MG-20094 *SV at the Blue Note,* MG-20219 *Wonderful Sarah,* MGP-2-101 *SV Sings George Gershwin* 2 vol, MG-20316 *SV Sings the Best of Irving Berlin* (w Billy Eckstine *vo*), 60645 *Golden Hits*

Músico Stereo MDS-1023 *The Greatness of SV*

Musicraft MVS-504 *The Divine Sarah* (reissue)

Pablo 2310 821 *How Long Has This Been Goin' On?* (w Oscar Peterson *p*), T-2312-101 *I Love Brazil* (1977), T-2312-111 *Duke Ellington Songbook, Part I,* T-2312-116 *Duke Ellington Songbook, Part II,* 2312-125 *Copacabana,* T-2312-130 *Send in the Clowns* (w Count Basie & orch; 1981), *Crazy & Mixed Up* (self-prod, 1983)

Pickwick 8003 *Broken Hearted Melody*

Polygram *SV* (reissue, 1954)

Rou R-52060 *The Divine One,* R-52070 *After Hours,* 2-103 *Echoes of an Era* 2 vol (reissue), 42018 (w Count Basie & orch), Birdland SR-52109 *The World of SV*

Trip 5501 (w Clifford Brown *tr;* 1955), 5517 *Sassy,* 5523 (w Cannonball Adderley *as;* 1955), 5551 *Swingin' Easy*

Vic/RCA 110.001B *O Som Brasileiro de SV* (Brazil)

MARLENE VER PLANCK   *vo*

Audiophone 121 *You'd Better Love,* 138 *MVP Loves Johnny Mercer,* 16 *A New York Singer* (1980), *A Warmer Place*

SIPPIE WALLACE   *vo/blues*

78s: Okeh; Sto 198, 214; Vic

Atl SD-2-502 (incl w Bonnie Raitt *bl;* 1972)

Spivey LP-1012

Sto 4017 *SW Sings the Blues*

CLARA WARD   *vo/gospel*

Pickwick 3251

Sav 7015, 14308, 14026, 14034 (w Ward Singers)

HELEN WARD   *vo*

10": Col CL-6271 *It's Been So Long*

Camden CAL-872 *Featuring Great Vocalists of Our Time* (HW incl on)

Col CL-525 *Benny Goodman Presents Fletcher Henderson Arrangements* (HW incl on; reissue)

Harmony LP-7190 *Swing with Benny Goodman* (HW incl on)

Sunbeam SB-128-132 (5 vols; HW incl w Benny Goodman & orch; air checks, 1935–36)

Vic LPT-6703 *The Golden Age of Swing* 5 vol (HW incl on) CPL1-3370 *Legendary Performer*

FRAN WARREN   *vo*

Mon-Ever MES-7205 *Claude Thornhill on Stage,* (w Claude Thornhill Orch)

Tops L-1585 *Here's FW*

Warwick 2012 *Something's Coming*

DINAH WASHINGTON *vo*

10": EmArcy MG-26032 *After Hours with Miss "D"* (1954)

EmArcy MG-36000 (1954), MG-36011, MG-36028 (1953), MG-36065 *Dinah!* (1955), MG-36073 (1956), MG-36104 *The Swingin' Miss "D"* (1956), MG-36119 (1957), MG-36130 (1957–58), MG-36141 (1958), EMS-2-401 *Jazz Sides* 2 vol (reissue of 1954–58 recs)

Mer MG-20247 *DW Sings the Best in Blues*, MG-20479 *What à Difference a Day Makes*, MG-20789 *This Is My Story, Vol I*, MG-2-603 *This Is My Story* 2 vol, 61119 *Discovered*, SR-60614 *For Lonely Lovers*, 60788 *Golden Hits, Vol I*, 60789 *Golden Hits, Vol II*, ML-8006 *Unforgettable*, 60244 *Two of Us* (w Brook Benton *vo*)

Pickwick 3043 *DW*

Polygram *Dinah Jams* (reissue, 1954)

Rou R-25170 *Dinah '62*, R-25180 (1962), R-25183 (1962–63), R-25189, R-25220 (1963), R-25244 (1963), R-25269 (1963), R-25289 *The Best of DW*, 42014 *Best*, 104 *Echoes of an Era* 2 vol, 125 *Immortal* 2 vol, 2-RE-117 *Queen of the Blues* 2 vol

Session Disc SR-106 *Count Basie & DW* (1948)

Trip 5500 *DW Jams with Clifford Brown* (1954), 5516 *After Hours*, 5556 *DW Sings Bessie Smith*, 5565 *The Swingin' Miss D*

Wing MG-12140, MG-12223, MG-20119

ETHEL WATERS *vo*

78s: Bluebird

10": Remington 1025 (w Mary Osborne *g*; reissue of 78s); Vic LX-999; X-LVA-1009 (reissue of Bluebird 78s)

Bio 12003, 12022, 12024, 12025, 12026

Col KG-31571 *EW: Greatest Years*, CL-2792 *Theatre & Film Songs of EW*

Good Times 12003 *EW On Stage & Screen: 1925–1940*

Mer MG-2005 *The Favorite Songs of EW*

Mon-Ever 6812

Sutton 270 *Blackbirds of 1928* (EW incl on)

Word 8044 *His Eye Is on the Sparrow*

PATTY WATERS *vo*

ESP SXF-0720, SXF-10720 (w Burton Greene Trio)

MARY WATKINS *p*

Olivia BLF-919 *Something Moving* (MW *bl*; 1979)

Palo Alto *Winds of Change* (1983)

FRANCIS WAYNE *vo*

10": Col CL-6049 (w Woody Herman; reissue); Coral CRL-56091 *Salute to Ethel Waters*

Atl 1263 *The Warm Sound*

Br BL-54022 *FW*

Epic LN-3222 *Songs for My Man*

L'ANA WEBSTER *reeds*

78s: Dec 1655, 1662 (w Mike Riley & His Round & Round Boys, 1937)

ST 111 *Women in Jazz: All-Women Groups*, 113 *Women in Jazz: Swingtime to Modern*

ELISABETH WELCH   *vo/blues-vaudeville*
  78s: Br (1928); His Master's Voice/HMV (London); Voc (London)

VIOLA WELLS   *vo/blues*
  78s: Sav
  Matchbox 227 (1972)
  Sav SJL-2208 (VW incl on; reissue of 1944–45 recs)
  Spivey *C.C. Rider*

BONNIE WETZEL   *b*
  Dis DL-3021 (w Beryl Booker Trio; 1954)
  MGM E-255 *Cats v. Chicks: A Jazz Battle of the Sexes* (w Terry Pollard *bl*)
  ST 109 *Jazzwomen: A Feminist Retrospective*, 111 *Women in Jazz: All-Women Groups*
  Sto SLP-302 (w Teddy King *vo*)

MARGARET WHITING   *vo*
  10": Cap H-209 *Rodgers & Hart Songs*
  Cap T-685 *Songs for the Starry-Eyed*
  Dot DLP-3072 *Goin' Places*, DLP-3176 *MW's Greatest Hits*
  MGM E-4006 *Past Midnight*
  Ver V-3039 *MW Sings the Jerome Kern Songbook, Vol 1*
  Vic/RCA CPL-2-0362 *The Big Band Cavalcade Concert* 2 vol (MW incl on)

LEE WILEY   *vo*
  78s: numerous on: Dec; Epic; Gala/Rabson; Liberty; Majestic
  10": Col CL-6215 *LW Sings Vincent Youmans*, CL-6216 *LW Sings Irving Berlin* (1951); Liberty 1003 *Cole Porter Songs* (reissue), 1004 *George Gershwin Songs* (reissue)
  Allegro LP-4049 (w Jess Stacy *p;* 1947)
  Col JCL-656 *Night in Manhattan* (w Bobby Hackett *tr*), CL-6169 (1959), CL-6125
  JJC 2003 *Cole Porter*
  Mon-Ever MES-6807 *LW Sings Rodgers & Hart & Harold Arlen*, MES-7034E *LW Sings Gershwin & Porter*, MES-7041 *Back Home Again* (1971)
  RIC 2002 *The One and Only LW* (reissue of 1939–40 Liberty 78s)
  Sto LP-312 *LW Sings Rodgers & Hart* (1954)
  Totem 1021 *LW On the Air*, 1027, 1033
  Vic LPM-1325 *Wide, Wide World of Jazz* (1956), LPM-1408 *West of the Moon* (1956), LPM-1566 *A Touch of the Blues* (1957)

EDNA WILLIAMS   *tr, arr*
  78s: Vic (1946)
  ST 111 *Women in Jazz: All-Women Groups*

JESSICA WILLIAMS   *p*
  Adelphi AD-5003 *The Portal of Atrium* (1976), AD-5005 *Portraits* 2 vol (1978)
  Clean Cuts CC-701 *Rivers of Memory*, CC-703 *Orgonomic Music* (1979)

MARY LOU WILLIAMS   *p, com, arr*
  78s: numerous on: Asch; Br (incl MLW's solo debut on "Night Life"/"Drag 'Em,"

1930); Col; Continental; Dec; Dis; Selmer; Vic

10": Atl 114 *Piano Panorama, Vol II* (MLW incl on); Concert Hall Swing CHJ-1007 *The Art of MLW;* Coral CRL-56019 *Souvenir Album, Vol I*

Ace of Hearts (E)AH-110 *Clouds of Joy* (MLW in *bb;* England; reissue), (E)AH-160 *Twelve Clouds of Joy* (MLW in *bb;* England; reissue)

Atl 1271

Avant Garde AVS-103 *Praise the Lord in Many Voices* (1969–70)

Blue-Star (F)BLP-6841 (Paris 1954)

Br BL-54000 (1952)

Chr CR-103 *From the Heart,* CR-146 *Live at the Cookery* (1975), CR-204 (w Buddy Tate *ts*)

Circle 3008 (1951), L-412

Cobblestone CST-9025 *Newport in NY, Jam Sessions* 2 vol (MLW incl on; 1972)

Dec DL-9232 *Instrumentally Speaking* (reissue of 1936–42 recs)

Festival Album 215 (w Dizzy Gillespie Quintet)

Fk FA-2966 *The Asch Recordings* (MLW *bl;* reissue of 1944–47 recs), FJ-2843 *MLW* (also released as 32843), 2860 *History of Jazz* (MLW plays & narrates jazz history), 32844 *Zodiac Suite*

Hall 607-E *King & Queen—Art Tatum & MLW*

IC 2043 *Free Spirits* (1975), Jazz Legacy 7006 *First Lady of the Piano* (reissue of 1953 MLW trio recs)

Jazztone J-1206 *A Keyboard History* (1955)

King LP-295-85 (reissue of 1949–50 recs.)

Mary 101 *Black Christ of the Andes,* 102 *Mary Lou's Mass,* 103 *Zoning* (1974), FJ-2843 *MLW Presents*

MCA 510033, 510121, 510122 (MLW incl on), 510133, 510178-80 (3 vol, w Clouds of Joy), 510088 (MLW & Her Kansas City Seven), 510090

Onyx ORI-210 *Café Society* (MLW incl on)

Pablo Live 2308-218 *Solo Recital: Montreux Jazz Festival* (1978), 2620-108 (IMS) *Embraced* (w Cecil Taylor *p*), 2310-819 *My Mama Pinned a Rose on Me,* 2310-856 *Best of MLW*

Pres 7647 *Jazz Pioneers: Coleman Hawkins & MLW* (MLW *p, celeste,* on one side; reissue)

ST 109 *Jazzwomen: A Feminist Retrospective,* 112 *Women in Jazz: Pianists*

Stinson 24 *MLW*

Sto STLP-906 *Messin' Around in Montmartre* (MLW on one side)

Stp SCS-1043 *Free Spirits* (1975)

Ver MV-2620-IMS (w Dizzy Gillespie Orch), 2-25141-IMS (2 vol), MGV-8244 (MLW incl on *Zodiac Suite* w Dizzy Gillespie; Newport Jazz Festival, July 1957)

Vic RCA (F)741106 *The Greatest of the Small Bands* (Black & White Series, Vol 96; MLW & Girl Stars; reissues of Vic 78s; France 1946)

Vogue (E)LDE-022 (London 1953; also issued in France as [F]LD-124), (F)LD-186 (France 1952)

EDITH WILSON   *vo/blues*

78s: Col (w Johnny Dunn's Jazz Hounds; 1921, 1922, 1924); Vic (1930)

Delmark DS-637 (1973)

EBM 3 (EW incl on w Eubie Blake *p*)

Fountain FB-302 EW (reissue of 1921–22 recs)

NANCY WILSON *vo*

ASI *At My Best* (1981)

Cap T-1319 *Like in Love* (1959), T-1440 *Something Wonderful* (1960), T-1657 (w Cannonball Adderly Quintet; 1961), T-1767 *Hello, Young Lovers* (1962), T-1828 (1963), T-1934 (1962–63), T-2012 (1963), T-2082 *Today, Tomorrow, Forever* (1964), T-2155 (1964), T 2321 (1964), (S)T 2351 (1965), (S)T-2433 (1965), (S)T-2495 (1965–66), (S)T-2555 (1966), (S)T-2634 (1966), (S)T-2712 (1966), (S)T-2757 (1967), (S)T-2844 (1967), (S)T-2909 (1968), (S)T-2970 (1968), (S)T-148 (1968), (S)T-234 (1969), (S)T-353 (1969), (S)T-798 (1969), ST-429 (1970), ST-541, ST-11943 *Life, Love & Harmony*, ST-11659, ST-12055 *Take My Love*, SM-1828 *Broadway—My Way*, SM-798 *But Beautiful*, SM-12031 *Can't Take My Eyes Off of You*, SM-11819 *Come Get to This*, SM-1524 *Swingin's Mutual*, SM-2495 *Touch of Today*, SM-11884 *Nancy—Naturally*, SM-11802 *Easy*, SM-11767 *How Glad I Am*, SKAD-2136 (1964), 16128 *Best of NW*, SMAS-11786 *Music on My Mind*, SN-16210 *NW/Cannonball Adderly*

NORMA WINSTONE *vo*

Argo (E)ZDA-148 *Edge of Time* (NW *bl;* England 1972)

Deram *Love Songs* (w Mike Westbrook)

ECM/War 1-1099 *Azimuth*, 1130 *Touchstone* (1978)

Incus *Song for Someone* (w Kenny Wheeler)

Regal Zonophone *A Symphony of Amaranths* (w Neil Ardley)

Vertigo *Labyrinth* (w Ian Carr)

MAMA YANCEY *vo/blues*

10": Jump 7

Atl 1283 *Pure Blues* (w Jimmy Yancey *p;* 1959), LP-134 *Chicago Piano, Vol I* (MY incl on)

Fk FJ-2802 (w Jimmy Yancey *p;* reissue of 1943 recs)

Oldie Blues 2802 (w Jimmy Yancey, reissue)

Riv RLP-403 *South Side Blues* (1961)

Ver-Fk 9015 (w Art Hodes *p;* 1965)

Windin' Ball LP-102 (1952)

MONICA ZETTERLUND *vo*

Col SEG-S47 (Sweden 1958), SEG-K1040 (Denmark 1958), OSX-20 (Sweden 1958), SEG-S64 (1959), SEG-S69 (1959), SEG-S70 (Sweden 1960), (E)SEG-7999 (England)

IC 1082 *It Only Happens Every Time* (w Thad Jones–Mel Lewis Orch)

Philips 433404-PE (Sweden 1961), 433410 (1961), BL-7647 (England 1964), 08222-PL (1964)

VICKI ZIMMER *p*

78s: Bullet 286 (1948)

ST 111 *Women in Jazz: All-Women Groups*

Bibliography

Albertson, Chris. *Bessie*. New York: Stein & Day, 1972.

_____, and Schuller, Gunther. *Bessie Smith, Empress of the Blues*. New York: Schirmer Books, 1975.

Allen, Walter C. *Hendersonia: The Music of Fletcher Henderson and His Musicians, A Bio-Discography*. Highland Park, N.J.: monograph published by the author, 1973.

American Society of Composers, Authors and Publishers (ASCAP). *The ASCAP Biographical Dictionary of Composers, Authors and Publishers*. 3rd ed. New York: ASCAP, 1966.

Anderson, E. Ruth, comp. *Contemporary American Composers: A Biographical Dictionary*. Boston: G.K. Hall & Co., 1976.

Anderson, Marian. *My Lord, What a Morning: An Autobiography*. New York: Viking Press, 1956.

Bailey, Pearl. *The Raw Pearl*. New York: Pocket Books, 1969.

_____. *Talking to Myself*. New York: Harcourt Brace Jovanovich, 1971.

Balliett, Whitney. *American Singers*. New York: Oxford University Press, 1979.

_____. *New York Notes: A Journal of Jazz, 1972–1975*. Boston: Houghton Mifflin Co., 1976.

Baraka, Amiri. *Black Music*. New York: William Morrow & Co., 1967.

_____. *Blues People: Negro Music in White America*. New York: William Morrow & Co., 1963.

Bebey, Francis. *African Music: A People's Art*. Translated by Josephine Bennett. New York: Lawrence Hill & Co., 1975.

Berendt, Joachim. *The Jazz Book: From New Orleans to Rock and Free Jazz*. Translated by Dan Morgenstern, Helmut Bredigkeit and Barbara Bredigkeit. New York: Lawrence Hill & Co., 1975.

Blesh, Rudi, and Janis, Harriet. *They All Played Ragtime: The Story of American Music*. Rev. ed. New York: Music Sales Corp., Oak Publications, 1966.

Block, Adrienne Fried, and Neuls, Carol, comps. and eds. *Women in American Music: A Bibliography in Music and Literature.* Westport, Conn: Greenwood Press, 1979.

Bordman, Gerald. *American Musical Theatre: A Chronicle.* New York: Oxford University Press, 1978.

Broonzy, William, as told to Bruynoghe, Yannick. *Big Bill Blues: William Broonzy's Story.* London: Cassell & Co., 1955.

Bruyninckx, Walter. *Sixty Years of Recorded Jazz, 1917–1977.* Mechelen, Belgium: published by the author, 1979–.

Buerkle, Jack V., and Barker, Danny. *Bourbon Street Black: The New Orleans Black Jazzman.* New York: Oxford University Press, 1973.

Burton, Jack. *Blue Book of Broadway Musicals.* Watkins Glen, N.Y.: Century House, 1952.

——. *Blue Book of Hollywood Musicals.* Watkins Glen, N.Y.: Century House, 1953.

Charters, Ann, comp. and ed. *Ragtime Songbook.* New York: Music Sales Corp., Oak Publications, 1965.

Charters, Samuel B. *Jazz: New Orleans, 1885–1963: An Index to the Negro Musicians of New Orleans.* Rev. ed. New York: Music Sales Corp., Oak Publications, 1963.

Chilton, John. *Billie's Blues: A Survey of Billie Holiday's Career, 1933–1959.* New York: Stein & Day, 1975.

——. *Who's Who of Jazz: Storyville to Swing Street.* London: Bloomsbury Book Shop, 1970.

——. *Who's Who of Jazz: Storyville to Swing Street.* Special ed. New York: Time-Life Records, 1978.

Claghorn, Charles Eugene. *Biographical Dictionary of American Music.* Englewood Cliffs, N.J.: Prentice-Hall, 1973.

Coryell, Julie, and Friedman, Laura. *Jazz-Rock Fusion: The People, the Music.* New York: Delacorte Press, 1978.

Dance, Stanley. *The World of Swing.* New York: Charles Scribner's Sons, 1974.

——, and Dance, Helen Oakley. *The World of Earl Hines.* New York: Charles Scribner's Sons, 1977.

Delauney, Charles. *New Hot Discography: The Standard Dictionary of Recorded Jazz.* New York: Criterion, 1963.

Deveaux, Alexis. *Don't Explain.* New York: Harper & Row, 1980.

Driggs, Frank. "Women in Jazz: A Survey." Pamphlet included with *Jazzwomen: A Feminist Retrospective,* Stash Records ST-109, 1977.

Erlich, Lillian. *What Jazz Is All About.* Rev. ed. New York: Julian Messner, 1975.

Ewen, David. *The Life and Death of Tin Pan Alley: The Golden Age of American Popular Music.* New York: Funk & Wagnalls, 1964.

——. *New Complete Book of the American Musical Theatre.* New York: Holt, Rinehart, & Winston, 1970.

——, ed. *Popular American Composers.* New York: H.W. Wilson Co., 1962.

——, ed. *Popular American Composers, First Supplement.* New York: H.W. Wilson Co., 1972.

Feather, Leonard. *The Book of Jazz from Then till Now: A Guide to the Entire Field.* Rev. ed. New York: Horizon Press, 1965.

_____. *Encyclopedia of Jazz.* New York: Horizon Press, 1960.

_____. *Encyclopedia of Jazz in the Sixties.* New York: Horizon Press, 1966.

_____, and Gitler, Ira. *The Encyclopedia of Jazz in the Seventies.* New York: Horizon Press, 1976.

Foster, Pops, as told to Stoddard, Tom. *Pops Foster: The Autobiography of a New Orleans Jazzman.* Berkeley: University of California Press, 1971.

Gitler, Ira. *Jazz Masters of the Forties.* New York: Macmillan Co., 1966.

Godrich, J., and Dixon, Robert M.W., comps. *Blues and Gospel Records, 1902-1942.* London: Storyville Publications, 1969.

Goldberg, Isaac. *Tin Pan Alley: A Chronicle of the American Popular Music Racket.* New York: Frederick Ungar, 1961.

Goldberg, Joe. *Jazz Masters of the Fifties.* New York: Da Capo Press, 1980.

Green, Stanley. *Encyclopedia of the Musical Theatre.* New York: Dodd, Mead & Co., 1976.

_____. *The World of Musical Comedy: The Story of the American Musical Stage as Told Through the Careers of Its Foremost Composers and Lyricists.* South Brunswick, N.J.: A.S. Barnes & Co., 1968.

Hadlock, Richard. *Jazz Masters of the Twenties.* New York: Macmillan Co., 1968.

Hammond, John, and Townsend, Irving. *John Hammond on Record.* New York: Summit Books, 1977.

Handy, D. Antoinette. *Black Women in American Bands and Orchestras.* Metuchen, N.J.: Scarecrow Press, 1981.

Harris, Sheldon. *Blues Who's Who: A Biographical Dictionary of Blues Singers.* New Rochelle, N.Y.: Arlington House, 1979.

Havlice, Patricia Pate. *Popular Song Index.* Metuchen, N.J.: Scarecrow Press, 1975.

_____. *Popular Song Index: First Supplement.* Metuchen, N.J.: Scarecrow Press, 1978.

Heilbut, Tony. *The Gospel Sound: Good News and Bad Times.* New York: Simon & Schuster, 1971.

Hentoff, Nat. *Jazz Country.* New York: Dell, 1965.

Holiday, Billie, with Duffy, William. *Lady Sings the Blues.* New York: Doubleday & Co., 1956.

Horne, Lena, as told to Arstein, Helen, and Moss, Carlton. *In Person, Lena Horne.* New York: Greenberg, 1950.

Howard, Brett. *Lena Horne.* Los Angeles: Holloway House, 1980.

Jackson, Arthur. *The World of Big Bands: The Sweet and Swing Years.* New York: Arco, 1977.

Jackson, Jesse. *Make a Joyful Noise unto the Lord: The Life of Mahalia Jackson, Queen of Gospel Singers.* New York: Dell, 1975.

Jackson, Mahalia. *Movin' On Up.* New York: Avon Books, 1969.

Jones, Hettie. *Big Star, Fallin' Mama: Five Women in Black Music.* New York: Viking Press, 1974.

Keil, Charles. *Urban Blues.* Chicago: University of Chicago Press, 1966.

Kinkle, Roger D. *Complete Encyclopedia of Popular Music and Jazz, 1900–1950.* 4 vols. New Rochelle, N.Y.: Arlington House, 1974.

Kitt, Eartha. *Thursday's Child.* New York: Duell, Sloan & Pearce, 1956.

Leonard, Neil. *Jazz and the White Americans: The Acceptance of a New Art Form.* Chicago: University of Chicago Press, 1967.

Lieb, Sandra. *Mother of the Blues, A Study of Ma Rainey.* Amherst, Mass.: University of Massachusetts Press, 1981.

Lomax, Alan. *Mister Jelly Roll: The Fortunes of Jelly Roll Morton, New Orleans Creole and Inventor of Jazz.* Berkeley: University of California Press, 1973.

Lyttleton, Humphrey. *The Best of Jazz, Basin Street to Harlem: Jazz Masters and Masterpieces, 1917–1930.* New York: Taplinger, 1979.

McCarthy, Albert. *The Dance Band Era: The Dancing Decades from Ragtime to Swing, 1910–1950.* Radnor, Pa.: Chilton Book Co., 1971.

———. *Jazz on Record: A Critical Guide to the First Fifty Years, 1917–1967.* London: Hanover Books, 1968.

McPartland, Marian. "The Untold Story of the International Sweethearts of Rhythm." Working Paper (1980) for *Jazzwomen.* New York: Oxford University Press, forthcoming.

Meeker, David. *Jazz in the Movies: A Guide to Jazz Musicians, 1917–1977.* New Rochelle, N.Y.: Arlington House, 1978.

Meryman, Richard, ed. *Louis Armstrong: A Self-Portrait.* New York: Eakins Press, 1966.

Moore, Carman. *Somebody's Angel Child: The Story of Bessie Smith.* New York: Deli, 1975.

Nketia, J.H. Kwabena. *The Music of Africa.* New York: W.W. Norton & Co., 1974.

Oakley, Giles. *The Devil's Music: A History of the Blues.* New York: Taplinger, 1977.

O'Day, Anita, with Eells, George. *High Times, Hard Times.* New York: G.P. Putnam's Sons, 1981.

Oliver, Paul. *Bessie Smith.* Cranbury, N.J.: A.S. Barnes & Co., 1961.

Olsson, Bengt. *Memphis Blues.* Hatboro, Pa.: Legacy Books, n.d.

Ostransky, Leroy. *Jazz City: The Impact of Our Cities on the Development of Jazz.* Englewood Cliffs, N.J.: Prentice-Hall, 1978.

———. *Understanding Jazz.* Englewood Cliffs, N.J.: Prentice-Hall, 1977.

Placksin, Sally. *American Women in Jazz: 1900 to the Present.* New York: Seaview Books, 1982.

Pleasants, Henry. *The Great American Popular Singers.* New York: Simon & Schuster, 1974.

Pool, Jeannie G. *Women in Music History: A Research Guide.* New York: J.G. Pool, 1977.

Rivelli, Pauline, and Levin, Robert, eds. *Giants of Black Music.* New York: Da Capo Press, 1980.

Rose, Al. *Eubie Blake.* New York: Schirmer Books, 1979.

———, and Souchon, Edmond. *New Orleans Jazz: A Family Album.* Baton Rouge, La.: Louisiana State University Press, 1967.

Rublowsky, John. *Black Music in America.* New York: Basic Books, 1971.

Russell, Ross. *Jazz Style in Kansas City and the Southwest.* Berkeley: University of California Press, 1971.

Rust, Brian. *The Dance Bands.* New Rochelle, N.Y.: Arlington House, 1974.

———. *Jazz Records, 1897–1942.* 2 vols. New Rochelle, N.Y.: Arlington House, 1978.

Schiedt, Duncan. *The Jazz State of Indiana.* Pittsboro, Ind.: monograph published by the author, 1977.

Shapiro, Nat, ed. *Popular Music: An Annotated Index of American Popular Songs.* 6 vols. New York: Adrian Press, 1964–73.

———, and Hentoff, Nat, ed. *Hear Me Talkin' to Ya: The Story of Jazz As Told by the Men Who Made It.* New York: Dover Publications, 1978.

Shevey, Sandra. *The Ladies of Pop-Rock.* New York: Scholastic Book Services, 1972.

Short, Bobby. *Black and White Baby.* New York: Dodd, Mead & Co., 1971.

Simon, George. *The Big Bands.* New York: Macmillan Co., 1967.

Skowronski, JoAnn. *Women in American Music: A Bibliography.* Metuchen, N.J.: Scarecrow Press, 1978.

Smith, Cecil, and Litton, Glenn. *Musical Comedy in America: From "The Black Crook" Through "Annie."* New York: Theatre Arts Books, 1978.

Smith, Julia, ed. *The Directory of American Women Composers.* Chicago: National Federation of Music Clubs, 1970.

Stearns, Marshall W. *The Story of Jazz.* New York: Oxford University Press, 1956.

Stewart, Rex. *Jazz Masters of the Thirties.* New York: Da Capo Press, 1980.

Stewart-Baxter, Derrick. *Ma Rainey and the Classic Blues Singers.* New York: Stein & Day, 1970.

Toll, Robert C. *Blacking Up: The Minstrel Show in Nineteenth Century America.* New York: Oxford University Press, 1974.

Tudor, Dean, and Tudor, Nancy. *Black Music.* Littleton, Colo.: Libraries Unlimited, 1979.

———. *Contemporary Popular Music.* Littleton, Colo.: Libraries Unlimited, 1979.

———. *Grass Roots Music.* Littleton, Colo.: Libraries Unlimited, 1979.

———. *Jazz.* Littleton, Colo.: Libraries Unlimited, 1979.

Ulanov, Barry. *A History of Jazz in America.* 1950. Reprint. New York: Da Capo Press, 1972.

Waller, Maurice, and Calabrese, Anthony. *Fats Waller.* New York: Schirmer Books, 1977.

Waters, Ethel. *To Me It's Wonderful.* New York: Harper & Row, 1972.

———, with Samuels, Charles. *His Eye Is on the Sparrow.* Westport, Conn.: Greenwood Press, 1978.

Wilder, Alec. *American Popular Song: The Great Innovators, 1900–1950.* New York: Oxford University Press, 1972.

Williams, Martin. *Jazz Masters of New Orleans.* New York: Da Capo Press, 1979.

———. *Jazz Masters in Transition, 1957–1969.* New York: Da Capo Press, 1980.

Wilmer, Valerie. *As Serious as Your Life: The Story of the New Jazz.* Westport, Conn.: Lawrence Hill, 1980.

———. *The Face of Black Music.* New York: Da Capo Press, 1976.

———. *Jazz People.* New York: Bobbs-Merrill Co., 1971.

Index

ABOUT THE AUTHOR

Linda Dahl has written articles on women in jazz for *Jazz* Magazine, *Sojourner*, and for general-interest magazines. She has also produced cable and local television shows on women in jazz. She lives in New York.